Paddy's Road

First published in 2003 by Aboriginal Studies Press for the Australian Institute of Aboriginal and Torres Strait Islander Studies. GPO Box 553, Canberra ACT 2601.

The views expressed in this publication are those of the author and not necessarily those of the Australian Institute of Aboriginal and Torres Strait Islander Studies.

The publisher has made every effort to contact copyright owners for permission to use material reproduced in this book. If your material has been used inadvertently without permission, please contact the publisher immediately.

© Kevin Keeffe 2003

Front cover image courtesy of National Library of Australia.
Back cover pic (From left): Patrick Dodson, courtesy of News Limited; Patrick Dodson and Kevin Keeffe, courtesy of National Library of Australia; and 'The lay-up', low tide in the creek at Broome, courtesy of Australian Inland Mission Collection, National Library of Australia.
Frontispiece: 'Roads meeting' by Rover Thomas, 1987.

Apart from any fair dealing for the purpose of private study, research, criticism or review as permitted under the Copyright Act 1968, no part of this publication may be reproduced by any process whatsoever without the written permission of the publisher.

National Library of Australia cataloguing-in-publication data:

Keeffe, Kevin.
Paddy's road: life stories of Patrick Dodson.

Bibliography.
Includes index.
ISBN 0 85575 448 6.
ISBN 0 85575 454 0 (pbk.).

1. Dodson, Patrick, 1947- . 2. Social reformers - Australia - Biography. 3. Aborigines, Australian - Civil rights. 4. Aborigines, Australian - Government relations. 5. Reconciliation - Australia. 6. Australia - Race relations. I. Australian Institute of Aboriginal and Torres Strait Islander Studies. II. Title.

305.89915092

Produced by Aboriginal Studies Press
Design and Layout by Rachel Ippoliti, Aboriginal Studies Press

August 2003

Kevin Keeffe
Paddy's Road
Life Stories of Patrick Dodson

Aboriginal Studies Press

August 2003

Acknowledgments

Paddy's Road is the family history and life story of Patrick Dodson, Australia's 'Father of Reconciliation'. It tells stories of his people, his family and his country; exploring the impact on his family, and his own life, of the laws and policies and programs that have historically shaped the relationship between Aboriginal and non-Aboriginal Australians. It is a family history and life story of seeking reconciliation. It seeks an answer to this question: why does this man, whose grandmother, grandfather, father, mother and sisters have at one time or another, because of their race, each been removed, relocated and institutionalised, believe so strongly in reconciliation?

This book would not have been possible without the generous assistance of people across Australia. In Broome, I would especially like to thank the Dodson family, the Wade family (especially Eric and Sharon, Ronald and Rosie) the Djiagween family (especially Stanley and Cissie), Fr Kevin McKelson, Howard Pedersen and Peter Yu. Paul Lane offered wise counsel and assistance. June Oscar was generous in her hospitality, encouragement and support and Patrick's daughter and son, Grace and Adrian, looked after me well. His sisters, Fay and Patricia read the manuscript and made helpful suggestions. Fay was especially helpful in telling her stories of the harrowing experiences she shared with her mother and in providing photos from her own albums. Mick Dodson gave me time, encouragement and helpful criticism.

In Darwin, I was grateful for interviews with: Jack Ah Kit, Jeannie Devitt, Maude Ellis, Norman Fry, Jamie Gallacher, Marcia Langton, Basil Roe, Max Stuart; and was grateful for the use of facilities at the Australian National University's North Australia Research Unit. In Sydney, Phil Glendinning and Mark Yettica-Paulson of the Edmund Rice Centre of NSW for Justice and Community Education were generous with their support.

In the research for this book I needed and received willing assistance from many people, including: Neil Andrews, Toni Bauman, the JS Battye Library of West Australian History (esp. Steve Howell), Aurora Beasley, Broome Historical Society, Des Carne, Kevin Cook, Robert Champion de Crespigny, Bishop Hilton Deakin, Geelong Historical Society, Heather Goodall, Dot Henry, Ross Howie, Elliott Johnston, Norman Katter, the Archives of the Missionaries of the Sacred Heart Order, Yami Lester, Darrell Lewis, Wendy Lowenstein, Fr. Brian McCoy, Siobahn McHugh, the National Library of Australia, especially the Oral History Library, the NT Archives Service, Vern O'Brien, Chris Owen, Fr Dick Pascoe, Howard Pedersen,

Peter Read, David Ross, Barbara Shaw, the SA Royal Geographic Society, the WA Department of Indigenous Affairs, the WA Police Academy Library (Jean Hobson), WA State Records Office and Jack Waterford. I am grateful to Wendy Lowenstein for permission to quote her recordings of Paddy Djiagween and to Carolyn Armstrong for preparing the maps.

For comments on drafts of various chapters I am very grateful to Barry Alpher, Mick and Patrick Dodson, Caroline Fisher, Darrell Lewis, Francesca Merlan, Daphne Nash, David Nash, Stuart Rintoul, Tim Rowse, Lisa Walkington, Bruce Wellington and Alexis Wright. Thankfully, Jane Simpson did not let her friendship and loyalty interfere with her forthright and insightful criticism.

For their practical support I would like to thank the Australian Institute of Aboriginal and Torres Strait Islander Studies who provided an initial research grant.

Aboriginal Studies Press was vital to completing the task and I thank Sandra Phillips, Rachel Ippoliti, Rebecca Morphy and Rhonda Black for their professional support and assistance.

I cannot give enough thanks to Daphne Nash for her patience, support and critical insights.

In telling the story of Patrick Dodson's family, I have respected their right to negotiate with me on how their story was to be shared. They have been generous, patient and open-minded in these negotiations and my thanks go to Patrick Djagun Dodson and his family. Any mistakes, however, are entirely my own responsibility.

Thank you to the following agencies and individuals who provided images: Battye Library, State Library of Western Australia; The National Archives of Australia; The Canberra Times; The National Library of Australia; The Australian War Memorial; The State Library of New South Wales; The West Australian Newspaper; The Herald and Weekly Times; The State Library of South Australia; The Council of Aboriginal Reconciliation; The National Gallery; The Northern Territory Library and Archive Services; Melbourne Diocesan Historical Commission; Fay Wade; Maude Ellis; The Dodson Family; Chrissy Grant; Peter Nicholson and Nick Nartgerink.

This book is dedicated to the memory of Patricia Keeffe and Patricia Djiagween. It is written for Michael and Jonno, Grace and Adrian in the hope that they will see reconciliation in Australia.

Patrick Dodson's ancestors

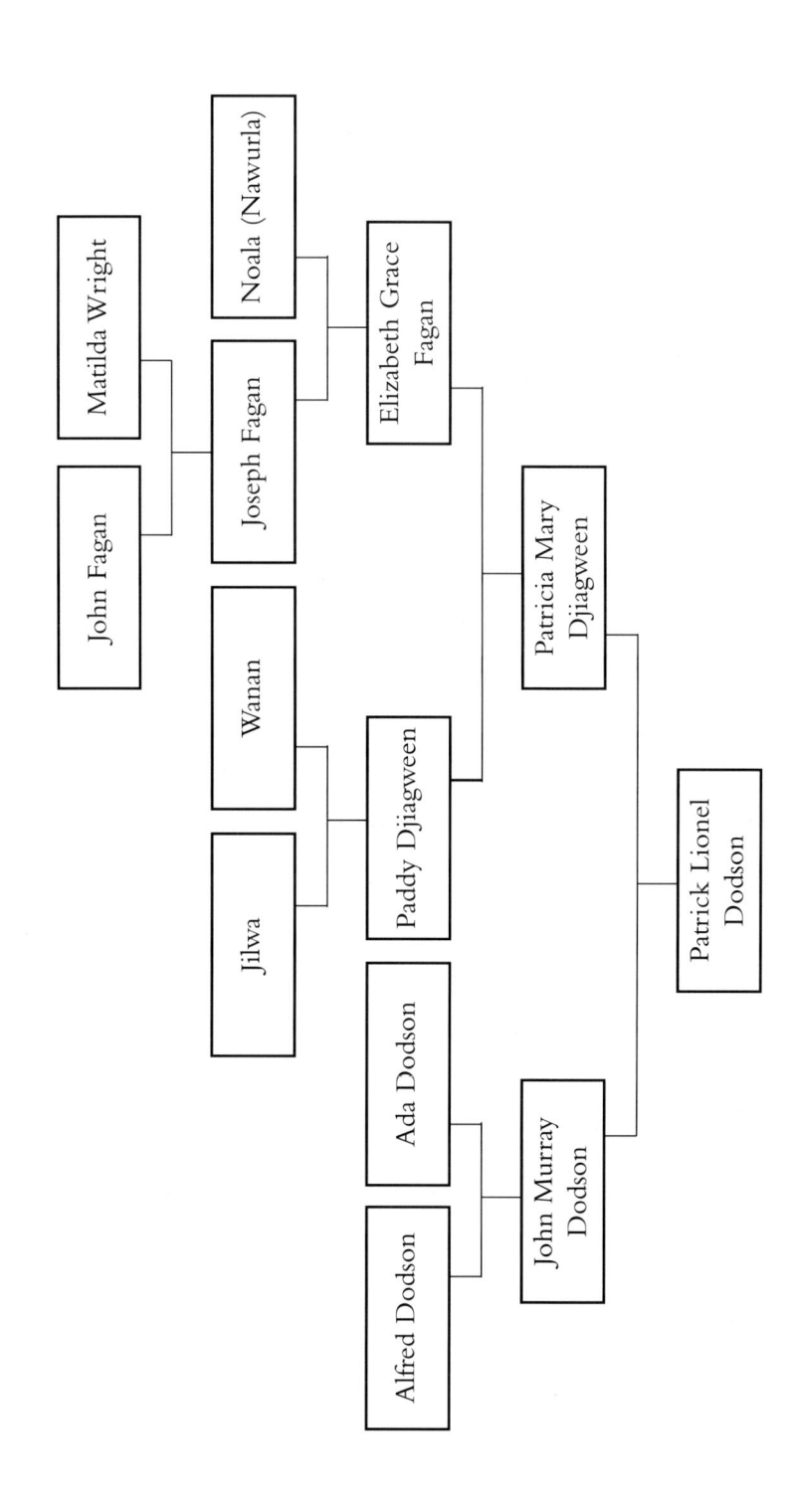

- John Fagan
- Matilda Wright
  - Joseph Fagan
- Noala (Nawurla)
  - Elizabeth Grace Fagan
- Jilwa
- Wanan
  - Paddy Djiagween
    - Patricia Mary Djiagween
- Alfred Dodson
  - Ada Dodson
    - John Murray Dodson
      - Patrick Lionel Dodson

Contents

Prologue	8
Map	20
Chapter 1: Yawuru country	21
Chapter 2: Pearlers, priests and pastoralists	37
Chapter 3: An Irishman at Wild Dog	65
Chapter 4: Two laws	89
Chapter 5: Crimes of love	122
Chapter 6: On the banks of the Katherine	155
Chapter 7: In the arms of the Church	190
Chapter 8: A troubled priest	227
Chapter 9: To the Centre	253
Chapter 10: Towards reconciliation	290
Chapter 11: The decade of reconciliation: an interview	304
Epilogue	321
Endnotes	327
Bibliography	348
Index	359

Prologue

Melbourne 1997

The winter morning of 26 May was cool and misty. Along the south bank of the Yarra River, commuters clutching newspapers pushed their way through the stream of delegates making their way to the Melbourne Convention and Exhibition Centre. In front of the Crown Casino, a group of excited students from North Queensland posed for photographs in front of the roaring gas flares. More than two thousand people had come from all over Australia to participate in the 'Renewal of the Nation', a major convention sponsored by the Council for Aboriginal Reconciliation. The Council sought to bring together Australians from all walks of life to help shape the agenda for the process of reconciliation between indigenous Australians and the wider community, in the lead-up to the Centenary of Federation in 2001. It was a milestone event on the road to reconciliation.

In the cavernous and echoing Convention Centre the delegates milled, picking up their identity tags, conference bags and programs. They looked through the list of participants and scanned the faces for old friends, colleagues, lovers and enemies. Captains of industry, senior politicians, lawyers and public servants, all dressed in charcoal grey or navy blue suits, jostled amiably with community representatives from as far away as Broome and as nearby as Fitzroy, many of them wearing shirts and badges in the red, black and yellow colours of the Aboriginal land rights movement. Bishops shared coffee with rabbis, while judges passed biscuits to musicians and policemen. The small area set aside for smokers quickly became shrouded in a dense cloud of cigarette smoke. As the Convention Centre filled, the hum of anticipation and excited conversation grew. The delegates had come together to have their say on how Australia could achieve the vision of the Council for Aboriginal Reconciliation for 'a united Australia which respects this land of ours; values the Aboriginal and Torres Strait Islander heritage; and provides justice and equity for all'. Like the process of reconciliation itself, the Australian Reconciliation Convention was ambitious, idealistic and energetic; it was also off to a late start.

The television crews hauled their cumbersome equipment around the room, seeking to capture images that could be broadcast to the nation to show what one commentator breathily called 'the most historic meeting between black and white since Captain Cook set foot on the continent'. There was one image that every viewfinder sought to capture. The lenses swiveled to follow Patrick Dodson, Chairperson of the Council, across the crowded room, their long grey woolly microphone booms hovering uninvited over conversations as Patrick personally welcomed the delegates.

It was easy for the camera crews to pick him from the crowd. They followed the black Akubra hat with the woven red, black and yellow band around the room, focusing on the trademark long, silver and black beard. They zoomed in as Patrick stooped slightly to shake hands and talk quietly and respectfully to an old lady who had come from Cape York to attend the Convention. She smiled up at him, completely engaged, and her discomfort in being in such a huge crowd dissipated. As he moved around the room, his conversational style shifted easily between the lilting rhythms of Aboriginal English and the formal tones of the Melbourne business and political establishment. Pushing down his own nervousness and tension at the scale and significance of the event, he worked hard to try to make every person he spoke to feel included, welcome and comfortable.

The media had crowned him the 'Father of Reconciliation': a label he disliked intensely. For every person at the Convention and many others watching on television Patrick Dodson embodied a process they wanted to succeed. Although they would be unlikely to agree on what success meant, or what it would look like when they reached it, there was a national consensus that reconciliation was a desirable thing.

For the Aboriginal elders who had come to Melbourne from distant, dusty and desperately poor communities in the outback he was a vision of hope—an Aboriginal man, polite and dignified, who could articulate their needs and concerns to the leaders of the nation and argue for change, for better treatment, for respect. The old lady from Cape York told me, 'He talks up for all of our mob'.

For the battled-scarred veterans of the decades of struggle for land rights and social justice he was a major player. It was his personal involvement that overcame their cynicism about the process of reconciliation. He pointed to a new way, focused on negotiation of common interest and mutual gain rather than the embattled but virtuous campaigns of yesteryear. They remained suspicious of the intent of governments of all political persuasions but saw his role as worthy of support. Geoff Clark, the Chairperson of the Aboriginal and Torres Strait Islander Commission put it succinctly, 'Patrick was our hero, our champion, dating from the days of the Federation of Land Councils. We saw him as someone with a strong view on our rights and ambitions'.[1]

But reconciliation was not simply for Aboriginal people. In the views of the Council for Aboriginal Reconciliation, established six years earlier by the Hawke government, it was part of a broader national movement intended to give benefits to the nation as a whole, and not simply to one sector.

Ray Martin, the television personality who saw through the decade of reconciliation as a member of the Council, believed that reconciliation provided a slender opportunity to establish a mature and confident Australian nation. Patrick often frustrated him. He would sidestep efforts by the media to personalise the process of reconciliation by focusing on the man himself as its figurehead:

> Major media stories were running, everyone was seeking a grab and Patrick was nowhere to be found. As like as not, he would be off in Broome fishing, or attending some small event in a local community Town Hall and the story would be allowed to run without him.[2]

The Australian business community was well represented at the Convention, with Robert Champion de Crespigny, executive chairman of Normandy Mining, heading a seminar that involved old protagonists from the Minerals Council of Australia, the Australian Council of Trade Unions and the Land Councils of the Northern Territory. For Robert, Patrick was absolutely essential to the reconciliation process:

> Here we are in Australia, one of the most resource-dependent nations on the planet, with our national wealth dependent on ongoing exploration and mining and with most major potential resource development projects located on land owned and controlled by Aboriginal people. For the first time we have been able to get the leaders of Australia's mining industry and the leaders of Australia's Aboriginal Land Councils sitting down and looking at each other across the table. Without Patrick Dodson there was no chance of us coming together like that. He showed us how we could talk the same language, pursue the same goals and enjoy each other's company while we were doing it.[3]

Australia, being a small nation in an isolated part of the world, surrounded by nations built on very different social and cultural grounds, is sensitive to the changing tides of international opinion and relationships. Indigenous representatives were present in force at the Convention, including Chief Ted Moses, Grand Chief of the Grand Council of the Crees of North America. He said quietly to me that Patrick's role in bringing all these people together was an amazing achievement that he could not see happening in the United States. 'I wonder, however, if it can last or reach a destination. Patrick's walking a tightrope, and I wonder if he can see what the other end is tied up to.'[4]

South Africa was also watching, with Archbishop Desmond Tutu sending a televised message and Dr Alexander Boraine, Vice Chairperson of the Truth and Reconciliation Commission, bringing a personal message from Nelson

Mandela, a man Patrick admires greatly. Dr Boraine addressed the Convention:

> I feel as though I am standing on Holy Ground, and feel almost as if I should be quiet rather than speak…I am witnessing here today with you, a people with a quest. Hundreds of Australians who are gathered together not to seek revenge but to search for reconciliation. And I want again, as someone who comes from outside, to congratulate you and all who have made this possible as warmly as I possibly can. In particular, I would like to thank Patrick. He is a leader, not only in your community but in the world. Would that his maturity and wisdom and open heartedness be as explicit in the political arena as it is in him.[5]

In the winter of 1997, the issues of native title and reconciliation dominated the political arena. Three linked issues captured the Convention: the national response on native title, dealing with the legacy of the 'stolen generation' and calls for a national apology for past injustices. It was these issues that Patrick had to juggle in the largest meeting ever held between indigenous Australians and the wider community. In this political arena, Australia seemed to be wrestling for its soul.

Native title was the primary contested issue. When the Council for Aboriginal Reconciliation was newly formed in 1992, the High Court issued a landmark decision in Australian legal history, recognising the ongoing existence of a form of native title in the common law. In the *Mabo* decision the High Court abolished the legal fiction of terra nullius, through which the prior and continuing ownership of land by Australia's indigenous people had been ignored.[6] This was a great legal and moral victory for Aboriginal Australians, but plunged many non-Aboriginal Australians, especially in regional and rural Australia, into a condition of fear. They were concerned that they could lose control over the land they occupied, and believed they owned. The definition of what could, or could not, be claimed through the courts in common law was open to wild and often ill-informed speculation. The Australian government, under Prime Minister Paul Keating, had established a consultation and negotiation process that sought to reconcile the different views of Aboriginal groups, state and territory governments, pastoralists and miners, in order to define a statutory regime that could identify, mediate and determine native title rights to land.

Intense negotiations followed, during which Patrick Dodson and his Council was often left on the sidelines, stranded by their over-riding need to maintain consensus and to avoid taking sides. Instead, they convened productive but politically marginal meetings of key decision-makers in an effort to find common ground. As the clock neared midnight, just three days before Christmas, the *Native Title Act 1993* was passed by the Senate. One issue left unresolved by both the *Mabo* decision and the new statutory regime would return. This was the vexed question of the potential coexistence of native title and leases, especially on the large pastoral leases of northern and central Australia. In the negotiations between Aboriginal groups and the Keating government it was agreed to leave this issue open. The preamble to the new Act noted the Government interpretation; recalling that the High Court had 'held that native title is extinguished by valid government acts that are inconsistent with the continued existence of native title rights and interests, such as the grant of freehold or leasehold estates'. The issue was left, however, for the courts to decide.

The High Court did so three years later. On 23 December 1996, in the *Wik* decision, the High Court ruled that native title could survive the grant of a pastoral lease.[7] However the Court also found that any action taken by pastoralists, that was inconsistent with native title, would extinguish that title. Claimants danced joyfully outside the High Court building with Gladys Tybingoompa from Aurukun claiming, 'Out of here we go, no one being loser'[8].

For the Coalition government of Prime Minister John Howard, elected in March 1996, this was a surprising and far-reaching decision of specific concern to key elements of his constituency, especially in rural Australia. The pastoral industry reacted with immediate alarm. The National Farmers' Federation announced the death of Aboriginal Reconciliation. The leader of the National Party criticised the High Court for being activist and called for 'bucket-loads of extinguishment'. During the first half of 1997, in the lead-up to the Australian Reconciliation Convention, the debates accelerated and intensified, with state governments calling for legislation to extinguish native title on all pastoral leases. Discussions between the Government and Aboriginal groups ground to a frustrated halt. By 1 May, when the Prime Minister released his 'Ten-Point Plan' to resolve the issues through legislation, the political arena of reconciliation was in the national spotlight and the heat was intense.

Three weeks after the Prime Minister's plan was released, Patrick Dodson had the task of introducing the Prime Minister for the formal opening ceremony of the Convention in the John Batman room of the Convention Centre. Together, they watched the welcoming ceremony arranged by the Kulin nation, traditional owners whose country covered the city of Melbourne, and whose ancestors had negotiated, in a manner of speaking, with John Batman. In his opening remarks, Patrick was unfailingly polite but unavoidably assertive, stepping dangerously along the bipartisan line that had been the hallmark of the Council:

> The ten-point plan in response to *Wik* is not acceptable. Why not? Because, taken as a whole, it does not treat coexistence fairly. It takes away the rights of Indigenous people which were recognised in the common law of Australia by the highest court in the land, and proposes at the same time to increase the landholding rights of those with pastoral leases, largely at taxpayers' expense. The nation faces a simple truth: if we cannot achieve coexistence, then we cannot achieve reconciliation.

Patrick articulated a different approach, consistent with the ethos of his approach to reconciliation:

> I remain convinced that with goodwill and generosity of spirit, all relevant parties can sit down around the table and negotiate a solution to *Wik* which will protect the legitimate interests of all stakeholders and preserve all existing rights. I am willing to contribute in whatever way I can to such an outcome.

The Prime Minister responded with increasing passion and barely contained anger, as several people in the audience turned their back on him:

> I know that the goals of the reconciliation process have been subjected to tension and strain as a result of the current debate on Native Title issues. You will all be aware that I have spent a great deal of time in trying to find a just, fair and workable outcome in response to the decision of the High Court of Australia in the *Wik* case. In working towards that solution, my Government's primary goal has been to strike a fair and reasonable balance between the rights of indigenous people and the rights of other Australians, in particular those in the pastoral and mining industries…I also need in the name of truth and in the name of a frank discussion of this issue to repudiate the claim that my ten-point plan involves a massive hand-out of freehold title at taxpayer expense. That is an absolute myth, it is absolutely contrary to the fact and I absolutely repudiate it.

In reviewing his first term of office, the Prime Minister would candidly remark that his presentation to the Convention was a personal low point, which he regretted. At the time, Patrick watched from the stage with growing dismay and disappointment. He noticed that the Leader of the Opposition, Kim Beazley, was silent on the issue of *Wik*. He could see little sign, at that moment, of the necessary goodwill and generosity of spirit from the political leadership of the nation. He recognised the authority and right of the elected government to determine the policy mix required to resolve decisions of land use and management. He could see the need for parliamentary leadership and statutory responses. He could not see, however, how to leaven that determination with a sense of respect for the connections that Aboriginal people continued to maintain with their land, with their cultural heritage and their sense of place. The road to reconciliation seemed even longer; the vision of the Council more elusive; his job even harder.

There was deep emotion at the Convention that transcended debates over words, laws and politics. The report of the Human Rights and Equal and Opportunity Commission on the policies and practices of the removal of Aboriginal children was released at the Convention.[9] *Bringing them Home* had been leaked to newspapers before the Convention and roundly criticised for its allusions to 'genocide', its perceived selective reporting and its calls for a national apology. Patrick's deputy on the Council in its first term, Sir Ronald Wilson, had worked with Patrick's younger brother, Mick, to prepare the report. They had shared the agonies of listening to hundreds of stories of grief and pain and working to start a healing process for all those who came forward. Sir Ronald made special reference to 'my colleague Mick, to whom I have grown so close, through this bonding experience we are more than brothers because we have been bonded by twelve months of listening to our fellow Australians and being deeply moved by those stories'. Some of the stories told have echoes in the Dodson family history: stories of pain, of discrimination, of suffering and of loss. Such events have shaped Patrick and Mick and their families, although neither of the Dodson brothers identify as 'stolen'. The stories are Australian Aboriginal stories.

The same emotional wavelength reached Patrick, generally a model of emotional stoicism and gruff practicality, in the closing session of the Convention. He remembered his friend Rob Riley, a 'stolen child' who had taken his own life. Tears filled Patrick's eyes and choked his throat as he recalled:

> There is one whom I would like to acknowledge and thank who is not here with us today. One who was always prepared to walk together with us no matter what the burden and hurt that entailed. He had the vision when others were still searching in darkness. He had the courage to walk without trepidation when others had difficulty finding the strength to confront the barriers that were raised before us. Our brother Rob left us physically 12 months ago, but where the candle of the stolen generations has burned in the corner of the stage over these days, his spirit has filled this auditorium. And we thank him for that.

The next night, at the Australian Reconciliation Awards Dinner and Presentations, hosted by Ray Martin, a different Patrick Dodson could be seen and heard. He was glowing with excitement and energy, despite the personal, political and organisational demands of the Convention. It had been a stimulating day, with a moving ceremony to recall the thirtieth anniversary of the 1967 Referendum and the heroes, black and white, who had pushed forward an overwhelming consensus on the recognition of Aboriginal people in the Australian nation–state. The Governor-General, Sir William Deane, noted that, 'perhaps most important for present purposes, the joint campaign of Indigenous and non-Indigenous Australians in support of the referendum and its carriage by more than 90% of the people constituted a first major step along the road to true reconciliation'.

An international guest panel had sparked a sense of possibility for Australia to join those nations that had formally recognised the reality of indigenous self-determination. The visitors praised Australia for its leadership on indigenous issues. A range of seminar sessions addressed the definitions of human rights as they were applied to indigenous Australians. Another series of seminars explored the nature, rationale and process for developing documents of reconciliation and entrenching the rights of indigenous Australians in the Constitution. In rooms across the Convention Centre, there was a buzz of excitement as diverse groups of Australians from a range of places, peoples and political persuasions worked together to discuss, define and deliver on the process of reconciliation. Patrick walked from room to room, tuning in to the wavelengths. As he listened, he began to see that reconciliation was not just a possibility but that it was becoming an actuality. In his closing remarks he would comment that, 'In these gatherings, people have rolled up their sleeves and got down to the business of looking for answers to the multitude of challenges encompassed in the notion of reconciliation'.

That night at the Awards ceremony Patrick sat, ate and talked with his friends and countrymen, sharing the spirit of commitment, enjoying the talk and laughter as people danced to the music of indigenous musicians Christine Anu and Troy Cassar-Daly and applauded the awards for reconciliation action. He commented that the efforts in communities and workplaces across Australia showed that 'political bickering, strident voices and ugly messages have not discouraged Australians from getting on with the job of reconciliation'.

One particular reconciliation award nomination pleased him. The Shire of Broome had joined with the Rubibi Land, Heritage and Development Council on a path of negotiation that resulted in an Interim Agreement, mapping a future for Broome 'that is reconciled in spirit and in reality.' The issue of native title, so divisive at the national level, was being resolved locally. Despite being 'on the square', not having had a drink for three years, he felt light-headed and joyful. Broome was his country, his place. It was showing the way forward, lighting the road ahead for the nation. He wanted to see a just and beneficial result for the native title issues on his own patch.

Apart from pride in his community, though, this award reached a part of his sense of self not readily visible to the television cameras or the crowds of supporters around the tables. It was his own reconciliation that was being affirmed. Patrick Dodson had spent most of the latter part of his life 'coming home', finding the road that would bring him back to his origins, his family, his people, his country. He was reclaiming his history and that of his grandfather, Paddy Djiagween. He was following Paddy's road.

In the months following the Australian Reconciliation Convention, the issues of *Wik*, a national apology and the most appropriate response to the findings of the *Bringing Them Home* report reverberated in the national media. The issues became divisive and politicised. There was little scope in such a climate for voices of reason, consensus and common ground. Patrick found himself increasingly at odds with the approach of the Howard Government, disagreeing with its primary emphasis on practical reconciliation and its disavowal of attempts to negotiate structural change in the relationship between indigenous Australians and the wider community. Negotiations with the Prime Minister and the Minister, John Herron, over the appointment of the deputy Chairperson of the Council ended in frustration on both sides.

Five months after the closing ceremony of the Convention, Patrick Dodson resigned from his position as Chairperson of the Council for Aboriginal Reconciliation. He 'rolled his swag' and returned to live and work in Broome, home of the Yawuru people. He returned to his roots.

Not long afterwards, on long service leave from my work as a public servant, I travelled to Broome and stayed for a time with Patrick and his family. I wanted to take time out to research and write. Patrick and I had known each other for some fifteen years. I had been employed by the Central Land Council, when he was the Director. At that time I was engaged as a newly qualified consultant anthropologist, carrying out sacred site research in the region where I had been a teacher in bilingual education programs. Patrick later press-ganged me into helping to organise the

'Come to Canberra' campaign of 1985, protesting against the Hawke Labor government's national land rights plans. Our relationship was renewed when I worked on the staff of Robert Tickner, Minister for Aboriginal Affairs and Patrick was appointed as the Chairman of the Council for Aboriginal Reconciliation. I joined the secretariat of the new Council, working in the Department of Prime Minister and Cabinet, before moving to a policy adviser role on issues of native title, heritage and environment for the Keating and Howard governments.

When I first turned up in Broome, I had a certain book in mind. In all the national media coverage of Aboriginal issues, I was frustrated at the lack of explanation or in-depth discussion on Aboriginal issues of land, heritage and culture. It was a political football, but no media interest was given to the history of the game and the reason it was being played. I wanted to write a book that explained the background to these issues set within the frame of Patrick's personal contemporary political history. As we talked through the research task and I learned more about Broome and its history, my research work changed. As I learned more about the history of the Yawuru people and his family, the shape of this biography and family history began to emerge.

The family story has its grounding in the life of the father of Patrick's mother. Paddy Djiagween is, in many ways, his role-model, mentor and life-hero. The story of this man, who lived for more than a century, is the story of the establishment, settlement and growth of the pearling port of Broome and the pastoral frontier of the East Kimberley. Paddy's life is a compressed history of colonisation, a case study in the Aboriginal experience. It is the story of the Yawuru people, Patrick's people, lived through the life of one man.

Over time, I began to piece Paddy's life story together from anecdotes, interviews and archives. Many of the fragments could not be found. They were missing, lost or forgotten. Some could not be told. Some of the pieces most important to Paddy Djiagween and Patrick Dodson are centred on Yawuru religion. This is religious 'business'; held tightly and closely. It is not for display to the world outside the Yawuru people and the holders of their law.

In the archives, I began to unravel the story of Patrick's Granny Liz, Paddy Djiagween's wife, Elizabeth Grace Fagan and her long struggle with a frustrating bureaucracy. Her Irish father, Joseph Fagan, was one of the early pioneers of the rugged and violent East Kimberley frontier. On the one hand, their story tells of generosity of spirit and frontier survival under difficult conditions. On the other, it tells of the negative impact of misguided policies directed towards the control of Aboriginal people in the early years of the last century.

I learned that the Dodson story is a love story; of love found by Patrick's mother, Patricia and his father, Snowy, and lost again in the harsh climate of assimilation and social control. I learned that they sought a new life, fleeing across a state border away from the long arms of a powerful and possessive bureaucracy. There were painful, sad stories of life, love and death. Losing both parents within months of each other has had a major impact on Patrick's approach to life, love, family and politics.

Much of the family story has been extracted from archival sources. The lives and loves of Aboriginal people in Western Australia and the Northern Territory were plotted and guided by powerful officials with mixed intentions and personal idiosyncrasies. The intrusiveness of policies and programs intended to improve and control the likes of the Dodson family, especially the women, was a major force in shaping life decisions for the family. The files make sorry reading today and still have the capacity to hurt and wound.

Once, after repeated requests for access, a carton of duplicate files from the Western Australian Government archives on the life of his Granny Liz arrived at Patrick's house in Broome. The files, carefully culled and edited in Perth, were personal records of wards of the state. They recorded the activities of state government agencies in sixty years of monitoring, considering and determining the fates of the Dodson family. The carton of files sat for over a year, gathering dust in a cupboard, until Patrick summoned the courage to deal with the contents. He firstly shared the papers with his family, especially his younger brother, Mick, and decided on how the information could be released for this book. Their courage in sharing these records is outstanding.

The brothers, Patrick and Mick, are public figures, their faces well known, if occasionally confused, in television and newspapers. Their siblings are not public figures and rarely engage in political life outside their communities. Fay, Georgina, Cecil, Jacko and Patricia have their own stories and histories, which this book does not attempt to portray.

The story is also a story about some heroes in Patrick's life. Men and women, black and white, rich and poor, who have looked at tough times and found laughter; have seen cruelty and responded with courage; have seen hardship and shown how to care. They are ordinary, decent Australians who have made a difference in the life of Patrick Dodson and his family.

The story is a personal story; of how one man has lived his life, from smiling schoolboy playing cowboy in Katherine to scholar, priest and national political figure. This life, however, is a frame for a larger story: the story of his country and his countrymen and their relationship with a dominating and often uncaring majority society. Always stressing the community over the individual, the political over the personal, Patrick has pushed this story into the shape it is. While being generous with his time, memories and reflection, he has been consistently reluctant to focus the story on his own personal life, career and political contributions. He argues that people can make up their own minds on these issues, while he is still alive and still contributing, and he has been careful to protect his children and loved ones. Over time I have come to recognise that such reluctance is consistent with the emotional patterns established in his childhood and youth, especially after the early loss of his father and mother.

The Patrick Dodson story has come into public prominence over the last decade, during the highs and lows of the decade of reconciliation, and the surge of media comment on issues of native title and reconciliation. Patrick reflects on that decade in an interview in the final chapter. The details of the complex and contested political processes of that decade and Patrick's role in the debates on *Mabo* and *Wik* are a long story, not explored here. I worked on these issues for both Labor and Coalition governments. Consistent with the professional code of conduct that guides my work, I have not included any information I have obtained as a result of my ongoing role as a public servant.

Paddy's Road explores the history of the Yawuru people in order to trace the political and cultural genealogy of the 'Father of Reconciliation'. It tells the story of the lives of members of Patrick's family, analysing the impacts of colonisation on one family over time, tracing the impact of policies and programs designed for their welfare. It looks behind the tall, bearded figure the nation saw at the Australian Reconciliation Convention to explore the shaping forces of one family history and one man's life in the history of our nation. It is an Australian story of reconciliation.

20 ● Paddy's Road

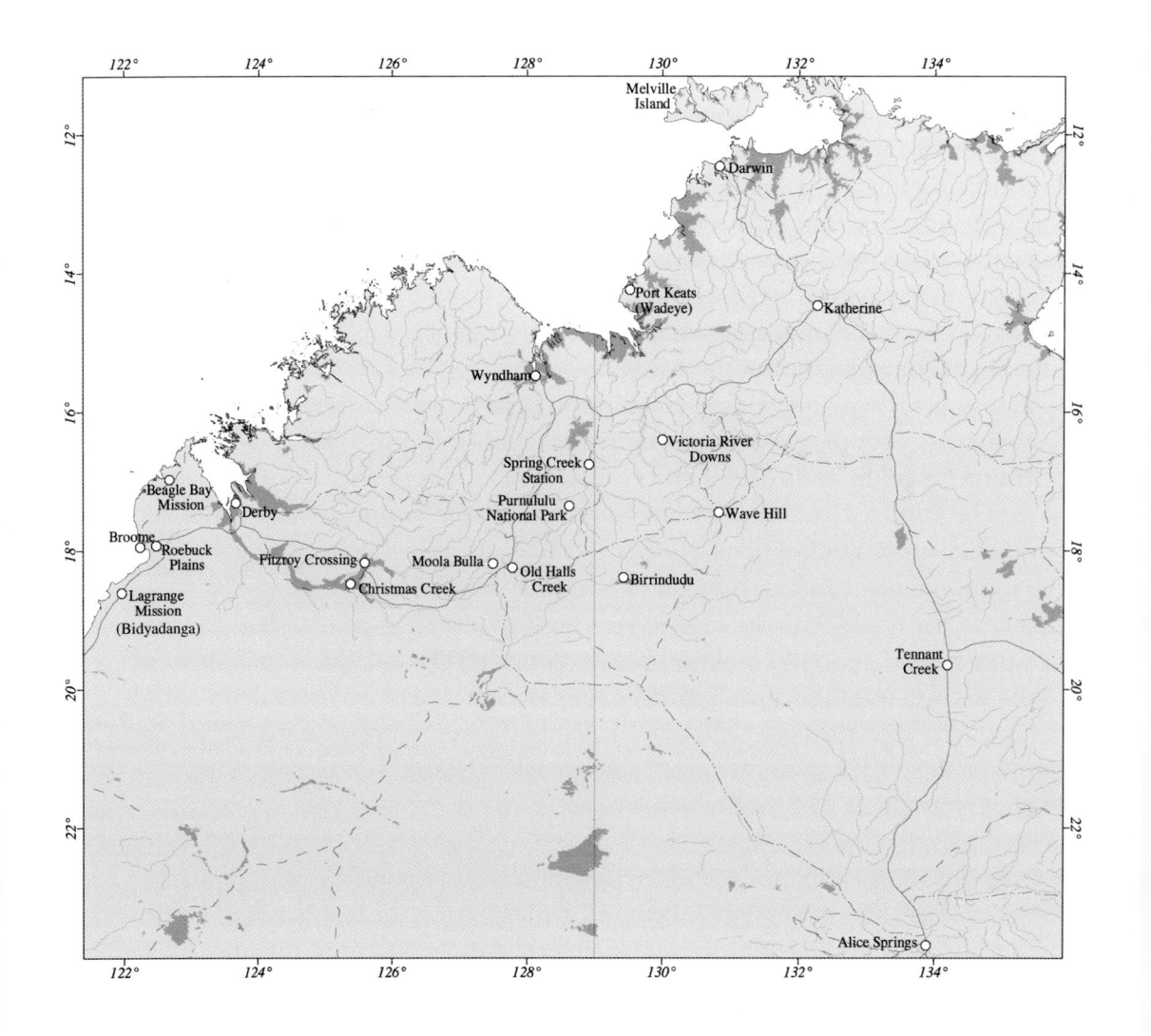

Paddy's Road: Places in North-west Australia

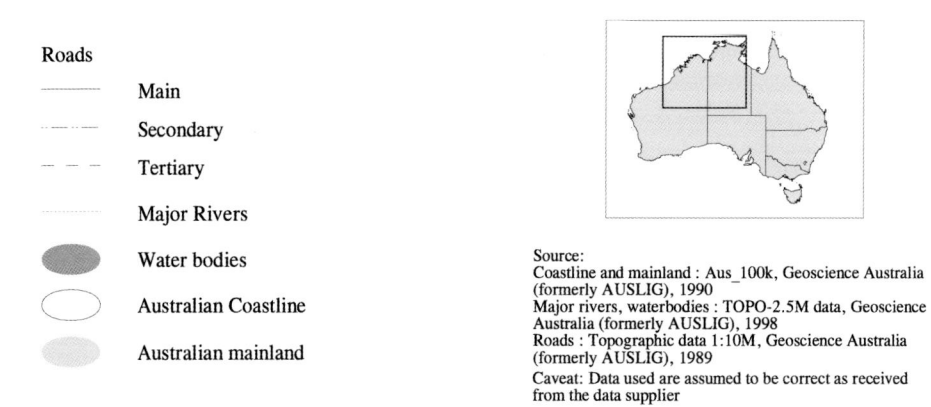

Roads
- Main
- Secondary
- Tertiary

Major Rivers
Water bodies
Australian Coastline
Australian mainland

Source:
Coastline and mainland : Aus_100k, Geoscience Australia (formerly AUSLIG), 1990
Major rivers, waterbodies : TOPO-2.5M data, Geoscience Australia (formerly AUSLIG), 1998
Roads : Topographic data 1:10M, Geoscience Australia (formerly AUSLIG), 1989
Caveat: Data used are assumed to be correct as received from the data supplier

Chapter One

Yawuru Country

'Nothing endured at all, nothing but the land… The land was forever, it moved and changed below you, but was forever.'
Lewis Grassic Gibbon, *Sunset Song* (1932)[1]

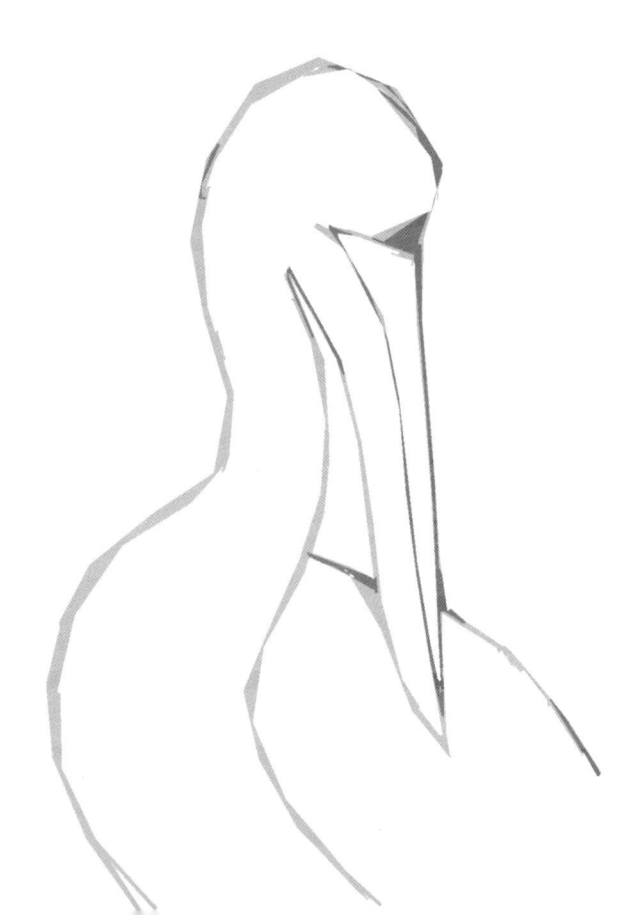

The Block, Broome, WA, April 1998

In the dry season from May to October, the population of the town of Broome more than triples to some 40,000 people. Tourists come from over the globe, seeking a taste of a tropical oasis on the fringes of the Indian Ocean in the northwest corner of the large dry Australian continent. At the airport is a sign that says, 'You can relax now. You're in Broome.' While many tourists come simply to enjoy the white beaches and blue waters of a luxury holiday at the Cable Beach resort, many are seduced by the romantic and flamboyant history and multicultural heritage of this Australian pearling port, situated in the exotic wilderness of the vast, remote Kimberley region. North of the Broome town centre, past the dusty speedway and the last caravan park, beyond the bitumen and the postman's route, visitors with good directions and a car that can clear the washouts will find themselves at 'the Block', Patrick Dodson's home.

Patrick is hard at it in the garden, digging, cutting back and cleaning up. He has lived here for more than ten years, sharing the rural subdivision with his niece, who lives in a neighbouring house with her family. Because Patrick is on the road for weeks at a stretch, there are always more jobs to do than time to do them. Years of work, however, and gallons of bore water have made a shady oasis in the dry, red pindan landscape fringing the tidal flats of Roebuck Bay.[2]

Under a pergola outside the house, a big, blue billycan, gift of a passing shadow minister, is in constant service. Large enamel pannikins of tea are poured for the flow of visitors. There is a pause in the gardening while Patrick works through next week's travel and meeting arrangements with his off-sider and business partner, Paul Lane. The mobile phone buzzes with requests for Patrick to talk somewhere, to meet someone, to write something, to be somewhere else. Paul fields the calls and tries to fend off most of the always-worthy invitations. Since Patrick resigned as Chairman of the Council for Aboriginal Reconciliation six months earlier, the demands on his time and presence have changed, but not abated.

Another dusty Toyota pulls up in the drive, avoiding the piles of besser blocks ready for the next big project, but disturbing Noah, the affable pig-dog sleeping among the blocks. A staff member of the Kimberley Land Council has made his way to the Block seeking advice on potential speakers for a forthcoming regional development conference. This is a weighty topic, its sensitivity measured as much by the number of cups of tea poured in the process, as the number of names proposed and rejected.

Managing the processes of reconciliation at the regional level requires a judicious blend of vision and pragmatism, of knowing who can deliver and what might be achieved. The track record and current positions of key factional players on Aboriginal and non-Aboriginal sides are weighed; interests measured; political alliances balanced; feuds, antagonisms and jealousies taken into account. Many of the names spark Patrick or Paul into a yarn, a story that perhaps gives a snapshot of personality and political persuasion, or simply tickles their sense of humour. The sun is setting behind thickening clouds by the time a workable list is drawn up for the first round of phone calls and invitation letters. The garden jobs will wait until the schedule allows another 'quiet' day at home.

June Oscar, Patrick's wife and partner for the last six years, comes home after a long day at Land Council meetings in her hometown of Fitzroy Crossing. She brings Grace, Patrick's daughter, from the school at Notre Dame in Broome where she works and studies, on an extended visit from her own hometown of Wadeye, Port Keats in the Northern Territory. Adrian, Patrick's son, is dropped off dragging his boots behind him after football training. The evening television news is interrupted by a few phone calls from family members in Broome or Fitzroy, arranging a fishing trip and exchanging news.

After dinner Patrick, June and I sit telling stories and sharing red wine under the pergola. I have come up from Canberra on long service leave to begin research on this book. Patrick and June have generously invited me to share their home, and given me a place to roll out my swag. Adrian, Noah and I share an elevated sleep-out and the world's largest mosquito net.

The evening brings the mosquitoes, causing Patrick to put some of the dried trunk of a conkerberry[3] shrub into the fire drum. A dash of water makes thick plumes of aromatic smoke drift across the table and the mosquitoes are repelled. Gungkara is the Yawuru term for the shrub, Patrick tells me. He and June talk about its uses, its fruits, sweet when black, its medicinal uses. They compare notes between the coastal Yawuru, Patrick's mob and the inland Bunuba, June's mob from the Fitzroy River. The sweet smoky smell and the Western Australian red wine complement each other and the mood is relaxed; Patrick is at home in his country.

Yawuru country

Patrick Dodson is a Yawuru man. He 'comes from here'. He tracks his story and defines his Yawuru identity and his Aboriginality through his mother, Patricia and her father, Paddy Djiagween. Another generation back is Paddy Djiagween's father, Jilwa, and his mother, Wanan.[4] Some one hundred and fifty years ago and more, Jilwa and Wanan lived in the country that Patrick now calls home.[5]

Any understanding of Patrick Dodson would be incomplete without some understanding of the Yawuru country and history. Any understanding of the issues of contemporary Aboriginal Australia would also be partial without an appreciation of the significance of this ongoing connection to country for Aboriginal people. The past, the place and the people are woven together in story and song.

Many Yawuru came before Jilwa and Wanan. Archaeologists trace the record of human occupation in the region back some 27,000 years.[6] Countless generations raised their children along the sandy beaches, coastal dunes and wetlands of their country. They called their place Jirrginngan; maps now show it as Broome. They called themselves the Minyjirr Yawuru, those who look after the Yawuru country around what is now the town of Broome at places called Gantheaume Point, Fisherman's Bend and the northwest of Roebuck Plains.[7] Today's place names tell of the colonial history of Broome. They sit uneasily imposed over the older names, with their deeper stories and longer histories.

Jilwa and Wanan, like other Yawuru, knew their country. They fished for salmon, stingray, turtle and dugong with spears and stone-fish traps, on the edge of the ocean and in the waters of the bay. Much of their country was marshy wetlands (*bundu*) rich in life and diverse in food supply even when inundated by king tides. They spent time finding oysters, cockles and crabs; gathering plants such as tubers and bush fruits; seeking the eggs of turtles and sea birds; hunting for turkeys, kangaroos and large sand monitor lizards. They knew how, where and when to find enough food to sustain a self-sufficient economy for a large population.

When reefs were exposed at equinox low tides, the Yawuru collected gold-lip pearl shells, grinding them on coral and carving intricate, religiously inspired designs on them. These were exchanged with their neighbours at the starting point of the trade routes that criss-crossed the continent. The carved shells (*jakuli*) were held in awe in the distant desert regions—said to contain, in their milky luminescence, the essence of water, of life itself.[8]

Jilwa and Wanan knew the power of the country and followed the *Bugarigarra*. Non-Aboriginal people refer to this time as the Dreaming. The collective memory of the Yawuru carried the songs, stories and designs that gave meaning to their country and their lives. Neither man nor woman was without country, without kin, without a place to call their own. Every Yawuru person belonged in the whole of the Yawuru country. Many could trace their origin to a special place (*buru*) where their spirit (*rai*) was found, emerging in the dream of their father and given to their mother. Sometimes this might be passed on through another senior relative. The *rai* were left at these sites through the deeds that took place in the *Bugarigarra*. There, the sisters in the Dreaming placed the stones on the beach; here the sea-spirit women became stone pillars.[9] At the time of the *Bugarigarra* the blue-bone fish swam, the dog howled, the pelican flew. These are the ancestors who transformed the land and water, leaving behind them the atom-like essence of all life. Everywhere, the *Bugarigarra* gave a specific shape to life, to country, to what it means to be a Yawuru person and how to relate to others through a kinship structure.

Patrick Dodson once asked Christian readers to imagine themselves as Aboriginal Australians before 'the white invasion':

> As to your knowledge of the land, your country, you would know every tree, every rock, because through the Dreaming, the great ancestors came this way. And they are still here. They live. They must be revered, appeased, paid attention to. It is they who cause conception as a woman walks near. When the child is born he calls that part of the country 'Father'.[10]

The actions in the *Bugarigarra* were recreated and rekindled in important ceremonies. Large groups of people flocked to the ceremonies to follow the *Bugarigarra* and celebrate life, culture and creativity. They shared their understanding of the *Bugarigarra* and its laws; singing and dancing to look after the country and its people. The older Yawuru lawmen and women were the guardians and interpreters of these laws, putting a wealth of intellectual energy, knowledge and experience into exploring the complexity of relations across social and cultural group boundaries.

The Yawuru had neighbours with whom they danced, exchanged marriage partners and shared songs about the *Bugarigarra* that crossed over their lands. The Nyikina, Mangala, the Karajarri, and the Ngangumarta carried the equivalent laws for their country adjoining the Yawuru.[11] At times, these boundaries, these complex relationships, led to conflict, dispute and violent death. Sometimes, following the Law meant fighting for the country. Further away, people were unknown strangers; some from so far away that they were rumoured to be not truly people at all. Some did not even have colour in their skin.

Dampier's Cargo

Three hundred years ago, the Yawuru world was visited by strangers from across the sea to the west. The men on the 30-metre wallowing tub, the *Roebuck*, were perishing for lack of water and suffering from scurvy after a voyage across the Indian Ocean.[12] The captain of the ship was William Dampier, once a buccaneer. In 1699 he was on the payroll of the British Crown as an explorer, seeking out the economic potential of lands unclaimed if not un-owned. He and his men came ashore and looked for water on the Yawuru land not so far from where Patrick's Block is now located.

Dampier wrote his story. He had a racy, opinionated and brash way with words that appealed to the London readers of the travel sagas he churned out on his return. He described the people he met in Western Australia in unflattering terms, regarding them as the 'miserablest people in the world':

> Setting aside their humane shape, they differ but little from Brutes...
> They have great Bottle noses, pretty full lips, and wide mouths...
> Neither have they any beards. They are long visaged, and of very unpleasing aspect; having no one graceful feature in their faces...
> They have no houses, but lye in the open Air, without any covering; the earth being their bed, and the Heaven their Canopy...
> There is neither Herb, Root, Pulse, nor any sort of Grain for them to eat, that we saw, nor any sort of Bird, or Beast that they can catch, having no instruments wherewithal to do so. I did not perceive that they did worship anything...

These people speak somewhat thro the throat, but we could not understand one word that they said.[13]

Twenty minutes after Dampier arrived, there was trouble. The inability to communicate led to a skirmish on the beach. The first shot was fired in anger, wounding a young Yawuru man. In retaliation, a 'nimble young crewman', not nimble enough, was speared in the face. Both sides withdrew to tend their wounded. Dampier stayed in the area for two weeks, getting water in the upper reaches of a creek that now bears his name, before setting sail for Timor.[14]

For William Dampier, the immediate aftermath of the trip did not go well. On his return, he was court-marshalled on charges raised by an officer of the ship, found guilty, deprived of his three years' pay and declared unfit as a commander. He turned to writing bestsellers based on his travels, books that sparked exploration fever in England and inspired the fantasies of Jonathan Swift. He also had a career as a showman (selling tickets to view the Tattooed Prince, a Filipino slave).[15] He may have been a rogue but he helped influence ideas and values. Dampier's views shaped European attitudes to Aboriginal Australians for longer than just his generation.

A Yawuru story of First Contact

Across Australia, interactions between traditional Aboriginal societies and the wider world created different stories, shaped different histories. A different story of that day has been passed on to Yawuru people such as Louisa Collins:

> When the first white men sailed into Roebuck Bay, the Yarru (Yawuru) tribe who was living in the sandhills didn't know what was happening. They thought the boat was some kind of fish monster. The men went down to defend and protect their people. Captain Cook and other explorers traded material and other domestic items for fresh water and food. One of the sailors was from India—his name was Congill. He went with the Yarru and lived with them for many years until he died. The story of Congill was told to us as children, and told to my mother and her mother. This story has been handed down over the years.[16]

In this story, the name of Captain Cook has become synonymous with all white explorers, but the emphasis is on reciprocal interaction and long-lasting relationships. The ideas of William Dampier and the ideas of the Yawuru on that first meeting could not be more different.

Cargoes of change

The *Roebuck* was the first of many ships that broke the horizon, carrying cargoes that would change the Yawuru way of life. The white strangers came again and again; then they came to stay. The holds of their ships were brimming with new objects, animals, tools but the ship also carried ideas. Some of this cargo would be absorbed into the Yawuru way; some would be rejected and resisted. Others would prove to have a devastating impact on their people.

Yawuru life would never be the same and Patrick's great grandparents, Jilwa and Wanan, were witnesses to the first rush of change. The pearlers came first, followed by the pastoralists, the priests and the policemen. They were the *kardiya*, the white people.[17] As groups and individuals they had distinct ways of working and living with the Yawuru and their neighbours. But most of the *kardiya* carried a common cargo. They shared a bundle of ideas and values that determined their position in dealings with the Yawuru and their neighbours. Boats, packhorses, camels, trucks and planes over the next three centuries would bring more loads of the same cargo, more people with the same ideas.

Patrick Dodson, in reading Dampier's words, saw them as signposts to the value system that shaped Australian interactions with the indigenous population:

> The Dampier view that Aboriginal people were somehow less human than their visitors and new masters has carried on. Time and time again in the history of the Kimberley, there were punitive killings, kidnapped labour, sexual exploitation and laws and policies that were brutal in their delivery while noble in their intentions. At its heart is that there was no recognition of humanity. It was always viewed as entirely appropriate, even by those sympathetic to Aboriginal people, that decisions should be made for Aboriginal people, not by us, giving us no right of choice, no power over our own lives. There was little recognition of the rights of our people, of our families, to be ourselves, to be allowed the dignity of human choices.[18]

Dampier 'did not perceive that that they did worship anything'. Without a shared language between the newcomers and the people, there were no shared ideas; there was no recognition of a religion without churches, statues and priestly garb. His failure to perceive the spirituality of Aboriginal society, especially its wellspring in the religion of the land, would be repeated throughout the Kimberley. As a consequence, land was appropriated without recognition, consultation or compensation. Families were uprooted and trans-located for administrative convenience. Ceremonies were forbidden.

Sacred sites were destroyed and sacred objects and human remains were stolen and sold. Not recognising the people's links with country and the religious dimensions of the Aboriginal experience enabled those links to be ignored or denigrated.

The perceived lack of 'Herb, Root, Pulse, nor any sort of Grain' told against the Yawuru. A people without agriculture, housing and the trappings of domestication were not seen as tillers of the soil or owners of the land. The land therefore, was ownerless, *terra nullius*, and its people denuded of any rights of ownership.

Dampier's cargo was a way of seeing the people and the country that did not recognise Aboriginal humanity, spirituality and land ownership. The *kardiya* values that led to this blind spot shaped Yawuru history. Across the continent, an historical script was played out that time and again saw Aboriginal people lose land, lose life, lose their human rights. In the Kimberley, and in the history of Patrick Dodson and his family, these attitudes would shape interactions and events, especially when the state, when government, was involved.

Other boats from Europe, although carrying much of Dampier's values about Aboriginal people, carried different ideas as well. These *kardiya* were influenced by values and belief systems that drew upon the romanticism of Rousseau, the independence of the Irish, the discipline of the Germans, and ideas and values shaped by different forms of Christianity. The boats came from not just Europe. They came from the islands of Timor, from the archipelago of Indonesia, from as far away as the Philippines, Japan and China. These people were not *kardiya* and interactions at the personal level were very different in kind and effect.

The Yawuru, however, had their own views on the processes of history and the mixing of ideas and values that occurred on their land. The Louisa Collins version of the first day of contact points to a less bleak and determined view of history—a different theme. She admits to ignorance and fear but also tells of resistance, defence, and of people fighting for their land. She also talks of accommodation, of trade, of a willingness to negotiate.

Louisa Collins talks of Captain Cook, as Aboriginal people do in other parts of Australia, as the archetypal leader of first contact.[19] The captain of a vessel between worlds, usually bringing with him a moral law that was out of step with Aboriginal morality.

And Congill, the sailor from India, who chose the beach instead of the boat? His strange story points to the possibility of ongoing cross-cultural relationships, of mutual dependence, of shared trust, even of reconciliation. It points to an important issue that Dampier's writing forgets; namely, the capacity of the human spirit to be decent, empathetic and willing to treat others, different from yourself, as human beings. Such a spirit is shown, by black and white, throughout the Dodson family history.

Jilwa and Wanan

Patrick Dodson knows the names of his great-grandparents on his mother's father's side. Jilwa and Wanan were born and raised in the bush around the turquoise waters of Roebuck Bay. Occasionally, ships came to the bay and their life was interrupted. Macassan fisherman and trepangers from the islands of Timor to the north visited the shores every wet season, trading alcohol, tobacco and brightly coloured cloth in exchange for the use of Yawuru resources. They were different people, but not strangers. These visitors did not stay, did not need to have ownership of the land, and did not need to convert, control or change the Yawuru. They did, however, culturally interact, to the extent that a Port Darwin Customs House report in 1903, noted that the trade had being going on for at least a hundred years:

> the natives on the coast visited by the praus have been so long in touch with the Malays that their habits have been entirely altered, they all speak Malay and in fact have become a dangerous and treacherous people.[20]

While there was frequent and significant interaction with other Aboriginal people in the region, the lives of the Yawuru were mostly free of external intrusion and imposed control. During Jilwa and Wanan's time this freedom was lost. The Yawuru would need to struggle in the future to hold on to their lands and their obligations under the *Bugarigarra*.

Early interaction

Jilwa and Wanan may have been too young to witness the 1837 exploratory voyages of one ship, the *Beagle*. The chronicle of the voyage was kept by John Stokes who wrote, 'our intercourse has been necessarily of the most limited character'. One of the Yawuru 'hurled a stone with great dexterity and force' at a search and mapping party coming off the boat and onto the hinterland of Roebuck Bay.[21] Searching for water, one of the officers was accidentally shot by another and left a pair of pistols behind him.

Stokes mused that 'tradition may serve to hand down the memory of our visit to the third generation, as the motive for the visit of those white men who came flying upon the water, and left some of the secret fire upon the peaceful coast'. He thought the pistols would be placed in fire and explode.

When reading this account a century and a half later, Patrick Dodson was more amused by the fact that the first gunshots in their country signalled that the *kardiya* were shooting each other by mistake.

Jilwa and Wanan could, however, have seen the 1864 expedition by Police Inspector Panter.[22] They would certainly have heard the stories. Panter and his crew were led to Roebuck Bay by the yarns of a transported convict claiming that gold was to be found in Camden Harbour to the north. No gold was found, but the expedition was to have a lasting impact on the Yawuru.

Panter travelled around Roebuck Bay, coming back to tell the young colony in Perth that land around the area of Roebuck Bay, 'would bear favourable comparison with some of the best runs in Victoria'.[23] The lack of running water was offset by the numerous native wells that he was shown.

Panter met the Yawuru. The expedition 'caught two natives (a man and a woman), brought them to the camp and after giving them some trifling presents, let them go again.' Panter's report noted that 'the natives at the head of the Bay were quite friendly,' giving them the 'names of several animals, water, etc. which may be of use to future settlers.' There seemed to have been a reciprocal, if forced, exchange and a beginning of communication, however limited.

Fuelled by inter-colonial rivalry, the promise of a great city rivalling Singapore, and 'homes for millions, land for nothing', the Camden Harbour Association was formed during the next few years. Graziers of Western Victoria, large wool-cheques burning holes in their pockets, rushed to invest.[24]

Not wishing to be beaten in the race for 'virgin land' by a crowd of well-off Victorians, a Western Australian group of colonists formed the Roebuck Bay Pastoral and Agricultural Association Limited. They attempted to establish a sheep station at Roebuck Bay against the fierce and organised resistance of the Yawuru:

> In the clash of interests there could be no compromise. The Aborigines needed all the land of their particular area, and freedom to roam as their fathers had before them. The settlers needed the same land for their flocks and herds and they needed to fence them in. Vital to both sides were the waterholes, billabongs and rivers. The stage was set for the Battle of Roebuck Bay and the central characters had already assumed the roles Fate had destined for them.[25]

In a rare occurrence in Australian history, the initial attempt to colonise the land was pushed back. The venture collapsed, not least through constant attacks by the Yawuru.[26] A revenge expedition was launched from Perth, dealing out 'justice' in a way that would become common in the Kimberley.[27]

Meanwhile, officials in Perth busied themselves with the formulation of new land laws under the watchful and mistrustful eyes of the officials in Colonial Office in London which was concerned about giving the young colony power over such a vast tract of land and was suspicious of their capacity to rule with justice.

Pearling

While the land resources of the Yawuru attracted southern interest, northern interest started to focus on Yawuru waters. Their precious trading commodity of pearl shell promised prosperity and fast fortunes to traders and adventurers from Portuguese Timor, China and the Dutch East Indies and from distant Australian colonies. In the far-off cities of Europe and Asia, a love of pearl-shell buttons and the fashion for pearl necklaces were to create new problems for the Yawuru.

By 1868, a decade or so before Paddy Djiagween was born, ten boats operating in and around Nickol Bay to the south had shipped away £6000 worth of mother-of-pearl. Most of the shell was gathered by Aboriginal women, 'diving naked to a depth of ten fathoms, emerging minutes later, their canvas neck bags crammed to capacity.'[28] Reasonably harmonious, negotiated relationships with payment by catch, started to break down into relations of force and reprisal and a consequent shortage of labour in the area now known as Roeburne. The pearlers began to look for divers further north, eventually reaching the Yawuru, transporting them to the pearling port of Cossack, on Nickol Bay.

Broome pearls were soon sought after and tales were told of quick wealth to be made for little investment. In 1884, a young Aboriginal boy, Thomas Clarke, found a superb pearl formation, the Southern Cross, with nine shells in the shape of a cross.[29] His father sold it for £10 to a friend who sold it for £50. A world exhibit in 1900 valued the pearls at £40,000 before an English lord made it a present to Pope Leo XIII, and it was locked away forever in the vaults of the Vatican.[30]

On the Boats

The boats were coming. The waters of the Yawuru had shell to harvest and pearls to seek, while the lands of the Yawuru had free grass, sufficient water and cheap labour. They would not be left alone. What began with William Dampier was set to continue, but now the *kardiya* were here to stay.

Another ship from England during this period of upheaval carried a passenger whose life would be central to the Dodson story. In 1856, the *David McIver* set sail from Liverpool Harbour on its long and perilous passage to Australia. On board, John and Matilda Fagan carried their young son, Joseph. A Presbyterian, or Church of Ireland couple, they were making their way from County Monaghan, just south of the present frontier between the Republic and Northern Ireland. Like so many of their countrymen at the time they sought opportunity and escape: the opportunity of a start in a new country and escape from the continued bitterness of sectarian politics in their home county. When they landed at Geelong in Victoria in April 1857, the Fagans quickly found work as agricultural labourers and established a new family home. Joseph would not see his ancestral home in Ireland, although he would carry the songs, stories and cultural identification as an Irishman all his days. Instead, Joseph came to know well the distant, dry back-blocks of outback Australia, from western Queensland, through the Top End to the East Kimberley. He would become Patrick's great-grandfather and shape the Dodson family story.

National Press Club, April 1996

Patrick Dodson was in a sombre mood. The Canberra morning had started, like many such winter days, with a grey shroud of fog that slowly melted to reveal intense and clear blue skies. His glowering frame of mind did not clear as quickly; anticipation and tension building as he worked and re-worked his speech to the National Press Club, for that April day of 1996.

The unit at Kingston, a short walk from the Press Club and a longer hike to the Parliament House building, was his temporary field office. The kitchen table was littered with drafts of the speech; each page had paragraphs crossed out, lines struck through, notations crawling across the pages like ants disturbed by a careless boot. Patrick's hand absent-mindedly stroked the strands of his grey beard, as he sipped at another cup of weak black tea and glared at the uncooperative pages. I was helping to edit and key in the final speech. A large, dry continent sprawled between the Canberra unit and Patrick's home in Broome, on the shores of Roebuck Bay in the Kimberley region of northwest Australia. He had travelled for three days to get there, stopping off along the way to talk to meetings in Perth and Melbourne. As Chairperson of the Council for Aboriginal Reconciliation for the last four years, he had travelled more than any other passenger on Ansett, addressing hundreds of meetings, listening and talking to Australians from every walk of life and any point of view. He was getting tired. A spur on the bones of his foot ached constantly, throbbing with unforgiving pain.

Patrick's job, selling reconciliation between black and white to a doubtful nation, was tough. He had to tell a story that, all too often, people did not want to hear. Politically, he had to weave a dancing line; as graceful as any he ran on the wing as a young footballer, ready for tackles from any quarter. Emotionally, he had to preach to congregations more reluctant than any he addressed as Australia's first Aboriginal priest. Practically, he had to persuade the depressed and worn-down Aboriginal communities of Australia that he had something to say worth hearing. These communities were like those in which he had worked as a priest, as a community worker, and as a political adviser. He knew their doubts, frustrations and concerns, for he too lived there, in his own community.

But reconciliation, as Patrick saw it, was a message for all Australians, for the nation as a whole. The non-indigenous people of Australia also had diverse and fractured communities that he had to talk to, to quietly sell a commitment to a new and idealistic approach, to get them involved in reconciliation.

That day's address, nationally broadcast and televised, was a major event at a turbulent time. The Press Club, the home of the formidable Canberra press gallery, was an important site for the contested terrain of Australian politics, abuzz with calls to overturn the High Court decision on native title and to extinguish the remnants of native title on pastoral leases. The Press Club was a place where Patrick could talk through the media, to all Australians, and he took the occasion with a serious sense of obligation and responsibility. While he generally spoke to diverse groups with only a few notes and could 'ramble on' for an easy hour, he had been working on the themes, pitch and agenda of this speech for several weeks.

The speech to the Press Club that day ended with the words of his grandfather, trying to convey a different world view to the media audience, and through them to convey to the broader Australian community some sense of the relationship that has survived between Aboriginal people across Australia and their lands. But in his speech Patrick also dedicated his grandfather's words to a 'local non-Aboriginal hero, Jack Clancy', who was being buried in Alice Springs on the same day. He was working to build bridges, between the divided people of the nation with their different views of the land and between the past and the present.

He told the Press Club:

> For all the importance of this event, I'd rather be fishing... I would really rather be out where the rivers meet the sea, near my hometown of Broome, in the country of my grandfather. These are places to sit and think. Think about people, think about politics, and think about the sort of country we are shaping. Many Australians don't know how to think themselves into the country, the land. They find it hard to think with the land. We Aboriginal people find it hard to think without the land.

My grandfather taught me how to think about relationships by showing me places. He showed me where the creeks and rivers swirl into the sea. The fresh water meets the salt, the different worlds of ocean and river are mixing together. He showed me the foam and the turbulence, pointed to the eddies and swirling mud, the colours intermingling. And he showed me where it was always good to put a line into the water and wait for a feed. The river is the river and the sea is the sea. Salt water and fresh, two separate domains. Each has its own complex patterns, origins, stories. Even though they come together they will always exist in their own right. My hopes for reconciliation are like that. [31]

Chapter Two

Pearlers, Priests and Pastoralists

'The struggle of man against power is the struggle of memory against forgetting.'
Milan Kundera

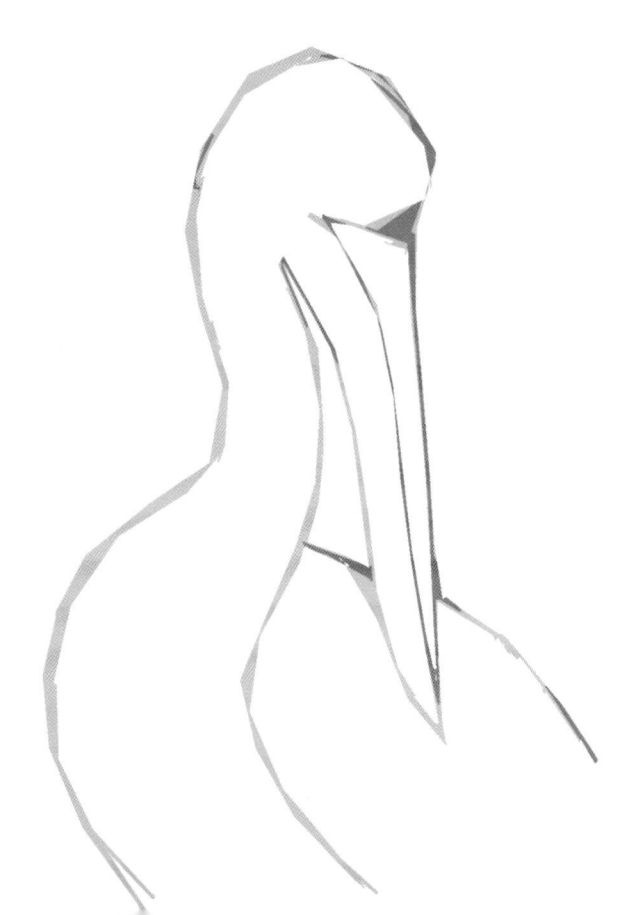

Patrick was sitting under the shade at the Block, talking about his grandfather, Paddy Djiagween. 'It's a shame you never met him,' he said. He looked across the yard before picking up his thread. 'When old blokes like that pass away, there's just such a huge gap. What they know can never be found again. For me, I was just away so long. When I came back here to live, he was getting on and there was so much I wished I had asked him. In his later years it was like he was on another plane of existence, getting ready to go back to the country. He would sing quietly in Yawuru, accompanying himself on the boomerangs and I would wonder at all the things going through his mind. He had so much knowledge that's just all gone now.'

When Patrick spoke of his mother's father, as we started work on this book, the talk would drift. Stories of the life of Paddy Djiagween became intertwined with Patrick's perceptions of race relations and colonial history in the port and hinterland of Broome and elsewhere in colonial Australia. He was thinking out loud, as he often does, turning anecdote into story, story into lesson. There were gaps, too, in his own knowledge that he would worry at like a tongue on a sore tooth.

I was having trouble as a newcomer to Broome, and as an outsider putting the pieces together. I was trying to understand enough to write about a Yawuru life that began sometime in the 1880s and ended in 1991. Patrick was usually generous and patient. He did not give voice to the frustration he must have felt as his parables missed their mark. I did not know the names and meanings of the places, did not know the people he talked of and had only a limited, second-hand, book-won knowledge of the history, culture and society of the Yawuru people. As I explored the holdings of archives and libraries and spoke to Paddy Djiagween's descendants, I came to realise that Paddy indeed had an extraordinary life that held many lessons for his often-absent grandson. In many ways, Paddy Djiagween's life shaped Patrick's value system, 'He was wise, but also well-grounded and practical, making him tremendously influential on me and to others too in a cross-cultural context. He gave me a sense of security and solace in a world of turmoil and dispute. I'm really aware of that as I get older and feel the lack of that presence.'

On his travels for the Council for Aboriginal Reconciliation, Patrick Dodson had been contacted by oral historian, Wendy Lowenstein, who had recorded the old man in Broome, some thirty years earlier. Back in Canberra, in the National Library's Oral History collection, I found copies of her recordings and heard his voice. Through the headphones, I was jolted back into 1969, listening to Paddy Djiagween telling stories and singing songs. Through his stories, I was catapulted further back in time, to Paddy's stories of the first contacts between pearlers and the Yawuru; events that took place even before his own time.

The early days

When Paddy Djiagween was born in the bush near Roebuck Bay, sometime around 1890, the pearlers were sailing into Yawuru waters and setting up their camps on the foreshores. The old man lived for more than a century, with some family members, including Patrick, saying that he was 111 when he died. He saw the port of Broome grow from a small outpost for pearling luggers to a thriving tourist port; from the age of colonisation to the recognition of native title.[1]

As a Yawuru person he had several layers of identity that showed his connections to places in the country and to people in his social world. Each layer was represented in a name, used in different contexts. At his birth in the bush, Jilwa and Wanan gave him the name, Djagun. He had his own spirit or *rai*, a stingray; seen in the dream of his father, or as a spirit child who found his mother. He had a section name, or 'skin-name', that classified his relations with countrymen and those from different places. His 'skin-name' was *Burungu*, from his father who belonged to *Garimba* section and his mother *Barrjarri*. Other *Burungu* boys and girls would be his brothers and sisters. *Garimba* men would be his fathers; *Barrjarri* women his mothers. Paddy told Wendy Lowenstein that his father had seven wives, 'and I seen all my mothers, I seen them.' Each of them, he said, had one or two sons; family connections that are lost today except in the extended family of 'country-men'.[2]

At his baptism in Beagle Bay, the Catholic mission to the north of Broome some decade or more later, the Catholic priests named him Patrick.[3] His parents were honoured with the names Mary and Joseph. In the non-Aboriginal world, he would always be called Paddy, although 'Tailor Paddy' was also used on occasion after the trade he learned on the missions. A version of his Aboriginal name became the family surname, Djiagween, and then a street name in Broome.[4]

Paddy Djiagween was to become a storyteller for the Yawuru, holding the experiences of the Yawuru for transmission to the young and to outsiders. One of his stories told about the first contact with pearlers in Beagle Bay:

> Now on Beagle Bay that big ship from England come in that afternoon. In there, there were oh, two, three or four hundred native people there. They saw the ship come in from Sandy Point and they thought that was some devil or something, that's what they believed. Coming in, and inside the Bay and anchored. Most of them ran away, into the scrub.
>
> Next day, the people went in off the ship, to land, to see those people. There were only a few there. They went to drink some tea, biscuit, tinned meat, and show them. They opened the tin and eat the meat off the tin and tea, drink a tea, and give them biscuit, eat the biscuit. So they did it.
>
> They were there for, that schooner was there, for three or four days in the Bay. And Captain notice, oh, that's a lot of native people there. Might be two or three hundred there. The captain notice.
>
> When that boat start to float, man, woman and children on the schooner, on the low tide. They play gramophone for them and a piano. Oh, they were happy listening to gramophone and piano play.
>
> Tide come in and captain ordered, take all the women and children ashore. Low tide they walk out. The boys was there inside, listening to the piano play.
>
> So he opened a keg of rum and he give them drink, so those boys got drunk.
>
> They find themselves on the Lacapede Islands, about sixty five miles from here, north from here, from Broome, that island is. When they find themselves there, oh, they don't know what to do. They think to themselves, well, we are finished. That devil has taken us away. Somewhere else.
>
> So next tide, that same day, they sail away. They have a few turtle on board and they sail away. They arrive in the first town, Cossack. Before Broome, before Derby, Cossack was the first town. Cossack. They were there, oh they were there for a week.

Neap tide came around, the boys getting a bit used to their boss. When spring tide started, he took them to the reef. Show them the shell which ones pearly shell he want. All right, that reef was full up with shell, nobody touched it, they cleaned that reef only in one spring. And when the neap tide come, they go to two fathom water, make them to dive.

They dive in, pick those shell and move further and further. And those people don't get any shell, he put them up, climb up the mast there. They all stay there, no tucker, nothing. Called them back and make them to dive. They have to get the shell…

Finish season, the captain brought them back to Beagle Bay. He took them back. These boys were all dressed up, got a trousers, shirt, hat, clay pipe in their mouth, began to talk yes maya, yes boss, says me. They call *wanyababi*, Derby native language, you understand.

When they come in there to home to Beagle Bay, oh everyone was glad. But before that, the people there, some paint themselves black and red. Red, mean losing their sons. Black, their fathers. All come back, all come back.

Not all, however, did come back to Yawuru country from pearling expeditions. Paddy told Wendy Lowenstein of young men drowning and being attacked by sharks in trying to swim back to the coastline from the luggers or the outer islands. He told of men escaping from Cossack, the port to the distant south, and being speared in hostile territory, attempting to return to their lands and families. They were hard times and not all violence came from white guns. The Yawuru and their neighbours held territorial demarcations seriously, with deadly consequences for transgressors.

But there is another theme to be heard in Paddy's pearling story. While talking about the hard times, of trickery and capture, Paddy also told of gramophones, pianos, rum and clay pipes. He allows for a less negative interpretation of frontier events, suggesting a sense of interest, possibility and material gain in a changing world. While not denying the painful side of the history, his story implies a practical acceptance of a changing world and the need to develop strategies for accommodation in order to ensure personal and social survival.

Paddy's account of lives lost while escaping capture and forced labour is mirrored in a letter to the *West Australian* from a young Irish priest, Matthew Gibney, who came back into Paddy's life in a significant way. While at La Grange Bay in 1878 he wrote:

> I was surprised to hear the heart-rending wail that went up from the crowd. I found, on inquiry, that some of the young men, who had been

forcibly detained, had drowned on making an attempt to escape from their captors. They believed they could swim to shore, a distance of about six miles, but only one man reached it, and I had a conversation with him. For a long time I believed the story of the employers of native divers that the blacks went with them willingly, but I afterwards found such was not the case.[5]

The protests of Gibney and other humanitarians led to changes in the law aimed at protecting Aboriginal people, especially women, from the worst abuses. A series of acts were passed between 1870 and 1875 to prohibit the employment of Aborigines in the pearling industry unless engaged under a contract witnessed by a justice of the peace or a police constable.[6] Over the next decade, Aboriginal 'bare-skin' diving was officially eliminated and Malay and Koepanger or Timorese divers, later Japanese, became the preferred workers in a dangerous industry. However, by the year 1884, there were still over five hundred and fifty Aborigines employed in pearling in northern Western Australia, increasingly out of Broome, compared to seventy-two Malays and nineteen Asians of unspecified ethnicity.[7]

As the young boy Paddy grew up, so too did the town of Broome. Its beginnings were modest and slow after it was declared a town in 1883. Charles Flinders[8] saw it in 1888, saying 'it had not one sheet of iron and the only water was a nigger well close to where the Roebuck Bay, the first hotel in Broome was later to be built…the natives were wild, and now and then made marauding trips into the settlement, stole what they could lay their hands on and disappeared into the bush.'

Originally a source of water and a rest camp for luggers exploring the King Sound area to the north, the waters of Roebuck Bay and the town of Broome rapidly became the preferred lay-up base for the mother schooners. Growth intensified as the town of Cossack to the south died and the pearling trade shifted away from Thursday Island in the Torres Strait. A long deep-water jetty was built in 1897 to allow the large steamers to dock and cart the pearl shell to distant markets in Singapore or London. Paddy recalled his childhood memory of the jetty being built, 'half-way down when I got my sense.'

With a burgeoning port came a service economy that aimed to provide, for the right price, any services that the lugger crews might require or desire. By 1890, a police inspector visiting Broome reported the presence of a few Europeans, several Asian pearling crews and seven or eight Japanese prostitutes. While the pearling boats were anchored in nearby creeks and the men drank at the make-shift public house, the brothels were among the first businesses in the new settlement. A small store and customs office had just been constructed.[9] The following year, Charles Flinders visited again and commented on the transformation with new hotels and stores, and the foreshore 'lined with the camps of the coloured crews'.

In this service economy, there was a place for Aboriginal labour as Paddy recalled to Fr Francis Huegal:

> My father would do any job. We lived in the bush near Broome, camping anywhere round there. There were any amount of Aboriginal people there, lot more than now. Plenty big, big corroboree.[10]

Life in the new town may have seemed, in these early years, to offer excitement and possibilities as well as challenges and troubles. Food, alcohol and tobacco were plenty, if 'any job' for any kinsmen paid enough for the needs of the group. The Yawuru started to cluster around the town, looking for access to new materials and goods, still engaging in ceremonies at every opportunity. As Hugh Edwards put it:

> Aborigines filled the lowest role in society, doing the most menial jobs for token wages. Begging and prostitution were the inevitable side effects.[11]

With the new town and the new people came new problems for the Yawuru. Social and health problems caused by prostitution and alcohol abuse splintered families. Cohesion and authority in the Yawuru community was eroded, as traditional processes of decision making collapsed under the weight of a new social order. Leprosy, influenza and venereal diseases raged.

It was around this time that Paddy was told that his father, Jilwa, died near the township. The young boy, looking at the body, hearing the wailing of his mother, was sure his father was simply asleep and would wake up in the morning.[12]

On the stations

Change was also rapidly unfolding in the Yawuru hinterland and the heartland of their neighbours. A new economy, ecology and social order were imposed. The 1881 Kimberley Land Regulations 'opened up' the area for lease-holding. In the next three years, station holdings were established throughout West Kimberley Aboriginal lands, including the Lower Fitzroy, Liveringa, Mt Anderson and Yeeda. These stations, by law, could not exclude Aboriginal people from passing through areas which were not enclosed, or were unimproved, in order to 'seek their sustenance in their accustomed manner'.[13]

The initial pastoral concern, especially from the south, was sheep grazing. Many of the Yawuru and their inland neighbours, the Bunuba and Nyikina, learned quickly to be shepherds, shearers and wool scourers. The Duracks were soon to drove cattle into the northern Kimberley from Queensland, followed by the McDonalds and Nat Buchanan.[14] Aboriginal people learned to ride, muster, rope and brand. On the stations in the foundation stage, a small local labour force was fed and clothed, while 'outside' Aborigines were regarded as hostile. In 1888, the King Sound Pastoral Company claimed to have lost seven thousand sheep to Aboriginal spearing in the one year. As the station groups dwindled and station boundaries expanded, these 'outside' groups were drawn into employment.[15] In 1886, the discovery of gold at Halls Creek led to a steady stream of miners along the Fitzroy River to the gold-fields, creating further pressures. Joe Fagan, the Irishman, was one of those on the trail of fast fortunes.

Many of the Yawuru, squeezed between the pearlers and the pastoralists, clustered near the homesteads of Roebuck Plains and Thangoo stations, and at Yardugarra, an outstation of Thangoo.[16] They shifted ceremonial objects to these camps to ensure their protection, and adjusted their ceremonial calendar to fit the station calendar. Their title to land may have been ignored, but their obligations to country remained strong. Moving away was not an option.

The influx of people and industry, over a relatively short period, was to lead to tension between the neighbours of the Yawuru and the new pastoralists. The debate between Aboriginal rights to land and the rights and interests of the pastoral and mining industry began early.

An uneasy coexistence, begun with the first sheep and cattle ventures, started to deteriorate. In late 1892, Anthony Cornish was speared while mustering sheep on Mt Anderson station in Nyikina territory.[17] Three suspects were eventually tried and hung at Rottnest Island for Cornish's murder. Some sixty years later the incident and its aftermath were described by Irene Shackcloth in a semi-fictional piece:

> 'Some of these black niggers will die for this,' he said grimly, 'even if it costs me my own life.' William nodded dumbly; and they all knew that it was to be a feud according to ancient rites—an eye for an eye and a tooth for a tooth. The death of the white man must be avenged.[18]

Debate in Perth raged between those who advocated longer, more severe punishment for cattle-spearing and absconding and those, especially from church groups, who argued for moderation. More severe floggings were called for, as the 'official "cat" used on a native simply wiped the dust off him…a native had a hide, not an ordinary skin like ordinary human beings.'[19]

It was decided that the police presence operating out of the nearby port of Derby should be increased dramatically. By the end of 1892 there would be seventy-seven prisoners at the Derby lock-up, chained together as road gangers building the wharf and rail tracks into the town, solving a labour shortage caused by the lack of convicts.[20] Prisoners in heavy, hot neck and leg chains would become a potent image of race relations in the northern frontier and Paddy would see them for decades to come. Charles White recorded this observation around the time:

> I speak of facts, and facts are stubborn things. In Broome in 1897, there were about 90 prisoners in Broome gaol, whose only crime was running away from their masters to whom they have been signed on by the Western Australian Government. These natives were assigned to the squatter (who was the local JP) for all time. After the shearing was finished the natives were driven away by cruel treatment and starvation, until compelled by the pangs of hunger to kill a sheep for food, and then, not only the real culprit, but the whole tribe, was hoisted on to the authorities for sheep killing. The local JP who was perhaps the party interested, would sentence the niggers to six months in gaol, to be kept by the Government until mustering or shearing came round again. These prisoners are kept in gaol and do all the necessary work around the township for those who are favoured by the Resident Magistrate. I have seen the prisoners with a warder standing guard over them digging the garden of the Resident Magistrate, and the next day removing rubbish from the local pub. The prisoners are chained round the neck by a chain that is strong enough to hold a bullock. These chains are not covered with leather, but are just plain, cold iron. They are padlocked to each other, and their padlocks are inspected by the warder each morning and evening.[21]

The police, under pressure from the pastoralists and from Perth, brought force to bear on outlying stations. Their official reports record the killing of twenty-seven Oobagooma Aborigines by a police party in 1895, while another seventy were 'dispersed by means of extreme measures'.[22]

Paddy Djiagween, the young boy growing up in the pearling town of Broome, would have heard accounts of the cattle-spearing, the murders and the reprisals. Word travelled quickly about the goings-on at the nearby stations and prisoners in chains passed through to the boats on their way to the hell of Rottnest Island. Few returned.

Laws such as the *Aborigines Protection Act 1886* for managing the 'Aboriginal problem' were now implemented more actively in the north, leading to an increased level of police involvement in the day-to-day lives of

Aboriginal people. In a recurring theme, laws intended for protection quickly slid into policies of control and restriction. The 'policing imperative' was set to become an entrenched part of official thinking, as Patrick Dodson would later discuss in his position as a Royal Commissioner for Aboriginal Deaths in Custody.[23]

Section 36 of the Act allowed a resident magistrate to bind any Aboriginal or half-caste child in an apprenticeship until he was twenty-one. Section 43 allowed a Justice of the Peace to order any Aboriginal person from towns such as Broome if they were not 'decently clothed from neck to knee'.[24] Failure to comply could call into play the *Aboriginal Offenders Act 1892*, allowing a Justice of the Peace to order twenty-five strokes of the whip for a male Aboriginal prisoner; unless the prisoner was under sixteen, when twelve strokes would suffice. The lash was in addition to any other sentence that may be imposed. Laws on whipping were not so severe at the time for non-Aboriginal people.[25]

There was resistance on the frontier. It is certain that Paddy would have heard stories about the exploits of Jandamarra (or Pigeon) in the Leopold and Oscar ranges, north-east of Broome. Jandamarra applied his police training as a tracker to hold the police at bay for years. Using stolen guns, his station training as a horseman and marksman, and, most importantly, knowledge of his Bunuba country and his prowess as a bushmen, he mounted a guerilla campaign of attack, flight and armed provocation. In 1897, a skilled and powerful Aboriginal tracker shot and killed Jandamarra because he knew that the outlaw's spirit resided in his thumb. In Jandamarra's short life he witnessed invasion by Europeans, the enticement of his people into their industries and resistance against them. What he never saw was the dispossession of his country. Shortly after his death, the Europeans were able to stock Leopold Downs Station, in the heart of Bunuba country.[26]

Non-Aboriginal men on stations felt compelled to assert their authority on their workers with violence, knowing that the law was on their side. For the Aboriginal people of the Fitzroy, these times would be remembered as hard and cruel. Even though there were always exceptional non-violent non-Aboriginal people, many were ' real mongrels', as Ernie Bird recalled:

> Back in those days, if anything went wrong, some blackfella would get a hiding from the boss… I was working for some rough men; whitefellas who would pull their gun out and kill any Aborigines who stood up to them. And there was none of this taking your time to pull your boots on either. No fear. They would use the whip on you. Those rough white people who were around in the early days treated the blackfellas as slaves… They were real mongrels.[27]

The Yawuru on the stations established at Roebuck Bay and Thangoo did not escape the violence, and it quickly impacted on their ceremonial life. Butcher Joe Nangan recalled these times to Kevin Lawton:

> The wandering life of the Yarro (Yawuru) was gone for good. Armed cowboys patrolled the bush making sure 'wild' Aborigines did not interfere with the cattle business. For the Yarro the only way to avoid being shot on sight was to camp near a station and hope for the best… Previously hundreds attended these sacred events (initiation ceremonies). Now only a few took their place around the fire. Of those that did come, many carried serious wounds. One man had a bullet wound in his shoulder. A woman's nose had been shot off. These survivors had a frightening story to tell.[28]

And yet, there were many Yawuru and others who took to the new way of things; who chose to survive through accommodation and incorporation, rather than active resistance. There were Yawuru men and women who gained widespread reputations as highly skilled divers, shell openers and boat handlers. There were many others who established their families on sheep and cattle stations and learned the skills and attitudes necessary to make a living out of stockwork by providing the labour the stations needed to make a living. The knowledge of country held by the Yawuru was essential to the survival of these stations. The major stations on Yawuru land lacked freshwater creeks and so bores were drilled in Aboriginal wells and soaks. The Yawuru, according to Patrick Sullivan, understood this as a reciprocal arrangement:

> The Yawuru perception was, and still is, that by allowing the whites to use these resources a relationship was entered into by which all traditional land owners could expect food and protection at the local homestead. At the same time they could visit and maintain their land, carry out essential ceremonies and raise children in Yawuru law.[29]

In hindsight, it can be seen that the choices open to the Yawuru at the time were constrained but real. They were not victims, although they suffered great cruelty and harm. They were not passive, although their power to effect change on their terms was steadily eroded. They did fight for their country, even if the Jandamarra message was that violent resistance was probably doomed. They did struggle to keep their families alive, fed and intact, even though the laws of the land empowered resident magistrates to remove their children. They did maintain their religious ceremonies, language and culture, particularly through the development of a separate domain for 'blackfella business' and the attempted negotiation of relationships with the newcomers based on mutual respect. The nature of work in the pastoral industry allowed space for the maintenance of language, culture and ceremony:

Although the station labour was hard and not properly rewarded at all, the people were able to enjoy the after-hours, jointly practicing traditional ceremonies, both secret and open, accompanied by vivid dances and songs. During the off season, camping out for fishing and hunting was extensively practiced.[30]

They remained Yawuru, even though acknowledgment of their rights, their privileges and their identity was rare.

A new century

The new century dawned in the pearling port with toasts to Queen and empire and grand celebrations for most of the town. Paddy Djiagween was about thirteen, the town of Broome was well established, the pearling industry was flourishing and the pastoral leasehold map of the Kimberleys was being steadily filled in.

In a short time, a new social structure had crystallised in Broome, with white pearling masters at the tip of a pyramid, Yawuru people at the very bottom, and a range of colours and classes in between. The families at the top have described the scene for posterity:

> In its heyday around the turn of the century Broome was still undoubtedly a world apart from the rest of Australia, a frontier town where lawlessness and luxury went hand in hand. But a more gracious side was emerging. Wealthy pearlers and their wives lived in elegant large houses with an abundance of servants and a second house in Perth or Melbourne where the women removed with the children during school terms. The women thought nothing of importing gowns from Paris and London. With the freedom resulting from the prevalence of domestic help they made full use of their finery at dinner parties, tea parties, tennis parties and an endless round of social events.[31]

The freedom provided by domestic help required someone else's loss of freedom. Aboriginal people, particularly Yawuru women, gave the pearlers' wives their freedom. Kevin Lawton depicted the scene after talking with a local Broome Aboriginal woman, Sophie McKenzie:

> In small groups spread across the immaculate lawn stood the master pearlers talking shop in their crisp white tropical suits…The wives sat in the shade of their parasols and exchanged gossip, dressed in the white frilly finery of the day. The garden party was set in an atmosphere of rich elegance. Across the lawn the elite of Broome society moved with an easy, self-assured grace. The Bardwells, the Gregorys, the Males and the MacDaniels were there. So too was Sophie McKenzie.[32]

Sophie McKenzie, dressed in a black skirt and a white frilled apron, was working eleven hours a day, seven days a week for eleven shillings, a far lower rate than was due to domestic servants in cities such as Perth. The social hierarchy would remain for decades. Paddy Djiagween's future wife, Elizabeth, would dress like Sophie and work for the Male family in future years, while Paddy would work for MacDaniel, or 'Long Mac' as he knew him, on his boats.

There was no shortage of Sophies. In 1901, in Broome there were 67 non-Aboriginal, European women. In the same year, there were 173 female Aborigines employed by Europeans or living in close proximity to European settlement. For every European woman, there were 3 Aboriginal women. Sixty-three women were unmarried Japanese, serving the needs of 303 Japanese men (and others), especially in the brothels that became a feature of the Broome township.[33]

Paddy Djiagween's family, like other Yawuru, somehow found ways of making ends meet in their niche of the pearling-based town economy. However, the options were decreasing. Aboriginal labour on the pearling boats had become increasingly regulated, so that firstly women, and then men were no longer given work on the boats. Increasingly, the male jobs went to the Asian men and the women were pushed into the domestic service employment market, if they were lucky. Aboriginal women often had the hot and heavy work of washing the white tailored drill suits of the pearlers in the hard, red town water filtered through drums, or rain water carried in buckets from the tanks.[34]

For those not working in domestic service at the big houses, the street life of Broome which centred on the Asian camps and Japanese brothels offered a life of sorts. This report from Inspector Tracer to the Aboriginal Protection Board tells of the times:

> From the camp we went to some of the coloured men's dens. The first we went to we found about four young native women sleeping with about six Malays and there were several other men of colour in and about the hut…In some cases I find native girls are employed by the Japanese prostitutes. These are appropriated by the men at night. That in many cases these women are kept by the Malays and others solely for the purpose of prostitution there is little doubt. I have it from the police and other respectable white residents that these men who have houses induce the girls by giving them food, clothes and other things.[35]

To survive in such colonial situations Aboriginal women often had a stark and unenviable choice between domestic service and prostitution. Older women, men and children had to live from day to day on the money and food that was left over, supplementing this with fish and bush food gathered around the mangroves of the bay.

The Mission

Into the melting pot around the camps and dens of the coloured world of Broome, strode a Spanish aristocrat. Fr Nicholas Emo, a Trappist monk from Patagonia, had a 'call from God' to serve the Aboriginal people in Australia. His particular mission was amongst the Spanish-speaking 'Manilamen' who served on the pearling boats, but he soon came to have a close connection to the 'other coloured folk' of Broome, including Paddy Djiagween and other Yawuru.

Mary Durack, in her history of the pioneering Catholic Church in Broome, has left us with a very human picture of the work of Fr Nicholas. She describes a 'short, thick set, black-bearded little man, devout, emotional and at some pains to keep his naturally extrovert nature within the bounds of Trappist convention'.[36]

Paddy was baptised by Fr Nicholas at around the turn of the century, becoming at that point what he would remain for the rest of his long life, a Catholic Yawuru; a Christian man while still truly Yawuru. As he recalled to Fr Francis:

> Fr Nicholas was in town, it was 1900. Governor came to Broome and Fr Nicholas ask for him in archway where Church of England is now. The old church was built. I was a big boy then, still with my parents. After Governor was here, the Sister's Point, the first one this side where the people camped. We camping then, all the boys, all the men and womens too, whole big areas. Manilaman, Andrew was caretaker for us.[37]

The big camp Paddy referred to was one of Fr Nicholas' many and varied attempts to establish alternative, Catholic institutions in Broome, both to protect and to minister to the Yawuru and other nationalities. He was partnered in these initiatives by Mrs Anabia, a 'half-caste' woman, brought up in Perth and returned to her mother's people as a Matron, nurse and lay missionary. These were people with a different outlook, of interest to the teenage boy on the verge of becoming a Yawuru man.

Before that life step, however, Paddy became an adult in the Church, being confirmed at the Beagle Bay Mission, north of Broome in Nyulnyul country. It was still the first year of the century and Paddy was tricked by Fr Nicholas into going to the Mission:

> We were camped there near the new jetty now, this side. We're staying there. And Father Nicholas asked us whether we wanted any sugar cane. We said yes Father. We didn't say yes Father, we said yes, *parta*. Well come on, we go to town. Seven of us walked into town with Fr Nicolas. In town we said 'where's the sugar cane?' Over here, he said. He took us to jetty. Schooner, mission lugger was anchored there. He put us in there and off we went to Beagle Bay. Without the sugar cane (laughs).[38]

The presence of Bishop Matthew Gibney at Beagle Bay accelerated Paddy's confirmation. The Bishop, as a young Irish firebrand priest, had earlier spoken out about the cruelties of the pearl-diving industry. He had also achieved a fleeting fame at Glenrowan in Victoria for being the first into the burnt-out, body-strewn hotel after the siege, and giving the last rites to Ned Kelly.[39]

In 1901 the Bishop was at the ten-year-old Mission, which was shifting from French Trappist to German Pallottine control, to ensure that improvements were made to the physical nature of the mission so that lease conditions were met. As Fr Huegal remarked, 'That a mad Irishman had joined two queer looking Frenchman must have been the talk of the town in Derby and news at the cattle stations and stock camps for quite some time.'[40]

His companion on the trip was Daisy Bates, just beginning her anthropological career. She described the confirmation ceremony, at which Paddy was accepted as an adult member of the Church:

> Knowing that he would probably never pay another visit to the Mission, the Bishop announced his intention of making confirmed Christians of all the natives in the district and I will never forget the occasion. Dean Martelli and the brothers rounded up the mob. Crowded into that little bark chapel and smelling to high heaven, 65 wild men and women and babies of the Nyool-nyool[41] stood before a prelate of the Roman Church, in all his ceremonial robes of lace and purple and mitre, to be anointed with the holy oils and receive the papal blessing and the little blow on the cheek of the 'Pax tecum'.
>
> Some of the men wore nothing but a vest or a red handkerchief, some a rag of a shirt, and the fraction of a pair of trousers. They had been told to keep their hands piously joined together and their eyes shut—and the flies were bad.[42]

Daisy Bates then went on to describe her amusement at the embarrassment of one young participant, trying to conceal his 'rear elevation' from her view while keeping his hands together in front. While she was embarking on her self-appointed mission to save his countrymen, she was mocking and disparaging the young man's embarrassment at the ceremony.

Another source of amusement for her came later in the evening of that day, when the Nyulnyul and their Aboriginal visitors were developing, through mimicry, their account of the day's ritual:

> Imagine my mingled horror and delight to find Goodowel, one of the corroboree comedians, sitting on a tree trunk with a red-ochred billy can on his head and a tattered and filthy old rug around his shoulders. In front of him pranced every member of the tribe, all in a line, and each wearing a wreath and veil that that were a bit of twisted paperbark and a fragment of somebody's discarded shirt. As they passed Goodowel each received a sounding smack under the ear with a shout of 'Bag take um!' Hilarious and ear piercing shrieks of laughter followed each sally. I went back in glee to tell the bishop. He shook his head. 'Ah the poor craytures!' was all he said.

Paddy and the other 'poor craytures' were having fun, enjoying communal theatre, recreating and celebrating the event. The play-acting was significant in that the mission residents were doing what Aboriginal people did all over the frontier, that is quickly incorporating elements of non-Aboriginal culture and ritual into their own cultural forms. To bring ideas and practices into their domain transformed them into Aboriginal things, Aboriginal creations, with Aboriginal people having power over them. This 'play-play', as Paddy called it, may have been fun for all the participants but it had serious implications.

Patrick Dodson, in discussing this account, remarked:

> Old Paddy would have identified with 'Goodowel'. Paddy would take on that sort of thing, using dance, song and his sense of humour to explore issues and tell a story about things that are happening around him. He had a reputation as a bit of a wise joker.

There were other adaptations to the influx of newcomers. Pearl shell pendants were still being traded along customary routes, but now they had carvings of boats, cattle and landscapes. Also traded were introduced material items of value such as glass (for exquisitely edged spear points), metals, money and the new drugs of dependence, tobacco and alcohol. Similarly, the serious rituals of Catholicism, with all the variations introduced by the multicultural crew of Irish, Spanish, French and German clergy at Beagle Bay, were incorporated into the local cultural life.

Of Paddy's initiation into Yawuru adulthood, no records or oral accounts are known, although Bates provides a description of the rituals of the time in Broome.[43] Stanner, in describing the initiation of a Nangiomeri man from

Daly River, sheds more light and explains more meaning than Bates. Even though the Daly is far away, he tells of universals:

> Durmugam was initiated as he says, 'in the bush' at a time when a relatively large number of Aborigines could be assembled and the full panoply of ceremonial forms could be followed. He emerged a blackfellow for life. He did not simply reach manhood: he was given it, was made a man by men who stood for and taught him to stand for a tradition in part only revealed
>
> ...
>
> The initiations teach boys to be men: to know pain and ignore it; to feel fear and master it; to want, but to bear the necessary costs; to grasp that outside society they are nothing and inside it, the masters, that through them the Dreaming is 'followed up'; that the tradition is 'the road'.[44]

The road of tradition was one Paddy would follow all his life, ensuring that his children would follow him. The slap on the cheek by the Bishop and the new name provided as part of the confirmation ceremony may have seemed a pale and limp equivalent, but the essence of transformation through ritual was the key to a shared meaning.

As a Yawuru Christian, one of 'plenty people Christian, nearly all Christian from Trappists,' Paddy spent most of his youth at the Mission.[45] Early on, he escaped with a group of other lads, taking off on the road to Broome. It was November, hot, and despite the watermelons they stole, he 'nearly perished there' on the way home.[46]

At the Beagle Bay Mission, life was strictly disciplined. Every morning from 4am, after sharing mass and cocoa, Paddy worked in the garden with Brother John Mary, a French Trappist who had the art of being able to call horses with a trumpet.[47] He went to school in the morning and learned the trade of tailoring in the afternoon from the several German tradesmen who were brothers at the Mission. After a midday rest, a bell would ring, 'and if we were even five minutes late,' we would 'get something on our backside'.

He slept in the dormitory with 'plenty boys, only seven half castes.' Many had been brought to Beagle Bay from places as far away as Halls Creek and Wyndham, because as Paddy recalled, 'the police inspector got em and send them there.'[48]

One family that was split up, with some taken to the Mission, was the family of Johnny Watson, who would become a mentor for Patrick Dodson:

> I never got a chance to meet my two eldest brothers because they were taken away before I was born, when they were only 9 or 10 years old. My sisters and another brother were sent away to the Catholic Mission School at Beagle Bay. My parents had no say in that, it was Government policy.

> Aboriginal children right around Australia were forcibly taken from their parents and placed in institutions. The police could take away any Aboriginal child with bits of colour in them, any kid with a bit of white blood in them. If they were taken away, it was often the last time their parents and relations saw them. It was a very bad thing! When it looked like the younger brother and I were going to be taken away as well, our parents got talking and decided that they weren't going to part with us. So, whenever a police party came out to Mt. Anderson they sent us off into the bush; sent us down to our father's and grandmother's country with some old people. That's why I'm able to speak my own people's language and several other languages. My sisters and other brothers missed out on that. Of course they can understand what's being said in language, but they can't speak it very well themselves.[49]

Along with everyone else at Beagle Bay, Paddy 'went to mass, all in Latin. We learned to sing. Only the Lord's Prayer was in English.'[50] As well as singing in Yawuru, he added a few French and German songs to his repertoire. 'We were good, so good, only one more step, Saint Peter would open the gates to heaven.'[51]

In 1907, the coastal steamer, *Bullarra*, huffed into the entrance of Beagle Bay with a cargo of nine Irish nuns from the Sisters of St John of God, led by Mother Antonio O'Brien. Paddy, now about nineteen, a man in Yawuru terms, but a 'boy' in the parlance of Kimberley missions and stations, was there to meet them. He told Fr Francis:

> They came by the steamship. The mission lugger came in. That day they couldn't get in, they stay floating. Next day they come in, in a little boat, Mother Antonio. Two men carried her. She went and kissed that ground. Then I came with hermit crab. She got frightened.[52]

His grandson was to laugh, a big, beard-shaking belly laugh in Canberra ninety years later when he realised that Paddy had seen her as a seagull in her long white habit, pecking at the ground; hence the offer of a crab. We later found that Paddy had indeed told Mary Durack that the nun was 'like a big white gull'.[53] Paddy travelled on a bullock dray pulled by eight bullocks, up top with Mother Antonio. Others walked. Along the way he pointed out kangaroos and dingoes to the Irish nun. There were church services to welcome them, and a few evenings later, a ceremony:

> Big corroboree, dancing, for the sisters. Fr Bischofs make me, after dark, turn on the 144 horse power engine, pitch dark. Cockatoo feathers on head. I go. Sisters. Mother Antonio O'Brien. Twenty to thirty men out dancing. Fr Bischofs was amongst them. When I spot Fr Bischofs, 'cos I

spot the white shorts, see, I tell Mother Antonio. 'See that man with the white cockatoo feathers on his head.' She didn't know. She make the sign of the cross.[54]

There was evidently a dialogue at Beagle Bay between Aboriginal cultural forms, themselves changing and adapting as Yawuru lived with Nyulnyul, and Catholic cultural forms. Hymns were sung in Nyulnyul; stories and songs were transcribed; wordlists were generated. The German missionary Fr Bischoffs began a scholarly tradition amongst the Pallottines, of writing about the customs and traditions of the people on the missions.[55] On Sunday Island, in Bardi country, one priest was even initiated.[56] But the terms of the relationship were skewed. Fr Walter, a later Pallottine missionary, summarised the outcomes of this stage of Beagle Bay from the perspective of his sunset years:

> The Trappists had excellent results. They did not encroach on the freedom of the Blacks and allowed them to follow old customs, enjoyments and dances as long as these did not conflict with religion and a moral life. They made the Blacks' stay at the mission pleasant so that after hunting expeditions into the bush, they gladly returned to the Mission which they regarded as home.[57]
>
> There existed a beautiful patriarchal relationship between the missionaries and their charges. This was to remain with the successors of the Trappists, and it is a beautiful sign both of the Aboriginal character, and of a right approach to missionary work.

The official history of the Catholic Church in the Kimberley is titled, 'From Patrons to Partners'[58] which captures the dilemma of the Church in the times, a dilemma that would haunt its work in Aboriginal Australia for generations. To be 'patriarchal', in the sense understood by Fr Walter and the other 'fathers and mothers' in the mission, implies control and authority at the expense of partnership, equality and real dialogue. The priests, not the people, made decisions about what did, or did not, 'conflict with religion and a moral life.' They determined and imposed the values to guide a changing society. They were the bosses.[59]

Aboriginal people granted the missionaries their authority. In the Aboriginal world view 'being a boss' for someone means 'looking after' them and their interests.[60] On the mission, as well as on the pastoral stations, non-Aboriginal people, who looked after their Aboriginal charges and were not cruel and demanding, were ceded an authority, a right to be a boss. They may have taken this right for granted, but it could have been withheld at the choice of senior Aboriginal men and women.

Such a vested authority had limits. One of the general no-go areas for white authority was Aboriginal law, especially sacred ceremonies, although adapting 'business' practices to fit with mission and station timetables was a common strategy. Ceremonial practices, 'proper inside business', deeper and more powerful than the 'play-play' seen by the Sisters, were in Beagle Bay and Broome, held on to with passion. Initiation ceremonies were a theological battle between the priests and the men for the souls of their sons. The ceremonial ground was contested ground, as remembered by Remi Balagai from Sandy Point:

> All followed the same Law. My father and mother followed the law, so did my four brothers, the next died, then me, six altogether…One day my father came and I knew that he wanted me for *Malulu* (initiation ceremonies). Everybody told me, 'You follow our Law. Proper we finish you *Malulu*, you can go back to the Mission. You must be man like first man and you will follow our Law. My father told Fr Alphonse nothing. I came back by myself. Fr Alphonse preached in that Church 'Stop that *Malulu!*' He talked outside to the men to stop. They said, 'We can't do that but that is our Law, we got to stick to that Law till we're dead, but all them boys can follow Christian'.[61]

Fr Worms, a Pallottine anthropologist of some note in the Broome region, recorded his view of the contest in later years:

> Having observed that young men are less inclined to conversion after they have passed the initiation rite with its instruction in mythology, we have successfully convinced the Aboriginal fathers that we are in the position of offering them and their sons something which still excels the good which their old religions and ceremonies could offer them. In our Christian native communities, baptism and subsequent liturgical consecration have been substituted for circumcision and subincision.[62]

Deciding where to draw the line between following the Church and following the Law would remain an issue for Paddy and his grandson, Patrick.

Roth Royal Commission

Paddy returned to Broome from Beagle Bay at some time after 1905. His return coincided with a shift in state policy towards Aboriginal people that would severely impact on the family. Policies of the time had a special focus on race, and the dominant belief was that it was inevitable that full-blood Aboriginal people would be 'effaced' or eliminated; while the remnant would require greater protection and control, for their own good and for the good of frontier society.

In 1905, a Royal Commission headed by Dr W.E. Roth, Assistant Protector from Queensland, criticised the 'most brutal and outrageous condition of affairs,' in relation to the imposition of justice, especially in the pastoral north. He decried the prevalence of inter-racial sexual relations, or 'komboism', saying that from La Grange to King Sound, 'drunkenness and prostitution, the former being the prelude to the latter, with consequent loathsome disease, is rife.' He condemned the poor state of administration of Aboriginal affairs in Western Australia. However, he refuted charges of deliberate cruelty by pastoralists. The Roman Catholic Church supported the findings.[63]

The *Aborigines Act 1905* was an attempt to solve the problems identified by Roth. The problem of 'miscegenation' was to be solved through prohibition. The problem of 'half-caste' children, especially the camp-dwelling offspring of pastoralists, was to be solved through separation and institutionalisation. The problem of disease was met through the tightening of control on sexual contact between the races and the provision of new health services. The best means of protection, it was argued, was control and existing laws were not adequate. The noble motives of care and protection quickly slipped into custody and control, and the level of police scrutiny and bureaucratic control over everyday lives was stepped up.

The Church acted as an agent of the Government under the legislation but was motivated more by the needs of Aboriginal people, especially children. Fr George Walter would write to the Chief Protector from the Beagle Bay Mission in 1906, pointing out that he was feeding and clothing some fifty children at the Mission and asking for assistance from the Government:

> If the Government will assist me for a few years in the maintenance of thirty of these children, I will gladly take, without question of remuneration, as many more as it will send me from the Nor-West. And I assure you, Sir that many full blood and half-caste children (your wards, according to Sec. 8, Aborigines Act) may be found roaming about Broome and other North-Western towns, beginning the worst and most unhappy of lives... It is irksome for me to be receiving money, given with much hesitation as an act of charity, that I claim should be given to the blacks as an act of barest justice.[64]

The definition of those caught by the legislation was widened. The Chief Protector was made the legal guardian of 'every Aboriginal and half-caste child' under sixteen years; his power delegated to police at the local and regional level. Portrayed as being for the 'better protection and care' of Aboriginal people, it was delivered as an 'instrument of control, and ruthless control at that.'[65] Bureaucratic machinery was geared up to carry out and implement the Act. Children of mixed race were a priority issue for the new administration. Patrick Dodson would write that, 'this Act, and the particularly oppressive measures it invoked, caused profound anguish, and the policies it introduced are still remembered with bitterness and repugnance by many Aboriginal people today.'[66]

This law, and those which followed in its path, would challenge the efforts of the Yawuru people to retain and build their culture, while accommodating the changed social environment. It would also severely restrict the choices and options of Paddy Djiagween's family. The machinery of *The Aborigines Act 1905* would later ensnare Elizabeth, the 'half-caste' daughter of the Irishman, Joe Fagan, Paddy's future father-in-law. When the Act was passed, she was safely living at his Spring Creek station, in the East Kimberley; country that Paddy would learn to know.

Regatta Restaurant, December 1997

The crowded restaurant overlooked Lake Burley Griffin; looking across the guests could see the lights of the National Library reflected on the inky waters. Every eye, however, was on Patrick Dodson and Gatjil Djerrkura, as Gatjil made a formal presentation to Patrick of a powerful and beautifully decorated ceremonial pole from his Yolngu people of northeast Arnhem Land.

This was more than a gift, Gatjil explained. It was a strong gesture of unification and commitment between the people of Arnhem Land, the bosses of that country and that law, to Patrick's people, the Yawuru people. The objects were passports of connection that bonded the Yawuru and the Yolngu. They gave Patrick full recognition as a man of Yolngu law and pledged Yolngu support for Yawuru law and culture.

The two big men came together in a rough and close embrace, pulling their bodies in to each other in the way of the ceremonial ground. They had never been personally or politically close, but tonight they celebrated brotherhood and affirmed each other's status. The occasion was a farewell to Patrick after his resignation from the Council for Aboriginal Reconciliation which he had chaired for six years. Over the last month the relationship between Patrick and the Prime Minister on issues of native title and the future of reconciliation had become tense and unproductive. Patrick had severed the ties by 'rolling his swag' and resigning. Gatjil was due to experience similar tensions as the Chair of the Aboriginal and Torres Strait Islander Commission. That night though, the mood was upbeat. The restaurant had been booked out for the evening and the speeches, anecdotes and reminiscences flowed with the wine. After a year of tension and bitterness, this was a night for letting go and celebrating.

For Patrick, leaning on a table groaning with bottles and talking over the loud music, it was Gatjil's gift that made the night and would be treasured forever:

I'll take it back home and show the old fellas. We always had our law, Yawuru law, coming up from the desert side and going across east. This is a whole new track coming across from Arnhem Land side. For the Yawuru, this makes our business even stronger. It's a whole new road for our law.

Then he got up on the dance floor to 'shake a leg', laughing all the while. I sat at the table, wondering how to get the ceremonial pole into the car for the drive home.

Patrick's Yawuru people had to adjust to life in a pearling port. 'The lay up', low tide in the creek at Broome, W.A. (photograph V. Nishioka, courtesy of Australian Inland Mission Collection, National Library of Australia).

Alcohol had a major impact on the Yawuru people. Outside the Bar in Broome ca. 1900 (photograph Anon, courtesy of Photographs Broome, National Library of Australia).

62 ● Paddy's Road

Yawuru women had to adjust to the new social order. Women in Broome, W.A. (photograph Anon, courtesy of the National Library of Australia).

Paddy Djiagween was always a ceremonial leader for the Yawuru. Paddy Djiagween (standing left) at a ceremony in Broome, ca 1965 (photograph courtesy Malos collection and Battye Library).

Pastoralism changed land use and society for the Aboriginal people of the Kimberleys. Cattle crossing the Ord River on the way to Wyndham, Kimberley, W.A. (photograph Frank Hurley, courtesy of Hurley negative collection, National Library of Australia).

With the cattle came new controls and a police presence. Bringing in prisoners for spearing cattle, Wyndham, Kimberley Ranges, W.A. (photograph Ernest Lund Mitchell, courtesy of E.L. Mitchell collection of photographs, Battye Library).

For the first time in their country, Yawuru people were imprisoned. The first gaol at Broome, W.A., 1894 (photograph Ernest Black, courtesy of Battye Library).

Chapter Three

An Irishman at Wild Dog

'There are a few fortunate races that have been endowed with cheerfulness as their main characteristic, the Australian Aborigine and the Irish being among these.'
Daisy Bates, *The Passing of the Aborigines* (1938)

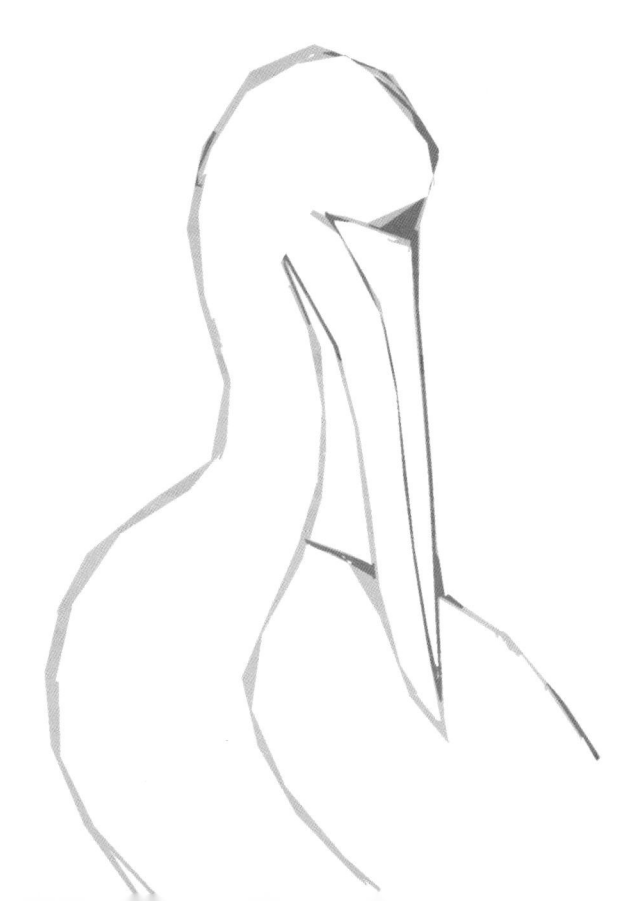

In Ireland, 2000

Patrick Dodson, like several contemporary leaders in Aboriginal politics, is quietly proud of the Irish side of his ancestry, often comparing the Irish experience with foreign rule and forced cultural change to his family experience. He knew that his mother's mother's father was an Irishman by the name of Joe Fagan. He knew of stories that Paddy Djiagween and Granny Liz had told. However he did not know Joe's country, and had not been able to trace his story until we began research for this book.

At the end of 2000, Patrick Dodson and Paul Lane visited Ireland as the guests of an organisation devoted to the goals of reconciliation. Siobahn McHugh reported on the visit for the Irish Times:

On a rainy Saturday at a school in Bray, County Wicklow, Ireland, a gathering of young people and students gathered for a conference on Exploring Identities, sponsored by an organisation called '80:20 Acting and Educating for a Better World'. Amongst the invited guests was Patrick Dodson, 'with his waist-length grey beard and trademark black hat, banded in the red, black and yellow colours of his people, one of the most easily recognised leaders of Aboriginal Australia.'

He had been meeting with leaders from all sides of the religious political divide in Ireland, seeking support for indigenous issues in Australia, joking that his reputation at home would be in tatters if it got out that he's met with the Unionist side.

A boy from Skerrie, north of Dublin, asks Patrick Dodson why the Aborigines have not resorted to armed struggle. Dodson points out that in the early days they did, but that that history, of spears against guns was, until recently, deliberately excluded. Now, numbering 1.5% of the population, taking up arms 'wouldn't be smart—far better to maximise the people of goodwill.' The teenagers are rapt as he addresses them with the same gravitas with which he meets world leaders. 'Violence breeds violence, as we've seen, but dialogue is a precious commodity. We're adept at picking out what we don't like about other human beings—your colour, the way you talk, the way you walk—but the harder challenge is to find out what we do hold in common… and find ways through the things that cause discord, train our minds, emotions and desires to find the common ground with people we might normally cross the street to avoid. That's what the future's about—create the space, find the common ground, develop it, THEN come back and look at the difference and see have they any substance or do they ring hollow now—because half the time they are not of substance if the essential goal is to see another human being able to live with pride and dignity and equality.'

As Pat Dodson sits down, a girl puts up her hand, full of moral outrage. 'Having heard the stories of the Stolen Children in the workshop, I want to know why you'd even want to be reconciled with people who did that?' Dodson gives a Mandela-like response: 'You need to liberate the oppressor as well as yourself. Because in doing that, you can construct a decent future for both of you. That doesn't mean you forget history, but don't let it neutralise you into remorse and being a victim, or you become totally useless to your cause, which is about liberating your people and enabling the oppressors to be better human beings.'[1]

Joseph Fagan

Joe Fagan's roots are found in County Monaghan, on the border country where Protestant and Catholic relations were inextricably locked in generations of conflict over land, religion and identity. In 1856, the *Belfast Banner* carried a notice seeking immigrants to the colony of Victoria:

> Persons wishing to bring their relatives and friends from the United Kingdom to Victoria, can secure passages for them in vessels chartered by Her Majesty's Government. The persons to be brought into the colony must be in good health, free from all bodily or mental defects; of good moral character, sober, industrious, and in the habit of working for wages at the occupation specified in the application forms.[2]

John Fagan and his wife Matilda Fagan, with their infant son, Joseph, first saw the shores of Australia from the deck of the *David McIver* in April 1857 when they made landfall in Geelong. The vessel had been dismasted during the three-month voyage.

Coming off the boat, John Fagan identified himself as a Presbyterian and was engaged by Thomas Gates as a labourer at a place called Moodewarre for six months.[3] He would have gained this position through the Geelong Labour Market and Shipping Office which advertised in the local paper, that 'great numbers of male and female servants of every description are daily in attendance, awaiting engagements at current rates.'[4]

The family adjusted to life in the farming district, learning how to work in the rural hinterland of Geelong, so different from their green home in County Monaghan, on the tumultuous border region of Northern Ireland. Their son Joseph, an infant when they set sail, grew up in the Victorian bush, learning to ride like the Australian-born and to work cattle.

While Ned Kelly and his gang were the focus of Victorian attention around 1880, young Joe was in his early twenties and itching to travel. A Sydney professional athlete came to Geelong challenging all comers in a sprint race. Joe borrowed £50 for a wager that returned good odds and he found his ticket out of Geelong and to a life in the bush. With money in his pocket and a stolen horse under him, he left Victoria, swam across the Murray River, according to Paddy Djiagween, and headed north for the outback.[5]

Along the road, Joe teamed up with Harry Twist, a man with a reputation that combined droving with cattle duffing and occasional bushranging. Harry had a droving plant, taking cattle to the Queensland Gulf country from north-western New South Wales. The men were on this road in 1881 when Jim Ronan, father of the outback author, Tom Ronan, joined them.[6] As the travellers passed through Thargomindah, in western Queensland, they spotted two 'mud-fat' horses in the yard of a Chinese market garden. These horses were added to the plant, although no money changed hands. Harry Twist and Joe Fagan had lifted them.

At Welford Downs in Central Queensland, the manager told Ronan that a young fellow 'ought to choose your company more carefully. You're in with a pretty shoddy mob.' Ronan looked at the horses, at Twist and Fagan; then decided to leave the droving team. The road into the outback crossed the Barkly Tableland and across to the world's largest cattle station, Victoria River Downs (VRD), east of the border of the Northern Territory and Western Australia.

Joe Fagan turns up once more in Tom Ronan's recollections, just before the turn of the century:

> One of the earliest head stockmen was that Joe Fagan who had been with Dad in Harry Twist's droving camp back in 1881. The original name of the Pigeon Hole, still the main outstation, was Fagan's Camp.[7]

The young Joe Fagan must have been skilled with horses and cattle to become head stockman at the world's largest cattle station. He was working there in 1887 according to the records of the VRD station. At the time, VRD and Wave Hill were important staging posts for stockmen droving cattle on the long and thirsty tracks across from Queensland and New South Wales in pursuit of fresh pastures and unalienated land in the East Kimberley. Joe Fagan would have seen and worked with a number of pioneer Irish drovers, such as Nat Buchanan in 1884 who brought 4000 cattle across to Ord River Station.[8]

There may have been another Irish connection at Pigeon Hole and VRD for the young Irish-Victorian drover. Anthropologist Debbie Rose was intrigued by the fact that Mudbura and Gurindji people, such as Hobbles Danayari, told stories of the Irish Victorian outlaw, Ned Kelly. Hobbles said that Ned Kelly came to the Victoria River District before other Europeans, taught them how to cook damper and make tea, and 'although there was only one billy of tea, and one little damper, all the Gurindji were fed.' Further research indicated that Isaiah 'Wild' Wright, Ned Kelly's companion and kinsman by marriage had, like Joe Fagan, made his way from Victoria to Pigeon Hole, before dying there of fever in 1911. On his death certificate, 'Wild' Wright was shown to have been born in County Monaghan, Ireland and came to Australia in 1857 with his parents. One intriguing possibility is raised by the fact that Joe's mother, Matilda, is listed on some records as Matilda Wright. If Joe Fagan and 'Wild' Wright had shared a campfire at Pigeon Hole and VRD, they would have had much to talk about. The stories of Ned Kelly, of County Monaghan and colonial Victoria would have formed common ground. The tales of Ned Kelly still alive today in the District may have had their origin around those campfire tales.[9]

Buchanan's droving exploits opened the track west for the Durack family. The droving exploits of the Durack family, also of Irish stock, are well known through the works of Mary Durack.[10] She has comprehensively recorded the histories of the big pastoral family in the region. The story of 'the battlers', like Joe Fagan, is less well-known, the records being scanty and contradictory. Paddy Djiagween recalled that Joe 'came together with M.P. Durack (Mary's father) somewhere along the road,' and Joe for a time managed a station for the Duracks.[11] Paddy remembered Mary and Elizabeth as little girls.

While horses and cattle formed the core of Joe's life, the promise of gold took him across the unmarked border into Western Australia and the East Kimberley. For a period Joe Fagan joined the search for gold with some 2000 other hopeful souls at Halls Creek in Western Australia on the southern portion of the East Kimberley after the discovery of gold there in 1885.[12] The rumours spread that 'there were not just reefs but mountains of gold in the Kimberley, nuggets the size of footballs waiting to be picked up in the creek beds, 'jeweller's shops' sparkling in the sun.'[13] The Irish diggers (as opposed to the Irish squatters) were not regarded as the cream of the new society in the East Kimberley:

> Native born or straight from the ould sod, these were the immigrants most disliked by the descendents of Swan river settlement government officers or gentlemen settlers of the Bunbury area. Whether they went out, as one of them boasted 'with our picks in one hand, our water-bags in the other, and our lives in the other,' in the mad and often hopeless search for gold, or whether they went into the grog-selling business, they were looked on with suspicion and a certain contempt.[14]

The gold-fields attracted those who sought to document the phenomenon. The photographer, R.T. Maurice whose collection now resides in the South Australian Royal Geographic Society gave one of his photos the caption, 'Pioneers of the East Kimberley Gold-fields 1886'. The photograph (now much copied by the Dodson family) shows 'Fagan' in the company of two European men, Kelly and McKellar, and an un-named Aboriginal youth.[15] If the 'Fagan' in the photograph was Joe, he returned to VRD by 1887 when he had to deal with an outbreak of the red-water disease that raged through the Territory's cattle.[16] Like many others, Joe Fagan may have spent the last decade of the century following the stock-routes back and forth between Wave Hill, VRD and the East Kimberley.

Joe's company, as always, was interesting. The 'Kelly' in the photograph is likely to have been the infamous stockman Jack Kelly who worked for the Duracks on Ord River station before taking up Texas Downs station, near Wild Dog, in 1897.[17] His young Aboriginal companion at the time was Major, who fell out with Kelly and became an outlaw, mounting a campaign of attacks in the district. Both Kelly and Major figure large in the oral history of the region, and were destined to play a role in the family story.[18] In 1892 the trooper in charge of the goldfields reported:

> Several have arrived within the last two months chiefly from Queensland. One a Mr Fagan who intends taking up a block of country for the purpose of breeding horses.[19]

The young Joe also found female companionship in the stock camps. It was towards the end of the century that he began his relationship with Nawurla at Wave Hill, the station south of VRD.[20] As Tom Cole recalls,

'Wave Hill was the jewel in the crown of the Australian pastoral division; being head stockman there carried a certain amount of prestige.'[21] Tracing Patrick's great-grandmother beyond the family understanding is a difficult linguistic and anthropological puzzle. Most references in the scanty records record her name as Noala.[22] For the Gurindji people at Wave Hill, this name would be Nawurla, one of eight female subsection (or skin) names. The name defines a social category and allocates her a place in a social network that defines classificatory sisters, mothers, fathers and brothers.[23]

We have no sure first-person record of her country, beyond the Wave Hill connection. Paddy Djiagween, some seventy years later, told Wendy Lowenstein that Elizabeth's people were Yarringadi from Wave Hill.[24] While this is not a known tribal or language name, it may be a reference to a group, defined by the anthropologist Mervyn Meggitt as the Waringari, from south-west of the Gurindji near Gordon Downs and Birrindudu cattle stations.[25]

Relationships between white stockmen and black women were commonplace but variable. Many such relationships, whether forced or voluntary, were fleeting and transient. Others were long-standing relationships of mutual regard and affection involving partnerships of sorts, in the saddle and the swag, with many Aboriginal women being highly regarded stockworkers.[26] In 1898, Nawurla gave birth to her daughter, who was given the name Elizabeth Grace Fagan, indicating that this was a long-term relationship. Certainly, Joe Fagan always acknowledged his daughter and sought to protect her interests.

The norm at the time in the region, however, was violent capture, as a Northern Territory policeman reported in 1898, the year Elizabeth was born:

> That if half the young lubras now being detained (I won't call it kept, for I know that most of them would clear away if they could) were approached on the subject, they would say that they were run down by station blackguards on horseback, and taken to the stations for licentious purposes, and there kept more like slaves than anything else… Some, I have heard take these lubras with them, but take the precaution to tie them up securely for the night to prevent them escaping. Of course, sirs, these allegations are, as you know, very difficult to prove against any individual persons.[27]

However at Wave Hill, the following diary entry from M.P. Durack around the time records that the women there were 'working the cattle' with their men.

Sunday on one of the most isolated stations in Australia…What a transformation! The many-coloured dresses of the women have given place to shirts, moleskin pants and stockwhips slung across their shoulders. They are not easily to be distinguished from the sterner sex but for their fuller posterial curves.[28]

The conservative Irish Catholic pastoralist was not approving. Later, he noticed a black stockwoman riding into Wyndham with cattle, a 'half-caste' baby in a coolamon strapped to her back, the first he had seen in the Kimberley. He worried that this would become commonplace, 'for the strain resulting will surely be no asset it's being common knowledge that the half-breed inherits the worst characteristics of both races, nor would I feel disposed to trust or to employ one of the kind.'[29] On hearing this diary entry, Patrick imagined Nawurla and her baby, his Granny Liz, riding into Wyndham with Joe Fagan and a mob of cattle.

Spring Creek, Wild Dog Road

After working for others back and forth across the track between Kimberley and Wave Hill, Joe Fagan was keen to get out of service to the large pastoral companies and look for his own land. Most of the good pastoral land had been taken up, but there were a few blocks as yet unclaimed. He went back to the Western Australian side, finding good cattle country in the southern basin of the Ord River. A small police outpost, also known as Argyle, was established at Wild Dog Soak in 1896.[30] This was the country of the Kija and Malngin people, who lived along the banks of the Ord, and between the domes and ridges of the Bungle Bungle range.

Joe took out a lease in 1901 for the Spring Creek station, adjoining the Durack and Hill Ord River properties, and extended the lease in the next year in partnership with J. Philchowski and R.A. Finlay, as the Turner Grazing Company.[31] The established Durack leasees did not necessarily welcome the new neighbours with Mary Durack commenting on the fact that:

> A number of tough Queensland stockmen with no capital began to drift into Kimberley and take up small holdings around the larger estates. One of these horse thieves in fact later became a small squatter who stocked his run almost entirely from his poddy dodging exploits.[32]

Joe Fagan, a stockman from Queensland, fitted the bill, with no money to his name and missing horses at Geelong and Thargomindah on the record.

Paddy Djiagween described the property as, 'Spring Creek, Wild Dog road, 46 miles from Argyle Station.'[33] The station adjoined the Northern Territory border and was on the track that led along the border from Halls Creek to the Wyndham meat-works and port, before the telegraph line route through Turkey Creek was established in 1890. While Paddy Djiagween was a boy on the west coast on his way to the Beagle Bay Mission, his future in-laws were establishing their home in the cattle country of the East Kimberley.

In two years, for an annual rent of some £29, Joe had gained possession of nearly 60,000 acres of pastoral land.[34] Future native title debates would argue that leases like Fagan's gave exclusive possession, but were constrained by conditions that officially recognised Aboriginal rights of access for hunting, gathering and ceremonial activity, keeping the sliver of native title rights alive. The property was not prosperous, and Joe Fagan had little in the way of cash for improvements. Most years he had to spend time away from the property earning enough money to pay himself a wage. For many years he worked at Springvale Station. He also relied on partnerships to meet the rental payments.

One early partner was Rudolph Philchowski, a Polish immigrant, reputed to be a count with distinguished military service, who 'ran a store at Carlton Reach, a place on the Ord River south of present-day Kununurra from which he sold alcohol and procured Aboriginal women for white travelers.'[35] According to Mary Durack, he later ran the mail service between Wyndham and Halls Creek, perhaps after M.P. Durack had him removed because of the delays in store deliveries caused by teamsters dallying at his sly-grog shop. Mary Durack recalled that Philchowski went with 'a man called Joe Fagan to Spring Creek and then took on the mail run.'[36] She elsewhere referred to his partnership with the 'astute but illiterate Joe Fagan with whom he had struck up an incongruous mateship.'[37] Philchowski was fatally speared as he slept, just south of the present town of Kununurra, near a creek crossing that bears his name.[38]

Deaths were frequent, and the Police Camp at Wild Dog became the last resting place for several early pioneers, victims of spears or illness. Before himself being speared, Philchowski found the body of Hugh McKenna, aged 33 years, speared while resting in the shade of a tree during the mid-day halt. Police Constable John Day, a 30-year-old Victorian died of fever and an internal complaint and was buried near the mill and tank. George Knight, a 44-year-old labourer on Argyle station, also died of fever and was buried nearby. Paul Hasluck, visiting the area in the 1930s with the Moseley Royal Commission would remark that:

> At Wild Dog Gorge on the Mistake Creek side of Sugar Springs, there lie near each other, making a grim jest, the last beds of men named Day and Knight. In the early days men were usually buried where they died. Sometimes they were laid down by a mate, at other times by those who happened to find them.[39]

Major, the outlaw

At the turn of the century, relations between pastoralists and Aborigines in the region were turbulent. The twenty-five years following the discovery of gold was marked by lawlessness, atrocities against local Aboriginal people, spearing of cattle and generally hostile relationships. To survive contact, Aboriginal people became the labour force for the new settlers, particularly in the pastoral industry where people could remain close to their traditional lands.[40] Most of the cattle stations in the East Kimberley relied on a core of Aboriginal workers, both men and women, who camped near the stations under the protection and control of the station owner. Outside that nucleus and at the corner of the runs, many Aboriginal people were attempting to resist their loss of land and autonomy, killing cattle and stealing gear, for which retribution was fierce and final. As Mary Durack remarked, 'Sooner or later the blacks would learn that if they wished to survive their choice lay between working for the white man on his own terms or keeping out of his way among the hills.'[41]

Violent interactions raged around the Spring Creek district and along the Ord River.[42] According to Bruce Shaw's interpretation of oral history accounts, much of the violence seemed to have been sparked as a result of failed relationships between individual whites and blacks, where trust turned to hatred and retribution after a breakdown in communication, especially where Aboriginal people felt humiliated. This was the essence of the story of Jack Kelly, whose Texas Downs station was close to Spring Creek, and Major, his 'working boy turned bandit.' Most oral accounts indicate that the stockman, Jack Kelly, brought an Aboriginal boy with the name of Major with him from the Northern Territory. Major may have come from the Wardaman people from the Delamere and Willeroo stations, north-east of VRD, although Patrick Dodson was told by Victor Vincent, son of Vincent Lingiari of Wave Hill fame, that Major was a Mirriwoong from the northeast Kimberley.[43] Bob Nyalcas from Warmun community at Turkey Creek says

Major was a 'Boy from that country, Darwin side. Blackfella you know, flash one, all along catch 'em up them *kartiya*.'[44]

Jack Kelly is well remembered in the district. A rock engraving near Purnululu National Park, west of Spring Creek, showing a man in a cowboy hat and pipe, is said to be Kelly and Queenie McKenzie recalls this incident from her mother's time working at Texas Downs:

> Jack Kelly was a hard man and he used to belt the people who worked for him if they did not do the right thing. All this time there were still wild Aboriginal people living in the hills and sometimes they used to kill cattle for tucker. One day Jack Kelly and some of his mates from the station went after them. They rode through Kilfoyle Gap and near One Mile Bottle Tree they came across some knocked up bullocks. Then they found some Blackfellas camped under high red rocks called Lajipany on Texas Downs. They had killed a bullock (a 'killer') and were skinning it and cutting up the beef. The *kartiya* sneaked up on them and started shooting everybody, men, women and children. Only two people survived, a man and a baby girl. The man was the grandfather of Paddy Rhatigan who is still living in the Pensioner's Quarters at Warmun. His grandfather escaped by hiding in the carcass of the killer. He crawled into the rib cage and hid in the guts until the shooting was over.[45]

Kelly and Major were close, even to the stage of going together to Perth, which was very unusual at the time. However, a violent falling out with Kelly led to a lengthy period of guerilla-like insurgency, murder and crime on the stations around Texas Downs and Spring Creek in 1908. The sandstone domes and deeply eroded chasms of the Bungle Bungle range offered an ideal hideout. Major, according to Queenie McKenzie 'used to hide away from the police by climbing a steep mountain in the Bungle Bungle country that no-one could get up to without a ladder.'[46] Back in Broome, the *Broome Chronicle* was alarmed:

> A well known squatter shot dead. Inquiries made at Perth show that the native murderer had been well treated by Kelly, who brought him to Perth last Christmas.[47]

Arthur Male, the master pearler and squatter had run his campaign for the West Australian Parliament from his pearling base in Broome, arguing that 'the question of securing efficient Police Protection throughout the district is one which I will continue to advocate.' The voters of the Kimberley supported his message, gaining 327 votes in Broome compared to his nearest rival O'Donoghue's tally of 49.[48] Responding to the Major crisis, he sent a telegram to the Premier:

> Reported from Turkey Creek, two more whites murdered by blacks. I should strongly urge that you authorise magistrate or police at Wyndham to have special party organised and sent out at once. Protection of whites must be attended to irrespective of cost.[49]

A police expedition, including trackers from Wild Dog police outpost, set out after Major and his party. Special constables were sworn in at the local court in Wyndham, organised by M.P. Durack. They were issued with 500 rounds of ammunition for Winchester Carbines and 100 rounds for pistols. A telegram from the Commissioner of Police declared that 'police searching for Major on no account are to resort to force or to use firearms unless in service defence.'[50] Legal and moral niceties such as these were given scant attention in responding to the state of ferment, outrage and terror.

The posse assembled against the protests of Bishop Gibney, who demanded to know, 'Has the Government any authority under the constitution of the country to send armed men into the wilds to slay, until the blood-lust of the police is sated, the innocent with the guilty?'[51]

Stories of Major's life and death are conflicting. Bruce Shaw has attempted to untangle the variations in the oral and written accounts.[52] In one version, Major's gang was joined by a woman with the name of Naula (or Nawurla), from the Northern Territory. She was said to have been either Major's wife or his mother.

Nawurla stayed with Major on his raids and in the final police pursuit, reloading his rifle in his last siege at the Nine-Mile near Spring Creek until being shot in the breast. She died a few days later. Jack Sullivan told the story to Bruce Shaw:

> One of the old girls was loading a gun for him. They ended up shooting the old gin, who was loading the gun, through the bub (breast). That buggered her, and one feller sneaked around and got him, shooting him in the arm. When that happened he could no longer load his gun. He lifted up his hands: 'You got me,' and they walked up and did him in. They shot him little by little—it was not a clean death—and cut off his hand and took it back. They could have taken him alive, poor bugger.[53]

The *Broome Chronicle* reported 'great relief that Major and his party were exterminated by police.' They noted that, 'Major's gin Knowla stood by him and handed him cartridges, and while fighting was going on she got a bullet wound in the chest. She was the only gin in the party that got hurt in the engagement.'[54] The four police and special constables were given rewards from the Commissioner of £20 each, while the same amount was extended in 'purchasing presents for the six native trackers: Charlie, Dickie, Quartpot, Nipper, Diller and Negri.'

Joe Fagan did not join the manhunt occurring in the ranges around his property. However, it is possible that his partner, Nawurla from the Wave Hill region, may have joined Major in his last stand. Major's final companion, Knowla, may have been Patrick Dodson's great-grandmother, Nawurla. We know that Fagan, Nawurla, Kelly and Major came from the Northern Territory to the East Kimberley around the same time. They settled on stations in the same district. Nawurla may have chosen to join Major and support her countryman or relative. If this was the case, Major's companion left behind her ten-year-old daughter, Elizabeth Grace Fagan. In the same year as Major died, the authorities relocated the little girl from Spring Creek to Broome. There is no record of Nawurla Fagan's death, nor any other information of her after 1908. She disappears from the official record at the same time as Major's Nawurla.

Major was no hero. His violence, his stand-over tactics and his thefts of women frightened Aboriginal people of the time.[55] They often assisted the pastoralists and police to protect them and pursue Major. Aboriginal descendants today know the Major story and can show where he travelled, but he is not recalled with the respect given to the likes of Jandamarra, in Bunuba country to the west.

Kelly, although he lived and worked with Aboriginal people in the region for decades, is also remembered with bitterness and resentment. Like other squatters at the turn of the century he valued a 'killer' more than a life, and dealt out justice with a Winchester. Estimates of the number of Aboriginal deaths vary wildly.[56] It is now impossible to ascertain either the pre-colonisation population or the extent of the killings. It must be concluded though that, thinly veiled under the romance of the Durack sagas, the colonisation of the East Kimberley was violent and brutal. For Aboriginal people, it was the imposition of a police presence at Turkey Creek that allowed the country to settle down, and a measure of control to be introduced over the rifles and tempers of the squatters. As Jack Britten recalls:

> When sergeant (constable) was there he bin stop every *kartiya*. Stop every *kartiya* 'don't trying to cruel thing on blackfella. I got a word from government,' he told them.[57]

But the East Kimberley also saw relationships of mutual respect, co-operation and co-existence. For every Kelly there was a Fagan. There were men who shared a time and a place but did not impose a value system. Other station managers were remembered with respect and gratitude. From the scanty records available, it is reasonable to accept Paddy Djiagween's recollection of his father-in-law as a good man, who got along well with the people on Spring Creek by giving them meat, supplies and shelter in reciprocal exchange for the use of their land and labour.[58] With the nearby Wild Dog police station, his corner of the Ord River basin may have been a peaceable refuge from the killers of the region—black and white alike. In 1889 the Government Resident of the Northern Territory expressed a bleak view on the hopes for a peaceful frontier:

> I am well aware that there were many odious things done by whites, but I believe I express the opinion of nine-tenths of those who have taken their lives in their hands and gone into the back blocks when I say that occupation of the country for pastoral purposes and peaceable relations with the native tribes are hopelessly irreconcilable.[59]

While the frontier came quickly to the East Kimberley country, reconciliation, if possible at all, would take a longer time.

Elizabeth and Paddy

The ten-year-old girl, Elizabeth Grace Fagan, was taken from her father at Spring Creek station in 1908 and sent to Broome, going from the grassy black soil plains country she knew to the saltwater pindan country of the Yawuru. The local Aboriginal protector, James Isdell, signed the papers that authorised her relocation. According to Fr Bischoffs at Beagle Bay, the father was 'forced to do so by Mr J Isdell, who otherwise would have sent the girl to the Mission.'[60] Isdell described his policy outlook:

> The half-caste is intellectually above the aborigine, and it is the duty of the State that they be given a chance to lead a better life than their mothers. I would not hesitate for one moment to separate any half-caste from its aboriginal mother, no matter how frantic her momentary grief might be at the time. They soon forget their offspring.[61]

The Church gained custody and control over these children. Sr Mary Mechtilde, one of the Irish Saint John of God nuns recalled:

> Mr Gale the chief protector of aborigines, visited the mission and set to work collecting all the little waifs and strays of the Kimberleys, bringing them in to receive the care and attention of their future guardians. It was nothing unusual for a policeman to arrive at the Convent door with a little darkie wrapped in his own coat or shirt.[62]

Elizabeth was left in the convent school dormitory in Broome, established by Mother Antonio to care for the 'swarms of neglected, idle and uneducated children around the port.'[63] At the school the nuns of the St John of God order educated the Catholic children of the town of all races, giving them valuable literacy skills:

> Despite the heat the nuns taught in a pleated habit of heavy cloth and stiffly starched cap and white collar. They were desperately poor and distance seemed to mean they were largely forgotten by the Church. After a day of teaching some of the nuns, after just an hour's rest, would start a shift in the government hospital.[64]

Their work in the hospital, nursing Japanese divers crippled with the bends, led the Japanese community to build them a school in 1912 to replace the makeshift school held on the Church verandah.[65] At the convent, Elizabeth was to be trained and civilised in order to gain a position as a domestic servant and be protected from the immorality and vice of the camps, either on the stations or around the pearling luggers. Fr Bischoffs argued in a letter to James Isdell that separation was necessary, for 'surrounded as they are by vicious influences they cannot but grow up immoral and criminal.'[66] It was in the convent at Broome that Elizabeth (Lizzie or Gracey as she was variously known) grew up and gained a lifelong love of Irish songs that she passed on to her family. She also came to know Paddy Djiagween, her future husband.

On his return to Broome from Beagle Bay, Patrick's grandfather had settled into a relatively independent life but maintained his Catholicism. He worked with Fr Nicholas Emo and Mother Antonio, whose humanity and poverty contrasted with the value sets of the time. Paddy's eldest brother died in Broome. He had come in from the bush sick, was baptised by Fr Nicholas, and died the next day. Paddy had already lost his only sister who died after being wounded in a domestic argument in Broome, near where a bottle shop now stands.[67]

Paddy worked hard to make a living. He tried to turn his tailoring skills learned on the Mission into a commercial proposition, despite the stranglehold on the trade held by the Chinese in Broome who fashioned the distinctive white tailored drill suits of the master pearlers:[68]

> My trade was tailor but I couldn't get any job. There were too many Chinese tailors. They wouldn't give anyone any job.

For many in the growing town of Broome, he would be known as 'Tailor Paddy'. The venture never got very far, although his skills were used on work with sails and nets on the pearling boats to which he turned for a living.

One of the master pearlers he worked for in the early years was Francis Rodriguez who owned some seven luggers but never went to sea, spending his days holding up the bar at his Continental Hotel. For Rodriguez, Paddy worked as a shell opener and sailed a schooner, serving the outgoing pearling boats with fuel and food, carrying:

> Rice and meat, Globe brand meat in a two pound tin, and Richmond tobacco. But I never smoked, nor drink at all. I was a good boy those days.

Paddy preferred travelling to and from the pearling boats, rather than staying out at sea for months at a time. He especially disliked the job of manning the hand compressor that pumped air down the hoses to the diver walking on the seabed. Working the pump left 'my heart on my lip' with effort. He once found a £20,000 pearl for Rodriguez and received the shell opener's cut of £200, a very healthy sum at the time.

While the pearling trade grew, the town prospered, but little benefit flowed to the Aboriginal community. Paddy was unusual in finding constant work in the town while an editorial in the *Broome Chronicle* in 1910 complained about 'the number of indigent lazy natives that are allowed to roam about at their own sweet will, and do more to entice the industrious natives from his quarters than any other cause.'[69]

The town's prosperity was built on a system of social and legal control to ensure that the white population (of less than 700) was secure while the larger Asian and Aboriginal communities provided the labour force and serviced their needs. The establishment of Asiatic communities in Broome, Darwin and Thursday Island was viewed with concern by the national government, as eroding the white Australia policy and threatening the jobs of Australian workers. In 1911 the Minister of External Affairs declared that from January 1913, only white divers would be allowed to collect shell. John Bailey tells the story of twelve ex-navy men experienced in deep-sea diving brought out from England in a tragic attempt to establish a new labour regime in the tropical north. The experiment failed and the multicultural communities of northern Australia continued to evolve.[70]

On Good Friday in 1913 Paddy refused to go out on a lugger, the *Valadero*, swapping his tasks with a Filipino diver less concerned with Church holy days. The next day the lugger went down, with two lives lost and a few survivors who swam twelve miles to shore. Rodriguez assumed that Paddy had been lost at sea. When he turned up in Broome, Captain Gregory sent him up to the Continental, to tell 'the missus', Mrs Rodriguez, 'cos she was worried for me. I was favourite for them.' The boss, Mr Rodriguez, shook his hand and 'the missus' was relieved. Favourite he may have been, but he had to refer to her as 'Ma'am', as if he had called her by name, 'they would jump on our throat.'[71]

Kevin Lawton reports that Paddy later worked as a skipper, managing an all-Japanese crew on a lugger. It was unusual for an Aboriginal man to be given such a role; to be trusted with authority. On one expedition, a rare and enormously valuable pearl was found. Paddy placed the pearl in the safe. The crew ganged up on him and demanded he hand it over to them, threatening him at knife-point. Paddy went to the safe, reached in and brought out a revolver. Holding the crew at bay on the deck, he took the tiller and entered Roebuck Bay by nightfall. There, frightened by the desperation of the crew, he jumped overboard with the pearl in his pocket; swimming to shore through the treacherous and shark-infested waters. He ran to the Catholic Church and collapsed on the altar. The master got the pearl, the crew were sacked and Paddy decided to avoid the boats and the Japanese crew for as long as he was able.[72]

Late in 1913 Fr Bischoffs wrote to the Chief Protector, inquiring whether the permission of Elizabeth's father was necessary to authorise her request for marriage, noting that 'if your consent should only be required for the marriage, please grant same for Patrick Djiagween and Gracy Fagan.' The Protector replied that his permission was not necessary, unless the girl was under the age of sixteen. 'If she is under that age, my permission is readily given on your recommendation. With regard to the supposed father… it is not necessary to get his permission, as no male person has any legal claim on his illegitimate children'.[73]

With the permission of their State father-figure, Paddy and Elizabeth stood together at the altar of the small Broome church before Fr Nicholas Emo in January 1914. They had raised enough funds from Paddy's work on the boats and Elizabeth's work in the laundry of Mrs Male, the wife of the master pearler and chairman of the Roads Board and Member of Parliament. Elizabeth was sixteen-years-old; Paddy was probably twenty-two.[74] They bought a house in partnership with Lawrence Hunter, who had also married a girl from the Broome convent.

Fr Emo talked a great deal with Paddy and was a close mentor. With his own money the priest had bought allotments in the town which he gave to Aboriginal people starting their married life. He had also rented ten acres within the town boundary at Gantheame Point where he cared for the sick and homeless. As he told the Roth Royal Commission through a translator, 'I have often found the old and infirm blacks … dying in the absence of a little care and kindness … how many must there be in other centres occupied by aboriginals.'[75] Fr Nicholas Emo died in Lombardina in 1915; buried in a blanket in the sandhills, in keeping with his vows of poverty and his identification with the people he served.[76]

Paddy Djiagween had lost a mentor and his people had lost a friend. Paddy and his new bride, Elizabeth, set out to leave Broome to return after a seven-year absence to her father's place at Spring Creek in the East Kimberley. Paddy was ready to take his place as Joe Fagan's book-keeper, scribe and son-in-law.

Interview with Patrick Dodson, National Library of Australia, 2001[77]

We wanted to talk today about some of those characters in your family history. We might start off with you great-grandfather, Joe Fagan, who was an Irish cattleman, a pioneer, who took up a cattle station in Spring Creek in the East Kimberley towards the end of the last century. How do you feel about Joe Fagan?

He's always loomed in my life through the stories from my grandmother, Grace Elizabeth. She obviously was very fond of him and spoke of him in glowing terms as a man who was a good man, as a man who obviously worked hard because he was a cattleman and a man who obviously had a great deal of love for her. The sense of sadness and sorrow when he died is something that she probably carried in her life. Finding out about Joe Fagan, my great-grandfather, has been an absolutely wonderful endeavour. Things have been confirmed from the stories that my grandfather, Paddy Djiagween told about him. About him running away from his own people in Geelong, stealing a horse and crossing the rivers and gradually getting up into the Kimberley.

He never made much of that though, money, did he?

Never made much money. He was obviously a battler. He tried his hand at gold mining in the early period. He was a man who lived on his own, in the sense of away from where the major camps were, with my great grandmother. She was known as Rosie, I think, but Nola (or Nawurla) is a name that's often recorded in the transcripts. Nola came from Spring Creek country with a Gurindji or Malngin or Jaru sort of background.

The exciting thing was finding a photograph of old Joe and seeing the stature of the man, a tall sort of a man. Obviously you could see he was a man who worked and a man who had very clear bearings himself. He seems to be a very strong kind of character in his bearing.

At the time he was living around Spring Creek it wasn't a peaceful time in the East Kimberley around from 1890s to 1917. I mean, that was, for instance, when Major was attacking white homesteads.

Certainly Major is in the vicinity and seen as a major guerrilla fighter, or a bandit, whichever way people wanted to look at him. He was a man who may have had some association with Joe in the sense that he might have worked in that region. Certainly he was killed right near the Spring Creek homestead, on a hill not far away from it. He was obviously a man who had his disagreements with non-Aboriginal people, for whatever the reason. Whether someone had stolen his wife or offended his mother or whatever, it led to a vigilante-type response, which was the way things were in the Kimberley in those days. Not only in the East Kimberley regions but also further in the Fitzroy Valley region with Jandamarra and in the north with the battles brought about, or the massacres brought about in the Forrest River region through Lumbia. There were some real outstanding Aboriginal people in the sense of coming to notoriety or fame that were feared by Aboriginal people as much as they were by white people.

So how did Joe Fagan survive in that sort of context, do you think? I mean, he was a border country man. Is that relevant?

I think he probably didn't take sides. He probably would've known what the injustice was that led to Major taking up arms to a bloke who was his mate, Jack Kelly. He would've known what the blue or the fight was about. He would've stood back from engaging in that. I suppose if there'd been any animosity between Joe and Major then Major would've come after him, but there doesn't seem to have been.

Your grandfather said he had good relations with the Aboriginal community in the district.

Very good relationships with people in the districts. So good, I think, that the Duracks described him as more of a blackfella than a white man. For the Duracks that was probably a form of criticism. From the Aboriginal point of view he was seen as a man who stood by his Aboriginal wife and stood by the principles that he lived by, which were things of justice and fairness it seems to me. He payed the rent and made his own way in life without relying on others to do things for him.

The Fagan family first saw Australian shores from the decks of the David McIver. The David McIver accessed from http://www.users.bigpond.com/mbrettell/cuttler /cuttler_Frameset.htm.

Joe Fagan always kept interesting company. 'Pioneers of East Kimberley Goldfields 1886' (courtesy of Maurice album, Royal Geographical Society Library).

Major eluded capture in the hills of the Bungle Bungle Range, southwest of Spring Creek (photograph by author).

On his way to Spring Creek, Joe Fagan camped at Blue Hole on the Ord River (photograph by author).

Granny Liz Fagan sought to gain exemption from the Act in order to hold title to her own home. Granny Liz at home in Broome (courtesy Fay Wade album).

Granny Liz Fagan was always surrounded by children. On the Broome jetty, ca 1974. Granny Liz with Seema, Aziz Sulamein, Debra Wade, Ronald Dodson, Veronica Wade, Ronald Wade, Eric Wade, Hannah, Julie Djiagween (courtesy Fay Wade album).

Paddy Djiagween and Michael Jalaru, Kennedy Hill, Broome, after collecting cockles (courtesy Fay Wade album).

Granny Liz provided home and a refuge for many in Broome. Granny Liz Fagan and Mackie Sariago, Broome, 1976 (courtesy Fay Wade album).

Chapter Four

Two Laws

'The force of white men's wills, which dispensed and withdrew life, imprisoned and set free, fed or starved, like God himself.'
Nadine Gordimer, *Six Feet of the Country* **(1956)**

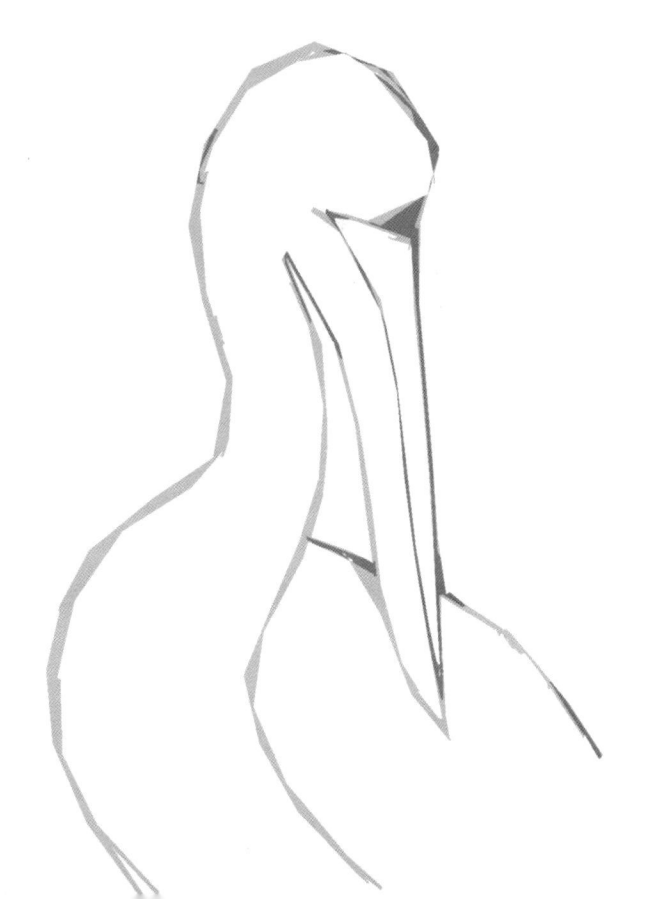

Spring Creek, WA, 2001

Patrick swung the Toyota off the Duncan Road, which snaked its way along the unmarked border of the Northern Territory and Western Australia. He let the sixty-wheeler road train thunder past, as it pulled three trailers of live cattle to the docks at Wyndham. It was mustering season; helicopters chopped across the skies, pushing skittish mobs of Brahman cattle to the yards where station hands on motorbikes waited. Clouds of thick dust rolled over the country that Patrick's great-grandfather and grandfather had called home. The three of us, Patrick, Paul Lane and I, were looking at country.

The feel of the place reminded Patrick of Wave Hill; it was soft country. He liked the look of the grassy, black-soil plains, traversed by limestone ridges and dotted with bloodwood trees and anthills. Patrick was on his way to Kalkaringi, the home of the people who had worked for Vesteys at the Wave Hill station until 1966, when Vincent Lingiari led the celebrated walk-off that gave birth to the land rights movement. Patrick was going to talk to the family and community about the Lingiari Foundation, a trust he and others had established to support Aboriginal land and cultural initiatives. Along the road, he wanted to turn into Spring Creek station, the station Joe Fagan had originally established. He also sought to find the location of the elusive Wild Dog soak, and the site of Major's last stand.

At the Spring Creek homestead gate, the manager's wife was friendly but firm, curious about the history of the place in which her family now lived, but cautious about protocol and precedent. The men were mustering; she had children to look after; the head office in Perth had to give permission after an application in writing; and there was nothing to see at Wild Dog anyway. She had never heard of Joe Fagan, but she said that the Turner Grazing Company he had established was still trading. As they talked, Patrick looked around at the homestead on the site selected by Joe Fagan. On his way up he had seen the remains of old yards and imagined the old man, helped by a young Paddy Djiagween, cutting the posts and sinking the post holes. Patrick left the station polite but disappointed; turning back on the road south.

Evening shadows were growing longer as we pulled into Mistake Creek station, an Aboriginal-owned property south of Spring Creek, on the Northern Territory side of the road. Here Donald and Linda Cameron, bosses of the Malngin Land Trust were pleased to see him, recalling his time at Central Land Council when Donald was an executive member and Patrick was the Director. The owners of the station asked their visitors for meat and tobacco; rich in land, poor in basic supplies.

Talking about the country and times gone, Donald told us where the Wild Dog police station was and where Major fought his last battle, near the Nine Mile. Linda recalled old people telling her that Nawurla was with him at the death. Linda surprised Patrick when she said, 'That Wild Dog, where Victor Vincent father (Vincent Lingiari) been born. That old man who passed away along Wave Hill.' Donald confirmed the story, saying, 'Oh, yes, old Vincent, he born there, his mother must have come across working for Vesteys.'

On his way to discuss the Lingiari foundation with Vincent Lingiari's family, Patrick had found Vincent's birthplace. A 'borning-place' is a special connection; one shared by Vincent and Patrick's grandmother. The hairs on the back of his neck shivered.

World War One

Paddy and Elizabeth Djiagween, newly wed, travelled by boat to Wyndham, and then by bullock and donkey teams down the long road following the Ord River to Spring Creek station, the country of the Kija people. Along the way, in the northern port town of Wyndham, the Beagle Bay Mission priest, Fr Bischoffs forwarded him a letter with bad news about his brother Charlie serving with the Australian Infantry in Gallipoli and Egypt.

> Another brother, 1914 war, he went over seas, and lost his life there, a soldier. I got a letter before they took Fr Bischoffs, you know, before they took him, and Father forwarded the letter to me while I was in Wyndham, 160 miles the other side of Argyle Station.[1]

Paddy felt this loss of his last sibling deeply. He knew that his brother Charlie now rested in an unknown foreign grave having died for a country that denied him citizenship and equality because of his race. This, in a war when southern newspapers urged their soldiers to show 'all the high patriotism and self-control of a ruling race,' and when Banjo Paterson would write of the 'mettle that a race can show' in his poem, 'We're all Australians now.'[2]

Archive files, originally secret documents, reveal that the Mission, staffed by German priests, was thought of by officials as a potential source of information for German authorities, through wireless or mail via Manila or Timor. The British consular agent in Timor wrote a classified report in 1916, saying that Fr Bischoffs was regarded as a:

> Disloyalist and a dangerous man worthy of close attention. Trappist missionaries at Beagle Bay have, for a number of years, used their influence with Manilamen (Filipinos), who are mostly bigoted Roman Catholics … at the mission, most of its (Aboriginal) members were unable to speak English, and so ignorant, that it could well be a mask for hiding any treasonable actions.[3]

Father Bischoffs was interned as a German alien in a camp at Liverpool, New South Wales. Conflicts of race and religion escalate when the nation is perceived to be under threat.

Spring Creek station

Paddy and Elizabeth Djiagween arrived at Spring Creek in the early part of World War One. Much of the active resistance in the East Kimberley had begun to subside, and life was quieter on the stations, although not yet peaceful. Cattle-spearing declined when the Government provided cattle and meat to Aboriginal people from Moola Bulla station in 1910 and Violet Valley in 1911, and the police presence at Turkey Creek and Wild Dog Police Camp restrained both pastoralists and Aboriginal people.[4] However, violence was a simmering presence.

In 1913, Joseph Fagan's partner, Philchowski, had been speared to death on the old stock route, near where Kununurra now stands. Bruce Shaw compared oral Aboriginal versions with the European written versions provided by the scribe of the pastoralists, Mary Durack.[5] According to her account, Philchowski was on his way to Fagan's place at Spring Creek when he was speared while he was asleep in order that his rations could be stolen. According to Aboriginal oral accounts, the spearing was sparked by a confrontation between Philchowski and an Aboriginal man, Wallambain, after Wallambain was refused food and tobacco. Another man, Jillambin, was put on trial in Wyndham, after being found with Philchowski's revolver. Durack quotes a contemporary account of the trial:[6]

> The trial of the blackfellow for the murder did not take long. Parker had a hopeless job of trying to defend him, especially with a jury of bushmen. They found him guilty in about three seconds.

Life on the stations has always been tough, and in the period during and after the World War One was very tough, especially for Aboriginal people. Work was demarcated along racial lines, with whites taking up, as a matter of right, any positions that paid a wage. This generally included the positions of head stockman and bookkeeper. Through oral and archival accounts, Mary Anne Jebb has analysed the development of relationships on the pastoral frontier of the West Kimberley. She describes how some people found protection from the dangers of white occupation in their relationships with white stockmen. While recognising that these relationships often involved violence, coercion, social dislocation and fear, she points out that:

> These white men also kept some people alive, introduced them to the world of work, and occasionally fathered and maintained their children and members of their families. This complex dynamic between violence and protection formed the basis for paternalism, which was an enduring characteristic of station culture and life with a white Boss.[7]

Paddy's job of bookkeeper and store-man was, as Tom Ronan's fictional account of a bookkeeper on the stations illustrates, a key bridge between the white roles of authority and control and the black roles of labour and service.[8] He had control of the rations, the source of food and loyalty on the frontier.[9]

Paddy's mission education and his relationship with his father-in-law marked him as unusually able to walk the boundary line that separated black from white. Joe Fagan's acknowledgment of his daughter and his recognition of her husband also marked the man as unusual for the times and the place. Spring Creek was off the track; here they could make their own laws and allow for Joe Fagan's skeptical view of authority.

Joe Fagan could neither read nor write. Paddy would sit up late and read to him from old newspapers and a handful of novels, both maintaining a face-saving fiction of fading eyesight for the old man, now close to sixty years old.[10] Paddy amazed the local Aboriginal community by riding a bicycle around the yards, something no black man had been known to do. He also stunned a cheeky white ringer at the Halls Creek races. When the ringer punched Paddy to the ground after an argument, Paddy's hand grasped a rock, coming back at the ringer with the stone in his fist, leaving him to taste the dirt while Paddy walked away. When you had to fight, you fought with what came to hand.[11]

Paddy told Kevin Lawton, a popular historian of Broome, of another event at the Halls Creek races:

> Paddy bet a camel driver four cases of King George Whiskey he couldn't push his camels over a certain trail in a certain length of time. Paddy knew the trail and was sure it was impossible. It was, and Paddy won. The whiskey he gave to his father-in-law.[12]

Paddy and Elizabeth looked to escape the strictures placed upon them by the legislation of the State. In early 1917, Paddy Djiagween sought, under section 63 of the *Aborigines Act 1905*, to be exempted from its provisions. The Resident Magistrate asked the local Turkey Creek constable, John Franklin (Jack) Flinders, to comment on the application. Flinders seems, from this distance, to have been a decent man. He tried to do the right thing by Paddy and Elizabeth, writing favourably to the Chief Protector as a file note shows:

> Djiaween is married to Fagan's daughter a half-caste—issue one child—and that Djiaween lives entirely at the house and does not consort with aborigines. Flinders says Djiaween is hard working man and of good character, his father supposed to be a Malay, mother an Aborigine,[13] Djiaween received some education at Beagle Bay mission and was taught tailoring. Flinders further states that Fagan has practically adopted Djiaween & may make will in his favour. From other inquiries the above seems reliable … in the circumstances, as Djiaween appears to be living practically in the same state as many whitemen in Kimberley I would recommend that he be granted an exemption from the Aborigines Act.[14]

A tall, fair Englishman who came to the East Kimberley in his early forties, Constable Jack Flinder's was destined to spend some twenty years in the district, nearly all of it as a Constable.[15] He seemed to be a friend to Joe Fagan and certainly supported Paddy Djiagween's efforts to escape the strictures of the legislation. However, the evidence suggests some ambiguous relations with Aboriginal people as Perth researcher Chris Owen told Patrick Dodson:

> It appears he had quite a fearsome reputation amongst Aboriginal people, and accordingly, (as has sadly become very apparent in my research), was considered a 'very effective police officer' by the department. In 1922 Flinders was on patrol near Fitzroy Crossing in search of Banjo Billiluna. He had been accused of the murders of Timmy O'Sullivan and Joseph Condren at Bililuna Station, nearly 400 kilometres south of Halls Creek. When Bililuna homestead was reached on 22 October, at Lawford Hole, Banjo's camp was surrounded and the fugitive shot dead. The Halls Creek

coroner gave a verdict of wilful murder against Banjo. He complimented Flinders's party on a job well done and recorded Banjo's death as inflicted by the police in the execution of duty. The Bililuna Pastoral Company wrote to the Commissioner on 29th November, thanking police and adding that, 'the pastoralists of the district are lucky in having a police officer of Constable Flinders ability.' Flinders was seen as the model of the mounted police of the outback. He could handle the blacks to the satisfaction of the pastoralists who believed that errant blacks must always be 'taught a lesson.'[16]

In the Djiagween case, the bureaucracy was slow to act, deciding to send more forms for Constable Flinders to fill in. The station, despite Paddy's book-keeping, was running up debts, including nearly £300 owed to the Durack company. Joe Fagan's health was rapidly declining, as was Elizabeth's after the birth of her first daughter, Mary.[17] Bert Ogden, who worked six months of the year at Springvale Station, came into the picture with cash and a longer-term strategy, not necessarily beneficial to Paddy and his family. Bert Ogden and Joe Fagan agreed on 7 June 1917 that Ogden could have a half-share in the station for £1,000, paid in quarterly deposits. Paddy witnessed the deal.

Joe Fagan's bequest

On 18 June, Joe made out a will, asking Constable Flinders to be a witness. He left his entire estate to his 'presumed daughter' Elizabeth Djiagween.[18] This would have been a normal thing for a father to do; but a rare act when the morals of the time and the rules of convenience weighed against any recognition of paternity. On his death-bed the old man asked Flinders to be his executor and to act as trustee for Elizabeth, looking after her interests. Being a state employee, he declined the old man's dying wish and Bert Ogden took on the role.

At Wyndham hospital three weeks later, on 29 June, Joseph Fagan died after a cerebral haemorrhage, aged sixty-three years. According to the death certificate he had been ill for seven days. The certificate also claimed that his father, mother, wife and sons and daughters were unknown. He was buried in the Wyndham cemetery by his daughter and son-in-law.[19] Forever after, Paddy Djiagween would speak highly of old Joe Fagan, knowing that in a difficult and unsettling period of history, he was one of the men who acted with dignity, kindness and respect.

If Elizabeth Grace Fagan did not have an Aboriginal mother, the law would have been clear and straightforward from that point. Her rights and entitlements to the estate would have been unchallenged. However, her Aboriginality meant that she and her husband had to battle for years against the laws, regulations and policies of the state to claim her rights. They had to fight their protectors for their inheritance.

The day after Joe Fagan's death, Jack Flinders forwarded an application on Elizabeth's behalf for exemption from the Act, writing in support:

> This half-caste is a respectable girl and to my own knowledge her application was approved of by her late father. She has now inherited a property of about £2,000. She has never received during her life any benefit from the Aboriginal Department.

Paddy and Elizabeth knew that the laws put in place to protect them would harm their interests. To escape from the Act they had to deny their connection with their Aboriginal families. To claim their inheritance, they had to deny their heritage.

Mister Neville

The application was sent to Mr A.O. Neville in Perth. From 1915 through to 1940, the laws and regulations aimed at the care and control of Aboriginal people were personified in Auber Octavius Neville, the Chief Protector of Aborigines. As for Aboriginal people, particularly those of mixed descent such as Elizabeth Djiagween, 'Mister Neville became,' according to Anna Haebich, 'the symbol of the system of authoritarianism and control under which they were obliged to live.'[20] There were few decisions taken on the course of West Australian Aboriginal affairs in those twenty-five years that did not bear the stamp of his personal views; views which irrevocably shaped the destiny of Patrick Dodson's family. Neville summarised the essence of his policy, after his retirement:

> The native must be helped in spite of himself! Even if a measure of discipline is necessary it must be applied, but it can be applied in such a way as to appear to be gentle persuasion ... the end in view will justify the means employed.[21]

Paddy and Elizabeth Djiagween stayed on at Spring Creek for another two years, badgering lawyers, welfare authorities and Neville to gain access to the money. The amount was variously described as being between £2,000 and some £7,000, a huge sum for the time, sufficient to keep the family in some level of comfort for generations. With it, they could buy houses, land, invest in business and gain a measure of independence from a system that rendered them permanently dependent. To put the figure into perspective,

Mr Neville was operating his department on a total budget of under £25,000 in 1916.[22]

Under section 33 of the *Aborigines Act 1905*, Neville had the right to manage the property of Aborigines with their consent; or without if 'to provide for the due preservation of such property.'[23] It was the commonly assumed view by all the officials dealing with the case, that Elizabeth's funds should be placed in a trust fund to be managed by the Chief Protector. Her gift from her father, a promise of freedom and autonomy, was to be kept out of her hands by her State-imposed father-figure, Mr Neville. He was, no doubt, aware of the irony when he later wrote:

> It has to be said to their credit that some few white men have taken pride in their coloured illegitimate children, have paid for years of upkeep and schooling and even remembered them in their wills.[24]

Elizabeth, being of Irish and Aboriginal descent, was defined as a 'half-caste'. Elizabeth and Paddy and their children were accordingly restricted in their options and movements at the discretion of the Protector and his agents. They lived their lives with the constant and very real threat of being institutionalised, against their will, in the settlements sponsored by Neville in places like Moola Bulla, near Halls Creek. Not only did they risk losing their inheritance; they risked losing their children.

The Djiagweens again sought exemptions from the Act, feeling either that the inheritance might save them from surveillance and protection, or that exemption was the only way to prevent the money being scooped into trust funds.[25] Again, they did not succeed. Neville decided that they needed to wait the granting of probate before a decision on exemption could be made. Meanwhile, he had already decided that 'it is considered desirable in the interests of the beneficiary that I should undertake the general care, protection and management of her property,' and sought Crown law advice on the mechanics of the probate process.[26]

Bert Ogden, as executor of the estate and half-owner of the station, wanted to buy out the Djiagweens, sending them away in order to have the place to himself. Undoubtedly under pressure, Paddy and Elizabeth were willing to go along with this arrangement, but sought to have enough control over their lives to keep the money from any sale of their share. Jack Flinders tried to argue the case with Mr Neville late in 1917:

> I have interviewed the Djiagweens who are anxious to dispose of their remaining half-share to Ogden for the sum of £900. Mr Ogden purchased a half share from Fagan six months ago for £1,000; and as we have experienced the worse season here for years I consider this a very fair

> offer, and taking into account the estate would be put up for auction necessitating more expense, and in my opinion Ogden would be the only bidder unless the Aborigines Department decided to bid. Elizabeth Djiagween suffers a good deal from bad health here and both wish to return south …
>
> If the Aborigines Department are guided by me I advise that Ogden's offer be accepted and the money held in trust by the Aborigines Department for the benefit of Elizabeth Fagan.[27]

Ogden peppered Neville's offices with letters and telegrams throughout 1918, urging a sale. On 22 March he sent a telegram to Neville saying that Gracie (as Elizabeth was now known) 'now all about to become mother advisable she be allowed to go back Broome. She does not care leave until something fixed up estate. Const Flinders visits once month and is of same opinion that the girl requires medical attention reply urgent.' Neville replied three days later that he had the matter of the Fagan estate in hand and Gracie 'might proceed Wyndham for medical attendance if necessary.'[28]

There is no record of the birth of this child in official records. The family understanding is that Elizabeth had only three children, Mary, Patricia and Joseph. However, Fay Wade (Patrick's sister) was told by people at Halls Creek that her grandmother had another child between Patricia and Joseph that may have been 'taken away'. The file appears to confirm their story and leaves another branch in the family tree unknown.

After probate was granted in late May 1918, by F.A. Moseley in the Supreme Court, the legal wrangling continued.[29] Ogden transferred the lease to himself as executor, presumably paying what he owed the estate for his half of the lease to the Department, which maintained the funds received in trust. Paddy and Elizabeth continued to seek their rightful inheritance.

In 1919, Paddy and Elizabeth returned to Broome, leaving the station to Ogden, while trying to seek help for their case. They settled into life in the coastal port, now blessed with its own picture theatre where admission price and seating was based on race:

> Sun Pictures: White people 2/6, Japs 2/6, Chinese and half-castes, 2/-; Koepangers and Malays, 1/6 and the humble black Binghis 1/-.[30]

Having spent some £60 on telegrams and £400 on lawyers (who surprisingly were also acting for Ogden) without seeing a penny, Paddy and Elizabeth went all the way to Perth to argue their case. Paddy managed to persuade the Protector to issue a special permit for him to travel to Perth to claim their rights, at a time when unsupervised travel south of the Murchison line was against the law for all Kimberley Aboriginal people.

Paddy and Elizabeth went all the way to Neville's office in Purfett Street. They argued with him: 'We can read, write, we know the value of money. He told us to clear off.'[31]

Neville later begrudgingly agreed to release £150 to Elizabeth, as payment for a house. Paddy got nothing because, as he described it:[32]

> Me and my wife had a row. Now just walk away. Roll up my swag, camp, haversack, wipe my pants and walk away.

In flight, 1997

Not long after starting work on this biography, I was travelling on a long plane flight from Sydney to Darwin, reading an old, yellowing copy of Xavier Herbert's short novel, *Seven Emus*[33]. I remembered that one of the last ceremonial acts performed by Patrick Dodson as a Catholic priest (although he was certainly not in favour with the Church hierarchy at the time) was to bury the notorious Australian author in Alice Springs in 1984.

As I turned the yellowing pages of the small book, published in 1961, I realised that the north-west port of 'Dampier' in the story was thinly based on Broome. Coincidences started to accumulate. Seven Emus station in the story was the same distance from Turkey Creek, as Joe Fagan's Spring Creek station. As I read on, I realised that the starting point of Herbert's novella could well have been the story of Paddy Djiagween, Patrick's grandfather. Like Bronco Jones in the novella, Paddy inherited a station from his Irish father-in-law (Paddy O'Hay in the story). Herbert wrote in language that would not be used today except when quoting original sources:

> 'The term boong is originally Malayan, meaning 'brother'; but it doesn't mean anything like that in Australian usage. To those who know anything about the social set-up in outback Australia, the idea of a boong ever coming to be classed as a squatter must be absolutely fantastic, as indeed it must have seemed to the unassuming Bronco Jones himself, who'd had his beginnings in a blacks' camp, than which there is no place humbler in human existence'.

I reflected, gazing out the jet window on the red earth scrolling beneath, that Paddy Djiagween and Elizabeth Fagan nearly achieved such a feat, but for a stubborn and cantankerous bureaucracy that could not allow Aboriginal people to achieve autonomy and independence. Xavier Herbert, the man Patrick buried, spent time around Broome and the northwest and could well have learned the story of Joe Fagan and Paddy Djiagween. For a big continent, Australia was a small place.

Patricia's childhood

In the coastal town of Broome, Patricia Mary, Patrick's mother, would never live with both her mother and father. From her birth in 1921, she had to make her own road.[34] Paddy and her mother, Elizabeth, had just separated acrimoniously. Her early childhood was spent between their homes in Broome and with other relatives, including times in Beagle Bay Mission. The times were not easy. Throughout the Kimberley, although the pastoral map was filled in and the industry established, the frontier was still caught in a persistent cycle of violent resistance and exaggerated reprisal. Her family watched events in the Kimberley region with concern.

In the year of Patricia's birth, punitive expeditions were reported from Durack River, after the death of a boundary rider.[35] When Patricia was a toddler, in 1924, murders were reported from Bedford Downs, supposedly in reprisal for the spearing of a favourite milking cow. This was in Kija country, near the Spring Creek station once held by Patricia's grandfather.[36] In another two years, when Patrick Dodson's mother was four-years-old, seemingly more killings in the Kimberleys came to light, this time at Forrest River on an Aboriginal reserve. A Royal Commission titled the 'Royal Commission to Inquire into the alleged killing and burning of bodies of Aborigines in East Kimberley' was called in response to the determined advocacy of the missionary, Ernest Gribble.[37] The report of the Commission concluded:

> A bare denial or the extremely weak suggestions offered do not refute the very strong evidence on the other side; nor do they account for the indications of intensely hot fires, burnt bones and human teeth that at intervals marked the trail of the police party almost from the start to the finish through country scarcely visited by anyone but the blacks.[38]

Despite these findings, for lack of evidence a magistrate acquitted the police constables, Regan and St Jack, three weeks later, to the applause and cheers of a large public gallery. The police were later re-instated, transferred and promoted.[39]

These events in the early life of Patrick's mother point to the fact that in the Kimberley the Australian historical frontier was neither distant in time, nor remote in significance. They took place in the living memory of senior members of the Aboriginal community. These received traditions shape the response of Aboriginal people today in dealing with issues such as policing, the justice system, native title and reconciliation. For Patrick Dodson, who heard stories of frontier cruelty in the arms of his mother on a tarpaulin outside their house in Katherine, and from his grandfather and grandmother, it came as no surprise when he learned Kija stories of violence from Peggy Patrick, Paddy Bedford and Terry Timms while he was working for the Kimberley Land Council in the late 1980s.[40]

Patrick remembers his Granny talking of a fear that ran through the country at the time. He recalled those times in a speech in 1995:

> My grandfather saw rights to land being trampled by the hooves of cattle, rights to fair treatment being strangled by iron neck chains, and rights to life being dispensed with by the muzzle of a gun. He lived that period of history, which people now say is so far in the past it should be forgotten. I say it should not be the subject of guilt—a wasted emotion—but should be the subject of honesty, a reminder of what has happened, in order that the thinking behind those events does not have a legitimate place in the present.[41]

When Patrick's mother was a young girl, the city of Perth celebrated a hundred years of white settlement. As Geoffery Bolton has shown by describing the 1929 centennial exhibition in Perth, there was a vast gulf between city perceptions and frontier realities:

> It was three years since an armed posse went out of Wyndham to revenge the death of a cattle man with a shovel nosed spear in his back. Wyndham was a long way from Perth and the city dwellers who planned the procession saw the Aborigines not as objects of hostility, nor even as comic relief, but as problem children deserving kind and charitable treatment.[42]

Epidemics of influenza and whooping cough had raged through the community. Many regarded Aboriginal people as the source, or because of poor hygiene, at high risk of spreading the illness, and demands for greater controls on their movement increased. People in the towns and cities of Western Australia looked at the 'Native Problem' with a mixture of concern, pity and fear, with widespread support for measures such as sunset curfews preventing the entry of Aboriginal people into the towns where they lived, and the prevention of Aboriginal enrolments in public schools.[43]

The economy in the Kimberleys did not provide the conditions for generosity of spirit. The pastoral industry was at a low, with beef prices insufficient to cover rising transport costs; the first motor trucks were replacing the bullock and donkey teams.[44] The demands of a post-war depression and the political necessity to provide ex-servicemen with a stake in the land, jobs and training eroded the meager public funds available for Aboriginal affairs. Large areas of land were arbitrarily sliced off Aboriginal reserves in the northern Kimberley for selection by ex-serviceman.[45]

Strict economy measures were introduced into missions and settlements, such as the Moola Bulla reserve. These measures made meager efforts in care and education even more miserly. Aboriginal inmates on settlements such as Moola Bulla were rarely provided with adequate housing or food, and never provided with the kind of skills-training to the levels achieved by missions such as Beagle Bay in Paddy's time. Conditions on the reserves reached a point in 1928 where a delegation of Aboriginal men, led by William Harris, met Premier Collier to argue that conditions were appalling and that 'The department established to protect us is cleaning us up. We were far better off under administration from England. Under the present Act Mr. Neville owns us body and soul.'[46]

Elizabeth's life under the Act

While care was lacking, control was readily available. The *Aboriginal Act 1905*, and its continually amended regulations, provided the means for that control. It remained firmly in place until it was further extended in the *Native Administration Act 1936*, and was not completely repealed until 1963.

In 1929 Elizabeth started working as a domestic servant and laundress for Mrs Hatfield, the wife of a master pearler. Her duties, amongst others, required her to keep immaculate the starched linen suits and white shoes the pearlers wore as a uniform of status. Many of them kept numerous pairs of shoes, so that, even in the red pindan dust and mangrove mud of the dock area, their shoes could remain sparkling white.

The next year, Elizabeth went cap in hand to Mr Neville's representative in Broome seeking £150 of her own inheritance 'to buy a house from Antonio Ozies, a Malay,' as her file in the department scrupulously noted.[47] The same file records that two years later, Elizabeth was charged at Broome with 'receiving liquor and cautioned. Ozies who is not an indentured man was fined for supplying the liquor.' The file catalogues relationships that Elizabeth is purported to have shared with non-Aboriginal, Asiatic men in the next few years despite police raids and official warnings triggered by anonymous letters from people, some of them Aboriginal, seeking to ingratiate themselves with officials.

Elizabeth was a mature woman but not entitled to manage her own affairs. While she had the freedom to choose her partners and friends, she risked the heavy-handed intrusion of an official morality, underpinned by legislation with draconian powers. Her adult private life and relationships were, because of her race, the business of the Broome police, bureaucrats and busybodies.

There was little congruence between the file kept in Perth, and the life lived in Broome, just as there was little congruence between the ideal sought by the Protectors and the reality as experienced by the wards. The file-keepers sweated to record the lives of their wards. However, inaccuracies and distortions crept in and remain trapped in the amber of bureaucratic history. In the present, such errors and concealed facts have the capacity to wound descendants, grieve families and rupture relationships.

This is so not least because Mr Neville and his staff were attempting to control issues of race and sex, rather than welfare. By the 1930s Neville had refined his policy framework for integrating indigenous people into the broader society, focusing his efforts on biological 'absorption' or 'assimilation' utilising what is now regarded as the pseudo-scientific theories of eugenics.[48] Eugenics had its roots in, and complemented, the social Darwinism that dominated European attitudes towards Aboriginal people at the time. Eugenics, however, was based on the widely accepted but now discredited notion that careful planning through proper breeding was the key to bettering society.

By ensuring that 'half-castes' were separated from 'full-bloods', and married with whites, they would lose skin colour and become 'just like white people' in a few generations. As the 1997 Human Rights and Equal Opportunity Commission report, *Bringing Them Home*, co-chaired by Mick Dodson described it:

> Unlike the ideology of racial purity that emerged in Germany from eugenics, according to which impure races had to be prevented from 'contaminating' the pure Aryan race, Neville argued the advantages of 'miscegenation' between Aboriginal and white people.[49]

In attempting to 'breed out' the half-caste population, any female Aboriginal relationships with 'Asiatics' and 'Malays' were anathema to Neville and prohibited under the Act. The prohibition was doomed to failure. The social reality in Broome was one in which Aboriginal people and 'Malays' were a part of a vibrant, dynamic community in which relationships were based on human, rather than racial grounds. People of all races would come together to party, to drink, to dance, to make music and, on occasions, to make love. For women and men of Aboriginal descent, state officials were obliged to make people's private business their own domain. The policy framework of biological assimilation was, at worst, genocidal, as the Human Rights and Equal Opportunity Commission report and authors such as Manne argue, or at best, a foolish, misguided approach guaranteed to result in non-compliance. Neville was aware of the problem when he reflected on the issues after his retirement:

> It has often been said that you cannot make people moral by Act of Parliament, or, as Hitler once put it, you cannot abolish intercourse by decree nor eliminate the instinct to possess. True enough, but laws and punishments are good in this way, serve to check illicit intercourse and regulate responsibility for the maintenance of children. We have attempted to regulate illicit intercourse because of its very often legal consequences, but it is doubtful if such measures could be defended today on purely ethnic grounds.[50]

Aboriginal reaction to the policies was muted by their lack of voice and political organisation at the time. Resistance was local and personal. In his 1931 Report, Neville was complacent that control was being effectively imposed, and that Aborigines had borne any 'sufferings ... practically without complaint' and that, being 'by nature inarticulate', they had been 'unable to assume a united front in the presentation of their case.'[51]

He may have spoken too soon. The 1930s were to see an upsurge in organised complaint and protest action by Aboriginal people in New South Wales, Victoria and Western Australia.[52] They managed against the odds of dispersal, poor education, general frustration and powerlessness to assert the injustice of their treatment under the laws of the land. They were complemented by a number of writers in city newspapers criticising the direction of Aboriginal affairs.

Moseley Royal Commission

In Perth, articles by humanitarians such as Mary Bennett relentlessly attacked Neville's administration and practice claiming, 'they are not safe until they are dead.'[53] She pointed out that 'we shall be better able to evaluate this policy when another race applies it to ourselves as the absorption of the white race and the breeding out of white people.'[54] Such articles led, against the will of Neville, to the establishment of the Moseley Royal Commission in 1934, with a wide ambit to review the administration of Aboriginal affairs.

Patricia was a young teenager attending school with the Irish St John of God nuns when Aboriginal women from Broome sent a petition as the 'Half-Castes of Broome' to Commissioner Moseley. They sought some recognition of their self-reliance in choice of marriage partner, employer, workplace, and in their private and family life. Particularly, they sought recognition of their already independent lives:

> Our intended employers have to seek the permission of the police to obtain a permit to work us. Many of us refuse to work on that account ...

Sometimes we have the chance to marry a man of our choice who may be in better circumstances than ourselves. A white man, or an educated Asiatic, but we are again rejected because that man does not wish to ask the Chief Protector's consent …

We ask for our freedom, so that when the chance comes along we can rule our lives and make ourselves true and good citizens. Instead of that the Department would and could call us immoral girls …

Surely if we can support our children and no husband like some of us are doing and which we might have had if the Act had not held us back, do you not think we are quite capable of being able to make either sensible wives or citizens if given our freedom…

We educated half-castes who have been sent to the missions have been taken from either our fathers or our mothers when we were children by the advice of the Department. And by so doing that has been the end of father and mother to us. Do you not realise the cruelty of this, would you white people like to think that when you send your children to school you would never see them again? …

Many of us own houses and land, and many more of us could do so. We who do own our own homes pay the rates when the time comes along. We can read, write, sew, crochet, laundry, also make our own clothes and for other people, also other domestic work. So that, sir, on that qualification alone we think we should not be classed as natives and kept in bondage by the Act, knowing or at least hearing and reading about half-castes of other countries of the British Empire that they are not classed with their natives. Give us freedom … and make us happy subjects of this our country.[55]

Freedom, respect and happiness remained elusive for the women of Broome, even when they framed their appeals in the context of the values and moral systems of the time. Like the Roth report in the early years of the century, the Moseley Royal Commission report in early 1936 did little to address the complaints made by Aboriginal people and their supporters, especially in the Kimberley. Moseley considered that reports of violence and conditions of slavery were exaggerated. He commented that:

With the exception of improved medical conditions there is little, I think, of importance which should be done to better the conditions of the Kimberley natives … They are well fed and clothed, and the huts in which they live made of bush material—bags and sometimes flattened petrol tins—are suitable for their needs; anything more elaborate would not be appreciated by them.'[56]

Paul Hasluck, later to become the Commonwealth Minister responsible for the Dodson family, and to be Governor-General, was a journalist with the *West Australian* newspaper at the time. He wrote a series of insightful articles while travelling with the Moseley Royal Commission. He saw the operation of a strict colour bar in Broome as producing an 'an annually increasing body of discontented misfits.' He asked the readers of the *West Australian* to consider whether the 'half-caste's' future was to be an outcast or to be 'helped towards a future that is linked more closely to that of the life of his white parent than of his black parent.' He pointed out that children taken to missions and government settlements were 'lifted out of blacks camps' but not given the 'opportunity to improve their white inheritance.'[57] Of course, Elizabeth, Paddy and Neville all knew that the Fagan's 'white inheritance' was kept safely locked away in the form of savings bonds, with the interest being occasionally distributed to a number of Aboriginal people besides Elizabeth at the discretion of the Protector.

Moseley agreed with Neville's view that the increasing half-caste population was a menace to be controlled and bred out, observing that 'at the present rate of increase the time is not far distant when (they) or a great majority of them, will become a positive menace to the community, the men useless and vicious, the women a tribe of harlots.'[58] Far from being chastised, Neville felt vindicated and remained in control.

Legislation was enacted to amend the 1905 Act in a partial response to the report. Haebich comments that the amendments 'showed the stamp of Neville rather than Moseley.'[59] Under the *Native Administration Act 1936*, Neville's power was increased, while Aboriginal peoples' control over their lives waned, particularly for 'half-castes'. Neville now had the legislative tools to put his theories of biological absorption into effect and the opportunity to disseminate his views beyond the state.

Biological absorption

Neville and Cecil Cook from the Northern Territory sat together at a national meeting of key administrators in Aboriginal affairs in Canberra in the winter of 1937, when Patricia Djiagween was not yet sixteen-years-old. Neville and Cook shared their plans, policies and programs as a team. They politically and intellectually carried the conference, gaining its unanimous support for a resolution on 'the destiny of the race':

> That this Conference believes that the destiny of the natives of Aboriginal origin, but not of the full blood, lies in their ultimate absorption by the

people of the Commonwealth and it therefore recommends that all efforts be directed to that end.

At that moment, the national policy approach to Aboriginal issues became racially, not socially, defined. Policy has personal effects. People like Paddy, Elizabeth, and Patricia were now to be categorised according to the labels 'full-blood, half-caste quadroon and octoroon', and to be treated and controlled accordingly. Their marriage choices were to be treated as controlled biological selections, and directed to the task of eliminating the Aboriginal strain. Robert Manne comments, 'If there exists a more terrible moment in the history of the twentieth-century Australian state than the Canberra conference of April 1937, I for one do not know where it is to be discovered.'[60]

Neville had the legislative tools in place to implement the national policy approach he and Cook had engineered. From a moral perspective, the 1936 West Australian legislation is disturbing reading today. The definition of 'native' within the Act was widened to include all people of Aboriginal descent, except for some classes of 'quadroon' who 'neither associates with or lives substantially after the manner of (natives).'[61] The pleas of the 'Half-Castes of Broome' were disregarded. No marriage of a native was to be celebrated without prior notice to the Commissioner and severe penalties were introduced for any non-marital sexual intercourse between races. Provisions of the 1905 Act were retained that restricted Aboriginal movements, enabled their transportation, controlled their employment, and restricted their access to alcohol. New powers flowed, enabling compulsory medical examination (not for their health but for control of their disease) and any refusal was penalised. As Haebich comments:

> The most disturbing aspect of the Act was that it empowered the Department of Native Affairs to carry out biological and social engineering programmes. Virtually any child of Aboriginal descent could now be taken forcibly from his or her family and placed in a government institution. The Commissioner, not their parents, had total control over their lives until they reached the age of twenty-one. From this age any person of 'quarter caste' or less was prohibited by law from associating with persons deemed to be 'natives'.[62]

The National Inquiry into the Separation of Aboriginal Children from their Families dealt with the legacy of these issues in 1996. Mission representative Chris Jones, the President of the United Aborigines Mission, gave a blunt perspective on the past to the Inquiry:

Government policy was dictated by anthropological research at the time, which considered Australian Aborigines to be the missing link in Darwin's theory of evolution. The full-blood Aboriginal people were therefore tolerated, but scarcely regarded as full human beings. Only the missionaries gave them the dignity of true human beings and believed that they were worthy of their love and friendship. The Government felt some responsibility for the part-Aboriginal children because they were fathered by white men. This gave rise to the die-out policy, which felt that the solution to the Aboriginal problem was to breed out the colour. These beliefs resulted in the segregation of part-white children from their parents.[63]

Those beliefs also resulted in a dramatic escalation of the capacity of officialdom to intervene in the lives and love of the Djiagween family. They created a legacy which Patrick Dodson was alert to in describing the underlying issues that led to the Royal Commission into Aboriginal Deaths in Custody:

> For most Aboriginal people, the memory of the past on reserves and missions, ruled over by non-Aboriginal people and all they were seen to represent, is not easily forgotten. Nor are the 'protector' and 'welfare' roles played by police as instruments of government policies, as detailed in my report, forgotten. There continues to be a deep sense of loss, injustice and denial of recognition that still pervades the societies of Aboriginal people.[64]

Paddy Djiagween's new life in Broome

After his relationship with Elizabeth collapsed, Paddy Djiagween began a new family with Mabel, a Bardi woman from the coast north of Broome, with whom he had five children.[65] Perhaps he felt it easier to marry a 'salt-water' woman, without ties to the pastoral industry and with stronger connections to the communities of Broome and the Dampierland peninsula.

To support his growing family, Paddy went back to the sea. He worked now with the master pearler, Dan MacDaniel, skippering his cargo boat, sailing fuel out to the pearling grounds and bringing back shell. He hired a lugger from MacDaniel and started to make some money, on one trip earning £70 in five days. This promising commercial venture ended when his cousin put the lugger onto the rocks near La Grange, losing five tons of shell.[66] For a while, he used a horse and cart to cut sandalwood and cart peanuts from a Government farm at Walcott Inlet. Despite the policy and legislative framework of control and dependence, Paddy always sought to be his own man.

Eventually, Paddy gained a steady job at £6 per week with the Roads Board, a shire council controlled by the master pearlers. He managed a work gang napping stone and making the roads of Broome, including Carnarvon, Wells and Hamersley Streets. Paddy looked after a team of nine horses, shoeing, blacksmithing and repairing harnesses. The labour on the roads and beach quarries was provided by some twenty-five native prisoners working in chained pairs. Many had been imprisoned for killing cattle. Paddy knew many of them from his station days. He was convinced of their innocence in many cases, and quietly angered by their working conditions.[67]

His work efforts did not exempt him from control under the Act. In 1927, Constables O'Connell and Johnston visited the small house in Napier Street and found:

> Black Paddy, a labourer employed by The Broome Roads Board and two native women slightly under the influence of drink; Black Paddy was very drunk. All were taken to the Police station together with one full bottle of Yalumba Port Wine and 3 empty port wine bottles, which were found in the room with the natives … The women were allowed to go, Paddy was detained and charged with receiving Port Wine.[68]

He was given one week to pay the fine of £1 or face 24 hours hard labour. The person who supplied the port wine was fined £50 or 5 months hard labour.

Paddy's personal fortunes were less bleak than for most of his countrymen. He had valuable skills and was determined to walk his own road. This combination gave him a personal authority recognised by many who knew him. Pastoralists, pearlers and local shire authorities found themselves yielding to this authority. Just as he had with missionaries like Mother Antonio and Fr Emo, and later with Fr Droste, he was able to assert his autonomy and rights through consistency and integrity, gaining respect and trust from any in authority with a modicum of goodwill.

Always his ability to speak up to those in officialdom was notable, he was remembered as both cheeky and clever. Stanley and Cissy Djiagween recall a time when one of Paddy's sons was hauled up to the Mission at Beagle Bay for some misdeed:

> The missionaries found the boy a little hard to handle and Paddy was asked by the police to take him back to Broome from Beagle Bay. Paddy's answer to the policeman was, 'Well you might as well go to London and shoot the Queen.' The policeman scratched his head, and asked 'Why?' Paddy replied, 'Crown law sent him there, you gotta kill the crown to stop it.' Again, the policeman was puzzled and repeated his question, 'Why?' Paddy looked askance and said, 'Why? "Y" is just a crooked letter.'[69]

The behaviour of his family was under continual surveillance, subject to the rules of police, missionaries and public servants and their stiff-necked notions of propriety and correct behaviour. His children could be removed without his consent, and could not marry without the permission of firstly the Chief Protector and then the Commissioner of Native Affairs. Paddy Djiagween was a black man in an increasingly intrusive white world. He was not a free man.

However, he could be personally influential. Paddy's relationships with significant leaders of the non-Aboriginal community were important tools for negotiating benefits for the Yawuru community. One close friend was James MacKenzie, President of the Roads Board, and Justice of the Peace, known as 'Long Mac'. Driving an oyster-tinted Buick with a mother-of-pearl dashboard, according to Mary Durack, Long Mac 'bore the white man's burden conscientiously and the coloured people of the district respected him for his sense of fair play; loved because he always knew their names and asked after their children.' After his death in 1957 she recalled his later years:

> The Aborigine, Paddy Djiagween, number one off-sider of his Road Board days, remained his devoted attendant. They were in full agreement about the youth of the day—both black and white, both bemoaned the good old days when Broome was Broome and pearls were fortune's favours to her courtiers.[70]

Paddy worked hard to be accepted by authority inside the system, while advocating the cause of those of his countrymen stranded on the outside of the system by a lack of education and skills. His relations with the men of the Roads Board, mostly master pearlers, was influential in gaining some improvements for the living conditions of Aboriginal people in Broome, despite general attitudes of complaint about Aboriginal lifestyles. In 1961 the Minister for Native Welfare, Police and Transport, Mr Perkins visited Broome and met the Broome Roads Board. The Roads Board complained to the Minister, 'that nothing had been done at the previous years in establishing the reserve for the natives the Broome and that their present camp sites were a disgrace.' The Minister committed to developing:

> A new native reserve one mile out of town which would take care of the most difficult type of native ... The control of the reserves would be carried out by officers of his Department, who are only administering the welfare of natives and were not police officers. Any difficulty arising from people on this reserve would be handled by the police department at the request of the Native Welfare Department, and he would also guarantee that on this reserve at the back of Kennedy's that the natives were allowed to be housed there under various rules made by this Department ... Any

complaints received would be immediately dealt with by the Department with the assistance of the police and the local authority. The plan outlined by the Minister was wholeheartedly agreed to by the Board.[71]

Shortly after this breakthrough, on 21 March 1963, Queen Elizabeth II visited Broome and was introduced to Paddy Djiagween as he stood by an old cattle truck, dressed in a white shirt and tie. Patrick Dodson described the event in a lecture given to commemorate the celebrated Irish Archbishop Daniel Mannix:

> Mannix knew that to get change sometimes you had to go to the top. When God was busy, or the Pope unavailable, he could always go to the Premier. Sometimes he would skip the junior ranks of the hierarchy altogether and just talk to the Premier's wife. My grandfather had to wait for his moment to get to the top brass. He waited until the Queen visited Broome in 1963. He shook the white-gloved hand and said to her 'Why can't we have the same rights as the white man?' The Queen promptly agreed and indicated her wish that he be given full rights. My Grandfather went across to the Continental Hotel and demanded a beer. The barmaid was startled and refused, as the consumption of alcohol was forbidden to those without a dog tag of citizenship rights. An aide of the Queen was summoned and confirmed the citizenship rights of the old man. He sipped his beer with a sense of gratitude—due more to the achievement than thirst I feel.[72]

In later life Paddy moved to the night cart, carting waste; not glorious work but he earnt a steady income, enhanced by the fact that he made clothes for all his family. He was to enjoy a secure position with the Roads Board for thirty-seven years. He later moved off the cart and onto a bicycle, riding around town reading the electricity meters and selling Chinese raffle tickets in a local popular version of the numbers game. His reputation for luck and skills in manipulating the results of the draw grew. According to the family, he was consulted by gamblers in the Broome community as a *Maban*, a shaman with gifts of healing, prophecy and traditional influence with the spirit world.[73]

Paddy's two laws

As his grandson looks back he believes that Paddy Djiagween asserted and lived his freedom to be Yawuru, to be himself. He maintained his religious affiliations in both Aboriginal and Catholic domains, obeying both bodies of law, without apparent conflict. He saw many changes in his life and found ways to adapt without acquiescence. He worked to find ways in which his stories, songs and law could survive, using his authority in law to negotiate constructive resolutions for the problems of massive social change, dispossession and dislocation. He did this externally, with white authorities, and internally, between different peoples moving into the Broome region. In Patrick's eyes:

> He lived his life and judged a person as a person, treating all as equals, and as good people until proven otherwise. There was no bitterness or hatred there, no spark of angry revolution, surly or real. He worked in his community with his people, through his law on his land, to show a way of survival, of adaptation to events he could not control or change. Bending but not breaking. He was always strong in his own position, certain of his authenticity, a lawman who followed his bush law and Catholicism, finding a source of spirituality and a rationale for life in both.[74]

As time went on and his seniority as a lawman was enhanced, he gained in authority and consequent responsibility. Paddy was given custody of the powerful 'Two Men' song cycle, holding the sacred objects that both contained and encoded the spiritual essence of this Dreaming. Patrick would not risk any breach of Yawuru law by describing that system of law, song and story for this book. Its geographical spread and significance, from the saltwater of Broome to the deserts of Central Australia, can be seen in several anthropological accounts and is powerfully portrayed in paintings by the Papunya School of artists.[75] The ancestors were those who gave the people languages, songs, and ceremonies and taught the most appropriate forms of initiation, leaving behind sacred objects charged with ceremonial power. Paddy held those same objects for those who would come after.

Paddy was, by his grandson's account, adept at using the Aboriginal laws to explore the overlap and pressure points with European laws, culture and society. He became particularly closely identified with the Gadaranya or Juluru song cycle, an innovative ceremonial complex that has spread from the Kimberley into Central Australia. Aboriginal participants have told me that the imagery of the Gadaranya tells of the transformation of Aboriginal people from prisoners of their destiny, in chains and victimised, into the masters of their destiny. Paddy worked to ensure that all initiation ceremonies included the Gadaranya cycle. He negotiated with his fellow law custodians to determine what should be included in the ceremonies, engaging in a theological and ritual debate to define the extent of 'inside' and 'outside' business.[76]

In the 1960s it was up to Paddy and his lawmen colleagues to ensure they had the space to continue maintaining their responsibilities. Paddy had a key role in negotiating with the Roads Board (the town council) to set aside the space needed to allow the law grounds to survive an expanding town. The changed world of the Yawuru required negotiation with white authorities to ensure the protection of this domain. Paddy used his personal authority with the Roads Board, including his relationships with master pearlers such as James MacKenzie, to influence the decision of the Road Board to allocate land at this important site. On 9 January 1968 the District Officer in Broome reported to the Superintendent of the Northern Division of the Department of Native Welfare:

> The Broome elders are most keen to have a repository erected on the Broome site. This has posed a slight problem as this is 'Shire Common Land.' The Shire president has been spoken to regarding this and he has verbally indicated that every assistance can be expected from the Shire.[77]

This was the first documentary example of Yawuru elders being consulted by non-Aboriginal persons in relation to the use of Kunin as a ceremonial law ground. It is also the first occasion in which non-Aboriginal people gave serious consideration to that topic. There was a positive result. The Shire of Broome, the Department of Native Welfare and the Western Australian Museum agreed in 1971 that Reserve 30906 be excised from the Broome common reserve as a 'Ceremonial Site'. The site was to contain two stores for sacred objects, which included objects necessary for the rituals identified in the notes of Daisy Bates at the turn of the century. Although the initial proposal considered the excision of an area of one square mile, the area reserved was slightly less than half a square mile.

Paddy Djiagween had succeeded. Working with his fellow lawmen, and building on his positive relations with people in authority, he had managed to establish a small portion of land, set aside in European law to protect the laws and ceremonies of his Yawuru people. Kunin was needed to ensure a keeping place for storing ceremonial objects and to continue the work of carrying out ceremonies to look after the country and society as a whole. In a life of many disappointments, he had this 'half a square mile' to call his own.

As Patrick later reflected:

> For all that he still had to watch the erosion of Yawuru land and authority as all the foreshores were taken up. As part of his role as a lawman, he had to ensure the protection of sacred objects and was instrumental in bringing them in from the pastoral lease at Thangoo to a place called Kunin on Fisherman's Bend, south-east of Broome, out near the Block, on the edge of town. He made sure there was a place there that was safe to use as a

ceremonial ground and as a keeping place for the things (sacred objects) that he had responsibility for looking after. This was the last remaining place allowed for the Yawuru people in Grandad's time.

According to Patrick, Paddy was successful in this complex negotiation because he was able to stay mostly on his own country and pursue a religious and cultural education that made him an authority on Yawuru law, songs and ceremonies, on Yawuru business. He also had the confidence and strength to negotiate with powerful interests, with whom he maintained engagement. In this, Paddy Djiagween provided Patrick Dodson with a moral, social and political template that would influence Patrick's life and pattern his future life choices.

Paddy Djiagween also worked to leave a legacy for his descendants that would allow them to maintain their law and give substance and reality to their Aboriginality and their Yawuru identity. The authorities and the legislative framework of the times held back the legacy left to Paddy and Elizabeth by Joe Fagan. Neville, with his restricted view of the 'destiny of the race' saw no reason to support the maintenance and protection of Aboriginal law and culture. The legacy left by Paddy Djiagween and the changing moral, legal and political framework of the modern era, has enabled his grandson, and his fellow custodians of Yawuru law and culture, to reclaim this inheritance.

Broome, 2001

At a native title claim hearing in 2001 before Justice Merkel of the Federal Court, evidence of the on-going significance of Kunin was attested to in oral testimony from a group of law-holders working together. As one of these men, Patrick gave evidence for a full day in camera. The oral evidence was supported by a few compelling written documents that dated back to the turn of the century.[78]

Also giving evidence was Paddy's son from his second wife, Francis Djiagween, who participated in ceremonies at Kunin in the 1960s. Francis remembers, as a young boy in the 1950s, being told by the 'old people', including his father, Paddy, that Kunin was an important law ground. His evidence was supported by Joseph 'Nipper' Roe, born in the early 1940s, who was told by his father and by other old people of Paddy's generation that there were law ceremonies at Kunin before he was born.

A senior Karajarri lawman recalled visiting Kunin with his father, who was attending to law business as well as a gumbali ceremony (where two people are given the same name) for his brother, when he was a young boy before the war. He told the court that his father had told him that he had been to Kunin himself for law business when he was a young man in the 1920s. Yawuru people and their neighbours had been carrying out ceremonies there for a long time.

The evidence was opposed by the state. They questioned whether Kunin had, as a matter of fact, fallen into disuse as a law ground with the consequence that any traditional connection with Kunin had not been substantially maintained. In response, evidence was given that the last first stage initiation ceremonies were held at Kunin in 1990 and the last second-stage ceremonies, which were for Patrick Dodson and Joseph 'Nipper' Roe, were held there in 1994. In the hearing, Patrick in support of the other lawmen took on the roles of claimant, anthropologist and lawyer, explaining Yawuru law to the judge. In the role of claimant he used the Yawuru name, Djagun, he had received from his grandfather.

Justice Merkel quoted the transcript of evidence in his final judgment:

PATRICK DODSON DJAGUN: Kunin is there from the Bugarrigarra (the Dreaming). His purpose is set, ngirpiri place for holding objects. That's there. Those objects are there. It's used when we go there, us four or five men, if we go there or we bring this lot. They can't go onto that ground unless we give them permission to come on. They can't just walk over. They come through us. Even though they (are) bosses, they have respect for Yawuru.

MR BELL: We know because you've told us that the last lawmen to be put through or the last men to be put through the law, more accurately, are you and Nipper which happened in 1994. Does the fact that no lawmen since then have yet been through the law mean it is not in use?

PATRICK DODSON DJAGUN: No, it doesn't mean that at all.

MR BELL: Why not?

PATRICK DODSON DJAGUN: Because the law is in the land there. The law is in the ground. Wherever you travel around here, anywhere on the country, you think of the law. The law governs you, by your behaviour, what you do, where you go, how you behave even if I go to some other country, some other place like Nyikina country or Karajarri country, Nyangumarta country, I got to worry about that place.

Later in his evidence Patrick explained why the process of getting young men to go through law at Kunin had been difficult. He referred to the two traditions of assimilation and Christianity which he said had helped to break down the process of young people going through law, but emphasised that that made the task of the elders in keeping the knowledge and practice of the law alive even more important. He was asked if it is unusual for men to be put through law at Kunin. His response was:

PATRICK DODSON DJAGUN: Well, when you say, 'unusual' to me, that's a small space of time. You're talking about 10 years or whatever it is. I'm not sure what you're talking about, 'unusual'. What's it relate to? From the death of my grandfather to now or from the death of my uncle until now or from the time these people went through? I'm not sure. It's a relatively short period in our culture because the law was put [there] from the Bugarrigarra.

Our belief and our responsibility is to maintain the law and that's our job, his job, his job and my job in the Yawuru country. We are supported by these men.

MR BELL: Well, let me put it to you specifically. You and Nipper were the last to go through the law. That happened in 1994 at Kunin. Does that gap in time say anything about whether the law is still observed at Kunin?

PATRICK DODSON DJAGUN: It doesn't say anything to me, no. It doesn't say. Because I know what we do. From the day we were put through that law to this very day, I know what we do and I know what sits over there on that ground. And that ground is alive.

In his summary judgment, Justice Merkel recognised that the native title held by the claim group confers upon them the right of occupation, use, possession and enjoyment of the area, as against the whole world, 'for ceremonial purposes'. He further added:

> 'There has been much misunderstanding and disinformation in the Australian community about native title. Although the evidence in the present case did not produce any new or startling revelations about traditional Aboriginal society, in telling their story the Rubibi applicants have articulated a cogent, rational and historically sound exposition of why a fair and just legal system does not refuse to recognise the unextinguished native title that they have established has existed since prior to European settlement of Australia. In a small but significant way that exposition has the capacity to better enable the Australian community to understand why the common law and the Australian parliament have recognised and protected the native title held by indigenous persons in Australia.'

Abu Kassim, father of Fay and Georgina, was indentured to the pearling company, Streeter and Male. Pearl divers, Broome, W.A. Abu Kassim gets ready to dive (courtesy Fay Wade album).

Race determined the seating arrangements at the Sun Pictures in Broome. An audience at the Sun Picture Gardens, Broome, W.A. ca 1920 (photograph Anon, courtesy Battye Library).

The Broome port serviced the pearling industry and the pearling companies controlled the town. Streeter and Male Pty Ltd no.1 Store and Garage, Broome, W.A., 1961 (photograph Western Australian Government photographer, courtesy of Government Photographer Collection, Battye Library).

Paddy Djiagween claimed citizenship rights from the Crown in person. The meeting between Paddy Djiagween and Queen Elizabeth II, Broome 1963 (courtesy of the West Australian Newspaper).

Paddy Djiagween, Patrick's maternal grandfather showed the young man how to find Paddy's Road. Paddy Djiagween (courtesy Patrick Dodson album).

Chapter Five

Crimes of love

'A pity beyond all telling is hid in the heart of love.'
W.B. Yeats, *The Pity of Love* (1892)

Oombulgurri, WA, 1993

Patrick and I were sitting under the shade of a tree in Oombulgurri, the Aboriginal community in the northeast Kimberley, on the banks of the Forrest River, near Wyndham. Patrick had been asked by Robert Champion de Crespigny, the wealthy and fiercely independent gold-mining magnate on the Council for Aboriginal Reconciliation, to facilitate negotiations between the community, the Kimberley Land Council and a diamond-mining company seeking exploration licence approvals. Negotiations had been dragging on for several years as sensitive and complex issues of site protection and royalty arrangements were discussed. During a break in the day-long meeting, we were talking through the negotiations, focusing on the always tricky issues of process and people.

Somehow, I started to talk about my mother; telling Patrick about her uncanny ability to defuse a family conflict or redirect a perceived slight with a flick of the head, a change of subject, a joke and a wink. Patrick laughed:

> Gee, not like my Mum. She would have been into the blues, giving it her best shot. She shirt-fronted any bloke that she thought needed telling off. All her life she was like that. Oh, she'd have a joke and tell a story; but wouldn't put up with any nonsense.

It turned out that our mothers had had roughly parallel lives. Both named Patricia Mary, Catholic of course, born around the same time, with fathers who had lost siblings in the war, they each had many children and lost some tragically early. And yet their lives were different countries. My Mum was not Aboriginal; Patrick's Mum was.

To show the difference: in 1944, Patrick's Mum was in chains in a truck being carted across the Kimberley to a reform institution. My Mum was likely to have been dancing with servicemen at the Cloudland Ballroom in Brisbane. Patricia Djiagween's life experiences, tough enough, were made a lot tougher, more strained, risky and traumatic, because of her Aboriginality and the laws, policies and programs that were forced into her life as a result. The archival files held by the Department of Native Affairs in Perth document the imposition of state control and the impact that control had on the lives of Aboriginal women, such as the young Patricia Djiagween.

A young mother

Patricia Mary Djiagween was only fifteen years young when the *Native Administration Act 1936* (the Act) came into effect. She was carrying her daughter, Fay Elizabeth who was born in December 1937. The Act would make her life, and her role as a mother, challenging.[1]

Patricia lived with her mother; surviving on the few shillings that Elizabeth Fagan earned scrubbing the white uniforms of the pearling masters. At times Liz sent telegrams asking to withdraw small amounts from the trust account of her inheritance in Perth. Paddy Djiagween didn't have much money to help; he and Elizabeth were estranged and he had his own young family to feed and care for.

Patricia also earned money from casual work when she was well enough and baby Fay could be cared for. Any such employers officially required a permit to employ casual native labour, but the top end of town turned a blind eye when cleaning and washing needed to be done. Too often, however, both Patricia and her baby were too sick for work. They were admitted for weeks at a time to the Native Hospital established by the St John of God Nuns but then run by Government officials, helped by the nuns. While the Act, established after the Moseley Royal Commission response, was generally onerous, the establishment of improved medical conditions in Broome was one innovation that saved many lives and reduced suffering. Patricia found herself at the Native Hospital in February 1938 and again in May with 'pyelitis and stomachitis' after the birth of her child, according to the files.

Fay's father, Abu Kassim bin Marah, was 'Malay', from the town of Ulu Beruang in what was known as British Malaya.[2] Abu Kassim was indentured to the pearling company, Streeter and Male. He spent long and dangerous months at sea on the two-masted luggers, diving for pearl in heavy suits and brass helmets. John Bailey described the experience of diving at twenty fathoms in the Roebuck Deep:

> He was aware of the immense pressure on his body, which squeezed breath out of his lungs and made it difficult to breathe. His throat felt dry. The thump of his heartbeat, transmitted by the compressed air around him, echoed in his ears … He began to feel cold. He signalled to the lugger to drag him along the line of the cliff, but for some reason he was taken lower. He felt a sharp pain in his eardrum, and then a buzzing noise deep within his skull. Stupidly, he tried to poke at his ear with his hand, but it bumped helplessly against the helmet.[3]

Coming into the mangrove port in March, 1938, Abu Kassim had willingly signed a declaration admitting paternity. He arranged to have maintenance funds of 10 shillings per month drawn from his earnings by Streeter and Male. Patricia was a ward under the Act and Commissioner Neville ordered that Patricia should not receive these funds. They were to be paid to Neville in trust and Patricia could ask him for access to them when required. She was expected to ask him for her rights. It seems that no one explained the arrangements to the young parents.

Abu Kassim helped his young family when he was in port by providing cartons of rations and essential supplies. While Patricia was in hospital, he visited morning and evening but it was a difficult and risky time for them. Their inter-racial relationship was prohibited under the new legislation. The child provided direct evidence of a breach; proof of an illegal inter-racial union. Patricia was at constant risk of forced removal and separation from her family. Being 'Malay', Abu Kassim risked deportation.

Dangerous contempt

Threats of removal and eviction were not hollow. The intentions of the authorities to remove Patricia and deport Abu Kassim are clearly documented in the files. In February, while Patricia was in hospital, having just emerged from the critical phase of her illness, she 'became insolent, disobedient and almost uncontrollable,' according to Mr Knight, the Officer in Charge of the Native Hospital. He reported to the Commissioner of Native Affairs, that 'investigation into her mode of living revealed that she was an undesirable character who had been warned on several occasions by the Police.'

When Patricia again sought help for Fay in May 1938, Knight noted that she had 'been persistent in breast-feeding contrary to directions' and he complained of her behaviour:

> When Mrs. Knight spoke to her regarding part of the feeding apparatus she refused to answer and when I was called she was collecting her belongings ... in order to restrain her I had to hold her by the wrists until she quietened. During this process she screamed hysterically and was violently abusive.

Knight informed the Commissioner that Patricia 'does no work; has always been the consort of the Malay element ... and treats the white community with dangerous contempt.' He recommended her removal to an institution for a year or longer, to 'establish the authority of the Department; save the girl from becoming nothing more than a public menace but (to) also act as a deterrent to the type and perhaps check some of the Asiatic crowd.' He also claimed that, 'whilst the lugger is in (Abu Kassim) and the girl occupy a room in the hut curtained off from the others'.[4]

In distant Perth, the Commissioner of Native Affairs, Mr A.O. Neville, scribbled an annotation on the report: 'this (Abu Kassim) is again associating with Patricia and he should be dealt with.' He ordered local police Inspector Timms, Protector of Natives, 'for these people to be kept under surveillance with the object of prosecuting under Section 46.' This section of the Act had a minimum sentence of six months 'for any person (except a native) who cohabits with or has sexual intercourse with any native who is not his wife or husband'. Eviction, deportation, removal and the forced separation of Fay from her mother, and Patricia from hers, were but one step away.

Sensing trouble, Paddy Djiagween intervened and arranged for his daughter to get out of town for a few months. By agreement with Elizabeth, he sent her and the baby to stay with relatives at Beagle Bay on her release from hospital. On her return to Broome in July, Patricia and her mother took the matter into their own hands. They walked into the Police Station and asked to see the police sergeant. They begged for another chance to be allowed to stay at home in Broome and promised to behave. Sergeant Drysdale reported to Inspector Timms that:

> Patricia has been a sick woman ever since the baby was born. She looks ill. That is the main reason why her mother is so anxious to have her with her. I informed this woman if she is given another chance and breaks her promise she will in all probability be sent to Munja Station without getting the chance to go to Beagle Bay.

Meanwhile, in the dusty ledgers of the Department in Perth, the maintenance funds paid by Abu Kassim were steadily accumulating in the trust account, being deposited by Streeter and Male and later deducted from Abu Kassim's earnings on his return to port. While there are comments on the file noting this fact, it seemed that none of the officials in Broome informed Patricia that she needed to apply for access to funds from the Commissioner for the welfare of her daughter. She continued to receive money and provisions from Abu Kassim when he was in port, arranging the supplies from a man called 'Dobson'.[5] This led Knight, now promoted to Inspector, to suggest that she was amply provided for with stores and had no need for funds. When Abu Kassim's lugger was at sea for some months he wrote twice when told his accounts were in arrears, including in October:

> To reply to your note and according to your request, I can't pay it by present times because being here on the big ocean. The time for us the sea

men are not allowed to come ashore whenever till our time is up. So then I will only cope if you will be mercy, but to boat lying up, I shall urgently fix it up.

He did, or he tried to. In December 1938, Abu Kassim went with Patricia to the police in Broome to try to sort out the situation. He complained that Patricia had not received one penny of the maintenance money he had paid, with the 'result that besides paying maintenance, he is keeping mother and child.' Inspector Timms was irate and took on the case, accusing the Commissioner of 'wrongfully detaining' payments. Neville replied in February 1939 that the police criticisms were unfair:

the word 'erroneously' would have been a much better term to use than 'wrongfully' although I admit my officers have been careless in not drawing attention to the accumulation of funds in her trust account.

Inspector Timms was not satisfied with Neville's 'endeavour to pass the blame on to someone else,' and chronicled the errors of the Native Affairs Department in the care of Patricia and her child. He attached a statement from Patricia:

I was kept by my mother who gets two pounds per month from the Court House and earns a few shillings going out washing. My father has not been living at home for about ten years and does not pay my mother anything. I was very sick all that time and some of the time my baby was sick. When I am well I earn a few shillings doing odd jobs. I have only been out of bed for two days before I came here. I was sick for three weeks. I have to pay a shilling a tin for milk and 6d. per pound for meat to make soup to feed baby with. She is well now. I did not tell anyone (Abu Kassim) was giving me stores, because I thought Mr Drysdale (of the Police) would make trouble for him.

Abu Kassim also made a statement, outlining his commitment to pay maintenance; his concerns when coming ashore to find that Patricia had not received any money; the fact that he was buying stores from Dobson and that he:

saw Mr Knight when he came back and told him, 'Patricia no get the money.' He said 'none at all?' I say 'no', and Mr Knight say, 'I fix it up before you go out again.' I not hear any more from Mr Knight.

Inspector Timms pointed out to Neville that 'the facts are well known in Broome and had anything happened to the mother or the child there are a few people here who would have only been too glad to have ventilated the circumstances in the Press.'

Neville chose not to respond to Timms, 'because he seems to be in a frame of mind which would render that course useless' and it 'was hardly a police matter.' He instructed the Department to pay the money promptly to the girl, 'before there can be any further comment levelled at us.' In March 1939, more than fifteen months after the birth of Fay, he authorised for 7/6d per week to be made available from the trust account for her care and maintenance. Mr Knight, whose personal antagonism to the young mother was evident and ongoing, chose not to comment.

The story in Patricia's personal file is a case study of bureaucratic bungling, buck-passing and blame shifting. It also illustrates the fundamental policy flaw of the state approach. The legislative and policy apparatus of the state, intended to protect the welfare of Aboriginal people, had the opposite effect on this family. The young mother, ill and malnourished, was unable to look after herself and her baby; was blamed for it and threatened with forced removal. The young father, an indentured seaman with limited rights in Australia, tried to do his duty and act responsibly for his family. His contributions were siphoned away and he was threatened with deportation if the relationship continued. The girl's mother was unable to access the funds left by her Irish father, which would have been more than sufficient to care for their needs. If the legislative regime had not been there (or if the girl and her mother were not Aboriginal), it is reasonable to assume that they would have had the capacity to take decisions, to make choices, and to manage the affairs of their family. The extra bureaucratic layer established under the Act foreclosed on all those options, leaving this family vulnerable, under threat of criminal proceedings and at risk of further trouble. They had to beg for their rights. They were not the begging kind.

Reading the files decades later Patrick is not surprised that his mother was said to be 'insolent, disobedient and almost uncontrollable.' The report by Mr Knight was the first of several comments annotating her unwillingness to be controlled, even when such control was administered by 'well-intentioned' authority figures with 'her best interests at heart'. It is only possible to speculate on the cause of her reaction, the wellspring of emotional resistance to authority, the nature of the 'bedside manner' that caused her anger, especially perhaps when told she was 'breast-feeding contrary to directions'. It may be true that her behaviour was inappropriate, that her anger was not carefully directed. However, reading the case files held by the Department consistently reveals that the authorities, as individual agents of the state, were impatient with their wards and held their task to be one of surveillance and prescription rather than care and custody. Many mature Aboriginal people were treated either as unruly, immoral children, or as threats to the moral and racial order of society in the tropics.

Removal and relocation

The surveillance and control of the young mother continued, as did her troubled lifestyle. In October 1939, Patricia gave birth to a premature child (named Gerald Francis). Gerald lived for just two hours. Despite urgent calls for help, the local medical doctor did not arrive until the next morning.

The authorities were not sympathetic. The new Inspector of Native Affairs, Mr Lew McBeath, interviewed the ill, frightened and depressed young mother. Patricia admitted that the father of her stillborn was Abu Kassim, also the father of her daughter, Fay. McBeath wrote sternly to Neville suggesting that Patricia had concealed the pregnancy by 'wearing very tight corsets, or had herself laced up in some way.' McBeath sought to control the situation. He recommended deportation of Kassim and the partner of another young woman, which 'deals with the principal offender, but it would have no effect on the half-caste girls, nor deter them from becoming intimate with others after the departure of their paramours.' Removal of the women was necessary, he said, 'as a very severe warning to the others and give me some control over an otherwise impossible situation.'

Commissioner Neville was inclined to agree with McBeath that forced removal and relocation to the Beagle Bay Mission was necessary for 'certain young girls in Broome who continually associate with Asiatics and produce illegitimate children.' He was not, however, without concern for the welfare of his wards or the unintended consequences of his actions. He was worried that there had been twenty-seven cases of leprosy in Beagle Bay since 1936, including five children in 1939, and he suggested exploring the option of removal to Lombadina Mission to the south of Broome. Neville also commenced proceedings for deportation of Abu Kassim, noting, 'although the child has died the fact remains that he has offended a second time with Patricia.' Somehow, these punitive actions were avoided for the time being.

By October the following year, 1940, a frustrated Inspector McBeath noted that Patricia was again pregnant, and sought the matter to be referred to the police 'as I cannot deal with it'. Sadly, this child also did not live. Unfortunately for the officials, more than six months had elapsed, and therefore a conviction could not be secured under section 46 of the *Native Administration Act* 'for sexual intercourse'. Nevertheless, the State Department of Native Affairs formally sought deportation from the Commonwealth

Department of the Interior, and Abu Kassim was charged with being in arrears on his maintenance.

Some in the town sought to inflame the situation. In December 1940, her mother Elizabeth's files record that Inspector McBeath received an anonymous letter stating that an Asiatic was living with Elizabeth. Early the next year the police 'raided her house but without result. They report that no Asiatics have been seen at her house for some weeks.'

Decades later, Patrick Dodson would chat to an Aboriginal lady in Broome, who expressed sympathy to him, 'for those horrible people who wrote anonymous letters about your Mum.' Patrick speculates angrily on the identity of the authors, believing them to be Aboriginal people trying to distance themselves from their countrymen and ingratiate themselves with the officials. In the Coles supermarket in Broome, he pointed out one likely suspect to me. I watched her hobbling down the aisles pushing a trolley, surrounded by her grandchildren. He said that Granny Liz had a phrase to describe them, 'Filthy stinking bastards, she'd say.'

In April 1941 the Commissioner of Native Affairs[6] briefed his Minister to take 'drastic action to suppress prostitution in Broome,' through removal of several women to Beagle Bay. Patricia Djiagween was on his list. He noted that 'some of them are "one-man" women and strictly speaking they are not prostitutes in the full meaning of the term.' In the family view, Patricia was a 'one-man' woman, and if given a fair go and left alone, she would have married her man. However, the Commissioner told his Minister:

> Something must now be done to indicate our bona fides and sincerity of principle, not only to the native women and Asiatics of Broome but also to the Commonwealth Government.[7]

The inevitable occurred. In May 1941, under section 12 of the Act Patricia and daughter Fay were arrested and relocated under warrant to the Beagle Bay Mission, along with some eight other women and children. Six months later, her second daughter, Georgina Frances was born at the Mission.[8] Abu Kassim's maintenance bill went up by another 7/6 per week. Her mother had earlier requested £120 to be placed in her own bank account at the Commonwealth Bank, Broome, presumably to assist Patricia. No record exists to show that the authorities approved or rejected the request.

The intervention of war led to a new calling for Abu Kassim. He enlisted and transferred his salary deductions for child maintenance from the pearlers to the military. Abu Kassim's physical strengths, language abilities and capacity for difficult work under trying conditions led to him being selected in the 'Z

Force' commando unit. After training in guerilla warfare on Fraser Island, he was parachuted into Borneo behind the Japanese lines. Sergeant Abu Kassim was a wireless operator in the secret 'Semut' (Malay for 'ant') operation, in which small commando teams trained the local Dayak people to attack Japanese positions.[9] It was ironic that the man the Australian authorities sought to deport on racial grounds should become a key part of the defence of the nation, utilising his cultural and linguistic skills.

World War Two

World War Two brought drastic change for the people of Broome. The pearling industry would come close to collapse and the Japanese families there were forcefully evacuated and interned; their luggers burned on the beach. Only the six hundred graves in the Japanese cemetery were left as a witness to their contribution to the pearling industry. In Broome, the town came under military control.

Aboriginal people, the majority of the remote northern Australian population, were to see more of the frontline than most Australians. As a refueller on 3 March 1942, Paddy Djiagween was helping fuel Dutch refugee flying boats en route from Java to Perth after the invasion of Java by the Japanese. Nine Zero aircraft strafed and bombed the flying boats and town, the first of three raids on the town, killing fifty-five mainly Dutch servicemen and civilians.[10] Paddy's son Ray (for Raid), was born to his second wife, Mabel on that day. After the Japanese raid, most of the women and children of Broome were evacuated in army trucks to the Mission. Paddy and Elizabeth were also at Beagle Bay for considerable periods, although Paddy and Mabel preferred to keep their distance, staying at Coconut Well, near Broome, for most of the war.

North from Broome, at Carnot Bay, a downed Dutch DC3 had been carrying a box of valuable diamonds from Java to a bank in Melbourne. After Aboriginal people from the Beagle Bay Mission rescued the pilot and crew, a friend of Paddy's named Jack explored the wreckage and the diamonds were discovered. Given a share, Paddy had another opportunity to feel material wealth in his fingers, even if he knew it would not stick for long. Family history has it that, when a search for the diamonds commenced, Paddy gave up his share to a white official who commended him for his honesty, and spirited the cache, never to be seen again.[11] Paddy told Mary Durack that a few had come his way as a gift from his tribal father-in-law. He secretly buried his treasure in a secluded corner of the Beagle Bay Mission but after the War found them replaced by a few common pebbles. 'He is still wondering whether someone discovered his hiding place or whether the substitution was a cautionary miracle.'[12]

Placed under military control during wartime, the town relied on Aboriginal labour. A visitor to the town in late 1942 was anthropologist William Stanner, given an Army commission as Lieutenant Colonel to advise on organising Aboriginal guerrilla schools. Three schools were proposed for the Kimberley at Mt House, Fitzroy Crossing and Liveringa. Stanner noted that it was 'odd and rather disturbing to realise that Broome could be taken so easily. There is nothing whatever to prevent a speedy ingress.'[13] Nothing that is, except the owners of the country. Paddy Djiagween recalled that the Officer-in-Charge of the military presence, Major Gibson, saw the prisoners in chains on the work gang and he 'tell the jail master, take those chains off. Those men belong to the country.'[14]

In September 1942, the Australian Armed Forces passed a proclamation under National Security Regulations requiring employed Aborigines over the age of fourteen years to be issued with a 'military permit'. Permits were issued in either red or black, with red indicating the bearer was believed to be 'subversive' and black indicating they could be considered 'trustworthy'.[15] Paddy received a black permit. Elsewhere, Aboriginal people were treated with suspicion; a letter to the editor in the Sydney papers claiming that Japanese could pass themselves off as Aborigines by adorning their face with burnt cork, and that Aborigines using smoke signals could give information to Japanese reconnaissance planes '60 to 100 miles off the coast of Broome.'[16]

Wartime at Beagle Bay

As in the first War, the multicultural mission at Beagle Bay was under suspicion and surveillance. In October 1940, the six non-naturalised German Pallottine priests and seven brothers were escorted to Broome under suspicion of disloyalty. They were held in the local jail, pending their internment in the south. Aboriginal men and women in Broome flocked to the jail bringing food, bedding and gifts. The master pearler families watched in stony silence.[17]

Bishop Raible, a charismatic German with a long full flowing beard, had been naturalised and escaped detention. He rallied support from many, including Archbishop Mannix in Melbourne, who intervened with the Prime Minister, reversing the decision after ten days' detention. Three of the priests, most recently arrived, were sent to Melbourne parishes for the duration.[18] Suspicion increased after the Japanese entered the war. A sizeable

Army presence was maintained at the Mission to ensure the compliance of the missionaries and their flock, now swollen by the addition of some 250 evacuees. The Mission's effort continued under the trying conditions. Six 'native sisters' were received into the order and three chaplains arrived from the Australian Missionary Society of the Sacred Heart in 1942.[19] They were the first members of the order in that region.

Patricia's older daughter Fay, remembered some of the times at Beagle Bay Mission. She recalled taking kangaroo ears to the kitchen for Theresa Hunter, the cook, and a friend of Patricia's. With her Uncle Joe she caught eels and trapped parrots by putting branches on the roof with honey and then grabbing the parrots. These she sold for hard-boiled lollies to the soldiers, coming through on trucks. Patricia, Fay and Georgina lived in the old community with Elizabeth in small bush huts near a spring.[20]

Sally Bin Denim was there, an age-mate of the young Georgina Kassim:

> I cannot remember too much about my childhood in Beagle Bay, other than going to their beautiful church with my mother and sister praying for the war to end, and celebrating their wonderful feast days. All the masses and benedictions prayed and sung in Latin still remain clearly in my mind.[21]

The rules of the Mission, stressing the need for work and church-going as steps to salvation, were under pressure from the new arrivals, as Mary Durack comments:

> The peaceful family atmosphere of Beagle Bay had been shattered by the arrival of over two hundred and fifty evacuees, many of whom gambled or otherwise idled their time away in open defiance of authority and scorn of those who respected it.[22]

Patricia and her mother were, as like as not, amongst their number. They were certainly soon in trouble with the authorities. Elizabeth attempted to get back to Broome at one point soon after the air raids, but was stranded and unable to enter the town. 'They were picked up by Mister Knight and fully realise the position and said that they will not leave the mission again.' Soon after, 'a fight took place between Kathleen Hunter and her mother Flora opposing Elizabeth Djiagween and daughter Patricia. They were all severely cautioned.'[23] In early 1943 Patricia requested permission to return to Broome, writing directly to the Minister in a letter kept on file:

> While I have the opportunity of writing a few lines to you. Please could you kindly let me know about my children and myself as we are anxious to go home as it is already one year and five month now. Hope you'll let

me know how we stand. Dear Sir hope you will let me know as soon as possible. As it's up to you and we are in your power.[24]

The Minister replied in the negative with regret, citing the war situation. However, the Commissioner had briefed him that 'there is an undesirable gathering of half-castes in Derby and possibly Patricia Djiagween has heard of this.' This gathering may have been related to the pastoral industrial unrest in the Aboriginal workforce at the time.

Later in the year the Minister approved the relaxation of Patricia's warrant but specified that she was to remain in Beagle Bay. The unrelenting Mr Knight protested against the relaxation, saying that she 'is incorrigible, and I cannot imagine lifting warrant from her with any idea of encouraging better behaviour.'

Her relations with authority, never happy, now deteriorated beyond repair. The priests at Beagle Bay tightened up their procedures, desperate to maintain control over their charges and restore order on the Mission. Compulsory masses were required before food would be provided. Patricia, perhaps in a mode of resistance and a mood of frustration, punched out at Fr Francis, knocking him to the ground. Winded and with pride wounded, Fr Francis made an example of her, reporting her crime to Inspector O'Neill at the Broome police. There is no doubt that punching a priest was a serious and unusual action, although no record of the incident has been found.[25]

O'Neill wrote to the Native Affairs Department, stating that she 'was regarded as a hopeless case at the mission,' was associating with servicemen in the area, and recommended her removal to Moola Bulla:

> She is regarded as one of the ringleaders and is a bad example and influence to the others. She deliberately flouts the rules and regulations of the Colony ... Mr. George would not appreciate her presence at the Station but at least he would be able to control her. There is no doubt she requires firm handling and I can think of nowhere else she would be likely to receive it. Patricia would regard such a move as a definite punishment and it would need a police escort to remove her.

As evidence he attached a letter from Patricia to a friend at Lombardina that had been intercepted and confiscated:

> Dear Friend. It was a wonder you wrote me a letter. I thought you have forgotten we. Because too (m)any kaki (khaki) suit around. Gee my kaki friend is on the transport truck he sure is handsome with beautiful blue eyes ... It is a pity to see all the children parting from they (their) people, it brought heart ack (ache) and tear, parting going to the hospital ... If you

write give it to the Air Force chap on the truck and tell to give it only to me. Closing now with love and kisses.

Here was clear evidence of Patricia's 'association with members of the various Military Units,' and her 'loose moral outlook'. The officials chose to make an example of the young woman. She was to be arrested, imprisoned, transported and relocated.

Arrested, transported and rescued

The story of Patricia's arrest, transportation and rescue is an important family story told by Patrick and Mick, but they defer to their elder sister Fay, as it is her story. She was there, with her younger sister Georgina.[26]

Fay, after months of negotiations by Patrick, sat down and told me the story in 1998, in Broome. She refused the tape recorder, so this is reconstructed based on my notes at the time and her memories as a six-year-old girl:

> It was wartime, and we were sent to Beagle Bay. Mum and we two kids were there. Georgina was born there, but just a baby. The priests there didn't like us then, called us 'Sheba lane sluts', because Mum followed the Malay man, like Dad. Our Dad, Abu Kassim had gone to war and he never saw Georgina till he got back. Mum got into a blue with Old Father Francis; we used to call him 'Well-well', because he was always saying that, 'well-well'. She upped and hit the old priest. That was Mum, hit first, talk later. So she got put into the Beagle Bay lock up.
>
> Then we three got taken to Derby on the boat and then in a truck to the Broome lock-up. We all went to jail, Mum, Georgina and myself. At the old police station, those first cells are as you walk into the tea room now. Georgina was just a baby wearing blue overalls. She was crying because it was dark and Mum sang to her. I remember she sang 'White Cliffs of Dover'. No-one was allowed to visit us. Granny Liz and Auntie Gracie Martin used to visit but only from outside. Mum lifted me up to look through the bars on the windows so I could see my grandfather outside.
>
> There was another woman in jail there, a bit silly, who was in the other cell and a man who was in the next one, blackfella who was there for murder I think. We were there for about two nights I think.
>
> Then, evening time, we went by truck to Moola Bulla. Wasson Byers was there. He was the most evil man I knew. Bert Sharpe was the driver; big man with guts hanging over his trousers. He chained us to the back of the truck for the drive out through Broome. On the road we stopped at

Christmas Creek, there was a pub there. Georgina was crying for milk. I had sandy blight, really sore eyes. Bert Sharpe stopped to get food and we were sitting down under the tree. We were frightened for white people, that time and that Bert Sharpe.

Then Snowy Dodson come up and said, 'What's this business?' Mum told him, 'We're going to Moola Bulla for reform.' He give Georgina milk, and by the time Bert Sharpe got back, Snowy had pinched us. We took off in the back of Snowy's truck, nobody in the front seat. We met up with old Curly Pascoe, Snowy's mate. I was with him and Mum and Georgina was with Dad.

We were hiding from the police, we were on the run for about a couple of months, around Fossil Downs and Go-Go. We used to camp in the bush. Dad used to park his truck on the riverbank, and showed us how to dig soaks. We went to Jubilee Downs, there was a big stone building with coloured woman married to white man. Dad used to do a little bit of job here and there, windmill, fencing.

They caught up with us and then took Mum, Georgina and me to Moola Bulla. Dad was sent to Fannie Bay goal in Darwin. When he got out he pinched us again. Mum jumped through the window of the dormitory and ran off with Snowy. Got caught and sent to Fannie Bay again.

Fay's story is, like many Dodson family stories, sad, poignant, and illustrative. It is also insightful into the motivation of campaigners for social justice and human rights such as Patrick and Mick Dodson; providing a window into their family experience. Thomas Keneally points out:[27]

Stories of love, paradox and malice across the racial and cultural divide are the most resonating of human stories. Imaginative readers like them. Because everyone has had some experience, in the classroom, at home, on the street, of the turned shoulder, the easy jibe, the cold eyes of a society that believes it knows all about you and won't be persuaded, whatever you do, to see you as just another human pilgrim.

It is true also that in oral traditions facts shift, stories become embellished, information is skewed and memory is unreliable, especially the memories of a six-year-old girl. With Patrick Dodson's co-operation, I began a long and frustrating search of archival and court records to document the family account. At first the situation was bleak. There was no record of Snowy Dodson at Fannie Bay gaol. There were no court records at Broome. The Bishop of Broome sent a letter saying that there was no record of the incident involving Fr Francis.

However, as a trained bureaucrat, I knew that where there was a Life there was a File, somewhere. Given the scope and scale of the legal and policy machinery set up in the west to monitor, regulate, control Aboriginal life choices, the files would have been extensive. Patrick eventually received permission to access copies of the personal files of his mother and grandmother from the Western Australian government. Much later he passed them on to me. The files confirm the fundamentals of Fay's story and tell another side; the official view of the time. They also provided access to file copies of intercepted letters, important for a biography of a family in which no letters were kept.

The official story

On 20 September 1944, a warrant was signed by the Minister for the Northwest for the forced removal of Patricia Djiagween and her child[28] from the palm trees and pindan soils of Beagle Bay Mission to the spinifex-covered hills of Moola Bulla Native Station near Halls Creek. Patricia had just turned twenty. The Commissioner recommended her removal on the advice of O'Neill, and the evidence of the intercepted letter. The Commissioner advised Alf George, the manager of Moola Bulla that Patricia was on her way, noting 'that she is quite a good type and is a competent domestic, however her conduct has been unsatisfactory for some years owing to her association with Asian pearling crews in Broome.'

The station at Moola Bulla was bought as a reserve and pastoral training camp, and was now used as a place of punishment for Aboriginal people proving troublesome to the authorities. As Mick described it to Phillip Adams in a radio interview, 'It was the Palm Island of the Kimberleys; a kind of slave camp where troublemakers were made to work.'[29] It was many miles inland, on the fringe of the Tanami Desert. No court was required; no hearing was necessary. Patricia's side of the story, apart from the poignant teenage correspondence, remained untold.

Patricia, Fay and Georgina were arrested in the early morning of 20 October at Beagle Bay, transferred to Derby on the *M.V. Koolinda* and then driven to Broome to await the cartage truck to Moola Bulla, operated by Bert Sharpe. For four days and nights the young mother and her two young daughters were locked in the cells at the Broome police station.[30] Mr Campbell of Broome received a shilling for each of their meals. In the cells, Patricia sang the 'White Cliffs of Dover', no doubt conscious of the irony of the lyrics:

> *There'll be blue birds over*
> *The white cliffs of Dover,*
> *Tomorrow, just you wait and see.*
> *There'll be love and laughter*
> *And peace ever after*
> *Tomorrow, when the world is free.*[31]

After receiving extra clothing of two children's dresses and bloomers, Patricia and her two little girls were piled into the back on Bert Sharpe's transport and driven off along the inland road towards Halls Creek. After a few days on the boggy highway, the truck ground to a halt at Christmas Creek, camping there on the night of 31 October.

Another intercepted letter presented as evidence in the trial records Patricia's version of events as told to her friend:

> We camped at Xmas Creek. So here was fun. There was six truck and all the men was drunk, so I camped nearby the house talking to a few gins when the Bozz came and look at us I thought now Hello there's somethings in this. He called a gins to carry his swag, Then he call a other chap. So they both came up to me and said to me well here you native to camp with. Tell you matey if I did get mad and told he off and then the chap said hang on I'll speak better to her so we spoke.

> He said this morning when I see you you remember me of a girl friend of mine. But you are nicer than her. I only laught. He was not drunk of. So I went over to his camped with the Kids and talk. Then came (the transport driver) full as an eggs and said things out of place so Snow got up and (Snow Dobson is his name) gave him a blow. He is a small thin chap alongside of (the driver) so he said get me my truck, so off we went matie he got heart of gold so I'm with him at present. But I'll be going to Moola Bulla. He try to get me out but I got to good my time first …

> Snow is always singing at like me. But he's got good voice. They call halfcast his yellow, so he always sing Yellow Rose of Mission for me. You think I got luck … They tell me you better have a good time Pat before you go to Moola Bulla.[32]

According to Sharpe's version of events told to the Police, he 'found Dodson in the company of the woman Djiagween and he told Dodson to keep away from her as she was his responsibility until they reached Moola Bulla. Dodson objected to Sharpe ordering him away from the woman and an altercation ensued in which Dodson hit Sharpe on the chin and gashed it about an inch long.' The next morning, Sharpe discovered his charges had absconded in Dodson's truck.

Constable Jensen was concerned that the truck driven by Dodson carried 300 gallons of wine for the hotel at Halls Creek:

> In view of the unsavoury records of Dodson (and Pascoe) I am of the opinion that the wine would be broached and a drunken orgy began, which if liquor was supplied to Djiagween, would be the corpus delicti of a major tragedy.

Instead, Snowy left Patricia and the girls in the scrub, dropped his load and returned. Patricia and her children were eventually forwarded to Moola Bulla from Lamboo station two weeks later. Their stay was a short one because Snowy Dodson went to Moola Bulla in his semi-trailer and lifted the young family again, less than a fortnight after that. Inspector O'Neill reluctantly reported that:

> She was taken out of the custody of Sharpe when en route to Moola Bulla and after spending some days with Dodson was eventually taken to Halls Creek. Dodson has again taken Patricia this time from Moola Bulla and has taken the children with her. I don't know whether the Police have been successful in locating her yet but no doubt they will do so.

An unsigned witness statement undoubtedly prepared by the Mission Superintendent from a 'half-caste married woman', told the official Moola Bulla Station version of events on the night of 25 November:

> A man came on the dormitory verandah. It was moonlight and I recognised the man to be Snowy Dodson. Dodson walked up to the window which is about eight or ten feet from where I was sleeping and he whispered something through the window. I could not hear what he was saying. He then walked up to the other window and I saw him take a blanket and a small suitcase through the bars of the window. While Dodson was gathering the things up at the top window I saw the girl Patricia Djiagween come and get through the windows near me. Her two children then got through the window. He and Patricia Djiagween and her two children all walked off the verandah of the dormitory together. I watched them walk away and they went over to the Halls Creek Road. Not long after I heard a truck start up and saw the lights of it going in the direction of Koonjie Park.

Snowy and Patricia kept out of the hands of the authorities, much to the concern of the Commissioner, for the next two months. The escapade couldn't last, of course. Police at Oscar Range arrested Snowy at old Brooking Springs. The law was tough on mixed-race liaisons in a time, where everyone had their place and the police had the job of keeping them there. A white man with a black woman and two kids couldn't be allowed to run loose in the bush, working their days to feed the kids at night. It may make fools of the police and the Department.

In mid-January 1945, Patricia and her two children were transported from Oscar Range to Halls Creek to give evidence against Snowy. She refused to sign a statement, declaring, 'I made up my mind to go with Dodson. I told him I wanted to get out of the dormitory. He did not ask or persuade me to do so. I took my belongings with me because I wanted to go away with Dodson and I asked him to take me.' Constable Andrews noted that, 'Dodson has refused to give any information whatever regarding his association with Djiagween. Her two children address him as "Daddy".'

Inspector O'Neill, not one to let a case go lightly, asked to attend Dodson's hearing, pointing to a:

> Strange reluctance on the part of Halls Creek and Fitzroy Crossing police to take any decisive action against Dodson and although he is not a popular man, nor a resident of long standing in the Kimberley, public opinion seems to be that he is being singled out for prosecution.

Compulsory sentencing was a feature of the 1936 Act. At 6am on 26 February 1945, John Murray Dodson had a hearing at Halls Creek before Magistrate Roberts. Despite Patricia's support, he was charged, pleaded guilty, was convicted and sentenced under legislation that defined a minimum term of six months for each offence. He was convicted of a breach of section 15 and with two breaches of section 46 subsection (b) of the Act:

> 15. Any person who, without lawful authority or excuse,—
> (a) goes or remains within the boundaries or confines of a reserve or native institution; or
> (b) removes a native, or causes, assists, entices, or persuades a native to remove from a reserve or native institution; or
> (c) transports or assists a native in or after his removal or escape therefrom, shall be guilty of an offence under this Act.
> 46 (b) Any person (except a native) who cohabits with or has sexual intercourse with any native who is not his wife or husband.

Snowy Dodson was sentenced to six months imprisonment (concurrent) on each of the first two charges, and twelve months for the third charge, to be served cumulatively. That is, he was jailed for eighteen months, with hard labour, a requirement of the Act.

The newspapers in Perth carried no report of the conviction. At the time, however, equivalent sentences were delivered on an elderly man found guilty of having unlawfully and indecently dealt with a girl of seven years old, and for grand theft from a house in South Perth. Meanwhile, Mae West was appearing at the Grand in 'Heat's On', and the readers in Perth were told of the long, hazardous trips inland by the North-West Mounted police, and bizarre stories that:

> Small bands of Albinos still roamed the plains. Their pink eyes and fair skins are typical Albino characteristics. They speak no English at all but never cause trouble and are found inland between Halls Creek and Wave Hill.[33]

The Dodson family was convinced that Snowy was sent to Fannie Bay Gaol in Darwin. In fact he was sent to Fremantle prison, south of Perth. The local police argued for his early removal, the lock-up in Halls Creek, being 'unsuitable for holding white prisoners for any lengthy period.' The court did not punish Patricia again; after all, she was on her way back to Moola Bulla, where she was taken that afternoon.

McBeath, now Deputy Commissioner of Native Affairs, wrote to the Commissioner of Police:

> I am pleased with the results obtained by the prosecution of Dodson and I have no doubt that this Court session will have a good effect generally in the districts concerned, and also deter others contemplating similar behaviour. Recently Dodson sought my permission to marry the native woman Patricia Djiagween, but the proposal was not approved.[34]

Snowy applied for permission to marry Patricia in April 1945. The application was rejected by the Commissioner who cited his conviction, 'and the circumstances of your misbehaviour in respect to those charges.' He also ordered all letters between Dodson and Djiagween to be intercepted.

In 2001, in the old cemetery at Halls Creek, Patrick stood over the grave of Charles Lewis McBeath (6/6/01 to 19/11/76) and read its inscription, 'erected by the citizens of Halls Creek as a tribute to his work for the community over a great number of years.' For Patrick, Charles McBeath was someone who set out to attack his family and persecute his father and mother. He was not working for Patrick's community. He recalled being told that McBeath had seen Snowy driving back from Moola Bulla on the Old Halls Creek Road, 'That's why they hated Snowy. He defied the laws'.

There is no doubt that the level of control, supervision and coercion applied to Aboriginal families in Western Australia was draconian, racially motivated and applied with vigorous force, in ways that non-Aboriginal families have rarely experienced. As Mick Dodson, Patrick's younger brother, said in a nationally televised speech on 27 May 2000:

> My father was jailed for eighteen months for breaching the Native Administration Act 1905-1941 of Western Australia in that he was 'co-

habiting' with my mother. I will never understand a social, political and legal system that could jail my father for loving my mother.[35]

Snowy Dodson

In a land of mysteries, Snowy was a mysterious man. In a land of hard men, he was known as a very hard man, who always worked with his hands and often talked with his fists. Mechanic, contractor, fencer, welder, he preferred to keep much to himself. He liked the backblocks country of the stations along the Northern Territory—Western Australian border, moving from job to job, station to station in an old Bedford truck, and later a Blitz, towing a caravan. Inside the caravan were some blankets, cooking gear and every tool ever likely to be needed to do a bush job and do it well.

Supposedly originally from Launceston, Tasmania, Snowy has left no track of his birth, family or schooling.[36] One old Aboriginal man told Patrick Dodson in later years that his father Snowy had been a stowaway on a plane that landed in Darwin, jumping out of the wheel-carriage before landing. Another had suggested he was a draft-dodger who changed his name on leaving Tasmania. The family wondered if he might have been a Tasmanian Aboriginal. They have no clues and no family connection has come forward.

It is known that Snowy worked for Tom Cole the buffalo hunter in southeast Arnhem Land on the Wildman Plains in 1938–9. Cole's published diaries are inclined to be laconic. Snowy's trail is faint, with entries such as:

> 25 November 1938: Arranged with Dodson to put up five miles of fence.
>
> 27 November 1938: Loading 115 hides. Left Dodson in charge and left with the Maroubra for Darwin.
>
> 8 December 1938: Big day. Got busy with the soldering iron and about five pounds of solder and made a petrol funnel. Snowy, out post cutting, brought in one boy unconscious- some kind of stroke.
>
> 1 January 1939: Snowy Dodson returned from line of fence. All the posts are cut and laid on the line.

In a letter of 28 January he tells a little more:

> I am getting through a lot of work just now and consequently I am feeding a lot of natives. There are 14 natives and Snowy Dodson and myself—three feeds a day—and a lot of rations are necessary … Christmas here was just another day, chiefly remarkable for the fact that I had a shave. I've got a chap named Dodson working here and we cracked a bottle of rum —'A merry Xmas', I said as we tossed a noggin down—it sounded idiotic.[37]

The December 1937 Tennant Creek Police journal of Monday, November 8 1937 has an intriguing notation:

> S.C. Littlejohn and Const. Mannion general police duties. Rec. mail from H.Q. — A/cs. re. cartage on Const. Sheridan's furniture etc.; Warrant of Commitment for Snowy Dodson, for execution, to be lodged Alice Springs gaol;[38]

The only earlier reference is October 30:

> Consts. Reid and Mannion general Police duties. Received mail (air) as follows: Posted air mail Darwin; re Dodson;[39]

What the warrant was for, or how long Snowy spent in the Alice Springs Gaol, remain mysteries. Patrick did not get to know his father or his father's family. The archival records and traces, while suggestive, are not conclusive. For an Aboriginal man, the cultural norm is one of inheriting your rights, knowledge and connection to country through your father. The experience of colonisation has transformed this expectation. Throughout Aboriginal Australia, men are now tracing their genealogy and their links to land through their mother's line. For Patrick, not knowing, for sure, his father's birthplace and family is frustrating; leaving a story unknown. It is another area of his life that he closes off; an unread book.

Moola Bulla

It would be another two years before Patricia and the girls were to see Broome again. Moola Bulla, off the track between Halls Creek and Wyndham, was a hardship post. People were brought in from all over the north, either as a punishment, as in Patricia's case, to hide away the illegitimate offspring of pastoralists and stockmen. Very few people chose to live there, except of course, for the traditional owners.

The stories of Moola Bulla, when collected and published by the Kimberley Languages Resource Centre in 1996 make difficult reading today. The stories are collected with the intention of supporting language knowledge and collective memory but there is a lack of historical perspective and context. The stories carry their own weight:

> We used to go to school on the verandah part every day. They built a bough-shade for us near the kitchen. That was our dining room, you see? We had to go to the dining room in the morning, lunch-time and supper-time. And after, we'd start having our meals in the dormitory now, on the verandah. This girl used to get to go and just get a tea, bread and beef, nothing else from the kitchen, bring it up to the dormitory and we used to eat there.

> Well you know how it was in the government times, everyone carried on, blacks and half-castes would sneak away in the night you know? ... Well, when the gardiya (white people) got up they weren't pleased. There was nobody there ... They took him to the electric shed you know, and gave him an electric shock. They just took his balls and splashed on some spirits and then gave him a shock. What do you think of that? Unbelievable isn't it? ... They'd just chuck them in the shed with handcuffs on and padlocks and chains on their legs, and then just touch them with the wire and ... Brrrrr! Brrrrr! Aaaaa! Aaaaa! That's all.
>
> During the Wet, the native boy used to go for holiday and the manager Alf George used to keep us back, never let half-caste go. So he kept us working.[40]

The reserve may have been established as a well-intentioned response to issues of conflict in land-use, providing a refuge in the midst of the pastoral stations of the East Kimberley where meat could be gained without attacks on the herds of the stations. It was also, from 1910 to 1955, an institution aimed at forced social change. The staff were separated, both spatially and socially, from the inmates, who had little control over their labour, their child-rearing and their love lives. In Neville's eyes:

> The moral effect of an institution of this kind is incalculable but some years must pass after its establishment before confidence can be restored amongst the natives and I think it may be safely said that one effect is to arrest the decline and re-establish family life largely destroyed through previous contacts with whites.[41]

The Dodson family life was difficult to sustain. Patricia and Snowy exchanged a restricted number of letters, carefully inspected by the authorities at Fremantle and later Pardelup Prison Farm, south of Perth. Copies were passed to the Commissioner, presumably to monitor the re-establishment of family life. Snowy asked her to organise tobacco from friends and complained of cold and carbuncles, telling her he was putting on weight. He told her that he was due out in February (1946) but was looking forward to some extra remission.

> I wrote to the Commissioner from Fremantle (re the marriage proposal) but he gave me no satisfaction. I'll go to see him when I am released. Well that's all for the present, Pat. I should be back before the end of the wet. With love to yourself, Georgie and Fay.

Patricia replied (in formal style, unlike her letters to friends):

> I was so glad to get your letter. After waiting so long, I have though(t) you had forgotten all about me. But I can see I was lasted in your mind to

write. But as you say you are sorry I forgive you dear ... I had also put on weight and I got fat. I suppose you won't like me now being fat.

She told him then of her ongoing worries about Fay's eyes, about Georgie's burned legs, about her work in the clinic ('I like the job') and a broken doll. She told him to keep smiling, and that she was counting the months and days until his release.

Patricia worked as a nurse, or health worker, at Moola Bulla, bathing all the big boys for scabies with a yellow, sulphurous powder, then rubbing them down with thick grease. Patricia's sister Fay remembers old people dragging spinifex in the water pools for fish, and the children chasing grasshoppers and cooking them. They would light a fire and when the grasshoppers were cooked, they would jump out onto the canvas. Fay was given the task of getting up and milking the goats at 5am, creeping from the dormitories, past the saddle shed to the yards. There were few visitors; only Granny Liz Fagan and Uncle Joe managing once to make the long trip from Broome.

Alf George, the fearsome manager of Moola Bulla, reported in August 1945 that 'she has not given the slightest bit of trouble since her return.' Commissioner Bray was pleased and permitted the couple to exchange letters, subject to George's censorship.

Elizabeth wrote to the Commissioner in November 1945 after 'waiting, waiting to see O'Neill but I have waited too long, so I am placing my matter before you hoping you will grant a Mother's plea.' She begged for Patricia's return to Broome, 'coming on in years I wish to see my daughter and grandchildren around me. Is it possible for her to leave the place?' Bray curtly declined her plea, noting:

> She has been involved with Asiatics and I feel it would be unwise to allow her to reside at Broome. She should make an effort to secure domestic employment on a station in the Kimberleys. This is my decision.

Snowy managed to get an early release, leaving prison in late 1945. The timing was not good. Patricia was pregnant once more.[42] It seems that she had formed a relationship with Cecil Rose, a non-Aboriginal head stockman on the station, originally from Dubbo in New South Wales. He and Alex Morton, Fay recalls, fought for Patricia's favours, always with the shadow of Snowy Dodson over their dispute. In July 1946, Patricia gave birth to Cecil Adrian at Moola Bulla.[43] Elizabeth rushed to Halls Creek to be near her daughter. She found work at the Halls Creek hotel, against the regulations of the Act, but was not able to secure the release of her daughter and grandchildren.

Instead, her grandchildren were removed. In September of 1946 the authorities decided that Fay and Georgina would be placed in the Orphanage in Broome, with Elizabeth's trust fund footing the bill for their relocation and care. Granny Liz, who travelled to Moola Bulla to collect them, managed to prevent young Cecil from being placed in the Orphanage, offering to care for him in order to prevent the possibility of him being taken away to any other institution the Department chose.

The family had fallen apart, and the bureaucracy had swooped, scattering the pieces, despite Granny Liz's frantic efforts. At no time was consent sought or assistance requested.

Commissioner Bray was concerned to identify the father of the child 'and the circumstances which led to a whiteman having intercourse with Patricia at Moola Bulla.' Alf George had to dob in Cecil Rose who by then was working at Lamboo station, but wryly noted:

> As to the circumstances of intercourse well I suppose they took the same course of action in this respect as they would in any other part of the world.

He and Patricia signed a statement for Alf George in November and said that they planned marriage. In early 1947, however, Cecil Rose walked out from Moola Bulla, refusing to sign a maintenance order for Cecil, stating that he was now uncertain of his paternity. He flew to Wave Hill in the Northern Territory and the legal advice was that he was beyond the reach of the law while across the border.[44]

Baby Cecil, with chronic otitis media, and his mother were also flown out of Moola Bulla to Wyndham, in March, staying there for several weeks. It was in Wyndham that Snowy and Patricia managed to meet up again and re-established their relationship.

Cecil Rose recorded his memories of Moola Bulla and told Charlie McAdam, 'It was Snowy Dodson welded up a steel table. He used to tie them on it and put 180 volts through it. Snowy got burnt to death in the end, priming a carburettor with petrol over at Old Halls Creek.'[45] According to Patrick Dodson, other inmates of Moola Bulla had told him that Snowy Holt, not Snowy Dodson, carried out this crime. It was Snowy Holt that ended up burned to death in what some Aboriginal people regard as a fair end.

To the Territory

Even after the retirement of A.O. Neville, the Aboriginal people of Western Australia needed the blessing of the authorities to choose their partners in life. Somehow, out of sight of the file clerks, Patricia and Snowy managed to put aside the issue of young Cecil and arrange their lives.

They were now, in an Aboriginal sense, married. In the eyes of the white law, their newly resumed relationship was punishable by imprisonment. Her children could be captured and institutionalised at the discretion of the officials. Another offence would have seen Snowy put away for three years or more, with hard labour.

About a year after the birth of Cecil, Patricia wrote to the Native Affairs Department, filling in the 'notice of intention to marry' form. Snowy was now working on Limbunya station, across the border. She followed the marriage request with an application for permission to go the Northern Territory to join him. In July 1947, her permit to travel was approved. It would not be until May of 1949 that the authorities belatedly got around to releasing Patricia from the warrant that sent her to Moola Bulla in the first place.

A month after their request, the young couple were advised that the Acting Commissioner of Native Affairs in Perth had no objection to offer to the proposed marriage under section 45 of the *Native Administration Act 1905/41*. Under the section, his possible grounds of objection included that: the marriage contravened tribal custom; one of the parties was diseased; disparate ages; or, indeed, any other circumstances the Commissioner may imagine. With a legal marriage, the books were clean. Snowy and Patricia could be Darwin's problem, not Perth's.

On 8 September 1947, after due notice had been given, Snowy and Patricia were married at Halls Creek, releasing her from the strictures of the Act. They now moved to secure the release of their children. Patricia went back to her family in Broome to await the birth of her next child. Cecil Adrian was with Elizabeth in Darwin at her daughter Mary Roe's house.

Snowy, at Patricia's suggestion, joined forces with Abu Kassim, who had come back safely from commando operations in the War. The two men ('my two fathers,' Fay called them proudly) had to gain the funds to buy the release of Fay and Georgina from the Broome orphanage. Apparently, the nuns were expecting Granny Liz to cover any costs for the children from her trust fund. For two nights until dawn, the two men played a form of dominoes with kaja kaja sticks in the Chinese gambling houses in Sheba Lane. They were playing an illegal game to regain the custody of their children and return them to their mother. They won.

Fay remembers the next day. She was doing her job of cutting the lawn of the orphanage with shears. She heard a woman at the fence calling out. It took her some time to recognise her mother. Abu Kassim went to the little office in the Convent and handed the money to the sisters. They were given some clothes and government blankets. Snowy pitched the blankets back over the fence, saying, 'I don't want your Government blankets. Shove them up your arse.'

A short time later, on 29 January 1948, Patrick Lionel Dodson was born at the old house in Mary Street Broome, where the pearler's laundry was rubbed, scrubbed, rinsed and starched to a pristine white. Patricia's child came out when she went to the just-cleaned toilet. The infant slid down, nearly drowning in the Phenyl used for cleaning the toilet pans. Granny Liz was called to help by Fay and Rosie Mahmoot, who were playing marbles outside. The little girls were hunted off, away from the women's business. For many in Broome, Patrick would be nicknamed the 'Phenyl Kid'. For his grandfather, he would be 'Minyirr bul' — Broome boy. Patrick would later say, 'Born in the shit house, always in the shit house.'

On the boggy tracks of the late Wet season, the family headed off to Katherine in the Northern Territory, looking for a chance of a fresh start and, perhaps, fairer treatment.

Canberra, 2000

The dining room table at my house in Canberra was piled high with files, tied together with the pink ribbons favoured by archivists as a softer form of red tape. He was going through his mother's file: WA Department of Native Affairs file number 469/43: Half-Caste Patricia Djiagween, now Dobson (sic) of Broome, Personal File. The cover was annotated with reference to 'Warrant Section 12. Married W/M (for white man) John Dobson 8/9/47'. Classification and categorisation by race led to treatment by race.

His mood oscillated as he read the official version of the life of his spirited and tempestuous mother. At times he would sigh and shake his head, overwhelmed at the scale of the bureaucratic apparatus put into place to control Aboriginal lives, sexuality and morality in the State. Occasionally he would get excited at learning something new, such as that his father had been imprisoned at Fremantle Gaol near Perth, as the family had always thought he had been sent to Fannie Bay in Darwin. At other times he was resentful and angry at the level of intrusion and pettiness exhibited by officials of that not so distant past. He took off his newly acquired reading glasses and said:

> It's just still so hard for me to believe that all this happened, not just to my family but also to people all over the State, all over Australia, for that matter. They never had a chance to get out from under. There was always someone pulling on the choker chain. God knows why they bothered half the time.

To a large extent, Patrick's access to these records was a result of his work from 1988 to 1991 as a commissioner with the Royal Commission into Aboriginal Deaths in Custody. A key recommendation was for governments to provide access to all archival records pertaining to the family and community histories of Aboriginal people. His brother Mick advanced those efforts in the 'Bringing Them Home' Report for the Human Rights and Equal Opportunity Commission in 1997, which recommended comprehensive access guidelines for the records of Aboriginal families and individuals subject to forced relocation and removal. Now the research on this biography had brought those recommendations and that side of their family history well and truly home. And it hurt.

For nearly two years, the box of files released from the Western Australian archives had accumulated dust in a cupboard at his home in Broome. Occasional prompting from me would result in a cautious dip into the volume of paper before putting it back where it sat, 'like a black snake curled up in the corner.' Now the files, the life of his family according to the State, were on the table. Putting away the file, he peered at me over his reading glasses and remarked ruefully:

> No wonder John Howard has trouble relating to me. Granny Liz and old Granddad forced into poverty. My Mum arrested and sent away more than once. My sisters chained up in the back of a truck. My Dad doing eighteen months hard labour down at Freeo. What is there in John Howard's life to let him understand that? Who else would he meet with that sort of form?

People in Broome saw the war at first hand. The Broome Aerodrome after Japanese bombing attack destroyed all the aircraft in less than 20 minutes during World War II in 1942 (courtesy News Limited).

Abu Kassim served with the Australian commandos behind Japanese lines. Sargeant Abu Kassim, on leave from Z Force in Perth. Fay used the registration numbers for lotto (courtesy Fay Wade album).

The Broome Lockup where Patricia, Georgina and Fay were imprisoned on their way to Moola Bulla (courtesy of the author).

A family picnic and swim to get away from the Katherine heat. Fay and Patricia, ca 1955 Low Level Bridge, Katherine, N.T. (courtesy Fay Wade album).

Patricia and Snowy Dodson on their wedding day, Halls Creek 8 September 1947 (courtesy Dodson family).

Patricia Dodson, Katherine Races, July 1960 (courtesy Fay Wade album).

Patrick's mother, Patricia Dodson at Broome jetty, wartime (courtesy Fay Wade album).

Cecil in the arms of his mother, Patricia, at Wyndham, W.A., ca 1946 (courtesy Fay Wade Album)

Chapter Six

On the banks of the Katherine

'In the little world in which children have their existence … there is nothing so finely perceived and so finely felt as injustice.'
Charles Dickens, *Great Expectations* **(1861)**

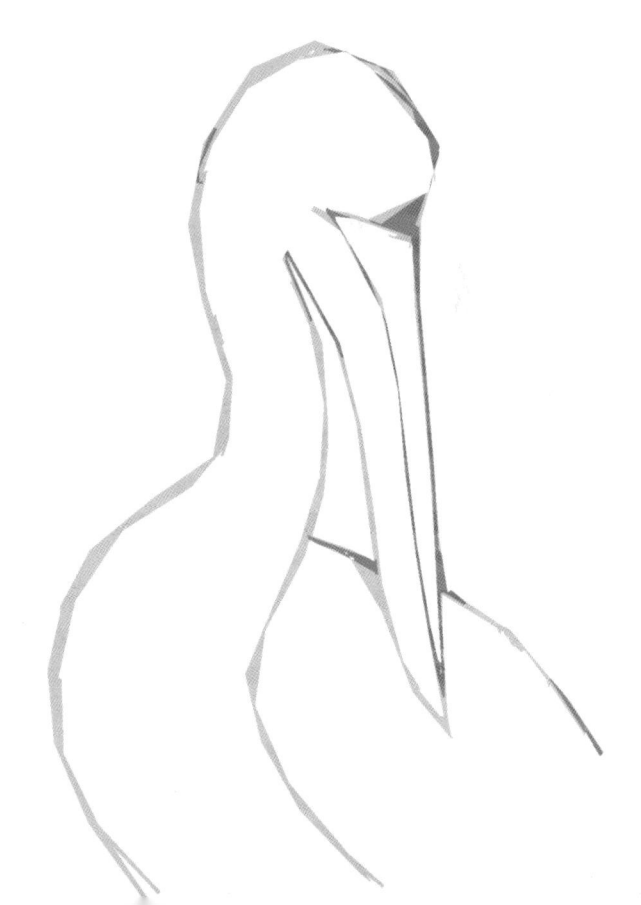

Katherine, NT, 1996

Patrick let the new Prado Land Cruiser shift smoothly down a gear as he coasted into the town of Katherine on the Stuart Highway. The odometer had yet to reach 500 clicks, and he was enjoying the smell and feel of his new car. Its shiny presence stood out in the mud-caked, flood-ravaged town of 11,000 people, still cleaning up after the horrific damage of the Australia Day floods. Along the main street, he watched queues of people lining up for basic supplies in the only open supermarket. The muddy waterline was still bold on the walls of the buildings in town; water-swept grasses were still draped around the light poles. The heavy stench of river mud clung in his nostrils.

In a way, Patrick had come home. This was the town where he had been a lanky kid growing up. Where his younger brother and sister were born. Where his Mum and Dad tried to scrape together a house and home. Where his mother died.

Katherine was the place he came to on holidays from school and seminary down south. Here he had sat through a 'Rights for Whites' meeting, and listened to men, who were boys with him in school, denounce the 'special treatment' given to blacks. Katherine friends nudged him, asking him to respond. He shrugged them off and watched closely.

Down the road to the southwest was Wave Hill, now renamed Kalkarindji, on land held by the Dagaragu Aboriginal Land Trust. His mother's mother's mother was from that country. His mother's mother's father had worked land there, building yards and mustering cattle. The contemporary Aboriginal land rights was born in the Wave Hill walk off, led by Vincent Lingiari, one of Patrick's heroes. Wave Hill was also where Patrick's father died.

The connections with Katherine and Wave Hill were strong; connections of kin, country and history. Aboriginal networks of people and place are, across Australia, dynamic and forceful. The networks are as alive as they ever were, but they change. They are shaped by the colonial experience, especially the forced movements of families, whether those forces are driven by Government policies or by economics. Families like the Dodsons.

Patrick was in country he could call his own, but he did not feel comfortable. There were just too many sad and unresolved stories. Characteristically, he pushed the emotion aside. Pausing for petrol and cool drinks, he turned the Land Cruiser at March's Corner and took the Victoria Highway out of town, heading west for Broome. Going home. The shift of gears was not as smooth as he would have liked.

Katherine, 1948

Late in 1948, Snowy's old Blitz truck bumped across the dirt track that unrolled from Halls Creek through Wave Hill station before joining 'The Track' to Katherine in the Northern Territory. Snowy drove, his arm out the window, while Patricia nursed baby Patrick and kept Georgina distracted from the boredom of the endless plains. The family had been reduced to four. Fay stayed in Derby with relations until the family settled. Granny Liz looked after the young Cecil in Darwin and Broome, on the move during the next few years, but always on the lookout for the police or welfare officials.

The small town of Katherine, perched on the banks of the usually sluggish but sometimes fickle and dangerous river, was the end of the railway line from Darwin. Like the river, the economy was generally slow moving. Long weeds grew over the railway yards and the holding pens next to the meatworks. The town was small. Some four hundred people, 'excluding full bloods' lived in the town or in camps around it.[1] Most of the non-Aboriginal population earned a living serving the outlying stations, and the meatworks employed more than a hundred men in the short killing season.[2] Big properties like Victoria River Downs (VRD) and Wave Hill were linked by dusty roads churned to bulldust by trucks carrying cattle where stockmen used to drove. The big stations were mainly owned by two companies, the British Bovril company which owned VRD, and the Australian Investment Agency, known as Vesteys, which owned Wave Hill and eleven other properties in the Northern Territory. Together, the stations in the northeast of the Northern Territory formed the basis of a global beef empire.[3]

Getting away from the west, Snowy wanted to make a fresh start in the railroad town and pastoral centre. Snowy never felt comfortable in the big towns and the War, especially the bombings of 1942, had hit Darwin hard. Katherine had been bombed too, with one Aboriginal person killed, compared to the twenty-five Aboriginal people killed in Broome. People were now starting to drift back after the wartime evacuations.[4]

Snowy had mates in Katherine from his time working on the plains of Arnhem Land and the stations; people who met the casual contracting needs of the railroads and the big pastoral stations to the west. There was talk in the pubs of expansion in the railway workshops and work had begun on a new plant to boil down beef for Bovril to serve the needs of the British Food Mission. Katherine had enough work for a man who knew one end of a spanner from the other. On this side of the border, perhaps Snowy could shake off the trouble that had dogged him in Western Australia. A fresh start.

When they arrived, the Dodsons set up camp under canvas at the back of the old meatworks. Snowy scrounged the wealth of the scattered army dumps to increase the size of the half-house, half-camp. Sheets of tin, coils of wire and rolls of canvas came in handy as the family grew. Most of the townsfolk did not turn their backs, but the Dodson family would never be fully welcomed as belonging to the town. People in the town saw them as being on the edge of either survival or chaos.

After the birth of John Murray (or Jacko) in 1949 in Darwin, two more children came: Michael (Mick) in 1950 and Patricia (or Tricia) in 1952. Fay helped her mother deliver both the Katherine kids. For some reason, Snowy had to put the wheels back on the ambulance for Mick's birth, with the wheel coming off as he drove along. Patricia was born on the verandah at the home. Fay had rejoined the family, coming over from Derby after a year with relations. She flew across the Kimberley and came down the track from Darwin on the train. Fay stepped out onto the platform, to be met again by her mother. Fay recalled:

> She hugged me on the platform and said, 'Happy eleventh birthday.' I didn't even know it was my birthday.

They were now a family of seven, although Cecil rarely stayed with the family while Snowy was in town and usually lived with Granny Liz. Granny Liz had spent some years in Darwin at the end of the 1940s shifting around frequently. She moved between the house of her daughter, Mary Roe, a pearler's camp on the foreshore and the Bagot reserve, only visiting the Katherine home when Snowy was out bush. In April 1948, the Director of the Native Affairs Branch wrote to the Western Australian authorities reporting that:

She had been living with relatives who had disagreements with her over her mode of living, resulting in her leaving them to reside at a pearler's camp, and from where she was removed by a Protector at her own request. Elizabeth states that her father, Joe Fagan, who died in 1917, left her a legacy which is held in trust with you. Would you kindly advise whether any moneys are held in Trust for her, from which the cost of her repatriation to Broome by first available transport could be made. It is not considered desirable that she should remain in Darwin.[5]

From Perth, acting Commissioner McBeath, the official family friend, advised the Darwin officials that 'she has considerable trust funds held by this Department, and I should be prepared to defray any expenses which your Department might incur.' She flew back with Cecil to her small house in Mary Street in Broome, beginning a lengthy battle for access to her funds in order to repair the house after the damage caused by Army occupation during the War.[6]

On the banks of the Katherine

Snowy had managed to scrape together £50 and purchased a three-acre block in 1952 on the corner of Fourth Street and Lindsay Street, back from the river. The land was sub-divided into agricultural leases. In the minds of planners in Canberra, cultivation farms, raising bananas, vegetables, mangoes or peanuts would spring up, providing new employment opportunities and income for the town. In reality, the lease gave the family enough room to build a rough but decent tin house and enough security to prevent eviction. The land would never be enough to provide an income. 'Every farmer but two in Katherine relies on outside work,' Snowy would tell the Lands Department.[7] They could stay on the land, however, as long as £6 a year rental could be found and the lease conditions met. These included fencing the block and clearing and cultivating at least one-tenth of the block in each of the first five years. These lease conditions would become an ongoing issue.

As the 1950s rolled out, the land along the banks of the Katherine River was taken over as the adventure playground of the Dodson boys: Jacko, Paddy, and little Micky. The Maher boys, Mano, Wiki and Billy,[8] moved next door and swelled the gang, joined soon by Graham Campbell. Every spare waking minute was spent on the river and its banks. The boys taught themselves to swim there, swinging out into the water on ropes, paddling canoes bent into shape from a single sheet of corrugated iron. They planned and executed occasional raids on the cultivation blocks, with egg tomatoes and watermelons from Knott's Crossing or Nixon's Farm a favourite target.

The pockets of their shorts bulged with ammunition for the shanghais in their waistbands. Once, on a rare return to Katherine, Cecil was caught in the peanut shed of Zimin's peanut farm by the scoutmaster and was relieved of his commission as a patrol leader.

No-one wore shirts or shoes, except to school and the major events of the week, the pictures on Friday night and church (at least for the Mahers) on Sunday. When they were needed, plastic sandals were sufficient footwear. Later, when they became conscious of girls, the boys would borrow shoes and long trousers in order to 'look the part'. Patrick recalls that Jack Neill ran the pictures in an open-air theatre, with a separate entrance on the side 'for the natives', while the 'toffs were under cover on their deck-chairs.'

The Redex car rally in 1953, featuring the famous Gelignite Jack Murray, was a major diversion on its way through to Broome and an early memory for Patrick:

> We watched the cars and were excited to think that they were going back to Broome, to the place we came from. Everyone told stories about Gelignite Jack blowing up obstacles in his path and blowing up dunnies. I wanted to go with him.

The Dodson and Maher lads did not have the riverbanks to themselves. Cattle waiting at the trucking yards near the railhead would be put out for water and feed in the early morning, before being returned at sunset. The boys would sometimes wag school, tailing the cattle and riding the stock horses bareback, more often than not, falling off in the process. They worshipped the Aboriginal stockmen as travelling heroes, admiring their skills and envying their elastic-sided boots, Tom Mix hats and rakish scarves. Some of the white stockmen were also friendly to the boys. Patrick stills admires the memory of Billy Doyle, 'a mystery man, a very decent man, a bloke with a big ten-gallon hat. He was always really nice to us.'

Patrick remembers a time with Cecil, when they were given the task of putting the horses in the racecourse enclosure. He may have been ten or eleven at the time. The brothers shared a horse, with Cecil in the saddle carrying the bridle to save a double trip. Between the two boys, a joke got up and kept going. Their laughter couldn't be contained and they slipped off the horse, which bolted away. A job that should have taken half-an-hour stretched to three hours as they trudged home in the dark.

Once in a while they would be given fresh or salt beef for 'hanging around all day and helping to tail the cattle', or the stockmen would use the boys as a blind, covering for them while the men made their way back into town and the pub. The boys would proudly take the beef home to their

Mum, working at the house described in a Land Department inspection in 1959, as a rough dwelling:

> Built of bush timber and covered with second hand galvanised corrugated iron. Concrete floor through main part of building. Not lined or ceiled. Shutter type windows. Attached to back is verandah with dirt floor. A garage with corrugated galvanised roof of 200 square foot. Good fence. 2 acres cleared and 1/2 acre cultivated but has deteriorated. Leasee's family resides on property while he is working at Rosewood.[9]

Maude Ellis, mother of the Maher boys, lived next door and was a mate of Patricia's.[10] She remembers the Dodson's tin house with a rammed antbed floor through most of it. A 'Flaming Fury' toilet[11] was out the back with cut-up newspapers on a wire. The Mahers had saved enough for a kerosene fridge but Patricia had persuaded Snowy to hook into the power line, paying scant attention to safety regulations. Patricia and Maude shared the tasks of the day while their kids went off to town or the river, only coming back for a feed or to scrounge soft-drink bottles to exchange for cinema tickets. The women washed clothes in a 44 gallon drum cut in half longways, and used a copper over a wood fire to get things extra clean; hanging the clothes out on the fences or bushes; ironing some with a petrol iron. They cooked in camp ovens, having 'rice with everything' in Broome style. They were 'all struggling' and shared sugar and flour, with Patricia's johnny cakes and syrup being a favourite quick feast. Sharing the work, the women shared jokes and yarns. 'Oh she was a great one for a story,' Maude recalled, smiling.

At night Patricia would tell stories to the kids, lying on tarps at the back of the house watching the stars. It was here that Patrick started to learn about Broome, 'as a place where mysteries came from.' Here he was told about his grandfather and his powers as a '*maban*', able to heal the ill with bush medicine and tell the future for the gamblers, giving out lottery numbers while cycling around Broome reading electricity meters. Sometimes relatives would visit from the west or visitors would come through town. They would bring pearl meat, which was kept hanging from wires on the roof of the house, ready for a meal, Malay style.[12] The kids would then stay up long into the night, listening to the adults exchange stories and emerging sleepy-headed for school the next morning.

School was not a greatly significant place in Patrick's memory. He 'never minded it' but remembered it more as 'half-time between the fights.' He performed reasonably well over the years, although mathematics was never a strong suit. Neither was homework. Sport, however, quickly became a lifelong passion. The boys between them managed to snare a number of trophies in the school sports days and swimming carnivals in the river. In 1954, the school took a train trip to Batchelor to see the Duke of Edinburgh and hold a sports carnival. Everyone wore green and gold in an early burst of Olympic fever. On another occasion, the Governor-General, Viscount de Lisle visited, with Paul Hasluck, the Minister for the Interior. The children were lined up on the platform to wave small Union Jacks, collected after the train pulled out again.

Snowy was a strong figure in the family, although his work took him away to stations in the west for most of the Dry. In the Wet season, the Blitz would return and Snowy would work on the house or fossick for steel, chains, wire and gravel at the old army dumps. Mick remembers him taking out the Blitz engine every season and replacing it with his spare, then grinding all the valves, reseating the head, reconditioning the engine for next season. For Patrick, his strongest memories of his father centre on work. Snowy kept his hands busy; never sitting down and telling stories, always working and always systematically. The messages were direct: 'walk the corners; finish the job, don't half do it.' All the boys had jobs: raking the yard, smashing antbed for the floor, helping pull fence posts and cutting wood. Slowing down or idle talk would get a 'ninni', a clip over the ear. They lined up to get haircuts with Snowy's hand shears that always pulled at their hair. The choice of styles was limited: basin cut or basin cut.

Snowy built a metre-high mesh fence topped with barbed wire inside the house as his office. Inside 'the cage', he kept his prized tools, his old bakelite wireless set and a marine-grey wooden trunk that held his secrets from inquisitive eyes. Kids were banned from the cage. The only exception was when the boys were fighting. They were put into the cage to fight with gloves. Jacko, who was always in strife, and Mick, who was Snowy's favourite, once had to solve a disagreement in the cage. Snowy coached Mick to always keep his guard up, never give an inch and to go for the first hit. Mick took the lessons to heart.

At night in the Wet season, as torrents of water dropped down outside, Snowy liked to sit in the cage, drink Bundaberg rum, read papers and listen to the radio. Paul Robeson was a special favourite, making the family speculate that Snowy had left-wing affiliations. He wrote many letters, to correspondents unknown, all kept in the wooden trunk. He was cooped up but safe; back in his Fremantle cell, perhaps detaching himself from the reality of his everyday life.

Fay had to present herself, a teenage girl, for inspection before leaving for the pictures. Makeup was banned, with Snowy saying, 'Coloured girls don't put all this shit on their face. If you want to paint yourself—paint yourself properly.' Her mother never went inside the cage, leaving Snowy to drink by himself and sticking to the tea. Fay recalls her refusing her husband's invitation saying, 'The day I start to drink, Snowballs, I'll drink till I die.'

Patrick, growing up, learned how to behave in the social structures of the small town. At the top were the 'big people' and the Dodsons had nothing do with those who would be on the town council, or the local doctor or justice of the peace. The 'big people' were level in status with the station owners and managers. He would see these red-faced, wiry men rolling bow-legged into town with a chequebook at the ready, buying supplies or labour; picking up and dropping off stockmen at the railhead. Teachers, shopkeepers and 'bank johnnies' were more human and approachable, but only with deference.

Snowy was never a boss; preferring to work alone and move around. Snowy's mates were men who worked hard and played hard: butchers, mechanics and drovers who made the pubs of Katherine their domain. They were often bosses for the black stockmen and labourers, including those men who drifted in and out of town in response to labour market demand or:

> Were busted flat in some way. They'd just come in from wherever they were and blow their dough and end up camping at home. They'd wait to get a lift back out or until the wet finished.

At times Snowy's temper, or the level of the rum bottle, would get the better of him. He never backed away from a fight and gained a lasting reputation in the Territory as a 'stoush merchant'. Some of these men became life-long enemies. It was a place of tough men, who, Patrick remembered:

> Drifted in and circled around each other like bulls in the paddock. Sometimes they'd drink with each other and sometimes they'd fight with each other.

One Queensland ringer, Jack Scanlon from the Dajarra side of the border, shot a policeman in the main street of Katherine near the picture theatre. For years after, the boys would poke their fingers through the posters for new movies, into the bullet holes, 'where the copper got shot.' Other tough men, like Wasson Byers, would strike terror into the town by their very presence, and cause Fay a shudder decades later, remembering him from when she and her mother were carted across the Kimberley to Moola Bulla. Patrick recalls a 'kind of electricity that went through the town when he arrived.' Geoff Allen described him at the Brunette Downs race meeting around 1950:

Wason Byers was at the races that year. He was a hard man. A solid six foot three in height, he had seldom been beaten in fights around the back of Queensland and the territory. Wason was a man known to be hard on blacks. His blacks hated and feared him but were too frightened to leave. Too often they had seen what happened to other runaways. Wason followed, brought them back in chains and flogged them with his whip. Sometimes the flogging went on for days.[13]

Jack Johnson recalls Byers at Flora Valley, 'making the women take all their clothes off and sit up on top of the roof, on that sheet iron. It was 40 degrees temperature and he made them sit there all day, and he was chucking rocks at them to make them move around.'[14] Men like Byers thrived in the system of power enforced by violence that characterised station life until the 1960s in the Territory. After the War, the winds of change started to blow, but men like Byers did not bend.

The Dodson boys soon found their own mischief. Wagging school when one of their mates had a slug gun to play with, Patrick and the boys saw a white man camped by the river. Full of cheek, they scared the man with an aimless shot from the slug gun and ran away, giggling and scared. The man rolled his swag and told the police who hunted the boys along the riverbanks until dark. They caught them and took them down to the old police station cells, accusing them of every local crime and prank that had been committed in the previous year. It was these boys, the police said, who had stolen wine from the Anglican church, smashed a statue in the grounds of the Catholic Church, stolen the taxi-driver's money box. They were sent home without a feed, well after the pictures had finished but ordered to return the next morning. The policeman locked them in the cells, parading in front with a stock-whip, demanding a confession. Patrick remembered:

> The policeman showed us the iron ring in the floor to which we would be chained if we did not confess. He said we would be sent to Adelaide by train and locked up for good. My mate, Graham Campbell answered him back, 'If you put us on the train, we'll jump off and kill ourselves. Let us go!'

Eventually, they were released but the police kept a watchful eye on them.

Outside the town boundaries, in ramshackle flimsy camps, put together with corrugated iron, petrol tins and scraps of cloth, lived the town's traditional owners, the Jawoyn, Dagoman and Wardaman.[15] Francesca Merlan describes the situation:

> After the war and the departure of the military, efforts at close control were resumed and even heightened by the modernization

and professionalisation of the Native Affairs Branch. Natives were to be in Katherine town and the surrounding rural area as properly managed labour. Only able-bodied adults were in theory, allowed around the town, housed, fed and paid a small wage by their employers. Children and the unemployable were to be kept out of town, on settlements or pastoral properties.[16]

Further out of town in the west and the north, Aboriginal people from the stations, especially Gurindji, Mudburra and Warlpiri, came in and stayed for the sly grog, food and family demands. In all, some one hundred Aboriginal people were counted in a 1952 census, living in thirty different locations in and around the town.[17] Many came to see relatives in the Aboriginal hospital, as Patrick recalls:

> I remember the blackfella hospital and that our mob weren't allowed in the main hospital. It seemed to be so controlled. Movement was largely organised by police, native welfare and station bosses. Only rarely would people get lifts with individual white truck drivers and blackfellas didn't have cars.

One Wardaman man cut grass for the Council and was the proud owner of a wristwatch, the hands permanently stopped. The boys laughed when they asked the time and he would answer, 'Half past two'. However, life was regimented and the police were all too ready to swoop on those Aboriginal people who were in town after the curfew, with Sergeant Mannion arresting twenty-two Aboriginal people one evening in 1953, 'for being within the prohibited area of Katherine', and hauling them away in a truck.[18]

Old Spud

Patrick and his mates learned respect for the owners of the country in which they found themselves. Once the boys came across a bush burial place, stunning them into a hushed and nervous silence. He recalled one tall, old Aboriginal man, by the name of 'Old Spud' or 'Potato' who worked in the yards of the white people in town. On his way back to his camp, carrying two drums of water on a pole across his shoulders as he limped along, he would look in on the family when Snowy was away; making sure everything was all right, looking after them. When Patrick asked him, 'Who's your *maluka* (boss)?' He answered, 'I got no *maluka*, I'm free.' Patrick did not know that the old man was Galambud (or Kulumput), a respected authority figure in Aboriginal law, consulted widely for decisions and the source of early anthropological insights into the cultural heritage of Aboriginal people in the region.[19]

Galambud was an informant for Walter Arndt, the German Queensland agronomist who managed the CSIRO agricultural research station on the south side of Katherine from 1947 until 1959. Arndt took an active interest in the traditions of the Aboriginal workers on the research station. Arndt's notes make mention of the fact that 'Spud', although celibate, was gifted with children, and frequently looked after Arndt's family during his absences. The hand-written notes record that Galambud worked across the cattle country, being born at Pigeon Hole, Joe Fagan's old outstation on Victoria River Downs. He lived in the bush with his family before his father went to work for Jim Ronan at VRD during Joe's time as head stockman. He then worked across the west and in the Kimberley, droving the long road with men like the Muggletons, who established the Bungle Bungle range station, and Jim Campbell, who designed the famous '_88' brand to cover all the existing stock brands in the Top End. He worked on a survey team and as a teamster on the wagon road out to the stations. This gave him the freedom of travel and the chance to cross over into the west, managing Aboriginal law-business in ceremonies across the Top End. His travelling days were cut short when he was in an accident while riding in a truck with a drunken white man. His knee was smashed and he was left to cure himself with 'bush medicine'. As Arndt noted, 'He was obviously intelligent and very concerned about the laws of his people. He realised that the old traditions which he was duty bound to preserve were no longer of interest to his people and lamented the fact that the laws would be lost.' The young boy was interested, however.[20]

Patrick remembers 'Spud' with a catch in his voice, recalling a boyhood brush with the traditions his grandfather carried in distant Broome. He remembers one time when the old man dug deep into the pockets of his shorts (he never wore shirts, trousers or shoes). He unwrapped a small cloth bundle to show the young Patrick a smooth, round moonstone, the colour of an egg yolk. 'This came from the Dreaming,' he told the wide-eyed boy.

> When I got to be a bigger boy riding a horse around Manbullo station, I found old Spud lying naked on the ground near a small fire. He was returning to his beginnings and his special place in his country.

The vision of his calm acceptance, the smile in his eyes in the face of death, stayed with the young lad. Arndt's notes record that Galambud died after being 'bushed' from the CSIRO station, 'from senility precipitated by acute malnutrition.'

Granny Liz

On her return to Broome, Granny Liz again applied, for citizenship, filing a statutory declaration that 'for two years prior to the date hereof I have dissolved tribal and native associations except with respect to lineal descendents or native relations of the first degree.' Her occupation was laundry work, which earned her about £1-2-0 per week. McKenzie of the Roads Board, and McDaniel, the pearler, friends of Paddy, supported her application with McKenzie noting that her intention to do laundry work, 'would be greatly appreciated by many'.[21]

Consideration of the application was initially supported by the Department in Perth. They noted that she still had over £600 in her trust account, and that the title deeds to Lot 117 in Mary Street, purchased in 1931 were held in the Departmental safe. If she was successful, the deeds would be handed over.

However, in November, the indefatigable O'Neill in Broome disagreed with the Department line:

> She is quite a good worker but is addicted to liquor if she can obtain it. Her normal associates are half-castes and Asiatics. Elizabeth owns a small house on the outskirts of Broome which is usually clean and reasonably well kept but is little more than a shack. I personally do not think the granting of citizenship rights would be to her benefit, as I cannot see what advantages she would receive. At present her money is cared for by this Department, and I feel quite certain that if that control was removed she would soon squander it.

Her application was rejected on the grounds that she had not dissolved native associations; had not adopted the manner and habits of civilised life; and was not reasonably capable of managing her own affairs. The fact that her standard of housing counted against her was ironic. The files show that Elizabeth spent years engaged in battles with the authorities trying to seek access to her funds in order to buy timber and recruit labour for her house repairs after the wartime evacuation to Beagle Bay. It was the Department that continually obfuscated her efforts to repair the 'shack' on Mary Street.

In 1952 Elizabeth again applied for citizenship. This time she was somehow successful, receiving a Certificate of Exemption, number A780. The intrusive Mr O'Neill made no comment this time. The Department handed over the deeds to the house, and, presumably, the £600 or so remaining from the Joe Fagan bequest. It had taken her thirty-five years to receive her entitlement.

Around this time, the six-year-old Cecil was in strife for 'ransacking and removing property and it is considered that this behaviour is a direct result of his environment.' Stanley Djiagween recalled that he was in trouble for stealing a watch with some other boys.

The District Welfare Officer, noting that his teacher considered Cecil to be a 'lovable and obedient child', though he needed, 'strict supervision as far removed from his grandmother as possible.' Being a '3/8 caste child, with a pre-ponderance of white blood,' Beagle Bay was ruled out. In August 1953, the Court declared him to be a neglected child and committed him to the care of the Child Welfare Department until 18 years of age, and removed to an institution as soon as possible. The Police, representing the Child Welfare Department, took him from his grandmother and placed him with Elizabeth Hunter, 'until the Child Welfare Department finds a suitable institution for him.'[22]

When the news reached Katherine, Patricia rushed back to Broome and somehow persuaded the Magistrate and the Child Welfare Department to allow Cecil to be released in her care. The threat was eliminated, for the moment.

When they moved from Western Australia to the Northern Territory, the Dodsons were determined to put the controlling forces of the Western Australian government behind them. Officially married, with highly employable skills and based in a town, there was less likelihood of their children being taken at whim. The risk, however, was still there.

The Dodson family shared knowledge of child removal and compared concerns with other parents of 'half-castes'. Snowy read the papers and listened to the radio, but most information came from word of mouth. Who were the Police and Welfare taking away now? Where were they taken? Where had your countrymen and family been sent? Were your children safe?

It happened on all the stations where Snowy worked; the progeny of the mobile and casual white workforce were swept away, as young as infants, as old as teenagers. The Patrol Officers, who complained bitterly at the task, hated the job. The Government Secretary advised that it would attract 'criticism for violation of the present day conception of "human rights" and would "outrage the feelings of the average observer".'[23] However, the removals continued.

The station run

The stations west of Katherine across to and beyond the Western Australian border were on Snowy's run. While the family was in Katherine, he worked at Limbunya, Rosewood, Inverway, Victoria River Downs and more often than not, the Wave Hill station. He would work at any job needing tools: fixing windmills, repairing generators, building yards, renovating motors. When the work was finished, or perhaps when the drinking and fighting made life in a closed social world difficult, Snowy would roll his swag, pack his tools and move on, towing a caravan behind the Blitz.

Sometimes, Mick would come along during the school holidays, sitting up front with his Dad, his neck straining to see over the dashboard. Patrick remembers once travelling with his Dad up a steep hill, following another truck labouring up the slope. Snowy reached for a large spanner, wedged it onto his accelerator, and told Patrick to steer the truck. Snowy jumped out of the cabin and ran past his truck to reach over into the tray of the truck in front and lift out a carton of beer. Grinning wildly, he threw the beer into his truck, jumped back in the cabin and started driving again, waving cheerily to the unknowing truck driver as he passed.

Also doing the same run were the officers of the Native Affairs Branch, or Welfare, as it was to become known. Patrol Officer Evans travelled around the stations of the Victoria River and the Kimberleys in 1951. He visited Wave Hill where Snowy often worked. Evans was the sole representative in the huge region of that sector of the Commonwealth government concerned with Aboriginal welfare. Against his personal reform agenda was the weight of a history of paternalism and control. Evans was optimistic of a change in labour relations on the stations, as most stations had introduced some cash payments, although at a lower rate than whites:

> The idea of 'ownership' is slowly dying and the principle that the native is a free agent and is at liberty to bargain his labour is gaining appreciation slowly.24

Change was slow. At Vestey's Wave Hill station Evans costed a fit-out (shirt, trousers, boots, blankets, swag, mosquito net, hat) at over £13. He commented that it would take three months work simply to pay back the credit owed the company store for the fit-out, saying, 'I doubt if some newly engaged boys would ever get in front on the present rate of pay.'

Freedom in the labour market was constrained by the cultural need to stay with and look after kin and country. For the Gurindji and Mudburra, the Wave Hill station was on their ancestral lands. Being able to stay on country enabled them to maintain their laws and traditions. Labour freedom and a measure of cultural space did not extend to personal freedoms. As well as identifying six children to be removed from their families in the camps at Wave Hill, Evans offered the suggestion that:

> Surnames be given to full-bloods to facilitate identity and eliminate much of the confusion existing with the use of an Aboriginal name, which could still be used as a middle name. The surname could be left to the discretion of the visiting patrol officer.

When Snowy worked on Wave Hill, the system was much the same as it was described a few years earlier by Ron and Catherine Berndt. These pioneers in applied anthropology saw Aboriginal 'stockboys' treated as serfs in a distinctly Australian form of the feudal system. They reported that women were available for casual sexual exploitation and domestic labour; children were 'broken in' on stock camps as young as ten years, families fed on scraps of gristle, dry bread and weevil-ridden flour. Babies were dying in infancy; old men and women were in abject misery:

> They lived in the camp, collecting the meagre rations allotted to them, too old to make use of the leisure at last available to them in collecting bush foods, until death in some form overtook them. They had nothing tangible to pass on to their children, who in turn looked forward only to a repetition of their parents' lives, accompanied by no personal economic security.[25]

The Berndt report was not written by publicity-seeking moralists—it was commissioned by the company, but suppressed by them and not published for forty years. It was the results of the research, not the rhetoric, which compelled attention and redress. Patrol Officers like Evans in the bush, and the critics in the cities, had their work cut out for them. They were pushed along by a strike of more than two hundred Aboriginal people in Darwin in 1951, demanding that the Aboriginal pastoral wage be doubled and calling for 'equal rights'. A Katherine man, Jack McGinness, was a railway worker and sportsman who cut an imposing figure in the small town. He and his brother formed the Half-Caste Progressive Association, campaigning for reform in Darwin and the south. They worked with the North Australian Workers' Union and organised strikes at the Bagot and Berrimah Reserve; pushing their case at the All-Australian Trade Union Congress in 1951. They sought equal treatment and a fair deal.[26]

Aboriginal people in the region had experienced a new labour system in Army Aboriginal settlements in places like Manbullo, at Pine Creek near Katherine. Here, Aboriginal people were paid for their work in cash at a standard rate, had discretion over the use of the money, and importantly, worked in a system not structured on race. The Army may have been authoritarian, but everyone had the same rules. This was a remarkable experience for Aboriginal people in the Northern Territory.[27] The end of the war marked a new phase in Aboriginal relationships with other Australians. On the stations west of Katherine the new phase would take longer to have effect.

Northern Territory policies

The policy framework of the Northern Territory did not spring newborn from a policy think-tank. Much of it came from the ideas and mind-sets of key figures in the administration, working with each other to achieve their common objectives. In much the same way as Neville's shadow had reached across the lives of Aboriginal families in Western Australia, Dr Cecil Cook's attitudes and views largely determined the life choices made by Territory Aboriginal people, especially those of mixed descent, like the Dodson family. Cook and Neville were not ideologically opposed. Cook, the Chief Protector and Chief Medical Officer from 1927 to 1939 argued as did Neville, for the absorption of people of mixed descent, to meet the perceived danger that such people might become a numerically preponderant 'under-class,' in conflict with the white population of the north.[28]

Robert Manne sees Dr Cook as 'a thoroughgoing eugenicist,' characterising his view that:

> If, as seemed to be the case, forced sterilisations or legalised abortions would never be countenanced in Australia, the most positive policy was to encourage actively the marriage of part-Aboriginal women and white males.[29]

To this end, the good doctor played marriage broker for some sixty sanctioned marriages between inmates of the Darwin home for 'half-castes' and European men. He also worked to thoroughly ensure that mixed-descent children were removed from station camps, often with siblings being separated and allocated to different institutions, based on the shading of their skin.

The police from Halls Creek in Western Australia around 1931 removed Myrtle Campbell, or old Aunty Myrtle as Patrick called her, at five years of age. Her father was Fred Martin, a stockman, who was away droving when the police took her. Patrick and the boys knew him well. In later years, they would often tail cattle with him on the north side of the low-level crossing, racing horses in the evening after the cattle settled down. Myrtle was removed with her three sisters (Maude, Maggie and Mary) to Katherine, and then placed on the train to the Half-Caste Home in Darwin. They sat in the Home and plotted escape and re-unification:

> We used to sit around and plan our escape back to Wave Hill … because that's where our grandmother was and we knew if we went back to Halls Creek they'd find us … We used to try to run away, but there was just bush everywhere and we didn't know our way out anyway, so we just cried all the time to go back to our country.[30]

Nevertheless, even administrators with total power over their wards had masters. For the Dodson family, the unlikely saviour from the policies of Cook was the short-reigning Minister of the Interior, 'Black Jack' McEwan. In 1937, he visited the Territory and was shocked by what he found at the Bungalow Home in Alice Springs and the Half-Caste Home in Darwin:

> I know many stock breeders who would not dream of crowding their stock in the way that these half-caste children are huddled.[31]

In 1939, McEwan announced a 'New Deal', shifting the emphasis away from biological absorption towards social assimilation; from controlling genetics and sexuality to controlling employment, education and social mobility. Dr Cook, shifted out of the policy driving seat, resigned. War intervened in the policy tussle and McEwan was promoted to the Defence portfolio. The New Deal was a forgotten document by the end of the War.

In 1951, Paul Hasluck became Minister for Territories in the Menzies Government and would hold the portfolio for twelve years. He took a strong personal interest in the Aboriginal aspects of his portfolio, drawing on his observations in Western Australia, particularly as a journalist during the Moseley Royal Commission. He explained his approach thirty years later:

> From the start I had urged that we should replace the idea of protecting the aborigines with the idea of advancing their welfare. Protection was a negative policy which showed neither faith nor hope in their future.[32]

Hasluck extended the McEwan 'New Deal' agenda, breaking step with the march of biological absorption sponsored by Neville and Cook. In keeping with the Menzies' vision of centralised liberalism and a strong emphasis on individualism, he proposed Commonwealth leadership of a joint national program aimed at a 'fair go' for Aboriginal people. Central to this program was the objective of assimilation, and his vision of the ultimate homogeneity of Aboriginal with non-Aboriginal Australians. Hasluck reiterated its core meaning in 1988, in language where the implications of choice and decision-making were notably absent:

> The policy of assimilation means that all Aborigines and part-Aborigines will attain the same manner of living as other Australians and live as members of a single Australian community enjoying the same rights and privileges, accepting the same responsibilities, observing the same customs

and influenced by the same beliefs, hopes and loyalties as other Australians. Any special measures taken for Aborigines and part-Aborigines are regarded as temporary measures, not based on race, but intended to meet their need for special care and assistance to protect them from any ill effects of sudden change and to assist them to make the transition from one stage to another in such a way as will be favourable to their social, economic and political advancement.[33]

As Minister for Territories from 1951, Hasluck was responsible for overseeing the native affairs branch of the Northern Territory administration, with Harry Giese being the Territory's Welfare boss.[34] The new legislation that Hasluck introduced (*Northern Territory Welfare Act 1953*) and Giese administered was intended to shift the labels from race to need, and to cease the use of racial types, like 'half-castes', although the language remained persistent. He emphasised the immediate needs of Aboriginal people in the areas of health, housing, schooling and nutrition.

At the heart of Hasluck's thinking was an emphasis on the Aboriginal person as an individual member of Australian society rather than as a member of an Aboriginal cultural group. Kinship links and community identification would dissolve as individuals were assisted to change their social and economic circumstances. He predicted, 'I feel reasonably sure that, more and more, we will have to think in our native welfare administration of individual persons of aboriginal descent. The behaviour of the individual, response of the individual, the aspiration or the effort at the individual, the heart and mind of the individual are at the core of our problem.'[35]

As Patrick grew up, however, it was the threat of being 'taken away by the welfare' that was used as the ultimate sanction:

> While we were often in strife, it wasn't getting into trouble at the school that was the worry. Teachers were a sort of buffer. The threat was that the welfare would intervene and take us away. Whatever that meant. It was a fear that we chose to challenge I suppose. It was not as immediate as being given a hiding. What was actually meant by being taken away was something we couldn't contemplate. Granny used to always say, don't mark trees or the welfare'll hunt you down, they'll take you away. She used to think they'll shoot you. They'll get your names and shoot you. Poor old Gran. But being taken away was very much the power that the white bureaucrats had. The men in white socks and short trousers. No grease on themselves. No dirt.

Granny Liz's warnings were not the idle threats of an old lady, invoking a 'bogeyman' that never appeared. Patrick remembered:

> I mean, as a kid I remember being dragged by another young girl who came running through our yard, grabbed hold of my hand, dragged me out and said, 'Run.' We ran and we hid in the long grass and watched the welfare and the police chase two other kids through the bushes and around the flat until they caught them. These kids were screaming and yelling and they bundled them into the back of a truck and sent them off to Croker Island. We were terrified that this was what was going to happen to us. So thankfully it didn't but the trauma of the lives of those people that have gone through these things is not a matter for litigation. It's a matter for courageous leadership and for a responsibility to err on the side of generosity in relation to these things.[36]

Things started to change

Patrick remembers that when he turned seven or eight, 'things at home started to change.' To this day, none of the children are really sure what happened. It seems that Snowy and Patricia started to drift apart, with Snowy spending more time in the bush. Out there, he had an ongoing relationship, and other children, with an Aboriginal woman from Wyndham.[37] He only visited Katherine for brief periods, often spending his money and time drinking, fighting and recovering. Patricia and Snowy officially separated in 1955. Patrick recalls that his father was not often on the scene in those years:

> There was the notion of him not being around, even though when he was around he was a pretty quiet sort of a bloke and never spoke much. Usually it was in association with his working mates that he was there. But he would always take us on picnics. Not only us, but collect up everyone else in the place who didn't have motor cars, go somewhere up to Katherine Gorge or down the lower level or places around Katherine or out bush.

Back in Katherine, Patricia now started to 'drink a bit', always being home to make dinner for the kids, however. She 'would pick up strays'; visitors to town with nowhere to stay. One of them was the young Max Stuart, an Arrente man, now Chairman of the Central Land Council, who remembers Patricia, her caring nature and home-cooking with warm regard, saying, 'she was a wonderful person, giving a home to people on the road.'[38] Patrick remembers that he always called his Mum 'Mrs Dodson.'

Max was travelling with a circus, Norman Keasman's 'Fun Land Carnival', part of the sideshow attached to the Snowy River Stampede, showing off trick-riding. Patrick hitched a ride to Darwin with Max. He helped him on the knock-'em-downs and the clowns, until Max gave him the job of running the hurdy-gurdy, a merry-go-round ride, 'for a few bob'. Patrick has three major legacies of that time: a scar on the forehead from running through a barbed wire fence; an ongoing relationship with Max Stuart; and a useful line in showground patter. Decades later, Patrick would frequently borrow a line of Max Stuart's, drawn from the carnival, 'Put sixpence in your hand, pat you on the head and watch your eyes roll.' It was a useful phrase for him to describe the ways in which ministers and officials would tend to deal with Aboriginal leaders.

When the circus moved on from Darwin, Patrick returned to Katherine. The circus reached Ceduna at the end of that year and Max was arrested and tried for the supposed rape and murder of a little girl. The family in Katherine was 'shocked to hear what it was he was supposed to have done.' The Stuart case would go on to become the subject of extensive news coverage, a Royal Commission and High Court appeal with Max being sentenced and serving more than fifteen years at Yatala Prison.[39]

Patrick would always call him 'Uncle Max' and remained convinced of his innocence. The family followed the saga of conviction, appeal, death sentence and reprieve with concern. The issue gave Patrick his first taste of understanding that the criminal justice system seemed weighted against Aboriginal cultural issues and language. Against that was a running concern that he may just have committed the crime. Family loyalty ruled out that possibility.

In 1985, when Patrick was Director of the Central Land Council, he gave Max a job as a field officer at the Council, which 'gave Stuart occupation, income and respect', according to Ken Inglis who also commented that, 'Pat Dodson contributed to Stuart's destiny no less significantly than that other Sacred Heart priest Tom Dixon.'[40] Max would later become Chairman of the same Land Council.

Shortly after the Dodson marriage break-up, Patricia moved into a new, ongoing relationship with a man named Mark Humphries, who had come up as a rider with the Snowy River Stampede and stayed to work on the railways. The kids moved with them down to Mataranka for a time, living in the fettlers' camp, while Patricia baked and sold bread to the tourists who were visiting the tropical springs. After a time the family moved with the Mahers to the fettlers' camp on the railway bridge at Ferguson River, south of Pine Creek, living under canvas and eating out of camp ovens for three months. Maude Ellis recalls that the kids took a lot of feeding and they 'got through a few bars of bread.' Kids would come and go on the train at weekends and holidays, the Dodson boys usually staying during school time with Fay in Katherine.

> One night, Mark and Pop Ellis went up to Pine Creek on the quad, coming back after a few too many beers, looking for a feed. Mum said, 'In the camp oven.' I remember him coming back inside the tent and saying, 'that was a beautiful feed, lovely soup.' And Mum said, 'that's just soapy water and the dregs of the feed, you dopey bastard'. She had been soaking the camp oven.

The river flooded the town in March 1957. Patrick remembers digging his toes into the ground to feel the water bubbling up from the saturated ground. The flood didn't worry Snowy. Patrick saw his father when Snowy parked the Blitz at the house in Fourth Street, sat up top with a few mates and drank rum, dipping his pannikin in the rushing waters for a chaser. He told Patrick to get out and go up to the old airport on high ground where they watched people on makeshift rafts floating down the back, navigating the treacherous flow. For days the town was locked up, with people unable to get in or out. After a few days, when the floods receded, the family came back to their house to see the wood stove floating around with the contents of the 'Flaming Fury'. Centipedes were everywhere. The rush of water took doors, windows, furniture and all Patricia's personal effects with it.

One day, Patrick was at home playing in the dirt around the front of the house, when the police turned up to arrest his mother.

> Mum walked in, looking very serious, came in and grabbed a few clothes or toiletries. The copper stood at the gate, we were all watching him. Mum just said, 'I've gotta go with police. You kids be good and Georgina'll look after youse. And she said to Pixie Scanlon,[41] 'Pixie, just look after the kids until Georgina gets here.' I didn't know where Fay was, whether she was in Katherine or where she was. The coppers bundled Mum into the back of the Toyota, with the cage on it. They bunged her into the back of it. Then they were gone, just dust, and we were wondering what the hell was happening. We were trying to ask Pixie and she was no better informed. She just knew she'd been arrested and we had to work out what we were going to do. That night Fay came back and we found out Mum had been shipped up to Fannie Bay. From that point we never saw her for ages. Seemed like ages anyway.

It seems that Patricia had been arrested in town, apparently for 'disgracing the Queen's Uniform.' She had walked into Mrs Peterson's cafe. As all seats were taken, she had to go right around the counter. Two men were there, staring her up and down. She grabbed one by the shirt, twisted it and said,

'What's the matter? Do I owe you sixpence, mate?' The policemen asked the men if she was drunk.

Apparently, the shirt belonged to the Queen, and inside the shirt was a policeman. She was sentenced to some six months in Fannie Bay. Fay had to look after the kids, desperately worried that they might be scooped up by the welfare net.[42]

As part of a formal settlement of the now dissolved marriage, Snowy purchased another agricultural lease (No 523) on the other side of the river from the old block on Fourth and Lindsay, now primarily used by Fay Wade and her new family. Snowy was on the move out west. He wrote in May 1958 to the Lands Department from Limbunya station (crossing out Inverway station as his address) after an inspection revealed that the lease conditions were not being met:

> Having separated from my wife in 1955, I bought this block for her to live on so as to have access to my children. Her de-facto husband undertook to fence it and extend the dwelling. I haven't seen the place in fifteen months. If the block is still unfenced when I return to Katherine at the end of the year, I will attend to it myself. As for agriculture, the most that can be expected is a kitchen garden. There are thousands of acres of cleared ground on the banks of the Katherine producing nothing because crops are uneconomical. With only two exceptions all the Katherine farmers have to take outside jobs to live.[43]

He wrote again from Birrundudu station in November 1959:

> I wish to advise that my wife, from whom I have been separated, has been living on this block since I acquired it—and I have since arranged for it to be legally transferred to her. When I was in Katherine last year I supplied building material and fence posts and wire, also necessary tools, for the fellow with whom she is living, to comply with the regulations … I would hate to see the block forfeited, as it would leave my children homeless, for whom I acquired it in the first place.

Snowy never got around to changing the lease over to Patricia's name.

Wave Hill, 1960

In early 1960, the ten-year-old Mick was out with his Dad for the school holidays. He had flown out on the mail plane to Birrundudu, and drove with Snowy in the Blitz, towing the caravan to Wave Hill station. Snowy's cheque for his work at Birrindudu was in his wallet and he was heading back to Katherine to take the ten-year-old back to his Mum and the school. They were held up by the flooded Victoria River, swollen after the heaviest March rains in sixty-two years.[44]

The layout of Wave Hill had not changed much since the Berndts saw it in 1944:

> The Old Station, about nine miles from the Wave Hill homestead … consisted of a couple of buildings beside the Victoria River. One was a public store owned and operated by an Afghan; the other a police station, the headquarters of the Wave Hill district police. A small group of Aborigines was camped here, mostly old people who received rations from the police station, along with several people employed there and at the store.[45]

Mick remembers, with some pain, an air of tension in the camp that his father set up near the river. Snowy had found out that an old adversary, one Charlie Swan, had camped nearby:

> He always made Dad edgy. I don't know why. After setting up camp and having a feed, he found out who was there. Dad said, 'Fuck you,' to him, and off he went.

On the morning of 24 March, after a few days in the camp, Mick found his father lying on the ground with a gunshot wound to his head. He ran, scared with heart pounding, to the police station nearby, seeking help. The Wave Hill Police Journal kept by Constable Coutts tells the police version of the story:

> 23 March: approx 7.45 PM to Drover's camp, then to Snowy Dodson's camp. Dodson behaviour seemed strange—I asked him if he wanted any stores bought over from Station—He said, 'I know I will get bashed and pushed around.' He spoke no more and stepped back into shadows. After returning from station tomorrow will try to ascertain Dodson's trouble. Constable to Swan's camp and talked with Jensen. The latter is an old friend of Dodson's. Jensen stated he didn't think Dodson had been in any trouble. Constable returned 8.15 PM.

> 24 March: Const Coutts departed police station 8.00 AM per horse for the cattle station—when near the jump up heard the police vehicle—travelled across to road and was there informed by Mrs Coutts that Snowy Dodson had shot himself at his camp. Const and Mrs Coutts returned to police station—picked up bandages etc and then to Dodson's camp. There saw Dodson lying on the ground and a large amount of blood around the head, a wound in the right side of the head—he appeared to be in a very low condition—a .22 rifle was lying on the ground nearby, an empty .22 rifle shell was in the breach of the rifle. Mrs Coutts attended Dodson.

> Const set up the portable wireless and contacted Dr Emerson at Kildurk Station—informed the Dr. of the situation and made arrangements to call him again in an hour. Dodson died at 10 AM. Conversation with Dr at 9.50 AM
>
> For all appearances the incident looks to be a definite suicide.[46]

More than three decades later, the family is unconvinced. They read the journal entry on Snowy's behaviour as being contrived after the event, no other entries in the journal showing the same level of behavioural commentary or direct quotation. They are baffled by the role of Charlie Swan and speculate on the root cause of Snowy's anxiety. They wonder what happened to his pay from Birrindudu. What happened to Snowy's trunk of personal papers, his box of secrets? Mainly though, they saw Snowy as someone who always packed and moved on from trouble, not as someone who would take his own life. Too much time has passed for these mysteries to be resolved. All that is left is a reservoir of hurt and grief as Mick said to me:

> I'll never forget it. A ten-year-old boy doesn't find his Dad dead everyday.

Patrick remembers his Mum coming home and telling him they had word that there had been an accident and his father had died:

> But it was as if, I suppose, something had just disappeared. You just didn't know what it was. You knew it was your father but didn't know what exactly was missing. That someone in your life had just disappeared and was not going to come back.[47]

Confusion reigned with the family unsure of what was going on. They did not know whether the young Mick was still at Wave Hill, or had been sent to Darwin. They were worried about the welfare moving in on him. In the end, Patrick thinks that Mick was flown to Darwin on the plane with his father's body. Patricia and Fay went with Ron to Darwin to collect Mick and arrange a hasty funeral service. Patrick did not attend his father's funeral. He stayed back in Katherine.

> I can't remember going to his funeral. I can't. I think it all seemed to happen pretty quickly. Trying to find people, trying to make sure that Mum could get up to Darwin and I think Faye and her husband took her because he had the car. We had no money, of course. There was no money in those days to simply get on trains or hire cars or do anything like that. Most of our relations were in Darwin in terms of my auntie's children, my cousins. So there was a long time to understand why and what had happened. Then later on to find where dad was buried was very close to his old mate, a fellow who we used to call Uncle Curly Pascoe, who was

his partner in crime, in a sense, in those days when he was running from the law and carting things across the Kimberley.[48]

'That Mongrel Bridge'

After Snowy's funeral in Darwin, when the roads had dried out, Fay's husband Ron Wade went out to Wave Hill to pick up the Blitz and the caravan, both unregistered. The twelve-year-old boy, Patrick, went along as a gate-opener, helping Ron to kill a plains turkey with a spanner on the road.

With five kids of her own, Fay had to take on a greater role in looking after the children, both Patricia's and her own. Cecil had gone out droving, Georgina had a child back in Broome but Jacko, Patrick, Mick and Tricia still needed some looking after, and Fay and Ron shared the load with Patricia. The kids would always remember that Fay's idea of discipline was tougher than their mother's, involving maximum force and minimal negotiation. 'Colonel Rockjaw' was the nickname that the family gave her.

It was in late July, some three months after Snowy's death, that Maude Ellis, Fay and Patricia went to the pictures to see 'Peyton Place.' At intermission, she was told that some relatives had come to town and wanted to see her. She went with a countryman, Lenny Edgar, a cousin of Patrick's and a nephew of Patricia, to cross the railway bridge back to the house across the river.

The bridge was narrow, carrying both car and footbridge traffic as well as tracks for the trains. Crossing the bridge was precarious, with large gaps between the sleepers that were difficult to cross in full daylight. Patrick remembers:

> If a car came along you had to sort of climb out on the edge of the sleepers and reach up for the pylons, unless you were next to one of those gaps they had for letting the train pass. You could climb under the sleepers and let the trains and cars roll across the top. In the middle of the bridge was a pipe that we used to slide down as kids into the water. It was a big drop down to the river-bed.

On that evening, the Angus family was moving house. The oncoming car caused Patricia to step to the side, the headlights glaring in her eyes. She reached out for a pylon, missed her footing and slipped. Lenny grabbed at her wrists. His hands were bandaged from an accident working with tar on the roads. He could not hold her. Patricia fell to the riverbank beneath, just missing the water, dying instantly.

The *Northern Territory News* had a small item, headlined '60 foot fall to death':

> A 38 year old woman crashed 60 foot to her death from the high level bridge over Katherine River shortly after midnight on Saturday. The woman was Mrs Pat Dodson, widow of a man who was shot dead at Wave Hill a few months ago. Police were told Mrs Dodson and a male companion were walking over the railway bridge when a car drove onto the other end of the bridge. Mrs Dodson is reported to have tried to step from the railway track to a catwalk at the side of the bridge. But she missed her footing and fell through a narrow gap sixty feet to the river bank.[49]

Patrick found this hard to take:

> I think the way the news came to me was pretty hard. Me and another young fellow who I grew up with, a fellow called Wicky Maher, we'd been babysitting my older sister Fay. We'd been babysitting her children, and one of Georgina's kids, Ronald, I think. They didn't come back after the movies because they got pulled out of the movies. Unbeknownst to me this was all happening because it happened at night. They eventually woke me up, or when I got up. It was early in the morning—I think they let me sleep until the morning. I got up pretty early. In that country you get up about five, six o'clock.
>
> They simply broke it to me that 'You're now an orphan.' I had to think about it a little bit. Then I realised what it meant was that I didn't have a mother as well as not having a father. That was pretty devastating. The sense of aloneness, the sense of wondering where life was going to go was the question. Not so much what's the next steps in this but… What's life going to be about now because I've got no-one to really guide me in that sense, to help me work out whatever the questions in life were going to be? Or someone to go and get advice from and seek guidance and be encouraged and someone to share whatever achievements there are in life. I was devastated.[50]

Children of the state

According to section 14 of the Welfare Ordinance 1953, a person could be declared a ward if by reason of:

(a) his manner of living;
(b) his inability, without assistance, adequately to manage his own affairs;
(c) his standard of social habit and behaviour;
(d) his personal association,

that person stands in need of such special care and assistance as is provided for by the Ordinance.

The Dodson children: Cecil (14), Patrick (12), John (11), Michael (10) and Patricia (8) were now all at risk of being placed in the care of the state and institutionalised. Cecil skipped the net by going droving, following the tracks of Snowy in the stations to the west. Georgina was living her own life, travelling between Darwin, Broome and Katherine with a baby of her own. The family scrambled to find ways to look after the four younger children.

Many discussions took place. Family meetings chopped and changed with decisions about what was best for the kids. With five children of her own, Fay could not manage them all. The day after the funeral in Katherine, Patricia's sister, Mary Roe and her husband Bill drove the kids up to Darwin in Bill Roe's one-ton Chev truck, the kids in the back in a large wooden box. The Roe family was a strong Catholic family and Mary was not well. They were initially persuaded by the priest that the Catholic reserve at Garden Point Mission on Melville Island, home of the Tiwi people, would be most capable of caring for the kids in the crisis. Their future would then be placed in the hands of God and his missionaries.

However, God seemed to have other ideas. While waiting in Darwin for the mission barge, the *St Francis*, to take the children to their new home, word came through to the Roe household. The barge had sunk. Through this accident Patrick avoided institutionalisation at Garden Point:

> It was the Catholic receiving depot for the stolen generation in Darwin, where the churches managed the placement of half-caste kids from all over the Territory. Jack Long, Michael Long's father (the footballer) was put there.

Michael Long today talks of the fact that he not know his living relations:

> Even today we've never met our grandfather, or our grandmother. My father didn't see his mother or father, so that just proves that the stolen generation did happen.[51]

Fay and Ron Wade, meanwhile had rethought the plan and had a change of heart. They drove up to Darwin and had a meeting with 'the Roe mob.' In thinking back on the family history and experience, it seemed wrong to give up now and send the children off to the mission, or for them to become wards of the state. Fay, in particular, emphasised the need for Patrick to ensure that he took the educational opportunities that were there 'so that we could take on the system and not lose every time.' It was decided that Patrick would go back to Katherine and finish primary school, helping Fay with her kids. Mick would stay with Basil Roe (Bill's son) and his wife, Janet. Jacko and Patricia would stay with old Bill and Mary Roe. This, at last, was a compromise plan that kept the kids in the family but spread the load.

After several visits to court by Janet Roe, the welfare authorities approved the arrangements. The children stayed with their family, escaping institutionalisation, separation and dispersal.

Mick would recall these traumatic events in a speech in the Year 2000:

> Both my parents died in 1960. I was 10. Mr Howard by then was a young man at university and I'm informed, a member of the Young Liberals. After the death of my mother, which followed that of my father, my aunt and uncle came and took us to Darwin on the back of my Uncle's Chevy truck. They had both been former mission victims and knew well the ways of the native welfare authorities. They did not wish the same fate to befall their young nieces and nephews. What ensued was a protracted battle with the authorities in and out of court with my family winning. We were permitted to stay in the guardianship and custody of family. I became a 'State Child' in my family's care. What kind of system is it that would define the ownership of a child by the state, while the child is in the care of its kin? They are dead now, but the courage and persistence of my uncle, aunt and grown up cousins saved us from institutionalisation. I will forever be grateful to them.[52]

Patrick came back to Katherine with Fay and Ron, subject to her discipline and control, but being the responsible elder child who helped her with all the kids. Patrick grew to respect Ron Wade, recognising him years later as a strong influence on his life, and treasuring his Unicorn watch and white rayon shirt. Ron Wade was the first adult to really sit down and talk to him about things. Patrick went back to finish primary school, with limited application and minimal ambition. At the time he saw his future in the stock camps, as soon as the authorities would allow his escape.

Another option appeared on the horizon when his mate Wiki Maher proposed a bold plan. They would go ringing with a drover they had befriended, chasing him up along the Barkly Stock route. Once before, when Patrick's Mum was still alive, they had run off to Willeroo station and worked with Matt Murray, droving cattle from Willeroo to Katherine. This was exciting work. With a good chance, Patrick, like Cecil, felt he could jump out of the control of school and welfare authorities and become a proper ringer, able to look after himself.

Patrick and Wiki met up with the Steve Daly's droving team at King River. With no swag, no boots and little experience, they were not really ready for a life on the road. Steve and his brother Mick had big hearts and made the boys welcome in their droving plant, giving them tea, a feed and a place to sleep. They also knew Ron Wade and sent a message back from the pub, letting him know where the boys could be found. Fay and Ron gave the runaways a serious dressing down when they caught up with them in the early hours of the morning.

The Daly brothers were no strangers to battles with the welfare authorities. Earlier in the same year, the readers of the *Northern Territory News* had followed the battle of Mick Daly, who was attempting to gain the permission of the Director of Welfare, Harry Giese, to marry Gladys Namagu. Giese raised various objections to the marriage, including the spurious and unsubstantiated claim that Mick was not a 'fit and proper person.' Giese was eventually overwhelmed by the persistence of the young couple, their insistence on running their own lives, and the stories in the press.[53]

Patrick dutifully but not enthusiastically finished primary school in 1961, the year Ron Wade died of a heart attack at Jasper Gorge. Boarding school was now the only option for the lad. Family meetings again determined his fate. Part of the thinking was the existence of a scheme, devised in cooperation with the churches, to send part-Aboriginal children south for education and training. The Commonwealth government provided an allowance of £300 per annum for each child selected by Mr Giese. The Melbourne affiliations of the Missionaries of the Sacred Heart Catholic (MSC) priests in Darwin led him to go to Monivae, the MSC boarding college near Hamilton in western Victoria. His dreams of being a ringer were put on hold. He was going south.

The Block, Broome, 1998

Patrick had headed off to another meeting out bush with the Kimberley Land Council. I was left behind looking after the Block, recovering from a nasty infection on my leg, presumably from a spider bite. Patrick was scathing about 'whitefellas' in the tropics: 'Your blood's too thin to cope. Useless in this country.'

Eric Wade, Fay's son, had driven over to the Block in 'Bluebell', the old Land Cruiser, carting some more besser-blocks to add to the pile standing in the yard, testament to the number of days Patrick had to spend away. Eric was fit, coach of the local junior footy team; skilled, able to turn the pile of blocks into an extension of the house; and ready to put in a day's work. Despite my injury, and a significant lack of applicable skills, I volunteered as his helper. We got some work done between cups of tea and balachaung (Malay shrimp chilli paste) sandwiches. Fay had made a huge batch of the family favourite to her secret recipe, jars of which were exchanged by Aboriginal leaders across Australia.

Eric was helping 'Dad', his term for Patrick, his mother's brother. His son called Patrick, 'Pop.' In the Aboriginal way, relationships of authority and reciprocity criss-crossed the family network, and the relationship of mother's brother is always close and significant. It gave Patrick some authority over Eric, but also an obligation to look after him and his family. Both had come back from Katherine to Broome and re-made their homes there, some fifty years after Snowy and Patricia drove off to the east as newly wed escapees. Both are connected through kin, country and history. In 1959, Paul Hasluck had talked of 'crumbling groups of aboriginal people bound together by ancient tradition and kinship and living under a fading discipline the tattered threads of kinship.'[54] He was wrong.

Forty years on, those threads are still strong and cohesive, despite generations of forced social change, intermarriage and cultural mixing. At the end of our working day, Eric called out to his wilful but charming ten-year-old son, 'Come on boy, time to go now. Get in the Toyota, Snowy.' Across the generations, across Australia, connections are maintained. The name of Snowy would live on.

186 ● Paddy's Road

The main road running through Katherine, N.T., 1943 (photograph W.D. Martin, courtesy of Australian War Memorial).

Wave Hill Police Station 1957 (photograph Ellen Kettle, courtesy of the Kettle Collection, Northern Territory Library).

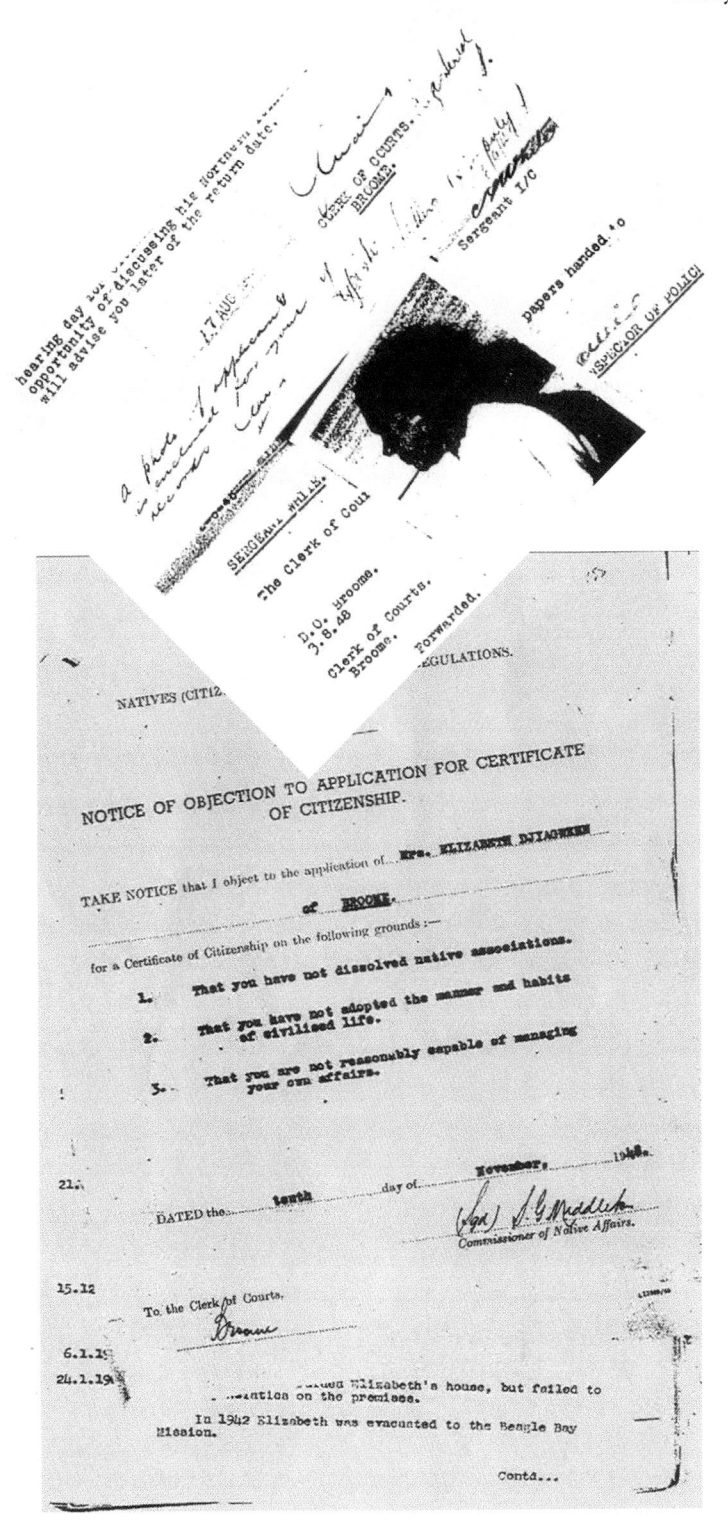

Top: Elizabeth's application for citizenship; Below: Rejection of Elizabeth's application.

From left; Pixie Birch, Patricia, Patrick and Cecil Dodson, Katherine, N.T., ca 1959 (courtesy Fay Wade album).

Faye Wade on her 11th birthday arriving in Katherine, N.T. (courtesy Fay Wade album).

Patrick Dodson in Katherine, N.T. (courtesy Maude Ellis).

The siblings: Cecil, Fay, Patricia, Pat, Georgina, Mick, 1998, Broome. In NAIDOC week Patrick and Mick jointly received the National Award for Aboriginal of the Year (courtesy Fay Wade album).

Chapter Seven

In the arms of the Church

'My object will be, if possible, to form Christian men, for Christian boys I can scarcely hope to make.'
Thomas Arnold, letter (1828)

Casterton, Western Victoria, 1997

The wind, whistling up from the Southern Ocean, eddied across the tree-stripped rolling hills in the valley of the Glenelg River. Hunched against the cold, Patrick walked slowly around the heavy concrete plots in the Casterton Cemetery, reading the inscriptions, imagining the stories behind the old engravings, searching for connections.

Patrick was 'showing me some of his sacred sites'; the places where he spent his teenage years. Eventually we found the plots he was searching for. He stood very quietly, hands behind his back, at the graves of the Gartlan family, paying his respects. Lying there were his first schoolboy friend, Tony Gartlan, and Tony's mother and father, Marian and Jack. In the 1960s the Gartlan family had brought the Katherine boy, boarding in nearby Hamilton, into their home on weekends and holidays, sharing life on their farm. They offered the orphan Aboriginal boy precious gifts: a noisy family dinner table, support, respect. He would always be grateful for the fact that this family took him in, gave him a home and stood up for his interests.

I left him to his thoughts, prayers and memories and walked back to wait in the car, out of the wind. In the car, I read an unusually frank tourist guide I'd found in the local newsagent on the local Kanalgundidj clans.[1] I read about the woman and child in 1836 who met the surveyor Major Mitchell and were given a tomahawk. In the 1840s in retaliation for what was seen as a 'theft' of sheep, a large massacre apparently took place using cannons loaded with bolts, nails and gravel at a place known as Murdering Flat. By 1856, twenty years after Mitchell, an observer commented that 'the tribe is nearly extinct.' The people of Patrick's adopted home had a brief, but sad, recorded history. There were no monuments to record their passing.

Melbourne, 1961

Patrick walked down the stairs of the DC3 plane that had brought him from the Northern Territory to Melbourne. A friend of Ron Wade's, a 'muscleman' named Norm Hack, was there to meet him at Essendon airport, reaching out for the small bag of clothes that Fay had packed. In the city, he saw huge buildings and busy streets with thousands of people, bustling like ants. He watched them rushing by, looking for the coloured people. He recalled:

> The neon signs, traffic lights and trams and the different houses fascinated me. I was taken to Luna Park and then later to Harry and Norma Grant's place in Preston. This was a proper *kardiya* place—a real city. They put me on the plane the next day to Hamilton.

At Hamilton, the Rector of Monivae, Fr J.J. McMahon picked him up and drove him out to Monivae. There was little to be found in the way of conversation as the man and boy drove through the prosperous rural centre of Hamilton, heart of the fine wool industry on the fertile plains of the Western Districts. Outside the town the land was green, but where were the grasses? Here the grass was like some sort of carpet. The huge red river gums, the majestic outcrops of the Grampians and You Yangs, the fat sleepy cattle, the clouds of sheep, the trees laden with fruit; all viewed with wonder by the wide-eyed lad. Fr McMahon told him, 'The boys are all looking forward to seeing the new black boy from the Territory.' Patrick was not sure how to answer that.

Just before suppertime the car reached Monivae College. They swung into the circular driveway around the statue of Our Lady of the Sacred Heart. Patrick saw her eyes fixed upwards, her hands poised outwards, her frozen expression quietly suffering. He looked up at the imposing, red-brick building with the marble steps; not yet realising that this was to be his new home. The brother in charge of the kitchen looked at Patrick's skinny frame and said, 'We'll have to feed you up!'

In his bed in the dormitory that night there was a 'stampede of boys running up the stairs and filing past my bed to have a look at me.' He pulled the red linen quilt and coarse grey woollen blankets all the way over his head, hiding. He shivered in the darkness and anxiously waited for the new day.

Monivae College, run by the Missionaries of the Sacred Heart,[2] was little more than a decade old. There were some four hundred students, most of them boarders, the sons or grandsons of squatters and cockies from the district. A few 'day scrags' made up the numbers. Some were the descendants of Victorian pastoral families who had been the first, foolhardy investors in the failed Roebuck Bay scheme that had alienated his grandfather's lands a century earlier. A few boys were overseas students sponsored by the Colombo Plan. There were no Aboriginal faces to be seen in the morning assembly.

On the first day of classes, Patrick learned that it was a tough school. The otherwise affable Fr 'Bomber' McPhillamy, dressed in long black robes, unlike anything Patrick had ever seen, meted out punishment that day to Patrick, and the boy who was to become his closest friend and confidant, Tony Gartlan. The two boys would stand together and talk whenever there was time in the regimentation of the school day.

> Well, he got me into strife. Or I got him into strife—one or the other. He was in front of me, sitting in front of me, and it was the first day I'd gone to school and I didn't have a uniform on and all these kids had uniforms on. This was all strange stuff to me. Anyway, I tapped him on the shoulder to ask him for a pen or a pencil or something so that I could write down what the priest was talking about. Of course, the mere act of doing that brought the attention of the teacher, the old priest, and he told us both to step out and we got four cuts across the hands each with a bit of linoleum strap. As I say, I hadn't met him before that but it gave us a lot to talk about. Had enough to talk about so we spent the recess condemning this particular priest for his barbaric style but we became friends then. Even though he didn't go right through to matriculation, he left at the old intermediate, form four, I then had developed a good relationship with the family and spent all of my holidays, apart from the Christmas ones, pretty much on their farm, working on the farm and enjoying it.

The Gartlans invited Patrick, or 'Paddy' as they called him, home for weekends and term holidays on the family farm. The farm, Koolomurt West was near Casterton, at the heart of what Mitchell had called 'Australia Felix.' The property had been selected in 1859, and been in the Gartlan family since 1931.[3] Not far away was the 'Nareen' homestead of future Prime Minister, Malcolm Fraser.[4] The farm became a place of refuge for the homesick lad. His times there punctuated the long sentence imposed by the school. The visits continued even after Tony left the school at the end of fourth form.

For the years of secondary schooling, Tony's mother and father, Marian and Jack, became like the parents that Patrick never really had. Without fuss or show, they gave him love and guidance over several crucial years of his adolescence. They offered warm support and security when he needed it. This was possibly his first taste of an intact, secure, functional family.

The extended family of brothers, sisters and cousins gathered noisily around a large table on weekends sharing food, talk, jokes and a 'misguided passion for the Collingwood football team.' They split wood together, hunted possums, and baled hay. He was warmed by the reception and grateful for the talk, the noise, the teasing. They let him fit in, sharing in the work that needed to be done and helping him to adjust to the new reality in which he had arrived.

Although his time with the family was not long in real terms, the Gartlans sparked in Patrick a sense of optimism about racial relations and a means of understanding the hopes, dreams and concerns of non-Aboriginal Australia. Decades later, Tony's brother, Buddy, wondered aloud whether the reconciliation movement began around their table.

In adjusting to life the south, Patrick had to come to terms with a new culture, a new system of values:

> It wasn't free fall but I had to work out how to make my own way in life, I had to work out the value systems. When I went to Monivae I didn't know what a bread and butter plate was and that you had these protocols that were associated not only with Victorian society but also boarding school society and I had to learn all of that without coming out of that family mould where these things were taken to be normal. I came out of the mould where your basic diet was stew and rice or pure meat. Whatever you had for the day, you got. No routine. Here dinner was called lunch, supper was called dinner and tea was called supper.
>
> I didn't know, when I first went there I had to learn all these things, adjust to them. That's just a simple example. I had to make judgements and had no-one except the Gartlans to get advice from. They gave me help but I had to rely on myself to know whether I was making the right judgements, especially about how to deal with things happening at home that Fay would write to me about.

State Child Number 165

Patrick was at Monivae through a program called the 'Accommodation for Part-Aboriginal Children in other States for Education and Training Scheme.' Two hundred and fifty children were removed from the Northern Territory in 1959. Mick was to follow Patrick to Monivae in 1963, while their sister Patricia went to St Anne's in Warrnambool.

The scheme was instituted by Paul Hasluck during his twelve years as Commonwealth Minister for Territories.[5] Hasluck recalled late in his life that this particular program evolved from a scheme in the 1930s that forcefully moved 'some children—described as "octoroons" or "quadroons" — out of the Territory into southern denominational institutions with a view to their ultimate adoption by white parents.'[6] Hasluck regarded the earlier scheme as ill-conceived. He argued, 'we should cease treating them as sub-normal people and regard them in the same way as all other Australians.' He claimed that this would require administrators 'to cease using a racial classification for Aborigines.'[7] Aboriginal children in need should be treated as welfare recipients, rather than as being subject to specific race-based laws.

In 1952 Hasluck saw a place for a revised scheme directed at what he called 'those light-coloured children who have no strong family ties in the Territory' as long as such a move 'is likely to be conducive to a happy future life for the child.'[8] He directed the establishment of procedures for the transfer, placement, inspection, after-care and eventual employment of the children.

The Dodson children, as orphans, were certainly in need. Their guardians, either Fay in the case of Patrick, or the Roe family in the case of Mick, agreed to their relocation in the south. Patrick felt that Fay made the choice because, 'she felt strongly that education was necessary to be able to fight the cruelty of the system. She had seen what had happened to kids who were taken to institutions and this was a way of keeping us in the family, even at a distance.'

While the scheme paid an annual allowance to the College, the relevant legislation legitimising their custodial care was the *Child Welfare Ordinance 1958*. Under this ordinance, they were placed in the care and control of the Director of Child Welfare, who was authorised to send them to 'a place within the Commonwealth to be placed under control, trained, educated, cared for and maintained.'[9] They were State Children—their files labelled with a large SC, and a number. Patrick Lionel Dodson now became State Child Number 165.[10]

In many ways, the scheme was a step forward from the earlier model of forced removal and controlled absorption. Hasluck set out to engineer a shift from the treatment of all 'half-caste' children as a uniform category to be managed at bureaucratic whim and convenience, towards a program that began to consider the needs of the individual. He de-emphasised the racial objective and emphasised the social and educational objectives of assimilation. As such, he contributed to liberalising the regime when viewed from within the values set of the time.

And yet Hasluck remained defensive on this issue in his later years, conscious of the horror stories of placements of children in homes where abuse was common and exploitation was rife.[11] The scheme in its general application was underpinned by the bedrock belief that the Aboriginal community and extended family were socially inferior and morally bankrupt, with no possibility of survival in a contemporary coherent Australian society. From this premise, the answer lay in stressing the needs of the individual, over and against the needs of the group and the individual's connection with that group, its identity, its culture, its evolving social reality. Hasluck later saw this dilemma at the heart of the debate on assimilation:

> It seemed to me at times that some of these persons who discussed the education with the air of being expert were not thinking of aboriginal children as persons but as a group. It was like talking about an ant-heap as though it contained no ants. Behind my hesitancy and their certainty probably lies the real division between the policy of assimilation and some of the ideas current today. I believe that in the long run, perhaps several generations ahead, the vestiges of an aboriginal society, in spite of many ingenious attempts to find a new cohesion, will gradually fade away, but there will still be aborigines in Australia. An education system or any other part of administration that looks to the future will give a chance for the aboriginal to be whatever he wants to be and is capable of being within an evolving society. He should not be held tightly within a group.[12]

To maintain the scheme and remove and detain the children, the administrators had to collude in supporting the unfounded assumption that every Aboriginal parent was an incompetent guardian and that the state therefore had the duty to undertake the care, custody and control of the children.[13] The officials charged with that task often lacked the skills and expertise to enable them to make the transition. Ministerial intentions and policy pronouncements were often insufficient to lead to change on the ground, especially when the machinery of the revised legislation was implemented by people entrenched in the thinking of the previous regime. As such, the transition from 'biological absorption' to 'social assimilation' was more a change in rhetoric than a change in practice. For example, the Minister's subtlety and good intentions to 'deracialise' the program were lost on senior officials like the Administrator of the Northern Territory, who wrote in a 1953 memo to Hasluck's permanent departmental head:

> The children under consideration for transfer to the South are quadroons and those with less than 25% aboriginal blood who will readily pass as Europeans or readily fit into a European way of life.[14]

The scheme was, in actuality, lacking a basis in law. Much of the archival file on the scheme is devoted to legal wrestling over the fact that the drafting of the *Welfare Ordinance 1953* gave the Director of Native Affairs the power to control all Aboriginal children, but only if their situation made such a decision necessary or desirable. The legal position was summarised in a 1961 memorandum:

> Present legal position of children committed to institutions by the Director of Native Affairs under the Aboriginal ordinance is not clear. These committals were normally until the child reached the age of 18 years. With the repeal of the Aboriginal ordinance and the lack of a saving clause under the Welfare Ordinance, it is possible that the detention of a number of children previously legally committed, is now illegal.[15]

For Patrick, the scheme worked, to a degree. It did 'give him a chance.' It gave him a grounded, broad education and expanded his career horizons, allowing him to move closer to being 'whatever he wants to be.' It gave him the opportunity to meet and interact with non-Aboriginal people on a more equal and decent basis than would have been the case in Katherine. It gave him the basis to develop individual educational and professional skills, choices and options that would never have been available to the boy in Katherine. These were strong gains. He would remark more than once in later years that he was 'so glad that he went to school in Victoria.'

However, there were costs. He was isolated from his family in Katherine and Broome, worried about Fay's ability to pay for his return on Christmas holidays, which the scheme did not support. The price of participation in the broader society was severance from the community; to succeed as an individual, assimilation required abandoning the group. In the longer term, Patrick would spend much of his adult life attempting to re-establish links and connections with his own home community, its cultures and laws, his by right. He had to work hard to reclaim his destiny; to find his way back onto Paddy's road. Recalling his time with Max Stuart, Patrick would often use the metaphors of the showground to explain an event or an issue. On this version of the hurdy-gurdy ride he worked with Max, it seemed there was a high price for admission and it was very hard to jump off.

Patrick makes it clear that he and his brother were not 'taken away', they were not 'stolen', although the family was always at risk, and Fay and Georgina suffered the brunt of forced relocations. Instead, the boys' links with family in Katherine and Darwin were maintained and their access to their home country in Broome was kept open. He does, however, acknowledge the costs of the assimilation process. Mick had to deal with these issues as an author of the *Bringing Them Home* report, which pointed out that 'during the 1950s and 1960s even greater numbers of children were removed from their families to advance the cause of assimilation … not only were they removed for alleged neglect, they were removed to attend school in distant places.'[16] He told a radio interview before the report was finalised:

> It might be arguable as a principle for example that because children were separated from their families, from their kin, from their culture, from their language, from their country, it now makes it very very difficult for them to prove their Native Title. Now it may be that the loss of that capacity underpins a principle that ought to apply to payment of compensation. But that's something quantifiable. That loss of culture, language and country is a principle that ought to underpin the payment of compensation because it's an enormous loss in my view.[17]

In a television documentary Mick spoke about these costs in his own life and his regret that he doesn't know more about his own people and his own traditions.

> Really, in a lot of ways I've neglected doing one of the most important jobs and that's getting better acquainted with my people and my people's culture … I have been so busy going off to school and going to university and all these other jobs and I've just been away too long.[18]

The two brothers shared a connection to each other, to their family and to their country in Broome. Patrick put more time and energy in his later life into maintaining and reinforcing those connections by going back to Broome and making his home. Mick found it hard to find the time and space to do so, and relied on Patrick to facilitate those cultural connections.

The inspections

Although the transported children were the official responsibility of Territory authorities, the distance from Darwin led to some serious supervision problems, especially during the school holidays. The southern welfare authorities had their own hands full and would not assist with what they regarded as an ill-conceived plan, sending children south and then more or less abandoning them. When some children in Adelaide committed a crime and were not represented in court, the state officials demanded a response from their Darwin colleagues. A Territory welfare officer was eventually posted in Adelaide to carry out a round of inspections of the children's schooling and living conditions. The Monivae children were also sent to Melbourne for an annual medical examination, no local doctor being approved for the purpose. This arrangement was costly and difficult for the school to arrange. The welfare authorities were also required to report on conditions of the places the students spent their holidays. This brought the authorities into a collision course with Mrs Gartlan.

Oh, they asked all sorts of questions but the one that really riled Mrs Gartlan was the fact of whether there were sheets on the bed. Now, you can imagine a Western Districts farmer's wife, who was fairly well to do, whether she had sheets on the bed for this kid to come and sleep on. So she turned up at the next visit from the welfare bloke out of Melbourne and my description of it, she basically just shirt fronted him. She tore strips off him. That was the last I ever saw the welfare basically. It was that sort of strength again and fairness that was part of that family that I think helped give me some really good understanding of the distinctions in the non-Aboriginal world. That there are decent people who, you know, stand for principles and whom you can trust and they're not all sort of the characters of the ones that were part of my mother's and grandmother's life. Even though there were some very good non-Aboriginal people that she knew, my grandmother and my mother knew. But basically they weren't part of these systems of welfare and they were good people and they still are.

But it was a time when assimilation was the policy in the country and any Aboriginal person who showed any ability was expected to assimilate into the western way of life and become some kind of beacon to help attract the rest of the Aboriginal people. It's not even sound social policy but it was a theory that was operated upon. But it worked the other way for me, I think. It sort of raised questions as to why so many of the Aboriginal kids that I knew left school in primary school and never had the opportunity to go to secondary school, even though it wasn't much of an opportunity. I mean, I was sent there; I didn't really want to go there. But after I got into the schooling I liked it, even though it was a boarding situation, I was away from home.[19]

In 1964, the appropriately named Mr Worthy (known to the boys from the Welfare Branch in Katherine) carried out the inspection and wrote up a positive report.[20] Patrick got a good school report for Form 3, as he did each year. He was older than his classmates, having repeated Grade 6 in Katherine, 'as there was no way for him to do the correspondence course.'[21] Worthy noted that Patrick was chosen by other students for a diligence award, played in premiership football and basketball at the open level and was regarded as one of the most popular boys in the school. Patrick nominated teaching, diesel engineering or medicine as future career choices. His vision had begun to shift beyond the ringers' camp.

Mick, in his second year, also received a good report, although Mr Worthy commented that he 'was uncomfortable, twisted his tie, looked down and spoke very, very quietly.' The next year, another inspector regarded Mick as 'more happy-go-lucky and more outgoing … he has no high expectations academically, wanting to return to Darwin and take an apprenticeship in motor mechanics.' Both boys were concerned to ensure that they could get back to Darwin for the Christmas holidays, if the family could afford it.

Land Rights and the Referendum

Patrick began to collect cuttings of short articles reporting on Aboriginal issues, pasting the cuttings in an art book, now long lost. In the art book were a few short clippings of the 1966 walk-off of the stockmen and station hands from Wave Hill station, a place name that echoed in his heart. He felt a pull to the stories from the country of his great-grandmother and the place of his father's death. He followed, as best he could, the efforts of Vincent Lingiari to lead his people to re-claim their land, including the public meetings held in cities such as Melbourne. He knew that this was the birth of something very important and Patrick would spend the next thirty years working to follow that lead. The name of Vincent Lingiari and the example of Wave Hill were locked into the mind of the Monivae schoolboy. He learned later about the Pilbara strikers and their efforts to recognise Western Australia's constitutional responsibility for Aboriginal people.

Patrick watched the events on the cattle stations of the Northern Territory closely. In March 1966, the Commonwealth Arbitration Commission ordered the Northern Territory pastoral industry to pay equal award wages to all its employees, regardless of race. Recognising the dependence of the industry on Aboriginal labour, the Commission provided a year of grace, to December 1968, and included annual increments and a slow-worker award in their approach. However, the result was massive social and cultural dislocation. As Andrew McMillan described it:

> The industry employed 1,300 stockmen, 1,110 of whom were blacks working for tucker, tobacco and blankets they couldn't keep. The pastoralists cried foul, arguing they'd go broke, paying blackfellas the same as whitefellas. Over the next couple of years most of the black stockmen were sacked, and families were forced to move off their traditional lands in search of work.[22]

The reality was the work was not easy to get, and fringe communities around the regional centres of Katherine, Fitzroy Crossing and Halls Creek became the new centres of the Aboriginal population and hotbeds of alienation, alcoholism and unemployment. At the same time the cattle industry was becoming mechanised, with road trains carting the cattle to market. The Aboriginal stockman, the backbone of the industry, who pioneered its establishment in northern Australia, was redundant.

On 1 May 1966, Gurindji workers on the Vestey cattle station of Wave Hill on the tablelands west of Katherine, went on strike for equal pay. In one of the first actions of the land rights movement, six hundred Gurindji workers and their families walked off the station and settled down sixteen kilometres away at Wattie Creek.

Patrick would recall in a speech years later:

> Months after the original strike began, Vincent Lingiari led his people to establish a settlement at Wattie Creek, known to them as Daguragu, within the Wave Hill lease. When Lord Vestey attempted to get the Gurindji to leave Wattie Creek and return to work on the station, with inducements including money wages, Vincent Lingiari told him: 'You can keep your gold, we just want our land back.'[23]

During the next year, the strike against work conditions evolved into a claim for title to land and maintenance of culture. In 1967 the Gurindji petitioned the Governor-General and asked for 1295 sq. km of their traditional lands to be excised from the Wave Hill station pastoral lease. They would have to be patient.

Patrick's growing political awareness started to focus on Aboriginal issues. He had found it hard to comprehend the school texts that insisted that Aboriginal people and their culture were extinct, when he felt very much alive. He recalls being amazed when the national vote for the 1967 referendum returned a massive majority in every state.[24] As he started to enjoy respect, recognition and reward in his adopted closed community, the wider nation was demonstrating that it could and would respect and recognise Aboriginal rights to equal treatment. The news stories on the referendum pricked the bubble that surrounded him in his school career, reminding him of where he had come from and where he his family had been. It forced him to reconsider the relationship between his Aboriginality and his Australian identity. He would recall:

> It just woke me up, I remember. Not that I was forgetting my people or my place but it forced me to realise how important those political efforts were and the fact that not only was change happening but that more needed to happen. I was starting to feel like maybe I could help somehow, though I didn't have a clue how.

In the long campaign leading up to the 1967 referendum, he read about Aboriginal leaders he knew like Joe McGinness from Katherine.[25] He read about others he did not know such as Sir Douglas Nicholls, Faith Bandler,

Kath Walker (Oodgeroo Noonuccal), Jack Davis and Bill Onus. He watched television programs about Charlie Perkins, originally from Alice Springs, leading a freedom ride through western New South Wales protesting against discrimination and living conditions. He saw that non-Aboriginal Australians were involved and that impressed him. Thirty years later, at the Australian Reconciliation Convention in 1997, he was proud to welcome many of the referendum pioneers as special guests and praise their leadership and vision.

At the convention, Dr Faith Bandler, one of the leaders of the referendum movement, remembered the odds against which they worked:

> In the Cold War which had penetrated Australia, when brave men and women who believed they should work for the first Australians, with the first Australians, and to help the first Australians to take their rightful place in the community, those men and women, true democrats and free thinkers, were conspired against from time to time. During the great struggle for the referendum, much was done to break their spirits but single-mindedly and with the drain of commitment weighing heavily, they set their eyes on the goal ahead: that the referendum should be held and that it should be carried.[26]

Patrick would always admire those who fought together, who fought against the odds, and who won the day, to change the nation.

The school captain

By 1967, Patrick was at the peak of his school career, elected captain of the school by popular vote, head prefect by the teachers, received the diligence prize for effort four years in succession and passed his intermediate and leaving examinations. Of major importance was his selection, two years running, as captain of the school football team, for which he won the best and fairest award and the Fitzgerald Cup. Decades later, he was honoured to be named as Captain of the Monivae Team of the Century in a group that included several prominent senior-grade footballers. His preferred position was at centre half-back, recalling that, 'Defence is always the best form of attack. I had to set up for the prima donnas up forward.'

As a cadet under officer he stood to attention during reviews of the college cadets by Malcolm Fraser, then Minister of Defence.[27] Having been told by Fr Prentice, the Principal, of an Aboriginal scholarship offered by Monash University in medicine, he announced that this would be his chosen profession. He told a local paper his 'greatest wish is to go back to the north where there is so much you could do for all the people there, regardless of colour.'[28] Not knowing as yet what it was that he wanted to do with his life he was influenced by the suggestions of others in considering a seemingly unrestricted set of opportunities.

He helped to shape the culture of the boarding school. Martin Flanagan and Patrick once discussed the problem of bullying and he told Flanagan, 'We managed to get rid of that.'

> He told me how he once found a big boy with a name like Jones holding a little kid out a second floor window by the ankles. 'Bring him in, Jonesie,' he had said. Even retelling the story years later, there was a sort of sad smile in his voice and I knew, as Jonesie must have, that if he didn't do what he was told, Dodson would make him.[29]

Patrick spent most Christmas holidays between Katherine and Darwin, where he laboured for the Department of Works, swinging a pick and shovel, and driving a truck in order to pay his keep and contribute to a scanty family budget. On the weekends, in Darwin, he played in the Wet Season Northern Territory Football League for St Mary's as a ruck-rover. They won the flag.

It was the Australian Rules field, the oval, that he loved most of all. As a young footballer, he was a solid, straight-through, focused footballer who could be aggressive when required, especially in defence. He won matches for his team with powerful punts from either foot. He was one of the hard-hitting men in any league he played. Mostly, he loved the fact that the footy was one place where black met white, even in Darwin, on level ground, equal before the umpire with the rules the same for both sides. As such 'the oval was sacred turf.'[30] Patrick's friend, colleague and fellow footy fanatic, Brian McCoy would remark:

> Indigenous footballers provide something that is distinctive and different for our Australian game. At the heart of what they bring is a great enjoyment for Aussie Rules. But they also bring their culture with them: hunting that low lying and flying object of desire, the art of skilled avoidance and holding to that fine line which puts pressure on an opponent but also offers him respect. Football can be an important area of men's business where skills and relationships are strengthened and the use of aggression is negotiated.[31]

For his school captain's investiture speech in 1967, Patrick chose to draw from President Kennedy, getting fellow students to 'ask not what Monivae can do for you, but ask what you can do for Monivae.' He also set out a theme to which he would frequently return:

> We realise the more we enter into these things (prayer, study, sport and community service) the more we become true Christians and true

Australians—men who will later on be capable of leading their communities and imparting to fellow citizens something from the store they have accumulated in youth.[32]

Thirty years later, without consulting the speech of his youth, he said much the same thing to the students of Monivae when invited to address the school speech night in October 1997. These were life truths he was learning and sharing. He was blending these truths with the important lessons learned in his family, especially in standing up for yourself, your rights, and your dignity. This period was the crucible of his notion of public service and commitment to community.

At Patrick's speech night in 1967, while he was inside, on the dais, he saw a ripple of commotion at the front door to the hall. An old Aboriginal woman was being gently but insistently removed from the building. He had seen the woman before, at the footy games, watching him play on the oval in town. She had come to see him, to hear him speak and for some reason he never understood, she was being turned away. Frozen in shock, Patrick could not move before she was whisked away. He never saw her again. Years later Geoff Clark told Patrick that he thought the old lady's name was 'Gracie' and that she was 'one of his mob at Framlingham.'

The vocation

While the school captain was starting to chat to convent girls at the cafe in the main street of Hamilton, he also started hearing a voice, starting as a whisper; the beginnings of a spiritual calling. He recalled:

> Fr Fyfe was a voice in my ear. He talked a lot to me about the need, or duty I suppose, to turn the privileges I had been given into an obligation of service to the community. I think more than anyone he persuaded me to do something useful with what I got, and that I could heal people spiritually as the highest form of service. This was more important than healing someone physically, as a doctor. That was just temporary. It was a dilemma for me, but I came out on the side of needing to contribute to something permanent and ever-lasting. But the moral challenge was hard, and I had to grapple with it when I had no real experience of life.[33]

It was the time, even past the time, when, if his family had been able to stay in their own country, with their own people, he would have been undergoing initiation ceremonies, being made a man by other men. He devoured the few books that were then available on traditional Aboriginal religion, gritting his teeth with frustration at the viewpoint of the authors.

There was nothing he could find on Yawuru religion, except for the work of Daisy Bates.

The road ahead for the big lad was not signposted. The Church had looked after him, brought him up, become in some ways, his Mother, embodied in the devotions to Our Lady of the Sacred Heart, 'our tender Mother; each of mankind dear to her.'[34]

Patrick was readily absorbed in reflections on the gospels and their teachings on the right way to live. He was drawn into the ceremonies, the rituals, and the incense and rich fabrics. He was a devout, practicing Catholic young man who started to think he was destined, rather than choosing, to be a priest. The senior retreat gave him an opportunity to pray and think about the calling, seeking advice from the fathers, who were only too supportive.

Jack Waterford has talked to me about the way vocations were handled in Catholic Schools of the time:

> There'd be a director of vocations come around and talk very seriously to the boys. Here boys, fill in the form and tick the box, and come around and talk to me at the Retreat. They would have been eager to score a lad like Paddy. The priest would stress that they wouldn't want any Holy Joe types, walking around hands in front of them the whole time. No, it was a muscular calling, you had to roll your sleeves up and get into it. That would have appealed to Paddy, too. Oh, he would have been under some pressure.[35]

He was handed small pamphlets, published by the Missionaries of the Sacred Heart, written to assist the process of following through on a vocation. They told him that 'a Vocation is nothing else but an interior drawing in the mind or heart of a youth, an interior yearning to leave all things and follow our Blessed Lord more closely.'[36] He was warned to guard his vocation jealously against the views of other boys and the temptation of vanity. He was told it would be a hard road, renouncing human love and affection, in order to pursue:

> The noblest career open to man. (God) invites him to the highest happiness, to a life more useful to his fellow man than any other and to duties that contribute most to the Glory of God.[37]

Perhaps for Patrick at this time, renouncing love and affection did not seem to be that large a sacrifice. He decided to join the order, despite a chorus of protests from those who held enough love and affection to say what they thought:

> Fay was furious, saying 'What do you want to go and do that for?' She saw it as a complete waste of my life and doing nothing for the family.

Mrs Gartlan tried very hard to talk me out of it. I remember she was in Melbourne at the time and dropped a plate. I didn't know, but that was when she must have been getting ill and going down for medical treatment.

A father of one of the girls I had been talking to suggested that I stay in his pub for the weekend. Mick said don't do it. The priesthood, that is, not the pub. I didn't tell him about that offer.

On the 1 August 1967, Patrick lumbered along with two fingers on the keys of an old Underwood typewriter, writing a letter to the head of the order, the Very Reverend Father Provincial:

Dear Father

This letter is to ask you permission to become a priest in the Society of the Missionaries of the Sacred Heart. Considered this question for many moths (sic) and have now decided that this is what I would like to do. If possible I would like to be member of next year's novitiate. I am at present studying for my matriculation and my 20th birthday will be on January 29th next year.

I would like to become a priest to dedicate my life to Christ and to assist in his work of saving others. Furthermore I have come to know and appreciate the life an MSC from living at Monivae over the last six years and seeing the dedication and community spirit here. Over the years the Priests and Brothers have been very good to me and have helped me in many ways for which I am very grateful. Their example has been partly responsible for my decision.[38]

Patrick always spoke highly of the example set by the Monivae clergy, especially the lay brothers, with their mission of domestic and manual labour, recalling that 'they worked hard, always did the shit jobs but willingly and positively.' The brothers were a key to maintaining the closed community of an MSC house, allowing the house to be 'independent of hired labour; free from many vexatious difficulties, making them smoothly running, happy families.'[39]

He would mention the selfless role model of the lay brothers in a lecture he gave about the influence of Archbishop Mannix, the demigod who ruled the Victorian Catholic Church and sparked the young boy's vision of social justice.[40] He would praise them thirty years later at the Monivae speech night. He told the students that his four major sources of motivation at Monivae were the Gartlan family, the inspiration of the brothers, the importance of his community and family in far-off Broome and Katherine, and a core group of mates he went to school with.

The gratitude the orphan boy from Katherine felt was also a strong stimulus for his decision. Patrick would say with a wry smile, 'This was my chance to pay back. To do something for others, as others had done things for me.' The emphasis on reciprocity was as much gospel in origin as it was Aboriginal.

It was also a fact that other choices would have been a little more difficult. His family was in no position to support his further studies. The holiday work with the Works Department did not pay well enough to make any savings. There was no system of Government support for Aboriginal participation in tertiary education, and university scholarships were hard to get and only allowed for a small stipend. Staying within the cloisters of the church allowed him to postpone a decision on his entry onto life's highways. He turned his back on the world and entered the novitiate.

Not long after, Marian Gartlan passed away and Patrick drew a veil over another part of his emotional life.[41] After losing his mother, and now his foster mother, he perhaps formed the view, unconsciously, that it was dangerous to become attached to people and, particularly, to relate closely to women. With his experiences, he considered that he should maintain his focus on his vocation and commit himself to the fraternal male world of the priesthood. It would be many years before he came to recognise the pattern and he was never comfortable in discussing it.

On 1 March 1969, after a novitiate year and his first year of seminary studies in Canberra, Patrick recited his temporary vows of chastity, poverty and obedience with fourteen other young MSC men before Bishop-elect Edward (Ned) Kelly and Fr John F. McMahon, the Provincial of the order, at Randwick in Sydney.

Patrick was the first Aboriginal young man to embark on a career as a priest in a Catholic religious order in Australia since Pope Pius IX clothed two men from the New Norcia mission in Western Australia with the Benedictine habit in 1849.[42] Neither man survived their trip to Italy, both catching tuberculosis and dying. Patrick would go on and become the first and to this date the only Aboriginal Catholic priest.[43]

Patrick was interviewed after taking his vows and said he chose the order because it was the only order of priests in the Northern Territory, and 'it has certainly got the spirit that fits onto the things I like. I feel pretty committed to it—not in any sense of obligation—I see it as a free choice. I've found a degree of peace already and it is certainly a very rewarding life.'[44]

Mick and Paddy

Mick and Paddy, the two brothers at Monivae, were warm but never close, tending to disagree about some fundamental approaches to life. At the time, Mick thought Patrick's decision to join the priesthood was wrong, and told him so.[45] Mick related strongly to the Darwin Roe family and was closest to his other brother, Jacko, while Patrick looked to his sister Fay in Katherine and back to his grandfather in Broome for his primary identity. Before then Mick was his 'father's boy', while Patrick was closer to his mother. Each boy reacted to the loss of his parents, and his removal to Monivae, in a different way.

At Monivae, the older brother tended to patch up fights, while Mick looked for them, as Jack Ah Kit recalled them doing in Darwin:

> I remember Paddy being a quiet reserved kid—a bit of a loner who kept to himself. He was independent. I don't remember him making shanghais with the other kids. I always had fights with Mick. Whenever we saw each other we'd get our shirts off. Paddy was never there, in the fights.[46]

While his brother was in the novitiate, Mick was elected vice-captain of Monivae. He had already become adjutant of the cadet unit, president of the St Vincent de Paul Society and starred in the school basketball and football teams. The *Melbourne Herald* carried a short feature article on the 'ever-smiling' 18-year-old boy, showing a photograph with his sister Patricia, 16-years-old. Mick told the reporter, 'First please tell the people about my brother, Paddy.' But he went on to talk about his motivation:

> When I first came to Monivae I had the impression the other boys were just being nice to me because I am coloured. But then I thought we are all God's people and he cares nothing about colour or race. At the beginning I was content to hope that I would get enough education to win an apprenticeship in some trade back home. Then I began to feel that I might be able to do better. Things like algebra and English were Dutch to me but my brother and the priests spurred me on. But the thing that spurred me most was my colour. I felt that the other kids were watching me and thought I could not make it. I couldn't give a darn what colour I am. People must learn to accept other people for what they are—after all, we have the same coloured blood.[47]

Mick's tendency to say what he thought was evident in that year when he gave his speech at the 1969 speech night. Rather than run through the usual courtesies, Mick hit out at the:

> Negative attitude adopted by some students, their criticisms have been destructive and they have shown no appreciation of anything that is done

for them, they are content to sit back and let others do all the work, while they 'knock' everything and everyone. These types have made it difficult for others and the sooner their attitudes change for the better, then we will have a much stronger and united student body.[48]

At his own speech night address in 1967, Patrick made the same point, but the difference in style and approach was plain:

Rather than see boys be over-critical of various features of college life, we would encourage those with worthwhile ideas to come forward and express them to us so that we can relay these to the appropriate authorities. In this way criticism is constructive and all of us can benefit from it.[49]

Even then, it was not hard to tell which brother would be the priest and which would be the lawyer.

The novice

Patrick went first to the Novitiate in Douglas Park in New South Wales. This was the location where the foundations of philosophy and theology were taught to the earnest and hard-working novices. Fay and Patrick exchanged regular letters (now lost) discussing family events. His contacts with Broome were tenuous. In May 1969, Sister Manetta from Beagle Bay forwarded Patrick a note, with his birthdate, 29–1–48 and his baptism date, 8–2–48 scrawled on Catholic Presbytery notepaper. In spidery script underneath:

God bless you Paddy love from your grand dad—Patrick Djiagween.[50]

A muscular vocation required exercise and he played football at every opportunity. The order combined mentoring and bushwalking with Fr Dennis Murphy walking with Patrick for four days in the Blue Mountains carrying a 40-pound backpack. It was on this long walk that the beard was allowed to grow and his face would never feel a razor again.

He completed his first year at the novitiate before he transferred in 1970 to the MSC House of Studies on Northbourne Avenue in Canberra and taught at Daramalan College in Dickson while studying at the Australian National University. He then undertook further study at Croydon on the outskirts of Melbourne, which had been opened by Archbishop Mannix at the beginning of World War Two. His studies would take seven years: four years of philosophy followed by three years of theology.

At the end of his first year in the novitiate, Patrick made the trip back to Darwin, Katherine and across the track to Broome for the first time since his birth. Granny Liz had been in Katherine with Fay and her new husband,

Cecil Fletcher. Family tensions were high as Cecil and Patrick clashed; Patrick sternly disapproving of the man and his relationship with his elder sister. Tensions were also high in the town as the Rights for Whites movement gathered force in Katherine.

Patrick went to one of their meetings and watched in bemused, baffled anger as speaker after speaker spoke out against the fact that Aboriginal rights and entitlements were being recognised. They were especially critical of the decision to award equal wages to Aboriginal workers in the pastoral industry. Kids he went to school with and their parents, people who knew the family after a decade in the town, all spat venomously about 'the blacks.' People at Patrick's elbow urged him to stand up and to speak. He couldn't.

He decided to get the family out and head back to Broome. Granny Liz wanted to return to her house in Mary Street, Broome, and in Patrick's increasingly judgmental eyes, things had deteriorated at Fay's place. Patrick, judging his sister's situation to be serious, lifted her and her children, semi-voluntarily; packed them into a borrowed HR Holden with a trailer overflowing with all Fay's treasured possessions, and took off for Broome. Granny Liz rode next to him in the front seat. A clandestine bottle of whisky was hidden in Patrick's bag, ready for a 'rip on the road.'

On the dirt road outside Fitzroy Crossing, a spring snapped on the trailer, flipping it and the car. They rolled to a halt, climbed out on the side of the road, putting all their gear in a heap. His grandmother, sister and nieces and nephews watched as he scrambled through the pile looking for the bottle of whisky. It was smashed; the only damage to the car, it's load and the occupants. 'Naughty boy,' said Granny Liz. Whether he was naughty for having, hiding or breaking the bottle, she didn't say.

His time in Broome, his 'borning-place', was too short. He loved the inclusive, relaxed welcome of the Broome community and his extended family. The feeling of belonging was strong. At first his grandfather did not know him as family gathered around, telling old Paddy, 'This one Pat's boy, born here, Mary Street. Young fella coming up priest now.' Once connected, Patrick was thrilled to be with the old man. Paddy Djiagween took his long-lost grandson under his wing, showing him their country, telling him the stories of the '*rai*' of his conception site and always singing the songs he learned from the Dreaming. It was at that time that Patrick learned his *rai*, the pelican and ever after, he sought to connect with that bird and its lessons, thinking of the pelican gliding before delivering a major speech.

Patrick sat under the shade of the mango tree with the old man and absorbed his presence. The experience stirred the novice. Here was another spiritual truth he could feel, that he belonged to, was a part of. Here was a learned man respected by his peers and juniors; a scholar in a religion who was consulted by many anthropologists; a master of ceremonies ensuring that the business of ritual was carried out in the proper manner. His grandfather seemed to him to be the Yawuru archbishop.

The family gently teased Patrick as Francesca (Topsy) O'Meara recalled:

> Paddy came to see me before he went off to be a priest. Patricia that's my proper aunty, so he calls me proper relative. I think it would be very good, the best thing, he always said that when he went to school. I think he must have seen how the people were going, in sin and everything, you know. He must have seen it because he said 'I'm going to be a priest.' We used to say, 'Oh you wouldn't be a priest!' teasing him, and he used to say, 'You will see!' It's only among our family you know and he did keep to his word. I said, 'If you become a priest will you come up here and see us? We want to see you at the altar.' He said 'Yes, but I don't think I will stop here.'[51]

He knew then, the church order he was joining would be able to send him, anywhere and any time, to any place of its choice, and would require obedience to the will of God and the order. He also knew at the time that he did not have the luxury of choice; he could have Broome, his family and his grandfather, or he could have the church and his vocation. He could not have both.

The seminarian

The winters of Hamilton were cold and hard to take, but good training for the long winters of Canberra, and Patrick's stay at the Australian National University. At the University, he recalled studying philosophy and theology and did fairly well, enjoying the classes and discussions, reading widely but not enjoying writing up his essays.

He taught classes as Brother Dodson at Daramalan College in Dickson, trying to get this rugby-obsessed school to try a bit of 'real footy' of the Australian kind. His frustrations were taken out playing as a wingman for the University team, winning a premiership in 1971, with the *Canberra News* reporting that he was 'outstanding on the wing with a solid game and constructive play.'[52] Gordon Briscoe the Aboriginal historian and scholar, was a team-mate at the time.

His experience of wet season footy in Darwin, which he still played on holiday visits, allowed him to handle the often slippery conditions, although a slip on the sprinklers at Manuka Oval cost him a season of injury time with a broken ankle.

Training for the priesthood in the early 1970s was also a slippery field. The era after Vatican II saw the Australian Catholic Church riven with division. The old church, built on tribal Irish conservatism, often looked inwards. Traditionally, energy and effort had been placed into consolidating the Catholic presence in Australia; bricks and mortar for new schools, new churches, new classrooms. The urging of Vatican II, led by Pope Paul and promulgated in Australia by leaders like Archbishop Knox in Melbourne, called for the church to turn outwards. This call was echoed by the many European Catholics beginning to take an active role in the church and changing its approach. The stress was on social justice and world brotherhood, on the need to act in the world. Many Catholic leaders were wrong-footed by the change in direction. They reacted with what Patrick described as 'tokenistic support for innovations like changes to the liturgy and the occasional folk mass' but change was glacial below the surface. The fundamental position of the Church in Australian society remained relatively stolid. When Archbishop Knox called for increased coloured immigration to Australia, the reactions of disapproval were loud both within the Church and outside.

At the same time, vocations began to dwindle and priests and seminarians started to leave the orders in droves. Seminarians at university were in a difficult position, living in a cultural milieu for which their training in philosophy and theology had left them unprepared. Around them student protest raged, especially against the Vietnam War; women were claiming their rights and controlling their sexuality; liberation, both social and personal, was the buzzword. For Aboriginal Australians, in the cities at least, calls for a more radical and assertive political stance were being made. Jack Waterford was a student leader at the same time Patrick was in Canberra. He recalls that the ANU student union had a bank account for emergency assistance to students in need:

> Half the money would go to women seeking abortions. They were still illegal, but we would put them in touch with a sort of underground railroad who would look after them. A hell of a lot of the rest went to help seminarians that wanted to get out. Their parents had disowned them, or refused to help. They had none of the essentials of life, no record collection, no mates to camp with, no clue really about how to organise your life.[53]

Times of change

The early years of the decade of the 1970s led to powerful movements and important political events that shaped the interaction between Aboriginal people in the wider Australian community. Some events were legal, defining the constraints of the European court system's acknowledgement of Aboriginal rights in land. In the Supreme Court in 1970 Mr Justice Blackburn heard the case *Milirrpum v. Nabalco* in hearings in Darwin, Canberra and Alice Springs.[54] The young Baptist Bible college student, Galarrwuy Yunupingu, translated the words of the old men from both moieties from the Yolngu country, establishing a powerful leadership role for him that would be maintained for the next three decades.[55]

Justice Blackburn found that, 'the evidence seems to me to show that the aboriginal has a more cogent feeling of obligation to the land than of ownership of it. It is dangerous to attend to express a matter so subtle and difficult by a mere aphorism, but it seems easier, on the evidence, to say that the clan belongs to the land than that the land belongs to the clan.'[56] This failure to recognise Aboriginal systems of land ownership would persist in the Australian common law until the *Mabo* decision of 1992.

In January 1972 the Liberal government of William McMahon overturned the long-standing policy of assimilation. It now believed that Aboriginal people 'should be encouraged and assistant to preserve and develop their own culture, language, traditions and arts so that these can become leading elements in the diverse culture of the Australian society.' This generosity of spirit did not extend to recognition of Aboriginal land rights. On Australia Day in the same month, a small tent was erected on the lawns of Parliament House in Canberra and was proudly proclaimed as the Aboriginal tent embassy. The protesters were reacting to a speech by the Prime Minister that rejected land rights for the Arnhemland people.[57]

After six months the federal government banned camping in the federal territory and police forcibly removed the tents and their inhabitants, only to have to repeat the effort a few days later when participants recreated the embassy with a number of protesters being arrested. A Cabinet Minute of 2 May 1972, noted that 'Cabinet was of the view that actions should be taken to remove the campers but this should be done with reasonable notice and tactfully and with the least disturbance.'[58] Scott Bennett points out that the McMahon Government's furious reaction to the embassy seemed inappropriate to the event, allowing it to symbolise, 'a new stage in the relationship between black and white Australians', symbolised by the visit to the embassy by ALP leader Whitlam, who promised Labor support for the land rights fight.[59]

In the same year, the Queensland National–Liberal government of Joh Bjelke-Petersen confirmed the historic paternalistic controls over their settlements in Queensland. They passed the *Queensland Aborigines-Torres Strait Islanders Act 1972*, which ruled that 'no aborigines shall—leave a reserve, settlement or mission reserve without permission of the protector, superintendent or other authorised officer ... every Aboriginal who disobeys an order of the protector or more superintendent to cease dancing (coroborees) and/or other native ceremonies (initiation etc) shall be guilty of an offence.'[60]

On 2 December 1972, the federal Coalition government was defeated. As Malcolm Fraser recollects:

> The coalition had run out of steam in 1972. Mr Whitlam came to power with a very different kind of government. It was a government that in a number of important policy areas changed attitudes.[61]

One of those policy areas was land rights. Gough Whitlam's incoming Labor government was quick to establish the Woodward Royal Commission to report on 'traditional rights and interests in, and in relation to, land.' His report would form the foundation for Aboriginal land rights in the Northern Territory, delivered, as it would turn out, by Malcolm Fraser in 1976. Land rights and self-determination for Aboriginal communities would shape the choices and priorities of Patrick Dodson for the next three decades.

Eucharistic Congress

It was in this heady climate of rapid social change that Patrick was given a job in early 1973. In attempting to change the direction and focus of the Australian Church, Archbishop Knox sponsored a seven-day Eucharistic Congress in Melbourne.[62] The Congress was a huge event, combining ritual celebration with a series of seminars on issues like poverty, social justice, world peace and development. The focus of this Congress was on the involvement of the Church in solving social problems. The Catholic liberal philosopher, Max Charlesworth, claimed that, 'I thought this was going to be just an extravagant display of Catholic tribalism, but it promises to blow a new breath through the Church.'[63]

Patrick explained the Congress to me:

> It's like the Olympics of the Catholic Church every four years or so, but it's more than that. It's a time when the laity have a say about the Church

and theology, rather than just have it handed down to them from the cardinals and the bishops and the priests. It was a time when all of the Church came together to penetrate more deeply into the mysteries of the Eucharist, finding liberation and celebration in God's word.

Patrick's primary task was to organise a three-day conference for some five hundred Aboriginal people from all over Australia to discuss the relationship between the Church and Aboriginals. The conference was held in conjunction with an Aboriginal liturgy at Sidney Myer Music Bowl led by dancers from Port Keats, Bathurst Island and Kununurra. Incorporating Aboriginal elements in the Mass was, in Patrick's view, an enormous accomplishment, acculturating the Church and allowing Aboriginal people who sat through Mass as passive observers to be participants in their own terms. He did not know how to achieve the goals they were aspiring to, but with the help of others, he wanted to make it happen.

Patrick and Margaret Valadian took on the job, working with a team of people, like Nola Ferguson, Anarella Charles and Phyllis Harrison and his age-mate, seminarian Brian McCoy. On the Church side, Fr Hilton Deakin was the main organiser. Patrick's plan for the conference as a forum for workshop-based discussions and a free exchange of ideas and experiences was not to be fully realised. The conference was held at Corpus Christi College Werribee, once the mansion of a wealthy pastoralist. For the first time, Aboriginal Catholics from the missions of the Kimberleys and the Northern Territory would meet and discuss issues with rural and city Catholics, from places like Fitzroy, Redfern and West End. A parallel conference of non-Aboriginal people was held at the Pallottine College, Kew. Patrick was optimistic at the outset and at the time was quoted as saying:

> For the first time, Aboriginals on a national scale will be able to offer the Church advice, criticism and guidelines about our ministerial actions in the area from which they come and for national matters that affect the Aboriginal people.[64]

Shirley Smith commented that it 'was the first time in Aboriginal history that there was a gathering of over 300 people from all over the country. I met people I had never met before and when we talked it was as if we had known one another for years.'[65] Patrick ruefully recalled the event while sitting under his bough-shade at 'the Block' in Broome, saying:

> It was as wide a cross section of blackfellas as you could imagine. You had people from the missions out of here and the Territory. Then you had people out of Redfern, Brisbane. You had this combination of the so-called radical elements and the mission elements. The first time ever that I know

of that anyone had tried to bring a conference together of such a diverse range of Aboriginal people. It made major practical recommendations on health, housing, land, employment and prisons.[66]

It was a major learning experience in my life at that early stage. I didn't expect it when some of the urban mob bunged on an act and 5 or 6 walked out. It would be considered tame today, but it was horrendous. I got accused of being a sell-out, an Uncle Tom, a white black man. I was a student, out of the seminary, used to the kind of reasoned, rule-bound dialogue, discussion and debate we had in the seminary, being tossed into the deep end with hardened street campaigners. They called the mob who were going to dance in the liturgy, exhibition niggers. I was surprised by the vehemence.

What they thought was tokenism, I thought was a huge break-through. I was already having my own blues internally (on the relationship of the Church to Aboriginal people, culture and law) and here I was being accused of being an Uncle Tom, as if I was sitting pat doing nothing. Nobody bothered to figure out what my thoughts were on any of this, just accused, you know.

Some of those who walked out and opened a new front to the media, which scooped it up, were the Watson siblings: Maureen, Lilla and Len, from inner-city Brisbane. They were joined by Bob and Kay Bellear from Sydney, and Ruth Wallace from Cairns. They claimed to the press that they had been discourteously treated by conference organisers who stifled debate, preventing issues such as land rights, discriminatory legislation and health issues to go forward to the Conference of Bishops. In the workshops they had argued against an internal church focus, rather than an external social justice focus, saying 'we're getting bashed by the coppers. What are you going to do about the coppers?' They had a different perspective, based on different (but overlapping) life experiences, from those Aboriginal people from north Australia who had flown in for the Congress.

Maureen Watson laughed when she recalled the event and then cut herself short:

Oh, real shame job, that one. I felt so sorry for young Patrick, so eager and bright-eyed. It was nothing personal, just that he was set up to be the stooge for the Church. We stood up for our principles.[67]

Their principles were born in the streets. The Watsons at the time were organising Brisbane Aboriginal people and their white, usually Catholic supporters, to take action against injustice, especially police abuse. They, with Pastor Don Brady, Dennis Walker and others based in Don's church and the

Born Free Club developed 'Pig Patrols.' The patrols were a scarcely documented attempt, before legal aid services, to observe and moderate police behaviour towards Aboriginal drinkers at the pubs of South Brisbane and West End. Sexual exploitation of young girls in the police cells was a relatively common experience. Aboriginal people, next to white middle-class young Christian students and workers, would stand as mute witnesses to the police as they bundled people into the 'Paddy-wagons.' The witnesses, including myself, handed out cards for referral to solicitors.[68] It was not a popular activity with the police. I discovered this fact when the Consorting Squad informed my father (a public servant) and the Principal of the Teachers' College I was attending about my nocturnal activities. The police told them to make me correct my ways or forget about my future career.

This was the urban scene in a conservative state. The Watsons were into direct action, rather than working through existing structures to change from within. That was the 'assimilation model.' Patrick recognised at that point that there were not only different means to reach objectives, but there could be different objectives. Any national political perspective, even in the one institution of the Church, had to accommodate a vast diversity of views on outcomes and strategies for Aboriginal Australia. There were lessons here that would be applied in the debates on land rights, native title and reconciliation.

The non-Aboriginal participants, as one would expect, have different perspectives on the Werribee conference. Fr Hilton Deakin remembered Patrick's role as less than central; pointing to his youth and inexperience.[69] Fr Brian McCoy thought that without Patrick's mediation abilities the whole conference would have fallen apart, but that Patrick was left 'holding the baby' after the walk-out.[70] Both saw it as a milestone in Patrick's life, with Bishop Deakin feeling that it started Patrick on the track to being a 'political priest.' He recalls advising the Church authorities to 'keep Paddy out of Aboriginal affairs for his own good and send him overseas to the Missions.' Fr McCoy felt that Patrick for the first time had to publicly address his Aboriginality and come to terms with where he stood as a person, as well as a priest. At Werribee and for every day after that, he would not be able to hide inside his habit.

Patrick would talk about it with Brian McCoy years later:

> There were all these serious emotional allegations being raised by political operatives about corruption, and discrimination and pederasty and they left me, like a mug, to handle it and defend the Church. The organising committee wouldn't be seen for quids. I wanted to shout, 'Why have you forsaken me?'

Back to Broome

During this period of growing confidence in his authority and key role within the Church, the seminarian was wrestling with his own doubts. He was particularly concerned with ensuring that he remained true to his own family heritage and the tradition embodied in his grandfather. There was much, he knew, that he didn't know, that he yearned to understand. He was 'in battle' within the MSC community:

> I was trying to get the order to understand the necessity of coming at spirituality and pastoral practice and missiology from within the perspective of the Aboriginal people, not the external perspective and therefore the necessity to have some standing within the Aboriginal community if you're going to have any authority. That's when I was saying to them that it's important I come back to Broome and at least learn some aspects about that side of my Aboriginal heritage and my family and the Law and the constraints of that Law and the view that people have on Churches and missions and whoever else. So I was already going down that track.

There were supporters of his view that the Church had to be an outward-looking Church, rather than serving its own clientele: its houses, churches, schools and hospitals. He expressed a conviction that the Church had to start dealing with the marginal people of society, the young mothers, the unemployed, the drug-takers, the homeless. He argued that the Church had to deal with these people and the priests had to be part of that community if it was going to have any sort of authenticity.

Holding his own against the silver-tongued orators of the order was satisfying but not enough. He came from practical folk, he believed in community action and saw a job to be done. To do it, he needed to live it, not talk it. Closing the circle required a homecoming and he eventually got the reluctant permission of the order to have some 'time out' in Broome, as a deacon serving in the Catholic Church in Broome, living in the Presbytery.

The Church elders were less than enthusiastic but eventually yielded to his needs. One senior MSC priest warned Patrick that he had to leave all that Aboriginal side behind and follow his vocation. He made Patrick do the sums, calculating what 'part of his blood was Aboriginal.' He was asked why he identified as 'Aboriginal', when racially, he was 'just an octoroon.'[71]

He came back to Broome and found, not to his surprise, that things were 'bit same, but different,' in Broome. The old social structure, pearlers at the top, natives at the bottom, was intact. Once, answering the Bishop's phone, he was spoken to by Mrs Male. The same Mrs Male for whom Granny Liz had laundered.

'The bishop is still on his plane, flying out west, Mrs Male,' Deacon Dodson informed her.

'Oh, that is most inconvenient. We were expecting him for tea and he is late,' she replied.

'Well, Mrs Male, perhaps I could come instead of the Bishop?'

'Oh, no. That wouldn't do at all,' she said through pursed lips, placing the receiver down.

Patrick and his fellow priest laughed long.

Change was in the air in 1974, nationally and in Broome. There was now some sense of the old days being gone, and gone for good. New Commonwealth Government services and representative organisations were starting to gear into action, following the recognition of Aboriginal living conditions and the legacy of decades of neglect.

Deacon Dodson started to 'say my piece, not hold my peace' while he was in Broome. He shocked 'all his aunties' in Broome when he dared to say during their Church retreat that priests were not always right. 'You must not talk like that,' the Aboriginal women of Broome scolded him, 'you have to talk like a priest.'

Paddy Djiagween, of course, was there. Now around 90-years-old and increasingly infirm, he would still take his rightful place among the lawmen, being consulted on matters of protocol and interpretation. He still sang in ceremonies, but would 'more often growl them for singing the wrong songs.' Paddy engaged actively in the politics of Yawuru religion and land ownership, being accorded the respect and deference due to his years and knowledge. He was one of three old men who were the major Yawuru lawmen at the time. They were the bosses. Patrick learned from them and other men, submitting himself to their authority. He started to go through their law. He was deacon in one domain; novice in another. Both domains could be described as male gerontocracies, with the authority of law being carried by the old men and the duty of the young men being to serve and learn.

As his pastor, Patrick took old Paddy Holy Communion and breakfast and then sat with him drinking tea and talking for as long as he could. He learned that, like the Church, debates over religious and ritual issues were commonplace. These debates were inherently political. Honour and authority went to those who could argue with knowledge, experience and forceful expression. Their arguments had to be within the law, always remaining consistent with known and agreed truths. Unlike the debates in the Church, the arguments in Broome centred on land and culture. Increasingly, 'traditional' politics were being exacerbated by the intrusion of Government policies and practices.

One specific case, over a small area of land, exercised the Aboriginal community at the time. Patrick learned the details of the ongoing dispute in Broome over the area north of Broome, known as Reserve 30906 to those who toiled over land maps; as Fisherman's Bend to most of the Broome townsfolk; and as Kunin to the Yawuru. After a negotiated arrangement between Paddy Djiagween and the Roads Board in 1969, the Native Welfare Department had excised the reserve from the town common to give the Yawuru a space safe from intrusion to perform ceremonies and to store their ritual objects in two iron sheds. Those sheds became the 'office' of Yawuru 'business.' Concealed carefully inside were sacred objects that were the 'title deeds' to the Yawuru lands. The deeds could only be read, understood and used by those with knowledge, who had been given that knowledge by other men. The boards give access to ritual knowledge and power, some of it very dangerous.

In 1972 the reserve was transferred to the newly established Aboriginal Lands Trust. Jack Lee, an Aboriginal man, wanted to establish a mud crab farm and quarry. He applied for title to part of the reserve. In the furore that erupted and continued for years, the sheds were raided, objects were stolen and sold, people were verbally and physically attacked. It went to court and a man was jailed. It was a terrible blow for the Yawuru. They had lost so much in the growth of Broome and the Kimberley. Now their last little pocket was threatened.

It seemed that the slender thread of Yawuru continuity, held in Paddy Djiagween's hand, was in danger of unravelling. Yawuru ownership rights were under challenge from those of neighbouring groups, with knowledge from different sources, both Aboriginal and non-Aboriginal. Custodial rights, once complementary to ownership rights, were claimed as separate and exclusive traditional tenures. Different ways of singing the Dreaming tracks, of reading the country, of interpreting the Law were proposed.

The political struggle had been waged in similar ways in countless Aboriginal estates over the continent, as land-owning groups changed over time. Now, however, the struggle was fuelled by the involvement of non-Aboriginal experts and cultural brokers such as the museums. Contesting anthropological and linguistic interpretations were raised on the nature and extent of Yawuru land ownership. Maps with boundaries, different to those in Paddy's mind, were drawn up.

Language was one issue on which the community was becoming divided. The relationship between Yawuru and Jukun was hotly debated. Claims were made that Jukun was not a dialect of Yawuru, but a separate land-holding identity owning its own language, traditionally responsible for the land around the town of Broome. As Michael Walsh notes:

> Language ownership is essentially a matter of birthright. To be a member of a language group is not a matter of making an application and paying a fee, as if to become a member of some local club. Typically one must be born into the group. An Aboriginal person can also be adopted into a group and thereby enjoy the privileges which would usually flow to those born into the group. Language ownership is rule governed, and, to a considerable extent, is permanent and non-voluntary.[72]

After close to a century of mixed marriages, multiple liaisons and rapid social and family transformation, the language associations of people in Broome were just as mixed and the subject of debates in bars, streets and kitchen tables. Paddy Djiagween had a view. He argued that Jugun was a dialect of Yawuru, and one, moreover, that he spoke. He had told Wendy Lowenstein the same thing in 1969. Patrick recalled a time when a Minister came to meet the old men and women for a discussion:

> I forget what the issue was and I can't remember the name of the Minister, some little fat bloke, might have been a Labor Minister. Anyway, he came there for a meeting on Kennedy Hill and Grandad said to him, 'If you could speak my language, we could understand what you're talking about. But if you can't, you'd better get someone to help you explain what you want to talk about to us.' Everybody laughed and the Minister didn't have a clue what to do or say.

Broome, 2000

Patrick drove me up to Kennedy Hill. The waters of Roebuck Bay glistened in the summer sun. A lacework of mangroves fringed the bay. Patrick pointed across the Bay to Thangoo; the pastoral lease that had once been the Yawuru stronghold. He pointed down to Kunin, the place that his grandfather and other lawmen of the time had been able to negotiate, and where Patrick, working with today's Yawuru bosses, now claimed rights of ownership against the whole world. We looked across to the distant east, and Patrick talked about lines of ceremonies, songs and custom that travelled through the heart of the continent to Uluru. He then talked about his Grandad.

Before leaving Broome to return to the seminary at the end of 1974, Patrick visited Paddy on Kennedy Hill, sitting with him as he stared out across the waters of Roebuck Bay. Together, they watched the smoke plumes of a bushfire rise up from Thangoo station. Grandfather and grandson watched over their country, their homelands. Paddy Djiagween told his grandson:

> I am Yawuru. I speak Jugun Yawuru. Little Yawuru. My people, the Minyjirr mob. From Jiringinngan, here in Broome right through from Willie Creek to Thangoo.

> You boy, you're same. From me. Come up same. You Minyjirr bul— Broome boy. When I go you gotta carry on. Djagun, that time you'll be. Djagun, like my name. You can follow grandfather. That track now. [72]

Patrick knew he was going away, again. He was a young man, on the verge of committing his life to Holy Orders and his Mother the Church. It would be many years before they would sit together again, and before Patrick could base himself on his grandfather's country. The Church, his Mother, had called him away.

*School captain and head prefect, Patrick Dodson, addresses fellow school leaders (*Daily News, *March 30, 1967).*

Reunion with the Gartlan family (courtesy of Paul Lane).

Patrick Dodson as footballer, 1975 (photograph Terry Phelan, courtesy of the Herald and Weekly Times photographic collection).

Patrick Dodson as Deacon, 1975 (photograph Terry Phelan, courtesy of the Herald and Weekly Times photographic collection).

226 ● Paddy's Road

Mick Dodson performing his last official duty as Aboriginal and Torres Strait Islander Social Justice Commissioner at Chittaway in NSW, 1998 (courtesy News Limited).

Halls Creek, the Kimberley Ranges, 1952 (courtesy of National Archives of Australia).

Chapter Eight

A troubled priest

'What bishops like best in their clergy is a droppingdown-deadness of manner'
(The Works of the Rev. Sydney Smith 1839)

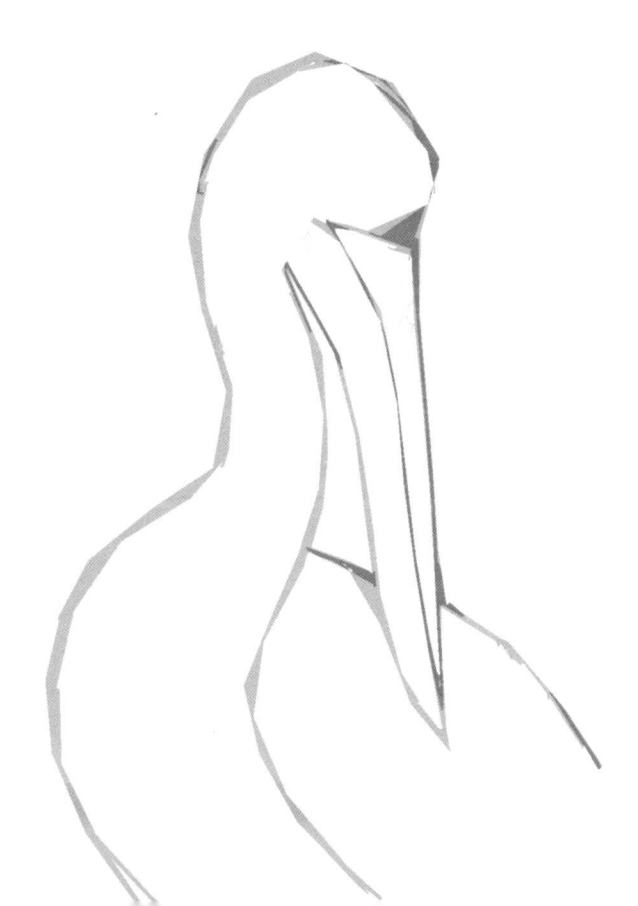

Broome, WA, 1975

In every bar, club, cafe and workshop in Broome; everywhere the Aboriginal people, pearlers, boat workers, shopkeepers and labourers met, large notices written in red, blue and black felt pens were nailed to the doors and walls. On 17 May 1975, everyone was invited to Patrick's ordination. No-one would be turned away.

In that week, every road on the Australian map seemed to run to Broome. Hundreds came from all over the Kimberley; across from Katherine and Darwin; up from Melbourne, Sydney and Canberra, from Hamilton and Casterton. From all over Australia, black or white, Catholic or not they came; in cars, trucks, buses, boats, planes and jets. Two bishops, thirty-one priests, fifteen of them from the MSC order and eight Pallottines, celebrated the mass.

Quite a turnout, swelling the small town population. Two thousand people crammed into the newly built, Asian-style Broome Civic Centre, overflowing onto the verandah and lawns outside.[1] The crowd was too large for the grandly named, but relatively tiny, Broome Cathedral. Those inside heard a choir of 50 boys from the mission at La Grange (Bidyadanga) singing in Karajarri, their language; saw the huge altar backdrop showing the country of the Kimberley; and watched the fans flap the big yellow banners. Each banner was designed to carry a story in black, red and blue of an Aboriginal spirit ceremony flowing from the dreams of Butcher Joe Nangan. He dreamed the story and the paintings. Patrick's nephew Ronald had designed the symbols and the cross. Across the altar was draped another banner with the Yawuru words, 'Gugu Hjamba Ingan—Father is here.' On the lectern, other motifs and the single word, 'Malingara' — Listen. The liturgy was based on the work done for the Melbourne Eucharistic Congress, aiming to incorporate Aboriginal cultural practices in the ceremonies of the Church.

The crowd was hushed as they watched the big, bearded Yawuru man prostrate himself, lying across the floor before Bishop John O Loughlin MSC, the Bishop of Darwin. At his side, another bishop, John Jobst, the

Bishop of Broome was assisting. Bishop O'Loughlin asked Patrick if he promised obedience and respect to his bishop. When the 'I do' answer was supplied, the Bishop said, 'May God who began the good work in you bring it to fulfilment.' At the acclamation, the new priest, Father Dodson led the congregation:

> Father in heaven,
> Remember Paul our Pope, and John our Bishop;
> remember all bishops and priests.
> remember all the people of God
> especially those who are here.
> Remember all your people
> who have died as your friends

The crowd responded, 'Father you are good', while the many Dodson family members present remembered the parents of the orphan boy and felt a tug of regret. Fay, Georgina, Cecil and Jacko were living in Broome. Mick flew up from his law studies at Monash University with his sister Patricia, recently married in Canberra. Their grandparents were first to the altar to receive communion. Paddy and Liz had been sitting together, for the first time in fifty years, as guests of honour in the front row. After the service, the old man, tears of joy in his rheumy eyes, led the young priest by the hand like a small boy down to the congregation to give blessings. It was a day of joy for the family, the Church and the town of Broome.

Father Pat

The Church media machine, overdue for good news on Aboriginal issues, swung into action and the event received wide coverage.[2] Pope Paul VI sent his blessings through Bishop Jobst of Broome:

> The Holy Father is pleased to be informed that first Aboriginal priest Fr P Dodson will be ordained at Broome and he gladly associates himself with this historic event in the life of the Church in Australia, invoking the multiple gifts of the Holy Spirit upon Fr Dodson and praying that as Christ's minister he may worthily make known among his own people the love of God and gospel of salvation, His Holiness warmly imparts to him and all assembled on this joyous occasion, special apostolic blessing.[3]

The interviews Patrick did at the time would induce a life-long aversion to answering the questions of journalists and playing along with the media's agenda. He saw and respected the journalists' purpose and function but was despondent at their lack of understanding of his cultural background and tendency to wrap their own words around his thoughts. They had no interest in history, or the need to explore the context behind the immediate issues. A journalist sought his comments on the perceived urban and rural divide of Aboriginal Australia. He replied cautiously:

> I understand the deep seated bitterness of the urban black activists. I sympathise with them, although I sometimes don't agree with everything they say and do. But I am a Yaroo (Yawuru) man. I prefer to stay out of the urban scene. My people have different problems.[4]

Others probed at his position on Aboriginal spirituality and how it fitted with the program of the modern Church:

> While the Christian hopes for a life hereafter he has to be concerned with the social issues of the day. Some Christians side step that—maybe some priests and ministers do as well. They tend to talk of society or community not caring for the poor and sick and those who are denied justice. I see my future as trying to bring about a greater sense of belonging among the Aboriginal people. I want to see that they're accepted for their own values for the enrichment of Christianity.[5]

The issues of the day would be the issues of his time in the priesthood and his future career. They were concerns that went to the heart of the reconciliation he was hoping to achieve within the Church, and within his own life.

These were fundamental issues for the Church. After the Werribee conference, the priest responsible for managing the Aboriginal component of the Eucharistic Congress, Fr Hilton Deakin, had been commissioned by the Bishops to write a report on Aboriginal relations with the Church. This was one outcome of the conference Patrick and Margaret Valadian had facilitated at Werribee. In the same week as Patrick's ordination, the anthropologist–priest presented a lengthy report to the Bishops.

Hilton Deakin had understood the need to listen, reflected in Patrick's ordination ceremony. He stressed 'very heavily that white people have got to adopt a posture of listening to Aboriginals during their process of self-determination', and adopt a more supportive and less directive role. He rejected the 'ordinary parish structure' as the way to operate in Aboriginal communities. He urged the introduction of Aboriginal studies in schools, the appointment of Aboriginal deacons as leaders, and the need to urgently address Aboriginal social conditions. Ultimately though, Deakin felt that the Aboriginal community should be encouraged to assimilate into the white society and culture, arguing his view that, 'in the long run, that is the only way they can go.'[6] In Patrick's view, the report did nudge the Church forward, but left much of their work in the Eucharistic Congress and the Werribee conference 'dead on the vine.' Patrick was learning the frustration involved in promoting institutional change from within.

Around Australia in a kombi

According to custom in the Kimberley and in the desert regions, a young initiand is taken on a 'grand tour.' The 'new man' is shown around related communities, makes contacts with other men and learns more about the Law, the country and the connections between people and places. Fr Patrick, after his ordination, had much the same experience, with a series of 'first masses' in the far-flung Catholic missions and settlements of the Kimberley.

Mother Church soon let Patrick know that it was time to stop touring the country and settle down as a priest. Darwin was his first assignment, living in the bishop's palace. Here he felt like the bellboy, answering the door, carrying the bishop's bag, living a strict, ordered daily routine. He was eager to get out into the community of Darwin where he had kin, footy and work mates, and where he could begin his work as a priest.

He did not sit for long. Fr John Leary had organised another job from the Bishops, this one on alcohol. Gaining funding through Pat Turner, from the NT Health Department, and Dr 'Spike' Langford, an ex-Territorian working in the Commonwealth Health Department, John and Patrick were to carry out a research project on the causes, impacts and amelioration of alcohol problems in Aboriginal Australia. Bernard Tipoloura, from Melville Island

and Diidji Bunduk,[7] from Port Keats, joined the team.[8] Just as the Church was starting, belatedly, to seek the advice of Aboriginal people in the management of the issues impacting on them, so too was the Commonwealth Government setting out to develop structures and processes through which to implement the policy of 'self-determination' and looking for Aboriginal people to advise them on the next steps.[9]

Patrick and John did the sensible thing for a group of young men touring Australia in the early 1970s: they got themselves a kombi van. Patrick was not the only kombi driver of the time who was bearded, pipe smoking, with hair long over the collar. However, he was the only one who was an Aboriginal priest. He and John carried out the research by moving around, finding people, sitting, talking and, mainly, listening. They visited bars, police stations, rehabilitation centres. They talked with drinkers and their families as they sat in parks, in broken down car bodies, in bombed-out empty houses. They followed the trail of despair, looking for answers. When answers could not be found, they sought reasons.

They saw that a large proportion of Aboriginal Australia was afloat on a sea of alcoholic numbness. Although a greater proportion of the non-Aboriginal population drank alcohol, those Aboriginal people who drank were more inclined to drink heavily in long binge-drinking sessions. They drank in public places, such as parks, where their noise and indiscretion was more likely to bring the attention of the police. They would then be moved on, inducing an escalation of conflict and criminal prosecution. He said later:

> It was a hopeless spiral. People were drinking out of frustration and hopelessness. They drank because they liked it, but kept drinking because they got locked in. Our report was just another out of the hundred and sixty odd reports saying the same things but nothing would change.

He also started to understand the need for people to drink; recounting later the story of a nine-year-old boy he met on a train going from Brisbane to Cunnamulla, saying he was drinking because 'I like it', and 'it knocks me out':

> This lad was in the company of his uncles at the time who were drinking and enjoying themselves. He was involved in the spirit of that time which was pleasant, warm, friendly and being made the centre of attention from time to time. It was obvious he felt accepted, welcomed and that he belonged. Maybe the seeds of his emotional life are planted in this sort of setting … When life pressures and the continuing colonising process threatens this lad it's to this kind of environment he will be attracted to. His memory will remind him where the seed bed of his emotional life was formed.[10]

Researching their project, John Leary and Patrick called in at La Grange Mission (Bidyadanga), south of Broome. Fr Kevin McKelson was the priest there, having arrived in the Kimberley in 1954 where he worked in the Broome Parish until 1961.[11] With the exception of one year spent at Beagle Bay, Fr McKelson had worked at the La Grange Mission. During that time he studied the Kimberley language groups, in particular the five languages spoken at the Mission.[12] Fr McKelson, who had assisted in the use of Aboriginal languages at Patrick's ordination mass, recalled Patrick's level-headed approach to the problems of alcohol:

> He impressed me the first time I met him. I had seen him previously dealing with drunken people, and he was very even-handed. He was very sure of himself—a moderate, level-headed man. I asked him why he thought Aboriginal people drank. He surprised me by saying it was not so much because they were suffering; they were drinking because they liked it.

At Fitzroy Crossing on this trip, a young Aboriginal girl came up and asked Patrick if he was a sinner. She told him that every smoker and drinker was a sinner, destined for the fires of eternal damnation. A strong form of fundamentalist Christianity was sweeping Aboriginal communities during this period, especially in remote Australia, to the accompanying rejection of Aboriginal culture. Patrick would see more of 'this plague of intolerant self-righteousness' in years to come and always found it distressing, saying, 'Today, even in death there is no escaping the rantings of these preachers about the evils of drink.' Many funerals would feature a preacher lecturing the congregation on the evils of drink.

Erich Kolig had a similar experience:

> I remember well the charmingly naive and disarmingly direct manner in which Aboriginal children being educated in the dormitory of the United Aborigines Mission at Fitzroy Crossing, asked me whether I was a Christian or a sinner. When I, somewhat facetiously, replied that I fancied myself as neither, they were left in giggling bewilderment unable to accommodate my strangeness. They had been taught to view the world in the white and black contrast between two true believers, i.e. those shaped in the mould of extreme Protestant fundamentalism, and those who were consigned to eternal damnation. This lack of any subtler nuances in assessing the world was symptomatic of the missionary approach up to that time, in which the crude racism of white settlers was replaced by an equally uncompromising division of humanity in terms of gnostic criteria. The hand of brotherhood extended to Aborigines had obviously exacted a price: the acceptance of the missionary world view with its rather limiting confines.[13]

For many communities, the problems caused by alcohol addiction (domestic violence, sexual assault, malnutrition) were beyond the capacity of the structures of the traditional religious framework and community decision-making processes to deal with. They yearned, sometimes, for the absolute certainty of the mission institution of earlier times to deal with these introduced problems. When that was no longer available, they instead were attracted to the absolute certainties of fundamentalist Christianity. Becoming a Christian meant swearing off the grog, and avoiding damnation into the bargain.[14]

Queensland

When the kombi rattled into Queensland, Patrick visited some of the settlements established under the legislation of that state. He found Woorabinda and Palm Island 'eerie places.' For him, Queensland was a 'complex cultural shock', and he came to believe that Western Australia had a spirit and sense of identity that Queensland lacked. He told Michael Pascoe of the *Courier Mail*:

> The people have no spiritual life. They have been forced into a materialistic way of living without realising they are a spiritual people. The effect of lumping people together, the fear of police brutality, the effect of drink on ceremonial life, the lack of acceptance by whites, the insecurity of not having land, all these things break down the spirit.[15]

When he walked around the beautiful beaches and shady lanes of Palm Island with Bill Congoo, Patrick felt he was in a time warp: back to 1955, 'like Moola Bulla with palm trees.' The desperation of the people reminded him of what he had been told by Granny Liz and his mother about Moola Bulla. The Island reserve was established in 1918, off Townsville, as a penal settlement, for the worst offenders from reserves all over Queensland. Now the descendents of the prisoners had only this place as their home. Their treatment at the hands of high-handed Queensland officials, standing behind their laws and regulations, moved the young priest to sorrow, sympathy and a quiet, brooding anger.

On Palm, he saw a community in crisis. He saw the drinking parties on the beach with sly grog smuggled in by boat, sometimes inside the fuel tanks of an outboard motor.[16] The fighting, the sexual abuse, the hungry children, the loss of control was stark and bitter. He was frightened by the hunted look in the eyes of the people on this spectacularly beautiful, tropical island. They were 'living but not living' he would say later.

He saw a community under control. They now lived under the Queensland *Aborigines Act 1971*. This legislation was a slight easing of the shackles of earlier acts such as the *Aboriginals Protection and Preservation Act 1939*. On Palm, Patrick met people whose income was still being kept by officials in trust without their consent, recorded in passbooks that resided in the Manager's desk drawer. Like Granny Liz, they could not be trusted to manage their own affairs. Under the old legislation, officials were legally authorised to make withdrawals from personal accounts and pay them into a Welfare Fund. The laws that were established to protect, had slipped into control and restriction, including a system of enforced sharing, so that the more enterprising workers under the Act had to contribute to the maintenance of others who exerted less effort.[17]

He met and talked to men denied the basic wage because they lived on Palm Island, and were under the authority of the Act. A study by Senator Jim Keeffe found only one in twelve hundred people on the island in receipt of the award wage.[18] It was only in the year that Patrick visited that restricted wages on Queensland reserves were made illegal through explicit Commonwealth legislation, in section 10 of the *Racial Discrimination Act* of mid-1975. It would be 1986 before it ended in practice and award wages would be paid to all Aboriginal workers on communities. He felt the threat faced by people who had nowhere else to go, but who were worried that their island home was to be sold as a tourist resort.

> The Act institutionalised a sense of insecurity, knowing they can be forced off. It's a sickening thing, the people who experience it are afraid.[19]

Patrick had to get a permit to visit Palm Island, not from the traditional owners, but from P.J. (Paddy) Killoran, Secretary of the Department of Aboriginal and Islander Advancement (DAIA), the contemporary Queensland incarnation of Neville and Cook. Patrick presented himself in the George Street offices of the Department, taking along as a witness a young Norman Katter.[20] Norman recalls that he was there as a parishioner of Fr Dick Pascoe's Graceville church, and as a lawyer, briefing Patrick on the workings of the Act.[21] They were lobbying the boss.

Rosalind Kidd has trawled extensively and systematically through their Aboriginal affairs archives.[22] She shows that for the twenty-five years to 1986 Paddy Killoran, only the third department head in seventy two years, exerted enormous personal control over the communities and the people who lived there. He was a skilled bureaucrat. He beat off attack after attack from other agencies within Queensland, particularly the Health Department, who were seeking to gain a measure of influence in community health on reserves.

Mainly, though, his enemy was Canberra, under both Coalition and Labor governments. He fought, mostly successfully, to resist award wages, self-determination, self-management, indigenous health programs, outstations, bilingual education and any form of Aboriginal land ownership in the state.

Killoran had no reason to label Patrick as one of the 'pseudo Aborigines who were disassociated from the mainstream of Aboriginal society' as he described the emerging national Aboriginal leadership.[23] He was polite, Paddy to Paddy, devout Catholic to priest. Norman Katter remembers that they received a 'pretty good hearing' and went back to Fr Dick Pascoe's presbytery in Graceville for a celebratory curry. Dick recalled the mood:

> Everyone was pleased at the outcome as a lobbying exercise, even Pat was happy. He tucked into a curry alright. He always liked a feed, but never got around to making one himself. He was a lazy bugger in that way. If there was no food cooked he wouldn't bother eating.[24]

Patrick said Mass that Easter Sunday and was challenged outside the Church when he drew an analogy between the holy places of Jerusalem and the sanctity of Aboriginal sacred sites. He was fairly disillusioned about the conservative attitudes in the Brisbane community, but he managed to communicate from the pulpit. One night, he preached a sermon at All Saints West End, in a packed church he held spellbound. As he preferred, he gave his sermon on the basis of a page of scribbled notes, extemporising at length.

Dick and his brother, Michael Pasoce, the journalist, organised for Patrick to attend a workshop on Aboriginal and Islander participation in the Catholic Church at Yeppoon in central Queensland. Gerald Brennan, later to become a High Court judge, heard him speak about Aboriginal association with land and told Patrick, 'You said it well, we've been wrestling with this for years.'[25] Brennan would go on wrestling with the same issues until he was required to write the lead judgment on the *Mabo* Case, some two decades later. Michael Pascoe wrote up Patrick's words:

> Land is the generation point of existence;
> it's the maintenance of existence;
> it's the spirit from which Aboriginal existence comes.
> it's a place a living thing made up of sky, of clouds, of rivers of trees, of the wind,
> of the sand, and of the Spirit that's created all those things;
> the Spirit that has planted my own spirit there, my own country.
> It's something and yet it's not a thing;
> it's a living entity.
> It belongs to me;
> I belong to the land;

I rest in it;
I come from there.[26]

Fr Brian McCoy says that this was the time, he thought, that Patrick began to put his own words around his Aboriginal beliefs and the potential synergies with Christian belief. He would later use similar words when speaking at memorial services for Aboriginal people at the Central Land Council.[27] Patrick's experience with the Queenslanders was pivotal. On the one hand, he was distressed by the persistence of a regime that brazenly denied rights to Aboriginal people. He locked in his view that a focus on title to land, community autonomy and cultural integrity was fundamental, giving his politics a harder edge. He rejected the foundations of assimilation, especially the widely held view that Aboriginal culture was in collapse, and that the future could only hold a merged identity.

On the other hand, he was starting to gain confidence in his ability to put a case to non-Aboriginal people at all levels that there should and could be change. He enjoyed moving around the nation being a catalyst for positive change and listening to Aboriginal people. He was learning to soften his political message, avoiding alienating his audience by using the language of moderation, reason, and the tones of priestly sincerity. He was starting to articulate for himself, through telling others, what it meant to be Aboriginal in a changing and diverse contemporary Australia, and what it meant, therefore, to be an Aboriginal priest. He was finding his own road.

A curate in Darwin

The kombi was left behind when Patrick was summoned back to Darwin, taking up the role of assistant priest, or curate, at the St Paul's Parish in Trower Road, Nightcliff. A large number of his parishioners were ex-inmates of the Garden Point Mission who had been 'uplifted and dropped in Darwin' in 1968. Garden Point was the Catholic Mission on the Tiwi home of Melville Island that had nearly become home for Patrick and Mick in 1960. The people from Garden Point did not have any other home or community, and were having problems coping with their new urban existence, as Patrick recalled:

> They came straight out of a closed mission environment, where they were living on the mission bells, to find themselves scattered across suburbia with their kids with no assistance to make all the adjustments that were necessary. The kids were all over the joint, their mission values were crumbling and they had to confront the dissolution of the bonds of family and community. They had lost their touchstone of authenticity. They

thought they were nothing. Nobody wanted them. For some they were too white, for others they were too black.

Bishop O'Loughlin viewed it differently, recalling that, 'In Darwin you will find over 300 people of mixed descent who owe their schooling and many of their good qualities to their experience at Garden Point.'[28] Patrick and his Bishop were operating on different models of Christianity, missiology and the politics of self-determination.

Patrick started to get the people from Garden Point organised, immersing himself in their community to promote and facilitate change. He brought the elders together and helped them make plans for a reunion at Berry Springs, south of Darwin. Most families attended and while they had a happy and relaxed picnic day, the nuns spoiled the occasion by saying they needed to take the girls back early for choir. Another planned reunion back on Melville Island was frustrated when they were told they needed a permit to visit their old home, alienated now by their Tiwi peers who held traditional ownership rights over the Island and the old mission. It would be many years before the Garden Pointers were sufficiently accepted by the Tiwi to be given Tiwi family names.[29]

Patrick was all too familiar with the dysfunctional lifestyles of the ex-mission inmates, trying to raise families when they had seen no role models for a family in their lifetimes. Many were scarred by the experiences, as 'Evie' told Mick in a hearing for the *Bringing Them Home* Inquiry:

> I was taken away in 1950 when I was six hours old from hospital and put into Retta Dixon until I was two months old and then sent to Garden Point until 1964. While in Garden Point I always say that some of it was the happiest time of my life; others it was the saddest time of my life. The happiest time was 'Yippee! All those other kids there.' You know, you got to play with them every day. The saddest times were the abuse. Not only the physical abuse, the sexual abuse by the priests over there ... There was four priests and two nuns involved. We were in their care.[30]

Sensitive issues such as these hovered, unsaid, at the weekly lunch with Bishop O'Loughlin, after Mass on Sundays in the Cathedral. Things were said, however, when Patrick started to negotiate a site for a club for the Garden Point 'mob', working on the Canossian Sisters for a piece of Church real estate. That Sunday, the Bishop told Patrick firmly, that he could not go down that road:

> He pulled me aside for a bit of a chitchat. He said that you can't have a separate place, that would not assist their assimilation into the community. They were brought over to Darwin to be assimilated, which was their only

chance. I started to argue with him, pointing down the road at the Italian club and the Greek club. Everyone else had a place where they could relax, seek advice, socialise. That's when we got into a tangle. He told me not to get too attached to the cause, into politics, that pastoral work should treat all parishioners the same. Separate organisations, he said, was not the best way to conduct pastoral care.

The young priest and the old Bishop were never on the same wavelength. Over the years, the Bishop would give the young, bearded priest carefully chosen Christmas presents: firstly a shaving stick of soap, then a razor without blades, then blades for the razor, and finally after-shave lotion. The message to shave and become respectable was clear, if not subtle.

A wider world

It was time once more for the Eucharistic Congress, this time in Philadelphia, USA, in July 1976. Patrick was selected by the Bishops to go as the 'missing link' with the Melbourne Congress. Fortunately, the Melbourne Archdiocese was footing the bill. The parish housekeeper, who took over the responsibilities of ensuring the young priest was fed and clothed, went into Mitchell Street, and came back with a blue safari suit.

He loaded his suitcase with Aboriginal paintings and artifacts and headed off for what was 'a really exciting time.' Most exciting was the Dominican Republic, site of Christopher Columbus' first landing. Here he briefly shared the lives of French-Canadian MSC missionaries and saw the disparities of wealth, power and communities under military control. Priests were followed and the sermons monitored for loose talk of social justice which risked rapid arrest and disappearance. The missionaries had a totally different form of engagement with their impoverished indigenous, 'Indian' parishes. The laity were empowered by the priests, anointed to carry out a range of ministries, such as marriage celebrant and counselling. The people had a greater role and function in the life of the Church.

> The priests invested in the laity, not pushing the classic clerical domination. They would leave hosts consecrated so that people could share communion without needing a priest. This was a real radicalism, a physical manifestation of a sacramental encounter. It allowed a greater expression of indigenous cultural forms than any dancing or singing in language could ever achieve.

His thinking moved beyond the possibilities he had been striving for in Australia. An Aboriginal liturgy was insufficient without fundamental changes in the relationships of power. It was the people who made the Church, not the priest. As a priest serving God in a global order, Patrick was inspired by the sense of possibility in adapting religious form and worship to blend with the economic, cultural and political realities of the people of the parish. In Australia, this sense of adventurous missiology and liberation theology was nearly unthinkable. As Bishop O'Loughlin said in his memoirs, 'We have learned in recent years that the Church is people. I don't think most of us would think there is a real church around unless there's a minister of the Church.'[31]

On his return from his 'jaunt' he was sent down to Tennant Creek, south of Katherine and north of Alice Springs, for a month, to act as the parish priest. He turned up there on 'the day that Elvis died',[32] and found it 'an eerie joint.' His parishioners talked about the devil running around, and told of seeing things that 'came out of Rosemary's Baby.' Watching him walk down the main street, the 'coppers bailed me up and asked me how long I was going to be in town and to state my purpose.' The next day, the circuit magistrate, Jerry Galvin, attended the early Mass, and Patrick took a ride with him down to the community of Ali Curung. On the way down, they talked about how customary law protocols could be integrated into the work of the courts, with senior elders sitting beside the magistrate to advise on sentencing. In Ali Curung, the Magistrate introduced Fr Dodson to the same policeman, who had the grace to be embarrassed when Patrick laughed and said, 'Oh yes, we met last night on the streets of Tennant Creek.' This time, they shook hands.

Port Keats, Wadeye

Southwest of Darwin, where three rivers flow into the Joseph Bonaparte Gulf, live the Murrinh-Patha people.[33] Their cultural neighbours had joined them on the mission station of Port Keats established by Fr Richard Docherty, MSC some forty years earlier. The mission station was roughly half-way between Darwin and the Spring Creek station where Joseph Fagan had lived and worked. Twice as far again would take you to Broome.

Fr Dodson was sent to Port Keats, now known as Wadeye, by Bishop O'Loughlin to act as curate for his old travelling companion, Fr Leary, and to 'settle Patrick down.' Patrick was pleased to go; he related more to the mission ideal of the MSC than the Parish role, and felt he had little support for his work with the Darwin Aboriginal community. He was eager to be back in a community and was fired by enthusiasm and ideals after his experience in Latin America. Also, he loved going bush. Geese eggs, barramundi and wallabies were in abundance, and fishing, hunting and camping was the best way to get to know the people and have a good feed. On one level, it was paradise.

One another level, it was a political, social, cultural tinderbox, regularly erupting in alcohol-fuelled riots sensationalised by the Darwin press. The priests, brothers and nuns were under pressure to do what they could in the tense situation. All too soon, Fr Leary left Patrick as the solitary priest, still officially the curate, to handle the load, while John did 'some sort of a gadfly' down to the Daly River. Patrick 'felt like the camp commandant in some episode of Hogan's Heroes.'

The MSC guides to missiology were not much help to the curate but pointed to the mission practice that had been dominant before Patrick's time:

> The moment you arrive at a station, you must not assert your authority as a master, indicating that you wish to be obeyed to the letter and that you are anxious to change the life-style and customs of the people. You must remember that they are not Christians and as a consequence, you will meet with certain irregularities, such as polygamy, the evil spells of the witch doctors, and others, which are quite repugnant to us. These are the most difficult things to root out and so we must not begin there. To destroy them we need to wait until the people are sufficiently instructed and your influence sufficiently strong.[34]

A Norwegian anthropologist, Johannes Falkenberg carried out anthropological research in Port Keats in 1950. He saw the mission having a major influence from 1945, 'when the serious work of conversion to Christianity was just beginning.' A dormitory system had been introduced with a strong impact:

> Among the consequences of the separation of the children from the other members of the tribe is the almost complete discontinuation of the boys' initiation ceremonies. The gradual admission into the secret life is one replaced by a systematic education in Christianity.[35]

Falkenberg observed that while the missionaries remained purportedly neutral in regard to the process of cultural change among the community, they were purposefully fighting the initiation ceremonies. These were central to the supposedly repugnant practices that Patrick should have been working to root out. One of those missionaries, Fr John Pye MSC, wrote a short history of the Mission published by the Bishop shortly before Patrick's arrival:

> At present Port Keats looks more like a modern town than an old time mission. There are new brick cottages, the people are living in them and looking after them (contrary to what many people thought).[36]

When he arrived in this 'modern town', Patrick saw the efforts to incorporate Aboriginal cultural practices into the church as witnessed by the intricate indigenous paintings in the church. The MSC missionaries, Fr Pye recalled, were very proud that Aboriginal women from Port Keats were admitted as nuns into religious orders in 1972 (the daughters of the first generation met by Fr Docherty) and that Deacon Boniface Pedjert was Australia's first married Aboriginal deacon, ordained the year after Patrick. These people were proof, as supposedly was Patrick, of the success of Catholicism in transplanting itself in Australia's indigenous soil. Fr Pye also commented on another form of Aboriginal-European interaction, close to Patrick's heart:

> MSCs take two things with them wherever they go—Christianity and Aussie Rules ... Football gave people a marvellous pretext for a fight, physical contact between two players would send everyone, spectators and all, and players alike scurrying for spears. Some were speared.[37]

Off the footy oval, the tensions between white and black culture, custom and law were razor sharp. In Fr Pye's view:

> Self determination is now the stated policy. It is the desired thing and let us hope it works and does not destroy all previous efforts by becoming self extermination.

This became the crux of the dilemma for Patrick, delineating the hard edge between his mission as a priest, specifically as it was conceived by Bishop O'Loughlin and other priests, and his identification with the Aboriginal community as the mission relinquished control of much of the day-to-day decision-making to Aboriginal councillors. For Patrick, the dilemma had religious, political and personal dimensions. The missionaries in previous decades had worked to minimise and marginalise Aboriginal traditional religious practice, treating it as suspicious and immoral:

> The bull roarer represented their Deity, a symbol of something that controlled their lives and was closely connected with the Devils and had some connection with sex.[38]

Instead of opposing, ignoring or seeking to eradicate these religious practices, Patrick sought to construct ways of incorporating, accommodating and reconciling Aboriginal ritual belief, in line with his thinking at Weribee and as he had seen in Latin America. Pushing across the track from Port Keats in a Toyota, Patrick took five 'old blokes' to Broome and La Grange to meet with his grandfather and other senior lawmen from the west. The old men sat together on the beach, drank tea and traded notes. In the way of such meetings they mapped the landscape between them, exploring where different Dreaming ancestors walked, sang and shaped the country.

On the surface, they had different laws, different customs. The Broome men danced with boards and had a minimalist approach to ritual; the Keats men played didjeridu, their songs had different beats and used a range of sounds not used in the west. But their common ground was greater than their differences, and they found a shared way of being and mutual authentication; discovering there was more in common in their law than was at odds. For Patrick, it was important for them to work out the common issues, in order to find a way of adapting Catholic rituals and theology to fit the cultural side of life. It was also 'very important in understanding me in the context of who I was.'

The vision was difficult to translate into practice, back at the Mission. It was run, supposedly, along the lines of an institution in which the roles, responsibilities and rituals of the place were as orderly and defined as the separation between inmates and authorities. At Wadeye, the clinic, community and school were controlled by the Sisters and lay brothers. They operated on the 'horarium', which defined the proper balance in any day between prayer and work as characteristic of a religious life. The common daily exercises of prayers, work; prayers ensured good order in the community and allowed the brothers and nuns to use their time well. Fidelity to the horarium was a discipline; they believed that the path to salvation was in keeping the rules. 'If you kept the rule, the rule kept you' as Patrick explained it. Meanwhile the priest, centrepoint of the balanced daily life, was off camping with the inmates.

The priest was supposed to be the pivotal point of the religious community, not to become embroiled in customary law and practice. At a practical level, the use of mission vehicles for camping trips, or for hunting and gathering, or for ceremonies, interfered with the orderly running of the Mission. Patrick used to go off fishing with Shane Fitzpatrick, the plumber from Toowoomba, and completely forget the 'horarium.' Once, the church trucks driven by Patrick and Mark Crocombe became bogged and were flooded by the incoming tide at the mouth of the Moyle River, near the beach where Nemarluk had killed the Japanese. Patrick's behaviour was not helpful to an ordered daily life. He relied on Brother Andy Howley, his offsider and right-hand man, to make sure works were carried out. Andy was the town clerk who managed the budget and attended to the practical tasks of infrastructure maintenance. The young men were organised in community efforts, such as tearing up the airstrip along which the town was built and back-filling it with topsoil and greenery.

At a theological level, Patrick's activities were giving privilege to customs and practices that people, in the view of the Church, had started to leave behind. According to the sisters, Patrick was being 'sucked into paganism', rather than 'rooting it out.' For Patrick, their view was blinkered; they were divorced from the social and economic context in which they lived and worked.

At a political level, the rationale of the place was still locked firmly into an assimilationist institution, a feudal fiefdom. The recently independent community, working its ways through the new process of self-determination, was officially no longer a mission, but an incorporated community. The title to land held by the Murrinh-Patha people was now recognised in the *Aboriginal Land Rights (Northern Territory) Act 1976* and they were learning that 'they were the bosses, not the priests, brothers and nuns.'

At a community meeting, when it was the time for the report of the priest, Patrick put a strong argument, asking people if they were ready to have real power. He strongly believed that they had the right and authority to take full control over the religious, political, economic and social life of the community. Boys could be taken out, if the community wished, to be taught their traditional Aboriginal values of manhood. The school calendar could be reorganised to suit community needs, not the white teachers who wanted to fly south for the wet—the very time the kids needed schooling because they could do nothing else.[39] They had the right to hire and fire staff. He would be there as adviser, not paternalistic overlord. The 'recently imposed' police presence would be there to support customary law, not establishing a layer of authority above the elders. The Church, rather than owning the Mission, could take out a long-term lease, not needing perpetual title over the lands on which their institutions were built. Visitors from the outside would require a permit to enter the community. This was radical change. Fr Dodson was handing over the institution to the inmates; throwing them the keys. He reflected:

> I suppose I was young, naive and idealistic in those days, not that all this wasn't true or necessary, but that you could just throw a switch and make it all happen. It was also true that there was no real leader in the community who came forward with the plan, and I was taking on too big a personal role. There was no Vincent Lingiari there.

Bishop John O'Loughlin heard the horrified whispers of the sisters. He spoke to priests, outraged to be told they now needed permits to visit the community. He heard the reports of the auditors, indicating that the revenue from the Port Keats stores, siphoned through Catholic missions in Darwin, would no longer flow to Bathurst Island. The Catholic Mission Headquarters 'the S.S. or Gestapo we'd call them', in Darwin, he was told, would no longer make decisions about the material needs of the community. The Bishop waited for Fr Dodson to come into Darwin for a little talk.

It was quite a talk. Patrick argued theology with the Bishop. He described the need for an indigenous mass, telling him that the encounter with God was the essential issue of Catholic theology; if you had a truthful carrying through of the cultural spirit, you could use that as the basis of the encounter. The form of the ritual was not important, and only became manifest as a system of order and control. Therefore, following Vatican II, if Christianity was to have any meaning, it had to be intelligible, to have meaning for the community.

The Bishop was outraged; declaring in ringing tones that Patrick's attempts at theological reconciliation were naive and foolhardy. Overstepping the mark for a curate. Worse, it was sliding down the slippery slope of a return to paganism, even Satanism. The words hung in the air, to be remembered by Patrick forever:

> It is not possible for an initiated man to be a practicing Catholic. I agree with an old man who once told me that once an Aboriginal is initiated into the old ways, you can wipe him off as a true Christian and a man who can survive successfully in the twentieth century.

Cut to the heart of his own identity, and ordered to abandon everything he held dear, Patrick was severely wounded. MSC priests I have spoken to had heard that the Bishop had made this definitive statement. They regard the statement as unsupportable, unfounded, insensitive and 'what probably led to his misbehavior.'

The Age newspaper would interview both the priest and the Bishop when the argument became public in 1981.[40] Patrick is quoted as arguing:

> A lot of conflict arose from my views on the power people should have in determining their own futures rather than being controlled by a centralised system. Plus my views on the need to allow Aboriginal traditional law to once again find a level of acceptability and to actively support and encourage that. I put self-determination into practice. I let the 1000 black people on Waderr (Wadeye) take back control over their own country and run their own community.

Bishop O'Loughlin said to *The Age* the next day that he had 'tolerated but not approved of the resurrection of pagan ways', and confirmed his view that an initiated man could not be a practicing Catholic. He traced support for revival of Aboriginal law as coming from:

> Certain artistic people who see some value in it because they can get some nice films of corroborees. There is also a group of old black people who are anxious not to lose their authority. They are brought hundreds of miles to initiate the young men into their wicked ways.[41]

Patrick returned to Wadeye, feeling the 'choker chain around my throat' but he continued to work and live with the Wadeye community as he had been doing, and building relationships with the families of the area. He immersed himself further in the way of life of the people, including joining in their ceremonial life. Fr Brian McCoy recalls arriving by plane at Wadeye. He was startled to be met by Patrick wearing a 'naga,' or loincloth, and painted up for ceremony.

Janet Hawley[42] described him in *The Age* at the time, as 'Fr. Dodson, 33, an articulate, magnificent-looking man with a flowing black beard and a physique like a front-row footballer.' Jack Doolan, the well-known territory identity, has recorded his memoirs with the Northern Territory Archives service. He also recalls Patrick in Port Keats as 'a big—well pretty big—strong handsome good looking young fellow.' Patrick had reminded Jack that they had met when Patrick was 'a poor little bloody, little black bugger wandering around Katherine', without shoes or shirt:

> And anyhow Paddy said he knew me and he did too, I got talking to him for a while. But he's a strange bloke, he's a very clever man. But I think the Catholic Church has done some really stupid things like particularly with Pat ... they put him down as a parish priest in charge of an Aboriginal settlement with all those luscious looking young ladies running around ... You know I can't understand their attitude. They want to keep a priest you know, they want to get some poor old bloke, about 98 not out (laughs).[43]

Out camping with the families from Wadeye, Patrick was relaxed and enjoying being with people in their country; a young Aboriginal man in a community that welcomed him, as well as being a priest in a diocese that was less welcoming. The differences between these roles and responsibilities would become difficult to reconcile when Annunciata Dartinga became pregnant with Patrick's child. In January 1980, their daughter was born in Darwin Hospital and given the name Grace Elizabeth Dodson Dartinga. Annunciata and Patrick would never live together and it would be many years before Grace shared a house with her father.

Fr Brian McCoy, Patrick's Jesuit 'age-mate', believes that it was not the relationship with Annunciata that was unusual or problematic. It was certainly not the first time a priest had fathered a child. Where it was different was that:

In Paddy's case, I believe Annunciata's pregnancy disclosed where Paddy's life had moved; there was nothing coming to birth in his relationship with O'Loughlin who continued to act like an autocrat and feudal lord. Many people in other places trusted Paddy and supported him, but Paddy was unable to ask for help and the MSCs were unable to give it. By this time, it was all too late.[44]

Some months before the birth of Grace, Patrick was in more trouble with the Bishop over the social and political direction of the community. There was another outbreak of violence 'sparked by underlying tensions of all the groups, where the mob went mad and blew the place apart, smashing the grader, leaving it with the two front wheels splayed in front of the Church.' The police next day were co-operative when Patrick asked them to put the guns away and 'let's just work through it.' The Bishop, however, wrote a stern letter to Patrick:

> Claiming the riot had brought the name of the Church into disrepute and asking me to explain why I couldn't control the situation. He said an Act of Repentance and Penance was required, and I was told to lead the community in procession with the Monstrance saying the Rosary and the litany of the Saints, culminating in a confession and general absolution.

Patrick's blanket refusal to obey the Bishop's directive on a community act of reconciliation became the final straw for the Bishop, who saw little need for patience. Patrick's stance was not supported by his MSC superior, Fr Fyfe, who was asked by the Bishop to deal with Patrick's 'sin of pride.' Fr Fyfe was amicable about the issues, agreeing to disagree with Patrick's position, but underlined the fact that the rules were there for him to obey. He needed to bow down before the will of his bishop, as he had done at his ordination. Patrick was invited to take twelve months leave of absence to think carefully about his life and his vocation, perhaps finding another field in which to be creative. Such a field, the Bishop and Fr Fyfe concurred, would best be found south of the Tropic of Capricorn. They considered that this would assist him to 'clean the terminals of his batteries so that he could communicate with God better.' He was temporarily relieved of his priestly duties, given $500 and an air ticket down south.

For the first time in his life, Patrick had to find his own road.

Canberra, September 1999

Patrick and I, between watching AFL finals, were talking about his time at Port Keats. I was taking notes for this book while he talked, reflectively running through the issues in his own mind. As usual, his focus was on the abstract and the political dimensions of events, rather than on the personal and emotional. Late at night, before he had to leave early in the morning for a flight back home, I asked him whether at the end of that time in Port Keats, he was frightened or scared. I knew that I would have been. He answered carefully:

> Not really. I was uncertain, I suppose. I mean, it was difficult knowing that I had to make my mind up about the nature of my vocation and the sacred call I still felt. But I was more concerned about clarifying what it was I was doing with my life and how I could best serve the needs of Aboriginal people.

The next morning on the way to the airport, as we drove through the gathering mists, Patrick said he had gone to bed thinking about my question and it was true, he was scared at the time. He had no money, no qualifications and no resources to fall back on. He was in a dilemma about not only what the right thing to do in the situation was, but what the best thing to do was. He knew that he was going to play a role on the public stage and he knew he could not ask Annunciata to leave her community and join in that life. He was scared that he could not look after a child, but knew that she and their child belonged in Keats and would be looked after. He was frightened that he might not be able to play a useful role, and maybe he would be better off becoming a lawyer, like his brother, Mick.

I listened and thought about his words. It occurred to me, but I did not say it, that he was still reconciling the events of the time.

Paddy's Road • 249

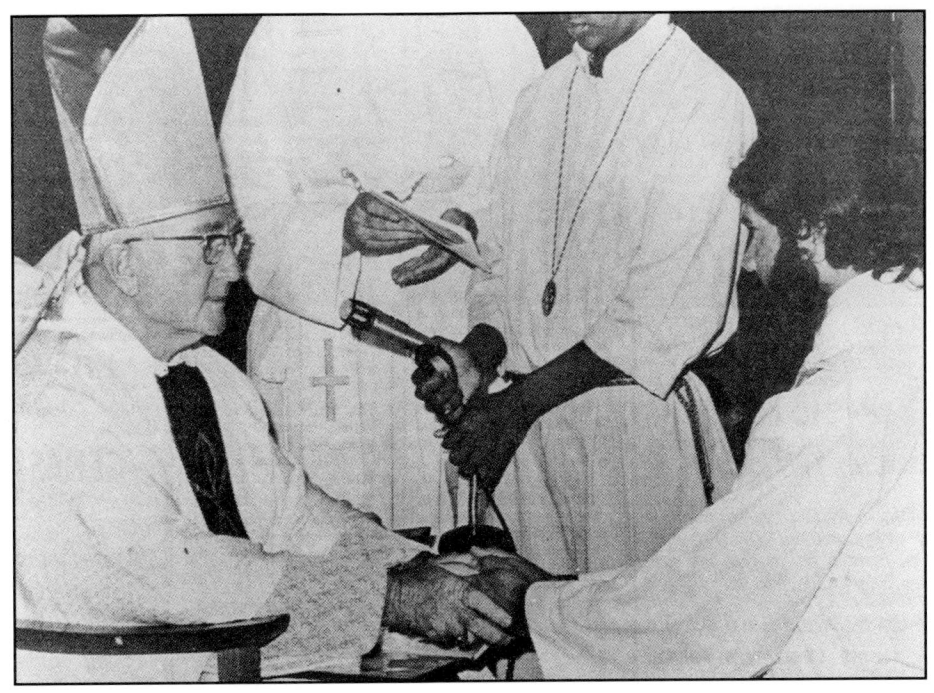

Bishop O'Loughlin of Darwin asks Deacon Dodson if he promises obedience and respect to his bishop (photograph by Les Teese, The Advocate *May 22, 1975, courtesy Melbourne Diocesan Historical Commission, Catholic Archdiocese of Melbourne).*

Fr Dodson joins in celebrating his first Mass with Bishop O'Loughlin, centre, and Bishop Jobst, right. On the far left is Deacon Boniface, from Port Keats, Australia's first Aboriginal married deacon (photograph by Les Teese, The Advocate *May 22, 1975, courtesy Melbourne Diocesan Historical Commission, Catholic Archdiocese of Melbourne).*

A group of men at the hand over of the Gurindji Cattle Station mining lease, Wave Hill, 16 August 1973 (photograph Government photographer, courtesy of the NTGP Collection, Northern Territory Library).

Land council meeting at Fitzroy Crossing, W.A., October 1979 (photograph Lyn Mcleavy, courtesy of the National Library of Australia).

'Politics should be kept out of paternalism' by P Nicholson, The Age, 23 June 1981 (courtesy the artist).

A pensive Patrick (courtesy Council of Aboriginal Reconciliation).

Chapter Nine

To the Centre

'The Australian ... will still live with the consciousness that, if only he goes far enough back over the hills and across the plains, he comes in the end to the mysterious half-desert country where men have to live the lives of men.'
C.E.W. Bean, 1911

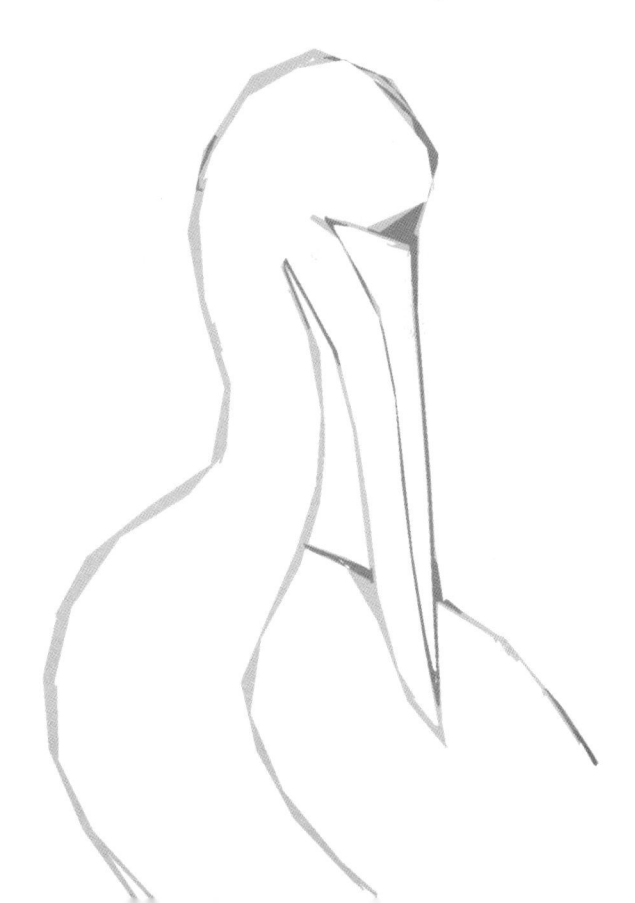

Hawthorn Station, Melbourne, Vic, 1980

The railway work-gang was gathering around the fire-drum, warming backs and hands before unpacking the tool-shed and getting on with the job. Big Joe, Little Joe and Bruce, or 'Yobbo' as they called him, watched the new bloke with the big beard walk along the track to their shed. He walked carefully, measuring his stride to the sleepers, a bundle of newspapers under his arm. The gang talked about the cold, the weekend footy games. Patrick parked himself on a drum, opened the newspapers and read the latest argument between Fraser and Hawke. He rolled a fat Log Cabin cigarette to start the day and sipped at the syrupy coffee brewed by Little Joe.

'Hey Paddy,' Little Joe called out, 'what you say to the boss first day?'

Patrick looked up from the paper and grinned, knowing that a good story was always worth repeating. 'Well, he reckon I'll get the sack if I get drunk on the job, 'cos I might walk into a train.'

'An' what you say?'

'I said, "If I get drunk and walk into a train, you won't have to sack me!".'

They all laughed. Even 'Yobbo' got that one.

Melbourne

Patrick took some time to settle into the working man's life. He warmed to the routines, the minor rituals, and the companionship. It gave him the undemanding space he needed for reflection while still keeping active. The railways were always one place where even a priest on parole could pick up work at a day's notice. Today, he points to the overpass at Hawthorn station and the walkway at Middle Park as monuments to his work. It was real work. Unlike social and political efforts, he said:

> You could look at the end of the day at what you or your mates had done and see a difference. Then you could go home, have a beer and forget about it.

He camped out at Ferntree Gully with his little brother, Mick and his wife Alecia and their daughter, Inala.[1] The brothers did not talk much about themselves. Mick half-suspected that something was wrong but 'Patrick didn't say anything. I thought priests did that sort of thing, taking time off and working for the railways.' Mick's view of the time was that the whole priesthood idea was a mistake. He would change this view years later when he recognised the skills and training Patrick brought to the process of reconciliation. Still, Mick and Alecia had been pleased that Patrick was able to be a celebrant for their marriage back in 1974.

Mick was now a fully fledged lawyer, working with the Victorian Aboriginal Legal Service, having been admitted to the bar in March 1979 by Chief Justice Sir John McIntosh Young after completing degrees in Law and Jurisprudence at Monash University and completing his articles at the Aboriginal Legal Service in Fitzroy.[2] He had also been appointed to the Victorian Equal Opportunities Commission. His vocational choice had been nearly accidental, the result of talks with Ian Heath, a Crown prosecutor living near the Roe Family in Darwin, over a Christmas holiday.[3] Originally enrolled in economics, Mick had shifted ground and found focus and a certain satisfaction. He still thought of himself as a Katherine kid and a Darwin man and knew he would head back up north at sometime. Speaking to reporters outside the Supreme Court after his admission to the bar as Victoria's first Aboriginal barrister he said:

> Because I am the only Aboriginal lawyer there will be a lot of pressure on me. The demands on me are far greater than for white solicitors. It worries me, but I know I can do it.[4]

Mick's legal experience met up with Patrick's hunger to 'be doing something meaningful' and the possibility of law filled the vacuum created in

Patrick's life. He enrolled at Monash University in 1980 to study torts, criminal law and contracts. He had barely bought the new books, when 'the cause' called, and Patrick found himself working with Australian Catholic Relief agencies on the campaign for Aboriginal land rights.

The times were busy for those, like the Dodson brothers, who had a passionate interest in Aboriginal politics and the law, especially in their home country of Northern Territory and Western Australia. The Fraser Coalition Government had made major changes to the policy landscape, building on the reforms of the Whitlam Government, while maintaining an uneasy truce with the states, especially Western Australia, on land issues. The watershed had been the passage of The *Aboriginal Land Rights (Northern Territory) Act* by the Federal Parliament in 1976. Carried across, with amendments from the Whitlam Government position, the Act provided recognition of Aboriginal land ownership to about 11,000 people, established the Northern Territory Land Councils and set the benchmark for statutory recognition of Aboriginal rights in land, particularly rights to control mining.

In 1978 the Northern Territory was given self-government by the Fraser Government and established itself as a perpetual opponent of the land councils. While it maintained electoral success through this opposition to land rights, its success in the courts would be meagre. For Fraser, 'the land rights legislation recognised an aspect of Aboriginals' affinity with the past which up until then had been ignored. Therefore it established a groundwork for future relationships with the Aboriginal population.'[5]

In the south, Aboriginal supporters and church groups initiated movement towards a treaty with Indigenous Australians. In 1979, when Patrick left the north, the Aboriginal Treaty Committee was formed by Dr H.C. (Nugget) Coombs. The National Aboriginal Conference, the official voice of Aboriginal people, called for a treaty between the Commonwealth and Aboriginal people. Fred Chaney, the Minister for Aboriginal Affairs, welcomed the initiative and funded a nationwide consultation process.

It would be the 'land rights' issue that dominated the agenda of the 1980s. Patrick would move out of his priest's collar and don the large hat with the red, black and yellow band that became his trademark. The possibility of a 'treaty', recognising prior sovereignty and accommodating and reconciling the existence of a contemporary nation state, was a goal for further down the road.

Nookanbah

It was the Nookanbah campaign, a prolonged dispute between the Western Australian government and the Kimberley Land Council and Western Australian Aboriginal Legal Service that dragged the half-hearted law student and part-time fettler away from his books. In 1978, the Kimberley Land Council was formed on a shoestring with the World Council of Churches providing enough money for a field officer and a part-time secretary. Peter Yu, a young man from Broome of Chinese-Aboriginal ancestry working for the welfare authorities, was interviewed before an entire Aboriginal community to win the field officer position.[6] The Nookanbah conflict began in 1979 and reached a climax in August 1980 when a police-escorted convoy of Amax trucks carrying oil-drilling equipment was blockaded by a large group of Aboriginal people and supporters at the Broome turn-off. The blockade failed to prevent the trucks from driving out to the cattle station owned by the people and drilling an area identified by the Western Australian Museum as a sacred site.[7] 'Land Rights, not Mining', became the catchcry and bumper sticker.

The cattle station on the Fitzroy River had been purchased in 1976 for the Yungngora community by the Commonwealth Government Aboriginal Land Fund Commission. However, their leasehold rights gave limited control over what could happen on their land. For the state Premier, Sir Charles Court, Nookanbah was 'the start of a massive land rights campaign in WA' and mining had to go ahead.[8] The Commonwealth Minister, Fred Chaney, also a Western Australian, watched anxiously, finding it difficult to keep in step with his state Liberal Party colleagues.

The churches, especially the Australian Catholic Relief organisation, had Patrick 'working the traps', speaking about the Aboriginal needs for, and rights to, land. He captured interest by situating the politics of the cause within a contemporary Christian theological perspective. He spoke widely, including in New Zealand for two weeks, explaining the dispute at Nookanbah and the need for land rights, to gatherings of interested churchgoers and Aboriginal support groups. Fr Dodson argued for the centrality of land rights as a social justice measure:

> One of the difficulties we have in trying to get across our concerns is that an Aboriginal person never thinks in terms of categories. We think of the total interacting factors on Aboriginal people and their life in society. Every other need of Aboriginal people is caught up in our understanding of land rights.[9]

For Patrick, the Nookanbah event crystallised his interest in seeking to gain support in the wider community for issues affecting Aboriginal communities that would otherwise be remote and vulnerable. He recognised the impact that media attention and international scrutiny could bring. He learned the value of coalitions of Aboriginal organisations and groups, such as union and church networks, to promote practical social action campaigns. The priest saw a larger flock, while he still missed the sense of belonging and purpose of the priesthood.

Nookanbah also crystallised a national approach for the first time, despite profound differences between the Aboriginal organisations across Australia. In September 1980, Aboriginal members of the land councils in the north, and Aboriginal leaders from other parts of Australia, joined forces at Nookanbah to form the Federation of Land Councils. This was an important organisation nationally, and an important group of people for Patrick, personally.

Many of the figures at that first meeting would go on to become mates and work closely with Patrick in the decades to come.[10] Galarrwuy Yunupingu, the urbane, regal and confident Gumatj Yolngu man was there. He held qualifications in Christianity, but from a Baptist background. Wenten Rubuntja, the cowboy-hatted master of the law was from the Arrente people in Alice Springs. Together, during the 1970s and into the 1980s, they were major bosses of the two large Northern Territory land councils. The two men would remain Patrick's bosses, in Aboriginal customary law and kinship terms and he defers to their authority. Both of them later joined Patrick on the Council for Aboriginal Reconciliation. Stan Scrutton was Chairman of the Central Land Council when Patrick was director. His long-haired, guitar-playing countryman, Peter Yu, and the irrepressible Daryl Kickett would remain close and work together on the Royal Commission into Aboriginal Deaths in Custody and at the Kimberley Land Council. Matthew Wonaeamirri from the Tiwi and Shorty O'Neill and Mick Miller from North Queensland were also at that first Nookanbah meeting.

It was this network, centred on the mining royalty supported and politically powerful land councils of northern Australia that became the core element of national Aboriginal politics and directed Patrick's work in land rights. The network transcended large divides to maintain a sense of momentum and purpose, although it was often in tension with organisations centred in the populous southeastern corner and represented by men such as Paul Coe, Les Malezer, Geoff Clark and 'Sugar' Ray Robinson. Kevin Cook at Tranby College in Sydney played a central role in bridging the north–south divide, as well as linking with church and union groups in the city, providing the donations that entered the bank account passbook Patrick carried. It is often not recognised that internal Aboriginal politics is vigorously contested and hard fought. Networks and alliances continually shift and fall apart; policies and positions are argued, attacked and abandoned; rivalries erupt and explode for reasons as often personal as political. In particular, male contests for supremacy and dominance often shape the political agenda.

In this ruck of competitive egos and contested agendas, Patrick built a reputation for his facilitation skills in large meetings with diverse stakeholders. In January 1981, the World Council of Indigenous Peoples, a United Nations-accredited non-government organisation, met at Patrick's old university in Canberra. While the official meeting took place, at which the National Aboriginal Conference was the endorsed Australian voice, an alternative conference was set up, with Patrick as a 'safe' chair. Patrick would remain wary of the value of the international road to social justice, while valuing the effort to ensure internationally recognised standards for the treatment of indigenous peoples. After the meetings, Patrick recalls:

> We'd adjourn to the Union Bar and get on the piss. I started drinking with a mob from Alice Springs, including Geoffrey Shaw and Dick Leichleitner. Pat and Lionel Turner I met there. Old Wenten Rubuntja was around, but he was never at the bar, of course. Marcia, wearing a red dress, I recall. It was in one of those sessions that Geoffrey told me I should come and work in Alice Springs, that it would be a good place to work.

Supporters in the southern churches found another role for the activist priest. The Catholic Church established a Task Force on Land Rights for Aboriginal People, under the auspices of the Catholic Commission for Justice and Peace and in cooperation with the Australian Council of Churches. Patrick was the ideal Chair, being able to bridge the political divides that existed between the members.[11]

One task they set themselves was the development of study materials on Aboriginal Land rights that could be used in church groups or adult education study circles. Des Carne, a recent theology graduate, was the chosen author. The work resulted in a book that explored the basis in Christian theology for supporting Aboriginal land rights. 'Many people said it read like a Marxist tract which of course it wasn't,' Des Carne recalled.[12] Patrick found it 'exciting that someone was able to write down and justify the ideas I had been wrestling with, not just in my mind, but in the mind of the church as a whole.' He would welcome the willingness of others to argue the issues with him and write up the results, providing him with texts to use in his campaign, backing up his often loose, if compelling, verbal presentations. It forced him also to clarify where he stood on key issues, such as the general malaise he saw whereby Aboriginal people and their supporters too frequently 'blamed the invasion and didn't do anything to fix things.' Instead, he argued:

> There is not much point in decrying what happened in 1788 and for the first hundred years. But we do want to say that Church people have it in their power today to know what is going on and to do something effective about it. That's the message our people want to get across to the churches. It's not a dredging up of past misdemeanours. The present situation is one of challenge to the Christian faith, and for that faith to be acted out in justice.[13]

Following a track of Aboriginal organisations and sympathetic parishes, he visited Melbourne, Adelaide, Perth, Alice Springs and Townsville, talking about the need for Christians to 'gain a better understanding of the need of Aboriginal people to have basic control of their lives free from interference, with security of tenure and permanency of occupation.' He stressed the need for local action, telling the Rockhampton community:

> If we are truly Christian in our hearts and minds we would be willing to try to understand the problems which face Aboriginals. I want to create a true sense of Christian commitment among the people of Rockhampton where they recognise Aboriginal people as their brothers and sisters. Working together to solve problems faced by Aboriginals will unite the community instead of dividing it.[14]

Elsewhere he praised what was being done to promote multiculturalism, but saw that 'traditional Aboriginal culture is pushed aside and unrecognised.'[15] The core message he carried was the need to protect land in order to defend culture, all within a framework of Christian beliefs and principles.

While on his 'sabbatical' he resumed work on the problems of alcohol, now working with the Brisbane-based Foundation for Aboriginal and Islander Research Action (FAIRA). He stayed for a time at Jeannie Devitt's house in suburban Indooroopilly, in Brisbane. Her neighbours were much surprised to see black people on the verandah, from which Patrick would cheerfully call, 'good morning', as they went scurrying past, averting their gaze.[16]

He regarded alcohol as the greatest problem and land rights as the great solution. He saw that the deep family and community crises caused by the grog threatened the cultural base provided by access to security of land. The priest was no 'wowser', being fond of a Cooper's lager or a bottle of red.

When there was more than a bottle available and men to drink with, he would always drink on. After a while he would reach a point of no return. He would then, more often than not, launch impassioned and uninterruptible tirades when someone made the error of challenging him on an issue or questioning a statement. 'Handing out a ferverino' was the phrase he used for this treatment, usually balanced by begrudging compassion, but not apology, the next day. There was no tolerance, though, for those men in the Aboriginal communities he visited who lashed out at Aboriginal women, saying later:

> When they abuse the children; when they abuse the women, the mothers they attack the future of our people—they abuse our heritage and our destiny.[17]

It was around that time that he received word that Granny Liz, his mother's mother, had passed away in Broome and he rushed back for the funeral. In Darwin, at an alcohol rehabilitation centre, he found Joe Soden (or Djiagween), Liz's youngest child, who had been 'ringing in the backblocks' working as a stockman, dodging the law, until a horse rolled on him and he was badly injured. Patrick gave his uncle Joe the bad news that his mother had died. Paddy Djiagween did not attend the funeral, in keeping with Yawuru tradition. For Patrick, who had not been able to go the funerals of his mother and his father, this was a poignant loss. The family sat around after the funeral telling stories. Patrick recalled the times with her, teasing her, sparking her cheeky sense of humour:

> Fay was bossy and used to make her sulk. I used to try and cheer her up. 'Jeez, you're looking lovely, darling,' I'd say to her. 'Would you like to come to the pub?' I'd give her a bottle of brandy when Fay wasn't looking. She didn't mind me being in trouble on her account.

Like many a family, Aboriginal or not, alcohol was a major social lubricant; a cause of pleasure and pain.

The law student 'gallivanting around the country' did not do well in his studies. When he opened the envelope from Monash University at the end of the year he saw that he had failed criminal law and scraped through contract law and torts. Then the phone rang with a message. Fr Dennis J. Murphy, Patrick's lecturer at the St Paul's seminary and a strong intellectual force in the MSC order, wanted to 'have a chat.'

They talked priest-to-priest and man-to-man. Whatever was said was persuasive. A meeting in Melbourne ran through the scenarios for Patrick's return to his ordained role. The Church and the priest negotiated what was required, what was possible and what was the ideal.

> I had a sore need and a strong desire to see if I could make this thing work. I needed to know for sure.

They suggested he could go to Papua New Guinea, or to teach at Downlands on the Darling Downs. Finally, they settled on the presbytery in Alice Springs, with an over-riding condition. Patrick was not to go north of the Utopia turn-off, some 100 kilometers north of Alice Springs. He had to keep well away from the Top End and the temptations of the north.

Alice and the dog collar

In early 1981, Patrick turned up at the Presbytery in Bath Street in Alice Springs, carrying a change of clothes and a box of books. They were an odd mix: books on theology, on law, on political empowerment. A few were special to him: *Seven Arrows*, the book on Indian medicine wheels, and the Irving Stone novel on the pre-history of Israel, *The Source*. Books like this reinforced his view that spirituality was grounded in cultural, historical form; authors like Illich and Marcuse helped shape his political approach to having this fact recognised and turned into social action.

By putting the collar back on, Patrick had 'rejoined the club.' He had doubts and nagging discomforts but wanted to satisfy his concerns and 'apply my mind to doing that, without being stubborn, or inconsistent.'

He fulfilled his parish role, serving Mass, carrying the sacraments out to the old people's home, organising sandwiches at 4.30pm every day for the pensioners, served from the Presbytery's side verandah. The priest hated the marginalisation of the Aboriginal community embodied in the 'sandwiches through the side door.' There was little constraint on his time and duties and he started to become involved with the local Aboriginal organisations as part of his parish work. He was welcomed.

Patrick joined the board of the Institute for Aboriginal Development (IAD) that guided the work of the Director, Yami Lester. Yami was a blind Yankuntjatjara man who had escaped from making brooms in the Royal Blind Institute in Adelaide to come to Alice Springs and work as an interpreter and then manager of programs for education and training of Aboriginal communities. Yami would always have a high regard for Patrick, saying:

> Oh I take me hat off to him and his brother too. Really smart men that could put the words together. They could argue any white man under the table. Every time I hear them on the radio, I want to drink to them. I would have been a sober man, but they're on the radio too much (laughter).[18]

Also on the board were David Ross, Geoffrey Shaw and Johnny Liddle. They were a formidable group, forming lasting relationships. They mixed humour with hard work and ideas. As individuals within the group, they might disagree but did not let the issue get in the way of the relationship between the men. The relationship between Yami and Patrick was a strong bond in the work of the IAD, with the blind man coaching Patrick:

> Yami used to say to me after I had given a talk at the Board or the woman's group or something, 'You're a very smart man with good words and strong ideas, but you got to draw a picture in my mind. You've got to talk about real things, paint a picture for me to follow.'

Michael Gordon, national editor of *The Age*, writing in 2001 showed that Patrick's speaking style had absorbed Yami's lesson:

> His is the voice of reason and there are very few in the country, black or white, that can match the power of his oratory ... Dodson is most potent as a speaker when he talks in pictures. It is how he speaks to his people.[19]

Patrick was given the job of Chairman, and the amount of time and energy he devoted to IAD increased. He went with Yami to Mimili, the Pitjantjatjara community in South Australia, to advise the community on holding elections, and saw Uluru for the first time. Yami remembers:

> We were talking away and then he went real quiet. I said, 'What's up?' He said, 'I'm seeing this place for the first time and it's amazing.' We drove around the Rock, keeping on turning left. I introduced Patrick as my Chairman, my big boss with the big beard. He still had collar on those days.[20]

A conference on Indigenous People and Multinationals in mid-1981 took Patrick, Yami and others to the United States, where they visited the Onandaga Iroquois people. Here Patrick met a little 'Eskimo lady with the biggest Colt 45 I'd seen in history.' They stayed on Native American homelands in Arizona and later walked somewhat fearfully through Harlem, with Yami Lester wedged inside a phalanx of minders, headed by Stan Scrutton, trained in karate. They met indigenous people from all over the world and shared their experiences. *The Multinational Monitor* interviewed Patrick, wearing a red, black and yellow beanie, and his travel companion from the Federation of Land Councils, Shorty O'Neill. Shorty told them:

> The only way that this struggle can end is when the governments and multinational companies realise that we are a sovereign people and that we must have our own self-determination. And by that we mean the right make our own laws, and the right to run our own country the way we want to run it.[21]

Permission to go to the Conference was sought from Bishop O'Loughlin. Patrick was told:

> 'Yes, it certainly sounds important, but not for you. You can go if you want, but don't bother coming back.' That was one thing that made me roll my swag.

It was Geoff Shaw, the grizzled and lively Vietnam veteran, who broke through the reserve of the priest:

> He made me confront my demons, I guess. He asked what I was doing committing my life to the Church and not the people. He persuaded me that I could do more, achieve more, if I worked with the organisations on the fundamental issues of land rights and social justice. He told me I was needed there more than at the Presbytery handing out sandwiches through the side door.

Barbara Shaw, Geoff's sister watched the two men talking under the trees after a day spent kangaroo hunting. By the time they were ready to shovel the coals off the shallow bush oven and take out the kangaroo, a decision of sorts had been reached.

It was no private decision. The rupture opened in the media when *The Age* newspaper ran the story of the 'outspoken black priest' and the issues of Port Keats on page one in June 1981. Patrick's quoted claims that he 'resurrected the Aboriginal ceremonial life that had been suppressed since 1935', and that 'he put self-determination into practice', were scorned by the Bishop, as 'self-aggrandising.' He said that Fr Dodson:

> Had gone through a period of uncertainty and confusion. I thought he was returning to normality. As a priest his work should be spiritual and liturgical, not political … I believe in spiritual liberation not liberation with machine guns, which has become a way of thinking among some Aborigines.

The Bishop said that after Fr Dodson had left Wadeye 'for personal and confidential reasons', he had worked for a group campaigning for land rights for Aborigines. He said that while the efforts of this group were 'sincere', they had 'given scant recognition to the people who saved them from extinction.' When asked about Fr Dodson's future, Bishop O'Loughlin said, 'We may just smile.' Nicholson accompanied the articles with a cartoon of a towering, fully robed bishop looming over a bearded cross-wearing priest and saying, 'Politics should be kept out of paternalism.'

Needless to say, media comment on church policy was not warmly encouraged under the terms and conditions of Patrick's return to the priesthood, or the canon law that had evolved over centuries. Under Canon

831, 'clerics and members of religious institutes may write in newspapers only with the permission of the local ordinary.' A page one 'over the fold' argument in a major metropolitan newspaper between a Bishop and his priest was going a little too far.

Under Canon 277, 'clerics are obliged to observe perfect and continual continence for the sake of the kingdom of heaven, and are therefore bound to celibacy.'[22] That precept was starting to unravel at that time in Patrick's relationship with Barbara Shaw. They would drive out of the town in the evenings, Patrick's beard concealed in his jumper; a disguise that fooled not one person.[23] There was a political as well as a personal attraction. Barbara recalls being impressed by Patrick's ability to shape a political vision for the organisations:

> I remember when he came to Alice he brought a freshness of vision. A vision for the future. He stimulated real changes with new positive directions for the organizations. All of a sudden this guy came along and there was a clear direction. It was a big shift in the political process and the tactical sense of the organizations.

Rex Scambary interviewed Patrick for the *Catholic Leader* a few years after the break-down in communication between the Church and the priest. His comments reflected a growing alienation, a failure to reconcile, between the interpretation of spirituality and social development embodied in Bishop O'Loughlin's views, and those that Patrick ardently believed in:

> The spirituality of the Missionaries of the Sacred Heart had a dimension to it that said no matter how bad you were, or how bad society was telling you that you were, or how rejected you were by that particular society, you were still a very important being in the eyes of Christ. That had a very important meaning if you are going to bring about some sort of reconciliation between Aboriginal and non-Aboriginal and a mitigation of the kinds of injuries that were done to Aborigines.[24]

He told Scambary it was not easy going through years of study and then to be confronted with a Church response to the social inequities of Aboriginal people that did not face up to the marginalised position of Aboriginal people. His argument was theological, saying that the Church at a local level did not recognise that, 'in all cultures, the seeds of salvation are sown within those cultures.' For Patrick, religion did not require uniformity of format, places and services, as witnessed by the differences between the Eastern and Roman rites. For the Church in the Northern Territory, a common ritual form was a primary requirement. They were 'pre-occupied with having better church-goers, not better human beings.'

His argument with the Church was also political; they were in conflict over the social structure, not recognising that 'Aboriginal people should have a very strong influence over the way any infrastructure was going to change their society, and have a strong say in how that should take place. For the Church this was a stepping back from the work of previous missionaries.

His argument was also about the relationship between Aboriginal people and the wider society:

> Trying to bring about a certain relationship between Aboriginal and non-Aboriginal Australians where we don't continue to go cap in hand to the Government, to go begging for our ability to assert ourselves in society. There's a fairly long struggle ahead of us.[25]

His arguments characteristically shunned any personal revelation, although he admitted he was 'now drawn to temporarily regard myself as following an Aboriginal spirituality.' He did not see conflict with the theology of Christianity in this spirituality, something the Bishop would never come to understand.

To this day, he holds no grudge against the Church. He 'continues to offer advice to them that they rarely accept.' Fr Brian McCoy asked Patrick one night over dinner with me, why he had never 'sunk the boot into the Church' and why he did not seem as bitter as other priests that had left. Patrick answered:

> People have gotta work it through in their own way. At the end of the day, it doesn't matter, its not where the focus of life resides, it's not the first issue. Some priests might think so, but life is an evolving process, you've just gotta work out how you deal with issues as they arise. You can't stay in one spot until the situation is resolved. There's no luxury to sit back or to fight a rearguard action. There's no choice. You have to move on to the next level of the fight. At the end of the day, you carry the load, you need to do it. No-one owes me anything, and in fact the MSCs gave me a lot. There's no point in closing the door.

Fr Pat Dodson never closed the door on the Church, but he would never say Mass again.

Central Land Council

Patrick moved out of the Presbytery and into a flat with Barbara Shaw, taking just his box of books and a change of clothes. He soon moved into a job in the Hartley Street offices of the Central Land Council, (CLC) then under the Chairmanship of the elusive cowboy figure from Borroloola, Stan

Scrutton. Stan had been a field officer, and now was a boss, as happened more than once in the Central Land Council.

There were some fifty people working at the CLC at the time, and Patrick was appointed to the position of Information and Field Services coordinator. He looked to his bosses for guidance, especially Wenten Rubuntja, Wenten's brother Eli, and Geoffrey Shaw. He looked to the quiet, intensely practical David Ross for support and comradeship. He soon set out to be a change agent from within the organisation, 'because the most basic need to was to enhance the level of recognition of the rights, authority and directive powers carried by traditional owners on the Council.'

This was in keeping with the style and ethos at the heart of the CLC: large bush meetings, open to all and sundry, with the meeting conducted using three Aboriginal languages in a large circular clearing. Attending such a meeting, it was impossible to know where the Chairman, or the executive was; everyone was equally placed in the nearest available shade. There were no visible bosses, because all the Aboriginal people were bosses, all with a right to speak and voice opinions, each had the authority to speak for their country. At the Northern Land Council (NLC), meetings were much more formal, with the Executive at a table under a shade, handing each other the microphone, while other traditional owners watched on, more spectators than participants. Patrick recalled a joint meeting between the land councils:

> We camped in swags; the CLC was very much like that, camped in a group everywhere we went. The NLC blokes all camped in motels up in Tennant Creek and they drove down the next morning and here we are, no showers, all looking flea-bitten, rolled out of the swags—no problem to the CLC—and the NLC blokes came down looking all clean, and spick and span, ironed trousers sitting down somewhere at Alekarenge having a meeting. The contrast between the styles of the two councils never ceased to amaze me.[26]

Partly, he thought these differences flowed form the higher levels of mining royalties that flowed to the NLC; partly also, it was a difference in cultural perspectives between the egalitarian desert dwellers and the more hierarchical top-end people. In the Centre, there were no 'big men.' In the north, men like Galarrwuy were 'big men' indeed.

There were other differences. The NLC was organised differently; they had an Aboriginal director, who coordinated the day-to-day operation of the Land Council, keeping in close communication with the Chairman. At the time it was John, or Jack Ah Kit, once a schoolboy scrapper with Mick, a Jawoyn man, nicknamed 'Buffalo.'[27] It was somehow the right name. Marcia

Langton, then an anthropogist working for the CLC, remembers the first day seeing Jack walk through the Hartley Street door:

> I looked up and saw Jack come in and went, wow, a black director.

The organisational structure of the CLC soon changed, with a shift of power from the 'white experts', the lawyers and anthropologists, to Patrick, David Ross, Marcia and other Aboriginal staff, working on Patrick's agenda. He was appointed Director in 1985.

The issues on the land council agenda, both before and after the change to a Labor Government in 1983, were dazzling in their complexity and pace. Land claims were proceeding, putting Aboriginal claimants through the hoops of proving their primary spiritual affiliation with areas of land. Some land claims were particularly complex, due to the impact of history on the knowledge and authority of the senior lawmen and women; others were complex in terms of competitive claims made by rival Aboriginal land-holding groups. The Northern Territory government opposed all claims not only tooth-and-nail but silk as well, with many senior lawyers employed.

Those Aboriginal people who had been able to establish their connection with land had to deal with non-Aboriginal commercial interest in their land: mining companies in Mereenie and Palm Valley and tourism ventures in places like Uluru wanted to keep, or bite off, their slice of the action. One ongoing difficult issue was the division and effective utilisation of funds received from mining royalties; an endless source of community discord. The funds received from the Mereenie oilfield were highly disputed, with one particularly prominent elder telling me at the time:

> Well, everyone was paid royalty last time and everybody just rushed into the garage and just buy all them junk motor cars, and a flood of grog, and some of them died in an accident the next day. A few days afterwards, they were running broke. They didn't have money in the bank, not even in the pocket. Aboriginal people should be using the money the right way, not the wrong way. My idea is to put the money in the bank or invest that money, and with that money we could develop our land or control that money to do it the right way, to save that money. If not, well we're going to end up nothing.[28]

Of particular and on-going concern for the Director and his staff on the Land Council was the plight of the 'people the Land Rights Act forgot.' These were the traditional owners unfortunate enough to have their country overlain by a pastoral lease, their rights denied and their interests marginalised as a historical, legal, factual consequence. Patrick helped to organise a 'convoy' to Lake Nash, the King Ranch property on the border of the Northern Territory and Queensland:

> There was a lot of tension about Aboriginal people living within two kilometres of a pastoral lease, which they had a right to. Lake Nash, which was an ongoing source of contention, no one seemed have done much to resolve the concerns … So in 1983, the organisations in Alice Springs decided they would take a convoy up there to show solidarity with the group there. But also, to do a practical thing, to put up a couple of tin houses which Tangantyere Council supplied … There was a crew of us that all joined forces and led off. We thought this was a circus. We had flags flying and horns blowing.[29]

This was the best of these times for Patrick. He was getting organisations and people together and working on direct political action that had practical effect for those who were left out of the mainstream of political concern:

> It brought out the best in all the organisations and key players. We had a lot of fun, people kicking football along the road, country and western music blaring. It was an absolutely great occasion and one of the most memorable things about being in the Centre.

Others, though, while interested in Aboriginal issues, were not as interested in the social and political agenda. They sought to gain access to the Aboriginal cultural world as a source of inspiration and authenticity in an increasingly homogenous world.

The writers

In February of 1983, the English author, Bruce Chatwin came to town, obsessed by his own interpretation of 'songlines', through which Aboriginal Dreaming roads could be described as a map; a long narrative poem and a series of dances that linked people and country. Chatwin spent nine days in the Centre and met Patrick at a barbecue at the lawyer Phillip Toyne's place. In *The Songlines*, Chatwin is a welcome guest and he and Patrick (described as an ex-Benedictine and given the name Fr Flynn) discussed the tracks of the ancestors to the small hours. In reality, 'not only did he (Chatwin) gatecrash, after being advised by Toyne, twice, not to come, but he monopolised the principal guest.'[30] The encounter was enough, though, for Chatwin to present a fictionalised account of a charismatic, brooding figure, wrapped in the dual mysteries of Catholic theology and Aboriginal spirituality. Chatwin invented a character, wrapping strips of fiction around the frame of Patrick's history:

> He was a foundling, dumped by an unknown mother at the store of an Irishman at Fitzroy Crossing. At the age of six, he was sent to the Benedictine mission at Cygnet Bay, where he refused to play with other black children, learned to serve at mass, and had the habit of asking questions about dogma, in a soft and reverential brogue.[31]

He reinvented Patrick's work at Port Keats and his role in mediating between Aboriginal law and mission rule. Of most concern to Patrick, though was Chatwin's reinvention of the Dreaming. Where the work of Strehlow on song and country was insufficient for his purposes, or when the facts got in the way of his thesis, Chatwin would take some of the insights given him by Patrick and others and embroider his own creation, justifying it by claiming it was a blend of fact and fiction. 'The camouflage of fiction did allow Bruce to do what he liked.'[32] Patrick was scathing and dismissive of the English author; angered at his unprincipled appropriation of Aboriginal religious belief. He saved both barrels of contempt though for:

> His camp followers, all the coloured shirt, hippy, new-age mumbo-jumbo crowd that wanted to know all about sacred boards and songlines but would not lift a finger when people needed it. Useless ticks.

Xavier Herbert was another author who sought inspiration and narrative colour under Centralian skies, spending the last months of his life there in 1984. Patrick had more time for him, although he was 'a difficult and cantankerous old fella when I knew him.' He respected the fact that Xavier had given evidence in support of the claim by the McGuiness family and others in the Finnis River Land Claim and had made impassioned pleas for a treaty with Aboriginal people.[33] According to Frances De Groen, Herbert was buried in the 'yellow ochre soil' of the Alice Springs on 15 November:

> Aboriginal activist Pat Dodson, member of the Central Land Council and former Catholic priest officiated. The moving funeral ceremony blended Aboriginal rites with Biblical and Catholic readings.[34]

Patrick remembered the occasion as 'an odd sort of turnout', in which he officiated at the request of the McGinness family, and had been asked to say a few words, but 'to keep any religious talk or prayers out of it.' He did so, and was surprised when others started to make the ceremony a religious one. He was still, in a sense, 'endorsed' to perform the sacraments, never having had his vows officially revoked. The Church has never taken the necessary steps of laicisation that were necessary to revoke the sacrament of Holy Orders. Neither had Patrick sought to formalise the severance. Ralph McInerney, the Catholic philosopher and author of the 'Father Dowling' mystery series, defines the issues:[35]

The priesthood is forever theologically, so, formally laicized or not, a man who leaves to marry is a married priest—although a priest who is not permitted to function as such. Under Pope Paul VI, Rome granted laicization almost for the asking. Paul was said to think that after the dissatisfied priests had left, things would settle down. But, as with divorce, the easy availability of laicization increased the instances of it. Pope John Paul II slammed the door on the procedure when he took office in 1978, and it is perhaps as difficult to get laicized now as it was in E. Boyd Barrett's day. That is to say, all but impossible. You can take the man out of the priesthood, but you can't take the priesthood out of the man. That is what the church has always taught, and it always leaves open a door of repentance for priests who, like the rest of us, are human and sin.

The main game

By 1985 Patrick needed more organisational skill and political savvy than the average parish priest to deal with the twists and turns of Commonwealth government policy on land rights. The Land Council was closely involved in what Patrick considered great achievements such as the hand back of Uluru Kata-Tjuta National Park, which Yami Lester recalled:

> I could feel a lump in my throat. I tried to talk but my lips went dry. I knew I had to say something just to control myself and stop the shaking ... I reckon there must have been four thousand people there. Sir Ninian Stephen, who was Governor-General at that time, arrived and he made a speech. Then they handed over the papers for the Mutitjulu people to sign ... So Anangu had Uluru for themselves—for about five minutes. Then they signed another paper giving a lease to the Commonwealth government for ninety-nine years. While all this was going on, there was an aeroplane flying over with a banner saying, 'Ayers Rock is for all Australians.' It was a nasty piece of work. We never found out who organised that.[36]

The honeymoon relationship between the land councils and the incoming Hawke Government soured quickly. The issue in contention was the best approach for a consistent national approach to land rights for Aboriginal people. Land rights legislation had been passed by state governments in South Australia and New South Wales and by the Commonwealth in the Northern Territory. The Hawke Government was committed to a policy of introducing a framework for a national approach under five principles enunciated by Clyde Holding as Minister for Aboriginal Affairs to the United Nations Working Group on Indigenous

People in July 1984, which included inalienable freehold title, protection of sites control over mining, mining royalty payments and compensation for lost land.[37]

In October 1984, Prime Minister Hawke, yielding to the demands of the Burke Government in Western Australia, dropped the benchmarking against the NT legislation in the national approach. In early 1985, Holding introduced a Preferred National Land Rights Model that, in the view of the land councils, fell well short of the five principles previously announced. Of more immediate concern was that the model would reduce rights available under the NT legislation. The land councils were concerned that under the model they would lose a conditional right to veto exploration and mining on Aboriginal land and their power to vest Aboriginal communities with access to mining royalty payments. They began to mobilise. Patrick recalled:

> We needed to organise on a number of different levels. We had to explain to the bosses out bush what was happening. That was a challenge, both logistically and conceptually, even though people always thought they had the right under their law to say no to anything on their land. We had to try to put pressure internally on the ALP machine to reinforce the party platform, which confirmed that Aboriginal people should have the right to refuse permission or impose conditions for mining on Aboriginal land. That required a lot of lobbying work in Canberra that we were not used to. And then we had to bring everyone else, across Aboriginal Australia, with us, to stand up with the NT mob despite the fact that they may have made small gains under the Model. Finally, we had to persuade the wider non-Aboriginal community that there was an important issue of national significance that they could not ignore.

The flying wedge

The Directors of the Land Council, John Ah Kit and Patrick Dodson, assisted by Warren Snowdon and Jamie Gallacher, took the concerns of the land councils to Parliament House in Canberra.[38] As Marcia Langton saw it, they 'made Parliament work for Aboriginal people, breaking down the invisible walls.'[39] With a Cabinet locked into a preferred position behind the commitment by the Prime Minister to the WA Premier, the land councils had to find new access points, and worked primarily through the various Caucus committees. Backbenchers such as Gerry Hand, Barney Cooney and Arthur Gietzelt opened some doors, particularly in getting the team unaccompanied passes which allowed them free access to the corridors of Parliament House:

> We were referred to, with Ah Kit in front, as 'the flying wedge.' We'd go down the corridor with Ah Kit in the front because he was the biggest and we'd all be going behind him in a 'V' shape. And whomever we saw in the doors, as we went past, and we'd just wheel in saying: 'We want to talk to you!' 'Make an appointment!' 'No, no, we haven't got time, we've got to talk to you now!'[40]

The land council negotiators, despite finding fertile ground and supporters in the Committees and the left factions, did not succeed in turning around the views of Cabinet, the Minister or the Department of Aboriginal Affairs. A large press and television campaign was mounted by the Australian Mining Industry Council claiming that Aboriginal rights were blocking development, especially in the Northern Territory and that national land rights would extend the areas of Australia closed to development. Opinion polls were seized upon by the Government, purporting to show that there was limited public support for the stance being advocated by the land councils. The 1985 polls also showed that over thirty per cent of respondents could not name one Aboriginal achievement of any sort, nor could they name an Aboriginal person who had impressed them.[41]

The land councils continued to lobby, with Jack Ah Kit taking on the role of 'the Master of the Compromise' as Patrick labelled him. In contrast Ah Kit recalled that he had to:

> Keep Patrick on a choker chain. We played good cop and hard cop. They were tough times. We had to figure out how to bend in order to stay upright. We learned a lot about lobbying and changed the game for other groups like the industry and environment groups.'[42]

The lobbying did not always go smoothly. One late night, the land council team, despondent after a frustrating meeting, called into the Kingston bottle shop as it was about to close. Patrick ordered a 'bottle of Boris' (vodka) and a bottle of gin for Ah Kit. Snowdon was aghast, saying they had meetings scheduled for the morning. Patrick turned to him and said:

> That's the trouble with you boys with a bit of mission in you, Snow. You can't stand it to see a good coon go bad. Don't worry; we'll be up in the morning … because we won't go to bed.

The land councils widened the base of the campaign, forming a National Aboriginal Land Rights Support group, with ex-Minister Gordon Bryant providing a figurehead role. Robert Tickner, a future Minister for Aboriginal Affairs, made the first donation to the group, while church, aid and human rights groups were pressured to offer support.[43] Patrick was learning to spread the networks and seek support from others outside their organisations.

Back in Alice Springs, the pressures of a complex organisation and the demands of the national lobbying campaign placed stress on the Director. The organisation was 'under siege' and the calls on Patrick's time and attention were numerous and varied. Patrick and Barbara Shaw were now living in the Mount Nancy Town Camp in a house a couple of doors up from her brother Geoffrey Shaw and his wife Eileen Hoosan. For Barbara, it was a particularly stressful time, when she was trying to cope with the illness and then loss of her very ill sister, Connie. Connie's infant son, Adrian, born in Derby, came to live with Patrick and Barbara. Patrick remembers the time with sorrow:

> She was a lovely kid, just a young girl. Back in Alice she walked around with an oxygen bottle. She had no resistance. It was devastating. The day she died, it was a tragic day. Just a tragic day. The poor girl. Adrian was just a baby, a month or two old. At home at Mt Nancy she asked us to look after Adrian and grow him up whatever happened to her. She was preparing for the future, whatever happened. Barbara was brilliant through it all, organising the funeral and everything. I tried to reassure her about continuing to care for Adrian, being his mother, while I carried out the job of father. It was very sad.[44]

Barbara felt lonely and hurt when the business of negotiation and political campaigning eventually overwhelmed Patrick's family responsibilities and her needs for care and attention. Tensions focused on the needs of Adrian, and Barbara became frustrated, trying to communicate with Patrick. 'Patrick has an ability to close off to anything and didn't let his emotional side come through. We were going through huge turmoil and he didn't want to open up and talk about it.'[45]

Come to Canberra campaign

The personal relationships between the men in the Federation of Land Councils were the driving force of the political movement of the time. The team was large and included at the core Patrick and David Ross from the Centre, Peter Yu from the Kimberley, Rob Riley from Perth, Kevin Cook from Tranby College in Sydney, Mick Miller, Terry O'Shane and Clarrie Grogan from North Queensland, Geoff Clark from Victoria and Michael Mansell from Tasmania. While they had differences and fallings out, they backed each other up and talked long into the night, drinking and smoking and laughing. This fraternity was the 'emotional seedbed' where Patrick found comfort and security, despite the daily personal costs on his health and on those who were working with him. With many phone calls, they managed to arrange a meeting of the Federation in Canberra in May 1985. The meeting evolved into a 'Come to Canberra' campaign to demonstrate against the Hawke government's preferred model for national land rights. It became the largest demonstration on Aboriginal issues ever held in Canberra.

Over several cold winter days in May 1985, hundreds of Aboriginal people gathered at the Blue Folk farm outside Canberra. Marquees borrowed from the university formed the central gathering place, while fires in drums went a little way to warming the travellers. They had come from every part of Australia, in trucks, in old cars, in Toyotas and in buses. The traditional owners from the Central Land Council had the hardest trip in a large cattle truck, one old man dying during the journey down the Stuart Highway. They were subdued and feeling the cold; grabbing onto the blankets and warm clothes distributed by welfare organisations. Their mood was buoyed however by the support they were given from countrymen they did not know. Their support was national; every state and territory, every major organisation was mobilised. Even those states without land rights were willing to come out and support the maintenance of rights in the Northern Territory. It was the high-water mark of a national Aboriginal consensus on land rights.

Their demonstration at Old Parliament House on 13 May was reasonably peaceful; some had rushed the barricades and tried to enter the building but had not created harm. Patrick remembers the funny side, with Clarrie Grogan from Yarrabah yelling out to people to cross the street and go up the steps, shouting, 'What are youse going to be, are you going to keep on keeping on like Berger paints; or are you going across the road?'[46] A poorly timed wine-tasting show at the Rose Gardens reluctantly provided a donation of a few bottles of Chardonnay to a few of the demonstrators.

Snowy Kulminya, an NLC field officer addressed the crowd in Ngaringman. Patrick had marched with the mob, not putting himself out front, and letting others gain the attention. When the rush across the road to the steps of Parliament House was on, he stood back watching and listening; Adrian Shaw, the toddler son of Barbara Shaw's late sister was in his arms, protected from the cold by a red, black and yellow beanie. From across the road he explained his passive response: 'I have to negotiate with them in the morning.'

The next day Patrick presented the position of the Federation of Land Councils to the National Press Club. He spoke strongly; inevitably too strong for some, too weak for others:

> We face the very real prospect that the Hawke Labor Government, under pressure from a small but powerful vested interest group, will turn back the clock and destroy this first and only token gesture by a Government since 1788. This present Labor Government, which likes to pride itself in giving people a fair go, and working for reconciliation has produced a draft model for national land rights legislation which could lead to a sell out of Aboriginal people.
>
> If our demands are ignored, and our existing rights dumped, the Government will be responsible for fanning a conflict, which could undo the small steps that have been taken towards reconciliation between Aboriginal people and the rest of Australia.[47]

Provocatively, he asked whether Aboriginal people had to go to Libya or some other country before the Government would come to terms with their prior rights. He stressed the continuity, persistence and survival of Aboriginal culture, religion and law, seeing the current issue as 'just another obstacle in a long struggle', warning:

> We will not continue to sit at the foot of your table and watch you grow fat off our land. We will not continue to accept the scraps which you choose to throw down to us, and threaten to take away. We will not give up our struggle for recognition, independence and dignity. Like our forebears, we will not die, we will not go away.

By the end of the week, after meetings at the farm in the cold rain with the Minister, Clyde Holding and the Departmental Secretary, Charlie Perkins, there was general agreement that the Preferred Model, while it eroded the Northern Territory Act, could not survive.[48] Patrick led a delegation that met with the Prime Minister who agreed to defer the proposed approach, and to provide funding for further consultation. The campaign was over; existing rights were protected at the expense of any new national statutory system of access to land, control over land, and compensation for land lost. It would be a costly victory, with the attempts to establish national land rights being completely abandoned by March 1986.

Patrick considers that the Federation of Land Councils acted correctly:

> We had to defend, to the end, the rights that Aboriginal people had gained in the Northern Territory from being watered down. They were under attack. The Seaman Inquiry had been rejected in Western Australia, the miners were advocating removal of veto rights, Hawke had his mind made

up and was doing deals with AMIC. But we had won the right for Aboriginal land to be protected from abuse and loss to mining interests. We had no authority from the bosses, the law men, to negotiate those rights away.

Through the rear-vision of history, this view could be challenged. If statutory national land rights had been introduced in 1985, land held in Aboriginal reserves, missions and other unalienated land would have been available for claim and the people in the south would have had access to inalienable freehold title. Importantly, the issues of native title would have been simplified and less divisive in the decade to come. Inalienable freehold title to Murray Island may have already been delivered to the people some years before the *Mabo* decision and the *Native Title Act* divided the country. Also, the vital qualities of bipartisanship and public support for land rights would have been maintained, at least to some extent. Patrick dismissed my arguments along those lines as wisdom in hindsight:

> You have to deal with reality not fantasy. If Labor governments in Canberra and Perth couldn't deliver on their platform because the miners snapped their fingers, what hope did we have relying on a regime that was dependent on states? There's a tension between the political track of statutory title and the other track of waiting for the courts. At that time, we didn't have anything from the courts. We had to do it.

For the men, and they were primarily men, at the frontline of the campaign in 1985, the experience enhanced their negotiation skills and their awareness of the means to utilise in seeking political and legislative change. They no longer had need for lobbyists and began to recognise the power to be gained through negotiation, especially through defined common interests. The return of Uluru in that year was regarded as a high point for the Aboriginal leadership, even though it was immediately leased back to the Commonwealth for ninety-nine years.[49]

For the ruling Country Liberal Party, it was a breach of sovereignty against the interests of all Australians and a useful campaign issue. The Chief Minister, Paul Everingham, criticised the Federal Minister for announcing that:

> He was to hand over title and control of Australia's premier tourist attraction to a disparate group of Aboriginals under the control of a handful of white advisers and lawyers … Aboriginal dignity and tradition were being trampled by the manipulators and their political allies, led by Minister Holding and the Socialist Left in Victoria.[50]

For the land councils of the Northern Territory, their negotiation skills were brought to bear in 1987 when the Hawke Government sought amendments to the mining provisions of the *Aboriginal Land Rights (Northern Territory) Act 1976*, and later when the negotiation of Aboriginal title to excisions on pastoral leases, stock routes and reserves was the primary issue. There were some tough all-night sessions, with Marcia Langton recalling that at a meeting with Gareth Evans and Clyde Holding, Patrick's plan was to 'keep them at the table and screw them for everything.'[51] When Evans asked how long it would take, Patrick replied, 'We've waited for 200 years, you can wait a night.'

She recalled Patrick kicking her under the table with his snakeskin boots at one point in the negotiation, and that a small group of them then set out to rewrite the mining sections of the *Aboriginal Land Rights (Northern Territory) Act 1976* overnight. Patrick remembers her on the floor next day with pieces of chart paper, explaining to Gareth Evans how the new provisions would work. As a qualified and skilled anthropologist, Marcia made a major contribution to disrupting the 'men's club' that had dominated the policy setting work of the land councils.

Two hundred years

Nineteen eighty-eight dawned with Aboriginal issues at the centre of the national consciousness. In Sydney on 26 January, while televisions blared with 'Celebration of a Nation', the harbour was crowded with tall ships that many Aboriginal people and their supporters regarded as 'Recreation of an Invasion.' The organisers of bicentennial celebrations had to deal with those who took the opportunity to demonstrate on Aboriginal issues, celebrating survival and the solidarity of their own nation. Even the new Minister, Gerry Hand, considered that he should boycott the celebrations in sympathy, while he worked to gain support for his new indigenous representation and decision-making structure, the Aboriginal and Torres Strait Islander Commission (ATSIC).[52]

On that Australia Day, the land councils took a central role in a Building Bridges concert at Bondi Beach, and joined in peaceful marches focused on Sydney's original La Perouse community and Hyde Park. Patrick marched with a large land council contingent, dressed in a loincloth and red ochre. With boomerangs in hand he was difficult to tell apart from the other warriors and lawmen at the head of the line of marchers. He shared a pair of thongs with another Aboriginal leader, hopping along on one foot on the hot bitumen through the city streets. Vince Forrester handed out spears borrowed from the collection of the National Museum; Patrick doubted if they were ever returned. David Ross from the Central Land council said he was:

> The mug in charge of the troops and getting them home without losing anyone or getting anyone into trouble. I had nothing to do with any of the rest of the organising or the meetings or anything, that was Patrick's job. My job was looking after the gang, and boy, what a job that was.[53]

The network of men at the heart of the Federation of Land Councils ensured that the march was a successful and peaceful demonstration of Aboriginal survival and organisational capacity. From the Territory, Patrick and Jack Ah Kit ran the meetings, Rossie looked after the gang, while Wenten and Galarrwuy connected the law and Dreaming roads of the north with the needs of the time and the location.

It was 12 June in 1988, though, that the Northern Territory Land Councils achieved their major political promise of the bicentennial year. The Prime Minister, Bob Hawke and his Minister, Gerry Hand, made a special trip to the annual Barunga Sports and Cultural Festival at the small Aboriginal community not far from Katherine, where Patrick grew up. While the large crowd watched the football, basketball and spear-throwing, a diverse but select group of Aboriginal men were working through a major drafting exercise, negotiating the text and art panels that would become the Barunga Statement. Patrick wielded the pen and talked through the words. Presented to the Prime Minister by Wenten Rubuntja and Galarrwuy Yunupingu, who had negotiated the designs that surrounded the statement, it asked the Commonwealth government to pass laws for national land rights, changes to the justice system, support for international principles of indigenous rights, and most importantly for Patrick, a 'Treaty or Compact recognising our prior ownership and sovereignty and affirming our human rights and freedom.' In accepting the statement, the Prime Minister committed the government to a treaty in the lifetime of that Parliament, and promised to display the statement in Parliament House, 'for whoever is the prime Minister of this country not only to see but to understand and to honour.'[54] Both commitments proved very difficult to meet.

Gerry Hand recalled the event at the memorial service for his adviser and one of Patrick's close friends, Rob Riley:[55]

> I recall the Barunga statement. The Barunga statement which now hangs in the Federal Parliament. We went up, we camped with the CLC, and this was the other side of Rob, he had a great sense of humour. And he said to me, 'You taking a swag?' And I said, 'Yes, I'll take a swag, and we'll sleep

out.' And he said, 'Well I've got a swag.' Well, it took about four people to carry Rob's swag. It had about a seven-inch piece of foam in it. He said, 'Well you can be a hero if you like; you can sleep out under the stars, but there's an empty tent over there, and there's a stretcher in it. I'm sleeping on my stretcher. I'm sleeping on my foam rubber. And I've got my blankets as well. So you have a good night out there, Boss, but I'm sleeping in here.' And he did. I woke up stiff and sore and feeling like a burnt-out hero, and Rob had a great night's sleep and was first up and never stopped whistling all day. But the Barunga statement, he saw that as a stepping stone towards achieving that understanding, that reconciliation, that treaty that he was grasping for on behalf of his people.

In the course of the national land rights campaign, Patrick and Gerry Hand had formed a good working relationship. The ties were cemented by the linking work of two of his advisers, Rob Riley, who represented the Perth Aboriginal community in Patrick's world, and Neil Andrews, who had worked as a lawyer for the Central Land Council.[56] Gerry began to turn to Patrick and his land council colleagues for advice and comment, rather than his portfolio secretary, Charlie Perkins, as he sought to restructure the various outposts of the Aboriginal Affairs portfolio into an integrated representative body, overseen by an elected Board of Commissioners, although with an appointed Chair.

One key area of the portfolio resisted incorporation throughout 1988. This was the Aboriginal Development Commission (ADC), chaired by Shirley McPherson, which was to be replaced by an Economic Development Corporation. After a series of disputes, critical media comment by the ADC chair, and a federal court challenge, in late May the Minister terminated the appointments of all members of the Board, except the Chair, McPherson, and appointed new members including Patrick Dodson, Peter Yu and Lois (Lowitja) O'Donoghue. Patrick became the deputy chair in what was an uneasy and contested relationship, in which, 'She would call me "my deputy", and I would say "I'm not your deputy, I'm the deputy."' The sacking of the ADC commissioners and the forced restructure of the economic arm of the portfolio is described by Perkin's biographer, Peter Read, as a setback for Aboriginal self-determination:

> Whatever Hawke had originally intended, a principal purpose of the bill now appeared to be to wrest back from the Indigenous people the semi-autonomous powers granted to them under the ADC Act. There was to be more, not less, ministerial power. There was to be less, not more, Aboriginal self-determination.[57]

In the months that followed, the issues would claim the job of the Secretary, Charlie Perkins, create animosity between Aboriginal leaders on either side of the 'north–south' divide, spark numerous press comments on waste and corruption in Aboriginal affairs and lead to several parliamentary and investigative reports. Importantly, the bipartisan approach that had applied to Aboriginal affairs over much of the past decade, weakened by the land rights and treaty debates, had been consigned to the past.

Another issue dogged the Ministerial term of Gerry Hand and cast gloom over the bicentennial year. Aboriginal legal services had been concerned for years about the over-representation of Aboriginal people, especially young men, in custody. They now began to focus their concerns on the number of these who were dying while held in police or in prison custody. The deaths seemed suspicious to many Aboriginal people and the numbers were escalating alarmingly. A Royal Commission was agreed with the states and territories, supported by the Opposition and established on a national basis late in 1987, with the interim report of Justice Muirhead received in late 1988.

The job was much larger than Muirhead or the government had first recognised and the 'true dimensions of the tragic situation' as Muirhead described it required the Commission be given extra time and resources. Five extra commissioners were appointed and Elliott Johnston QC was appointed as the national commissioner.

Patrick met Elliott and the new commissioners at Framlingham at a large meeting of the Federation of Land Councils, now co-ordinated by Geoff Clark. It was a vulnerable time for the band of warriors who had bonded during the 1980s, and a vulnerable time for Patrick:

> After all the hype of the Sydney march, and Hawke's promise of a treaty, the momentum seemed to die after a while. A lot of the focus started to change, with the Royal Commission being a big issue, and the push for an international declaration that was supposed to be a panacea. The salvation was going to come from overseas, from Geneva, they reckoned. There was also a tension building between those blacks going into the institutional type positions, with ATSIC starting up.
>
> Down south, the Aboriginal Provisional Government became a kind of rallying point for sovereignty campaigners like Les Malezar and (Geoff) Clarkie and (Bob) Weatherall. The whole movement represented by the Federation ground to a halt around then. There wasn't much national cohesion anymore and land rights were sort of lost as a goal. Fighting for culture and land didn't seem to be where the battle was. For that mob at least.[58]

A decision of sorts evolved. Patrick would leave Alice and return to Broome to work with the Kimberley Land Council with Peter Yu. David Ross could take over the reins at the Land Council, now his studies in Adelaide had finished. Patrick wanted to spend time with his centenarian and increasingly feeble, grandfather. Old Paddy now spent his days wrapped in a blanket sitting in a chair at the hospital, sometimes singing a Yawuru song as his mind drifted across the country. Fay had set up a house on the Block and Patrick and Barbara Shaw made the occasional trip across establishing a sleeping shelter and putting in some plumbing. He wanted to feel the pindan between his toes and reclaim his own heritage.

For Barbara Shaw this was a difficult period as their relationship, and Patrick's time in Alice, came to a close:

> All the time he kept things bottled up inside and didn't talk about it. I agonised over it. The man was like a stone. All that Church and seminary stoicism.

The relationship with Barbara Shaw was breaking down as she and Patrick increasingly differed over daily issues, especially the care of Adrian. At that time Patrick had become involved in a new relationship with Barbara Flick, the director of the Institute for Aboriginal Development. She is the daughter of Joe Flick, a man from western New South Wales greatly admired by Patrick.[59] Patrick married Barbara in 1989 and eventually divorced in 1994.

Around this 'about to finish' time, Elliott Johnston visited Alice and talked with the Land Council about gaining community involvement in the work of the Commission. Johnston recalled:

> We met over two days, with the national chair (Muirhead) and myself. We were very impressed with his practical approach and his attitudes to the questions we were wrestling with. When the need for a new Commissioner for Western Australia arose, after consultation with the Premier (Dowding) and the Commonwealth Minister, there was agreement that Patrick would be a good choice to report on the underlying issues affecting the deaths in custody, rather than the coronial issues of each case. We all felt that it would be important to have an Aboriginal commissioner to explore the deeper reasons and to really look for the way forward.[60]

After the drama and tension of the last few months, leaving the Land Council and handing over the reins to David Ross was a relief for Patrick. The party at the Pioneer Football Club in Alice Springs was a memorable occasion, with many speeches, several rounds of drinks and a presentation by

Yami Lester of a bundle of spears. A fitting present, Yami thought, for a warrior returning to his ground:

> I thought it was good, you know, even though we were going to miss him in Alice. He needed to go back to his country and settle down there. He was always fighting for other people's country. Now he could fight for his own. It'd be good for him and for his people, too.[61]

Central Land Council, 1983

I was introduced to the Director of the Land Council on my first day. Patrick Dodson was in his office in the old Central Australian style house in Hartley Street, working through papers with his offsider, Toly Sawenko, after yet another trip down south. The Land Council was taking me on during my University vacation to assist in a sacred-site clearance program. Although I had not yet completed my studies in anthropology and linguistics, I had been a schoolteacher in bilingual programs and outstations in the region. I knew my way around the Centre, could drive a Toyota, and spoke enough Luritja to get out of trouble and not enough to make trouble. Most importantly, I could fix my own flat tyres.

Patrick looked at Toly, 'Look at the size of him,' he said, 'Make a good half-forward.' I grinned and replied, 'Made a better second rower.'

'If you're going to work with us,' he growled, 'you'd better change your religion. We don't want any of that rugger-bugger stuff here!' I laughed until, looking up, I saw they weren't.

Soon after I travelled out west of Alice, looking for the traditional owners who were to accompany me on the site-mapping trip. The men I sought were located on a pastoral lease, squatting on a small excision from a large pastoral station. They had moved camp, setting up for the day on a creek bed where they could dig water from a soakage. The station owner had refused their many requests to drill a bore on the excision or to use one of the station bores. They were traditional owners for the country but without security of tenure, they could not get rights of access, take any water, run any horses or cattle, or establish any infrastructure. The family travelled to the creek on an old tractor, pulling a trailer that had seen better days. Crowds of kids, yelling excitedly, climbed on board the tractor and trailer for the trip back to their main camp. Also on the trailer was a large petrol-powered portable generator, brought to the creek for watching videos. I followed them back to the camp, in my Toyota, a senior custodian beside me.

We watched the tractor pull the trailer through a creek crossing. Halfway, the trailer tipped over, spilling kids and toppling the generator. Shouts and laughter suddenly turned to screaming and wailing and everyone ran into the scrub. One of the boys, a son of the senior traditional owner, had been pinned under the generator. We jumped out of the vehicle and raced towards him. Levering the generator off, I picked the boy up. The back of his skull was crushed. Hoping against hope, I drove frantically to the King's Canyon resort to make radio-telephone contact with the Flying Doctor, the boy lying across the back seat, the senior custodian beside me, muttering with concern and occasionally crying. On the radio-telephone, the Flying Doctor told us what to look for and confirmed what we did not want to admit. The boy was dead. The sad and unnecessary loss of a young life could have been avoided with a little commonsense, a smattering of goodwill and recognition of the need for co-existence on Central Australia's pastoral frontier.

On my return to Alice, Patrick listened carefully to my report of the incident, frowning and shaking his head, expressing sympathy for the traditional owners. Going out to the fridge in the Council office kitchen, he handed me a can of beer. He wasted little time though, organising the Tangentyere Council to assist with the funeral, and then he sent me back to finish the site-mapping work. The work had to go on.

Reconciliation March in Sydney 28 May 2000 (photograph by Wendy McDougal, courtesy of State Library of New South Wales).

Galarrwuy Yunupingu (far left) at the presentation of the Yirrkala petition on Land Rights to then Aboriginal Affairs Minister Ian Viner (far right), 1977 (courtesy National Archives of Australia).

Vincent Lingiari and Gough Whitlam at the handing over of a lease at Wattie Creek, N.T., 1980 (courtesy of National Archives of Australia).

Patrick and Galarrwuy Yunupingu at Yirrkala (photograph Nick Hartgerink).

In May 1985, Patrick held Adrian Shaw as he watched the demonstration at Parliament House, Canberra (courtesy Dodson family).

With family and friends camping out at Jarlmadanga in Nyikina country, July 1994. From left; Helen Sham-Ho MLC., June Oscar, Grace Dartinga Dodson, Chelsea Wade and Patrick.

Chapter Ten

Towards reconciliation

'The time for the healing of wounds has come.'
Nelson Mandela, Inauguration speech, 10 May 1994

Crocodile Hole, East Kimberley, September 1991

Patrick was standing on the sandy bank of the waterhole, talking to 'the mob' who had gathered at a large bush meeting hosted by the Kimberley Land Council to consult their leaders and form policy decisions. He was outlining the purpose of the two-day meeting, establishing the policy agenda after the important songs, dances and ceremonies of the evening before. The meeting was a time for putting complex policies and politics into purposeful and straightforward English. His pitch to his countrymen was direct:

> It is a time to think about where Aboriginal People in the Kimberley have got to after all these years of kadiya (white people) dominating and controlling our lives. Where do we stand and where do we go. Because you know each day there are officers in Perth and in Canberra who run around and make plans, send out messages and have studies and reviews. They have flying trips of people who come over here and look at things and you wonder what they are doing.[1]

I was on one of those flying trips from Canberra, dispatched from the office of Robert Tickner, the Minister for Aboriginal Affairs to carry a letter inviting Patrick to become the first Chairperson of the Council for Aboriginal Reconciliation. I was working at the time in his frenetic and over-committed office. The Minister was characteristically enthusiastic. The Act establishing the Council had been proclaimed two weeks earlier after passing unopposed in a rare display of bipartisan support, no one voting against it in the Federal Parliament. My job was to negotiate on the Minister's behalf with Patrick and 'his bosses' on the Kimberley Land Council to persuade him to accept the new position. Before he would agree to the Minister's invitation, Patrick needed to consult. He needed the permission and authority of 'the mob.' He talked to the gathered community members and sought to simplify the complexity of the reconciliation process:

> They started off talking about a treaty, that is recognising the rights of Aboriginal people. They just turned the pages of that book and

said there is another word on this other page called 'reconciliation' and that means let's be friends, let us forget about the past ... Reconciliation is about convincing the kadiya that it is important for them to come to grips with the way they treated blackfellas. To come to grips with the way they are continuing to do that. So that they can feel good. To say alright, I want to be your friend. It'll take a long time but we have got to work on it. But before we start working straight onto that let's fix up some of these outstanding things first. See what your goodwill is. We invite you to the ground here, you have been taking yourself here, take over the country, take over the river, take over the sea, take over the mineral. What have you given us?

We are not asking for much. We want access to our ground. To travel through free.

The Land Council delegates were not opposed to the idea of reconciliation, but found it elusive. It was difficult for them to come to grips with the reality of its practical application, leaving it up to long conversations around the campfire on the opportunities and the problems. Having spent most of his life circling back to his country, to his ground, to his bosses, the prospect of a decade of work on the national agenda of reconciliation was daunting for Patrick. A commitment to spending large amounts of time in Canberra was not attractive.

A group of us sat up late into the night by the campfire, talking it through. His partner, Barbara Flick, interrogated the practicalities. She asked some penetrating questions about other potential candidates. It was a very short short list, I told her. Patrick's main boss, Johnny Watson from Jarlmadanga, a community held by the Yawuru neighbours the Nyikina and Mangala people, negotiated hard. He wanted to ensure that the Land Council would not suffer if Patrick had to leave. He sought resources that were beyond my capacity to deliver and I had to respond negatively to his proposals. Johnny Watson congratulated me, I thought sincerely, on being the first representative he had met from governments who found it necessary to tell the truth when I said that something could not be delivered. Patrick's witness was Geoff Clark, at the time from the

Aboriginal Provisional Government. He provided a note of cautious cynicism and gruff scepticism. Patrick's friend and colleague at the Land Council, Peter Yu, was supportive. He saw an opportunity in this new 'reconciliation process' to advance the elusive 'treaty', promised by Prime Minister Hawke at Barunga in 1988. It was a friendly but challenging fireside discussion.

By the end of the Crocodile Hole meeting, however, Patrick was not fully persuaded, although he supported the need for the reconciliation process. In particular, he did not see direct benefit for the Kimberley community, and he did not want to leave his country. I completed my aerial circum-navigation of the continent to report to the Minister, who was less than impressed. Robert Tickner recalls:

> The most crucial appointment was that chairperson. The person proposed, Patrick Dodson, was the most difficult to persuade. Anybody who knew Patrick's record and the agenda of the reconciliation process knew that he was the person to take the position. My best efforts of persuasion left his agreements unresolved and, much to my despair, he went fishing.[2]

A few weeks later, a phone call to Patrick from Prime Minister Hawke tipped the balance and he became the first Chairperson of the Council for Aboriginal Reconciliation. One condition, agreed with the Prime Minister, was that he could remain based in Broome. When I heard the news I remembered his words at Crocodile Hole:

> We are not asking for much. We want access to our ground. To travel through free.

By asking for a base in Broome, Patrick felt he was not asking the Prime Minister of Australia for much. He wanted to keep access to his ground. He wanted to continue to travel through free. He wanted to work for the country while looking after his own country and claiming his rights to it.

Deaths in custody

Patrick rolled his swag in July 1989 and drove across the Tanami Track to Yawuru country, setting up camp on 'the Block', an area past the caravan park on the road out of town that had been leased as Aboriginal land. While Patrick had been to Broome several times for visits, he had not lived there permanently since he was a Deacon in the Church in the 1970s. The town had changed dramatically. An upsurge in tourism and the development of tourism infrastructure, especially at Cable Beach, escalated pressure on the Broome coastal strip and the land of the Yawuru. The local community was fractured; beset with discord and division. Their increasing economic and social marginalisation added to the pressure.

While he was immersing himself in his country, relearning the kinship and political networks of his hometown, he did not step back from the national stage. As soon as he arrived, he started work as a Commissioner inquiring into the underlying issues causing Aboriginal deaths in custody, while also assisting the establishment of the Rubibi Corporation to bring together those groups in dispute over law, language and custom.[3]

The Royal Commission would crystallise Patrick's thinking on the need for reconciliation and how it might work in practice. He was asked to investigate the backgrounds and histories of the twenty-nine Aboriginal men and three Aboriginal women who died in custodial settings in Western Australia from 1980 to1989. Patrick's objectives were explicit from the outset:

> Their lives and deaths should not end with this Commission. They offer to us all, the beginning of a new and better chapter in our relationship, and in the history of what is now known as Western Australia.[4]

For Patrick, the key underlying issues he was asked to investigate related to the historical and political dispossession of Aboriginal people. This was the root cause. Here could be found the basis of their impoverishment, their alienation and their lack of development opportunities. He listened to the stories of the young men and women who lost their lives with disquiet, seeing the custodial rates as a symptom of a much deeper malaise that went to the heart of the relationship between Aboriginal people and the wider community of Australia. Their tragic deaths provoked the inquiry; their tragic lives told a deeper story that touched Patrick's heart.

Patrick put a team together that included Paul Lane, Rob Riley, Daryl Kickett and Peter Yu. With input from other writers such as Howard Pedersen in Perth, Kate Auty in Melbourne, Marcia Langton in Darwin and Kathy Whimp in Adelaide, the team explored the history of racism in the state, analysing the far-reaching disadvantages in health, education, housing, income and employment that seemed to lead inexorably to a higher rate of contact and conflict between police and Aboriginal people.

It was Commissioner Dodson's task to explain why too many Aboriginal people found themselves in custody too often and how this fact could be turned around. To this end, they held over sixty conferences and meetings in town centres, lock-ups and prisons across the State, from Oombulgurri in the north to Esperance in the south, and from Kiwikurra in the east to Carnarvon in the west. There was little time spent in his new home and office in Broome. The garden on 'the Block' remained unruly and untended.

The Commission, and Patrick's appointment, did not receive bipartisan support. Shadow Minister for Aboriginal Affairs Warwick Smith, and Senator Grant Tambling, criticised the costs and questioned the necessity of the appointment. Peter Walsh attacked from the Labor Party. They pointed to the fact that alcohol was the primary issue, and the funds allocated to the Commission would be better spent on rehabilitation programs. Warwick Smith argued:

> Money is being soaked up by expanding bureaucracies. It is being hijacked by the mates of the Minister for Aboriginal Affairs, Gerry Hand. It is not getting through to the people in real need.[5]

In his report on the underlying issues for Western Australia, Patrick focused on the quality of relationships, both historic and contemporary, for those who died and on the social structures that made imprisonment inevitable:

> I can only conclude that the majority of Aboriginal people in this State remain not only in a destabilised and powerless position compared to the dominant non-Aboriginal population, but also in a position where their powerlessness remains remarkably unrecognised. This lack of recognition occurs at human, socio-cultural, economic and structural levels. In a sense, it can be argued that the 'scene has been set' for what we are witnessing today. This tragic state of affairs will continue into the future unless there is change on both the part of non-Aboriginal and Aboriginal societies.[6]

The national report

The National Commission of the Royal Commission into Aboriginal Deaths in Custody reported in April 1991. When Elliott Johnston's report was finally completed, it was to the surprise of many that the Commission did not substantiate allegations of murder or foul play. The finding was rejected vociferously by many of those Aboriginal people who had called for the Royal Commission. Aboriginal spokespersons such as Paul Coe and Helen Corbett claimed the report was a betrayal and a denial of justice. The Commission found that Aboriginal people did not die at a greater rate in custody, although the 'duty of care' shown by officials was a serious deficit. What was overwhelmingly different was the rate at which Aboriginal people came into custody compared with the rate of the general community.

The ninety-nine cases examined by the Royal Commission found that the Aboriginality of those who died played a significant role in their ending up in custody and dying there. It explored the history of Aboriginal people being regulated, controlled and monitored by the state and found a clear pattern of state intervention into and control over their lives, particularly through the criminal justice system, usually at an early age.

The Commission pointed to a need to understand the history of government intervention in many aspects of Aboriginal lives, a history not well known or understood by non-Aboriginal Australians. They pointed to the effects of the assimilation policy in the undermining of control by Aboriginal people of their lives, and the fracturing of families through the removal of Aboriginal children to be raised in institutions.

Patrick Dodson and his other commissioners saw the underlying issues as fundamental. They sought to identify and resolve the root cause of over-representation. The final national report tried to probe under the surface and looked to history for patterns:

> The history of Aboriginal relations with the broader community has impacted upon Aboriginal people in many ways. Collectively, Aboriginal people have been denied access to the social and economic power, which is essential to effective participation in mainstream society. The dislocation of Aboriginal people from their land and culture, and the intrusion of Western society into Aboriginal life have rendered many Aboriginal forms of social control ineffective. The dependence, which characterised the confined and controlled way in which most Aboriginal people lived for much of recent history, has left people poorly equipped to deal with the many social problems they experience.[7]

The Dodson experience

Historically, the experience of the Dodson family pointed to the truth of the Commission's bleak findings. The Commission described the collective experience of Aboriginal people. It reflected the experience of Patrick's forebears and his family. He looked at the cases, and saw his shared past.

Patrick's people, the Yawuru people, were rapidly and often brutally dislocated from their land, their sites and their livelihood. Their resistance was overwhelmed. The non-Aboriginal society of the Kimberley frontier devalued their culture, denied their religion and appropriated their land and labour. The pearling and pastoral industries reaped the rewards without recognition or compensation.

Patrick's grandparents, Paddy Djiagween and Elizabeth Fagan, suffered the pinpricks of bureaucratic humiliation, state intervention and official control. Historically, this process had been facilitated and enforced by the Catholic Church, acting as agents in carrying out the well meaning, but fundamentally misguided, policies of the state. Through the intervention of officials, such as A.O. Neville, his grandparents were denied access to the economic opportunities provided by Joe Fagan. Instead of autonomy, they were forced into dependence and subjected to the exercise of bureaucratic power over their everyday lives, moral choices and assets.

Patrick's mother, Patricia Djiagween, received cruel and vindictive treatment of a young mother in need. Some of her treatment was seemingly exacerbated by the personal efforts of individual officers who identified and treated her as a troublemaker requiring discipline, force and control. Patrick's sisters, Fay and Georgina, were transported against their will and institutionalised. Their father was threatened with deportation for continuing his relationship with their mother. Patrick's father was imprisoned for the crime of loving Patricia and the young family was forced into fleeing the state in order to make a fresh start away from harassment and brutality. There was no choice. There was no free will.

Patrick's life, while relatively fortunate on many accounts, was also not free of the structural impact of this history of denial and disrespect. He felt, deeply, the impact of authority figures questioning his identity, his Aboriginality, his cultural validity. He resented the attempts by welfare authorities to control, constrain and monitor his life and the lives of those who cared for him. He detested the fact that his siblings were under threat of removal and relocation. He saw a link between the policies of the times and his personal life; wondering if things would have been different in his family, in his home life, if the policy settings had been more humane and Aboriginal land, law and culture had been given respect and acknowledgement. He did not 'blame the invaders' for his life, but could see cause and effect.

In his adult life, he fought with passion the denial by the Catholic Church of the validity and legitimacy of the Aboriginal spiritual experience. He could not comprehend the unwillingness of Church and state authorities to accept fundamental rights of community control, self-determination and the maintenance of culture, language and ritual. He reacted personally, often not leashing his anger, when Aboriginal people in the west and the north were denied their rights to land and were not given equal treatment and fair dealing. These were not legalistic, academic battles fought for political gamesmanship—they went to the very heart of his personal, social and cultural identity.

And yet, Patrick Dodson saw the need for reconciliation. If one man whose great-grandmother, grandfather, father, mother and sisters had at one time or another been removed, relocated and institutionalised because of the laws, policies and programs relating to Aboriginal people could believe in reconciliation, how could the nation be persuaded?

Towards reconciliation

The Royal Commission, in its list of 339 recommendations, addressed the need for all political parties to recognise that reconciliation between the Aboriginal and non-Aboriginal communities must be achieved if community division, discord and injustice to Aboriginal people are to be avoided. The Commission pointed to the urgency and necessity of the task before the nation.

It was Elliott Johnston who drafted the final chapter, based on extensive meetings with his fellow commissioners, talking through the issues to reach an agreed view. His final comment in the lengthy report was prophetic:

> I would only add this. I think that great patience is required, especially on the non-Aboriginal side. It is the non-Aboriginal society that created the division and sustained it over a long period of time; we cannot expect the Aboriginal people to respond quickly. The non-Aboriginal society and culture is evolving and changing and the Aboriginal people must be allowed to develop their own culture in their own ways; clearly there is scope for the two to interact in a fruitful and mutually fulfilling way. The process may falter at times; appear to get lost; but it can be pulled up again and survive if we are cool and negotiate with open minds and as with equals. And in the end, perhaps together, Aboriginal and non-Aboriginal, the situation can be reached where this ancient, subtly creative Aboriginal culture exists in friendship alongside the non-Aboriginal culture. Such an achievement would be a matter of pride not only for all Australians but for all humankind.[8]

Patrick respected Elliott greatly, admiring his capacity to achieve consensus through reason and logic. For Patrick, it was the energy and commitment of people like Elliott, people he had met, lived and worked with throughout his life that convinced him of the deep reservoirs of goodwill that lay virtually untapped in the Australian non-Aboriginal community. He agreed with Elliott that the divisions in Australian society had been created and sustained by non-Aboriginal authorities and that his own family history was a demonstration of the legacy of that division; of the harm that had been done generation after generation.

Patrick also knew that there was hope. There were non-Aboriginal people in his family story such as Joe Fagan who acted out of the context of his time and place; who did the right thing. There were the men on the Broome Road Board who respected the Yawuru religion and cultural tradition enough to provide a place where the remaining Yawuru sacred objects could be stored and where the Yawuru could make men to carry those laws and rituals into the future. There were men like his father, and his mate Curly Pascoe, who stood up to laws that were wrong and paid a price. There were people in Katherine, like the Maher family, who recognised the common bonds of survival and need and shared food, drink and the human experience. The Gartlan family, especially Marian, opened their doors to an Aboriginal orphan boy and gave him a home where he had none, and a family when he needed one. There were, across the country, priests, lawyers, policemen and shire officials who saw that things could change, and who worked, with Patrick or with their local communities, to make change happen. This non-Aboriginal domain was not foreign to Patrick; he could see the decency and goodwill that was required to make reconciliation less of an ideal vision and more of a practical reality. As Paddy Djiagween had done, he had worked to gain credibility and authority 'inside' the system, in order to help himself, but also to assist his family and countrymen stranded on the 'outside', looking in. Paddy and Patrick used this hard-won insider status to seek change.

The process of reconciliation, 1991

The Royal Commission into Aboriginal Deaths in Custody National Report was tabled in federal Parliament on 9 May 1991. The last half of that year would be a dramatic time for the issues of Aboriginal land, heritage, and the establishment of the process of reconciliation. The Minister for Aboriginal Affairs, Robert Tickner, was campaigning to formalise the process of reconciliation, stimulated by the strong support given in the Commission report. Two weeks after the Commission report was tabled, the Council for Aboriginal Reconciliation Bill was introduced into the House of Representatives. The approach was bipartisan, after lengthy negotiations in meeting rooms throughout the nation. The Shadow Minister, Dr Michael Wooldridge, campaigned energetically inside the Coalition for support for the Bill while seeking to push the inclusion of benchmarks that would assess the progress made on key indicators such as Aboriginal housing, health and employment.[9]

In the next month, amidst intense Cabinet rivalry between Paul Keating and Bob Hawke, the Commonwealth government decided to prevent mining at Coronation Hill and incorporate the Kakadu Conservation Zone into Kakadu National Park. The dynamic nature of Aboriginal cultural beliefs and heritage issues became national discussion points. The slogan 'Land Rights not mining' appeared on bumper stickers as Aboriginal heritage was portrayed as the antithesis of development. Patrick's brother, Mick, as Director of the Northern Land Council, was actively involved in the Coronation Hill campaign.

Prime Minister Bob Hawke's control over the Cabinet was fatally damaged, however. His last act in December of that year was to speak at the formal hanging of the Barunga statement in Parliament House, surrounded by representatives of the land councils of the Northern Territory.

In mid-August, Michael Wooldridge and Robert Ticker shook hands across the dispatch boxes in the House, sending the Council for Aboriginal Reconciliation Bill to the Senate, which passed it without dissent. The Governor-General proclaimed the Act on 2 September 1991. The federal Parliament, the voice of the people in the modern Australian state, agreed to turn over a new page in the relationship. The process of reconciliation had begun.

In the same week, Paddy Djiagween passed away. The *Broome Bulletin* recorded the passing of Patrick's grandfather:

Sad Loss of Kimberley King

Kimberley character, Paddy Djiagween, thought to be the oldest Aboriginal in Australia passed away in Broome on Sept 5th. Paddy Djiagween, like all Aboriginals in his generation, was born in the bush, and although his birth was unrecorded, medical records in all accounts put Paddy at the ripe old age of 111.

A tribal Aboriginal, and former chief of the Yawuru community of Broome, he was known by its members as the 'King.' It was a title he was worthy of, being well versed in all aspects of Aboriginal knowledge and history, all of which, according to his younger son Francis Djiagween, he passed down through the generations. 'During his younger years, and right through to his golden years, Dad has made a tremendous contribution to our people. We are all very proud of him,' Mr Djiagween said.

Nephew, Paddy Dodson, claimed that Paddy was the most competent and capable person he had ever had the privilege to know. 'Paddy was a custodian—he developed the lore that dominated the life of the tribal people in Broome; he was a spiritual leader, the holder of the Lore (customs) which required the people to live by a code of ethics—you have to respect that' Mr Dodson said.

But as his years caught up on him, his health deteriorated and he eventually had to be cared for. Family members including Cissy and Stanley Djiagween, oldest living son and Fay Wade, granddaughter, nurtured Paddy into his twilight years. Four or five years ago, Paddy was reluctantly admitted to the Broome hospital, as he had become beyond the ability of the family to care for. Here he became the darling of the hospital staff, entertaining them with his clapping sticks, in primitive rhythm and sometimes singing in guttural tones. In his last two years, his music became his communication, as he partially lost his sights and hearing. Having been around for more than half of white settlement in Australia, and having seen Broome transformed from camel carts and donkeys to the tourism hub it is now, Paddy experienced more than most of us would ever hope to.[10]

Patrick told me, over the phone, after the funeral:

> On my grandfather's tombstone in Broome, we carved the words he said to me once when I was on my way back from Port Keats. He just looked up at me, looked right into me. He saw I was troubled about things and he said, 'The sun rises, wind blows, grass grows, the tide comes and goes. No-one can ever take your land.'

For the man who was to become the father of reconciliation for the nation, this was his touchstone; a connection to the past that shaped the present and future.

From left; Paul Keating, Patrick Dodson and Robert Tickner, Canberra 1991 (courtesy Council for Aboriginal Reconciliation).

Patrick Dodson with Kim Beazley (courtesy Council for Aboriginal Reconciliation).

At the Department of Prime Minister and Cabinet (courtesy Council for Aboriginal Reconciliation).

Patrick Dodson and John Howard light candle of reconciliation during the launch of National Reconciliation Week at Parliament House, May 1996 (courtesy News Limited).

Chapter Eleven

The decade of reconciliation: an interview

'Reconciliation presents us with two inherent choices. We have the choice of cooperating for the larger good through reconciliation or we have the choice of continuing conflict, which undermines our potential for national well-being and success.'
Marcia Langton, Speech to the Australian Reconciliation Convention, 1997

It was in the Oral History archives of the National Library of Australia overlooking the lake in Canberra that I first heard the voice of Paddy Djiagween. Wendy Lowenstein, one of Australia's leading oral historians, had recorded a series of interviews with Paddy and other personalities in Broome in 1969. While she lugged around her reel-to-reel recorder, her husband worked on the gang on the garbage trucks, the first non-Aboriginal man in Broome to do so.

When I brought the tapes back to Broome, Paddy's descendants gathered around to listen to the old man. They were captivated by the sound of his voice, delighted to be hearing his stories of early Broome and Beagle Bay history. They laughed when they heard children crying in the background, guessing at their identity. Of particular significance was the fact that Wendy Lowenstein recorded evidence, in Paddy's own words, of his connection to Broome. She recorded him describing the names of places of significance in Yawuru territory and singing songs that commemorated the movements and actions of the ancestors that shaped the land, sea and coastline of Broome and its hinterland. In a contested cultural landscape, this was powerful evidence. It gave the perspective of the past, of an earlier generation, to the shape of current conflicts over connection to land. Today those conflicts are between black and black as much as between black and white.

In the same studios at the National Library in 2001, I recorded a lengthy interview with Patrick Dodson in which he talked about some key issues in the decade of reconciliation from 1991 to the Centenary of Federation in 2001. What follows is an edited transcript of that interview.

The decade of reconciliation commenced in September 1991 when the Act establishing the Council for Aboriginal Reconciliation was proclaimed in the Commonwealth Parliament with cross-party support. In the same month your grandfather, Paddy Djiagween, passed away and you were asked to chair the new Council. How did you feel about that task when you were first asked?

I felt initially that the last thing I wanted to do was to go back and get involved at the national level. I did not want to deal with the attitudes and behaviours and assumptions and games that I'd seen some of in the time I'd spent as a Royal Commissioner into Aboriginal Deaths in Custody. I really wanted to consolidate what my intention had been in going back to the west after my time in Central Australia. I really wanted to re-steep myself in the Kimberley traditions or way of life; to become more knowledgeable in my own traditions, the Yawuru traditions. I wanted to deepen my understanding of language, law, customs and other things. To spend a bit more time in working from within the Aboriginal culture rather than trying to work from without it in the interface with non-Aboriginal Australia. My grandfather passing away gave me a sense of huge loss. Much of the opportunities to sit and talk with him were gone. Not that much hadn't been given to me by the years I had or the opportunities I had to talk with him and to be with him. But it signified a change in the era as well.

The Royal Commission into Aboriginal Deaths in Custody had finished on the note of reconciliation. The last recommendation was really about promoting a process of reconciliation with governments and bodies and with Aboriginal people as well. It was clear to me that unless we could shift some of the dynamics in the public sector in the way policies and strategies were directed at Aboriginal people, then all we would have would be a continuation of good intentions. Not necessarily leading to anything of a structural or systemic nature that would shift the nature of Aboriginal peoples' lives or status or position within the country.

So you saw reconciliation as an opportunity to do that?

I saw reconciliation initially as a great way to encourage the adoption and pursuit of the 339 recommendations that the Royal Commission had thrown up. If people could get better understanding, better opportunities of interacting with Aboriginal people, then hopefully that would reduce custodies. Also we'd get better enlightenment on the underlying issues and social justice matters. Beyond that, what reconciliation would do for major issues like land rights or the constitutional position of Aboriginal people, they were probably a bit further out. They were seen as a possibility that could be achieved.

There could be some real achievement because the legislation talked about a framework, a document or documents of agreement or documents of reconciliation. Underpinning that sort of discussion had been the promise of a treaty by the Hawke Government at Barunga. The need for some recognition, either in the Constitution or through some agreement, treaty or whatever else, to outline or to confirm the relationship between indigenous people and the broad Australian public was seen as a possibility. The practical steps to be taken weren't seen as easy ones. It was never going to be easy to get there. But there was opportunity. There was a good opportunity to progress the debate. If you could get sufficient levels of consensus in the public and support in the political domain then there was the potential to celebrate the position of Aboriginal people in the country rather being seen as simply recipients of what the public sector can tolerate.

But when it came down to it at the end of 1991 you still knocked the job back and it took a phone call from the Prime Minister, Bob Hawke, to persuade you. How did he persuade you?

Well, Bob Hawke's got some very persuasive characteristics about him. He's been a negotiator for years and he obviously had a keen interest in how Aboriginal people in this country might eventually find some acceptance or accommodation within the broader political fabric. At that stage I obviously didn't realise that he wasn't going to be Prime Minister for very much longer. There was a commitment to pursue what he'd said at Barunga about the treaty and agreement, subject to how the consensual basis across the Australian public worked. Putting back on the agenda some notion of a treaty or an agreement—not that that was the only thing. The significance of getting shifts in attitudes to reduce the racism and ignorance, to get better outcomes from the strategies or the directions that the Royal Commission had spoken about were also key things.

Was it important to hold the bipartisanship that was evident in the passage of the Reconciliation Bill? I remember when Robert Tickner and Michael Wooldridge shook hands across the dispatch boxes.

That was very important, that it wouldn't just be one party against another party. This would be a bipartisan approach, a cross-party approach. Aboriginal affairs wouldn't be thrown into the arena as a football and kicked from one end to the other. There would be a real ability to work in a cross-party way to find consensus to the complicated and difficult issues. To some extent the representation of the Council was to try and reflect that by virtue of the Government, the Opposition and the other major party (the Democrats) nominating people to the Council.

The Council was interesting in that while it obviously didn't have representation from every sector it had a fairly cross-sectional representation. We had people from the mining industry, from the Chamber of Commerce and Industry, National Farmers, Aboriginal leadership from ATSIC as well as from the Land Councils. People from the media, people who had a general interest in Aboriginal affairs, entertainers, people of all sorts.

What were the dynamics like when the Council first met?

It was very interesting. I remember one Aboriginal person saying that unless I have a treaty by the end of the next week I would be asked to come off the Council. That person stayed there for the full ten years. People weren't sure what the heck this was about. There was some sense that it was a bit of an adventure. I think some thought, 'Well, this will be just another sort of statutory body that would meet once or twice but be ineffectual. It wouldn't really set out to do anything.' I don't think that was the case for most. The deputy chairman in the first instance was Sir Ronald Wilson, so there were some serious-minded—not the other people weren't serious minded—there were some serious people. It wasn't just a group of ne'er-do-wells who were going to try and do something good for the country, but people that would try to think structurally.

The other thing that attracted was that this would be a strategic approach to progress this process of reconciliation. It would require the submission of plans to the Parliament for Parliament's agreement. In that sense, maybe naively at the early part, I thought that there would be a greater synergy between the Council and the Parliament to actually work a bit more cooperatively. To get outcomes that would have mutual benefits for government as well as for the community at large and for the process of reconciliation. I thought there would be good policy making out of this.

Was the Council weakened or strengthened by the need to have a consensus across these different groups?

I think it was strengthened. You could take any one issue, you know, particularly when the *Mabo* judgment came out. The need for some kind of consensual position on this issue tested it, really tested it.

The High Court decision was handed down very early, in June 1992, so it was a little more than a year old, the Council.

That's right. It tested it. Having to be strategic and to take a longer-term view rather than the short-term political opportunism of a comment or a statement was a bit of a tension point. Some of the members may have seen the Council as a lobby group, as a body that would make statements and condemn governments, be independent of government. It really was a challenge to get consensual outcomes from within the Council. But, by and large, when those outcomes were achieved there was a sense of common agreement.

The mining and the pastoral areas were interesting. We saw the resource industry and the primary production areas as the key sources of conflicts that arise in this country. Most people don't understand why conflicts arise over land and land rights and development issues. The notion of bringing senior executives from the mining industry together with senior Aboriginal leaders out of the land councils and getting them to sit around for a couple of days trying to understand each other. Ultimately they could clarify the ground they had in common rather than what divided them—and similarly in the pastoral industry. The focus on finding a common ground and developing mutual respect, even though we have different views, was a very early contribution that the Council members made to the notion of dialogue and discussion over contentious issues in Australia. And sought then to moderate in the sense of enlighten, if possible, but certainly to temper the extremism that flowed on some of the occasions about native title, *Mabo* and *Wik*.

Was there a need for tempering from the non-Aboriginal side or the Aboriginal side?

From both sides, from both sides. The Council was fairly courageous in its mode of operation. It was probably the first group of people that would meet with the community in the locations where it met. It would make sure that there was a community meeting where the representatives of the community, Aboriginal and non-Aboriginal people, could meet with the Council and express their views. It wasn't just a social occasion; it was an actual meeting. We changed and modified that a bit over time. We initially met with the Aboriginal community and copped a lot of their frustration about government policy or community attitudes. To the credit of most of the Council people, they would turn up to these things and bear that burden. It helped inform the work of trying to promote a process of reconciliation, create understanding, dialogue and discussion at regional local levels. It created interfaces where people weren't finding any reason to talk to each other or be in each other's company.

The Council was a catalyst to get other groups in the society to do things. To start doing things and to take some initiative rather than relying on the Council to have the blueprint for every source of division and discord that arises in our society. People started to realise that the Council didn't have the answers to some of these things. It provided a process to encourage people to find a way that would lead to some form of reconciliation of the differences. The responsibility for that was to be shared by all, not just by those who were on the Council. It than became a task for the Council members to engender that sense of responsibility across all sectors of society and more generally in the communities.

It wasn't program-driven. It wasn't a body to deliver funds to people or deliver certain programs. It had a small budget. It had to find ways to communicate at the regional and local levels when it was a Council that met just four times a year. It had no bureaucracy of substance to support it. It had a small secretariat in the Prime Minister and Cabinet Department. It had to set up a way of contracting people, to be the disseminators of information and be the source point for people in the states to get information about the Council. Those contracted agents become stimulators or agents to promote the discussion about reconciliation. We would create study circles, developing content material to get people to sit down in their own locations and deal with issues.

We identified what we thought were the key issues for debate and discussion, and they're still relevant today. We helped to articulate the focus for where debate and discussion ought to be without trying to control that debate and discussion. We always took the view that this wasn't just about Aboriginal people. This was about the nation of Australia. Australia itself had to be healed and in that process the divisions and discord between Aboriginal people and non-Aboriginal people was a very challenging dynamic. But there are divisions and discords between Aboriginal groups themselves and some of those had to be resolved and worked through. Often, though, the focus was on Aboriginal and non-Aboriginal relationships rather than internal Aboriginal relationships.

But reconciliation was a complicated word. It was seen by some people as threatening. They saw it as a jib for the breaking of the treaty promise. It was seen as another form of assimilation. It was seen as only to do with Aboriginal people becoming more socially acceptable and very little to do with change in the non-Aboriginal world. And certainly often it was not seen as having to deal with systemic change, such as constitutional or legislative change. The first test was the *Mabo* judgment, which led to polarisation in the community. The Council's response was to try and bring the stakeholders together, the miners and the pastoralists and the Aboriginal groups, to try and assist the government of the day to find some better legislative response, if that's what they were going to do.

But it was up to government at the end of the day to make decisions balancing the interests and coming out with a political legislative outcome?
It was very much the case.

So was the Council left stranded?
Well, the Council was left stranded certainly when the *Wik* judgment came to the fore. By that stage there had been a change of government. The Labor Government going out of power and the Howard Government, the Coalition Government, coming in. The Council articulated three ways in which to respond to native title. The first preferential way was to do it by way of agreement, to try and agree these processes at government level with Aboriginal people and at regional levels and local levels. But agreement making was seen as a fundamental platform or process that underpinned reconciliation. Finding common ground within the agreement-making process was seen as a key way of doing things in a culture in Australia where any agreement-making process with Aboriginal people wasn't seen as the preferred first option, or an option at all.

We did a lot of work with local government and other peoples in getting symbolic agreements, interim agreements. The notion that agreements are part of the political landscape was assisted by the Council's work. The legislative response was the second option in most of these things and ultimately the litigious response. If you're going to litigate then that's really the last straw.

Trying to get people together into forums or into workshops to find a way forward and trying to get government into a consensual mode of operating. I think that's where the Council was left out of the process. Whenever we sought to be consensual or to include government we were seen to be overstepping our mandate or charter or leaving ourselves open to be isolated because of the political process.

That happened in both 1993 with *Mabo* and 1996 with *Wik*?
Very much so. I can remember the face of a Prime Minister when I came along with the representative bodies, or the Aboriginal groups, at one meeting in the Cabinet room. The Prime Minister was obviously wondering what their guy was doing there.

That was Paul Keating?
No, that wasn't Paul Keating; that was John Howard. I think Keating had a bit of the similar view, although the dynamics of negotiation were quite

different then. There was at least a process for negotiation or consultation with the Aboriginal leaders around the country under the Keating Government, where there was very little of that with the Howard set up.

Just focusing in on the Keating Government and the passage of the Native Title Bill in December of '93. Looking back over the seven, eight years since then, do you think that the Native Title Act has really delivered fundamental change for Aboriginal people?

No, although initially it promised a lot. The Keating 1993 Act was very promising. The rights and interests on pastoral leases were left open for the courts to determine at some point. They did so under *Wik*, of course. The fact that the right to negotiate was central to the 1993 Act was a very important shift because it brought the Aboriginal people to the table. As with the nature of the change that *Mabo* brought and the legislative response brought, it was a period where extreme views on one side and the other resulted, and you had Aboriginal people claiming cities and towns. But the reaction to that was to limit the rights of Aboriginal people.

Looking back to the ten-point plan that Howard introduced, and over which I disagreed with him because it was going to reduce the rights and interests of the Aboriginal people in favour of the pastoralists. In my view, it lacked any integrity with what the *Wik* judgment had talked about when it spoke of the native title rights being concurrent and coexistent with the rights of a pastoralist or a leaseholder. But if there's a conflict then they (the native title rights) yield.

We had this hysteria to remove the right to negotiate. Howard ultimately caved in under the pressure from the National Farmers and other groups, the miners. It was a direct assault on the indigenous people and their rights and an assault on the Court. Ultimately the bucket loads of extinguishment stuff that Tim Fischer spoke about was a way of saying to the High Court of Australia, 'the political process will always have its revenge if it disagrees with your legal findings.' So the net effect of what native title stands for today is very minimal.

It's got nothing of the promise that it had back then. There was a real opportunity to not only get title to land for Aboriginal people and have land restored to them, but also a real opportunity for them to be at the marketplace. In terms of the economic marketplace, to be able to negotiate about their economic opportunities or futures in relation to the use of those lands. A lot of that has been taken out of the capacity of the Native Title Act today and the right to negotiate operates in very restricted domains. The process has become far more cumbersome and restrictive of what was the intent.

One of the good things about the Native Title Act, is when the states actually decide to enter into consent determinations. If they do that in any way of integrity and look towards more comprehensive outcomes at that regional local level, rather than just the black letter law of what native title says, then there's some real abilities or some real capacity to bring about what the intent of the native title decisions were about. That's not happening at the pace it ought to be and could be. But there are some indications that it might happen. That's in the face of what was done legislatively and that's really a question of political will and intent. Then, even with political will and intent there are still legislative consequences that make it difficult for governments to go as far as they might want to go without having to amend the Native Title Act. The inter-tidal zone will be one good example. Taking away the right to negotiate on the inter-tidal zone for Aboriginal people who live on the coastlines and whose culture and traditions relate to reefs and beaches and the low-water mark. Not having a capacity to have a say about those things is a fundamental denial of their human rights and their indigenous rights. That has to be restored at some point in the country.

Stepping back and looking at the long view, in 1986 you were involved with a campaign against the preferred model by the Hawke Government for national land rights on a statutory basis. In 1992 we had the *Mabo* decision, later the *Wik* decision, so instead of a statutory basis for land rights people were relying on a common law basis for land. If you had gone along with the national land rights model way back then would *Mabo* and then *Wik* have been as divisive as they were?

The climate was certainly quite different when the national land rights proposals came up. What that sought to do was to shift the higher benchmarks that had been achieved under the Land Rights Act of the Northern Territory. It sought to reduce rights that were part of that Act on the basis that the states and others wouldn't wear it. The finding at common law of the concept or the notion of native title is a matter that has made land rights a far more difficult thing to achieve. Land rights were really about the negotiation of a legislative arrangement in the uncertainty of whether there were questions of sovereignty or questions of common law title, the existence and to what extent the common law title existed.

What native title delivered was that capacity and the introduction of the heinous concept of extinguishment. You could extinguish the rights of indigenous people to their lands and waters and, in effect, extinguish them as people. As was found in the Yorta Yorta case, you could say that for this group of Aboriginal people, the tides of time have washed away their title. Without your land and your association, because your identity is attached to the land and the seas, then it is fundamentally a denial of your existence. While legally people will say, 'No, that's not what extinguishment's about', these are political as well as legal concepts and they run to the notion of a people's identities. The capacity to extinguish, or the notion of extinguishment, is a heinous concept. It basically says, 'The law of this land no longer recognises that you at any stage in your history have had any attachment to this land because you can't establish that you have a customary law base, that you're a common descent group, that you have a continuing custom and practice that identifies you as a group of people.'

If there's no further response by governments to the land needs of the Aboriginal people in a statutory way outside of the native title response then that's a terrible injustice to Aboriginal people. Many of the arguments today are really about trying to get native title outcomes and non-native title outcomes in the consent determination processes. But also to address the need to find land or other outcomes for those Aboriginal groups whose land has been extinguished, whose interest has been extinguished, or who will not be able to meet the registration test. The potential for that to create status and non-status sort of Aborigines in this country, as they've done in Canada, has to be fought against. Justice requires a real response to the rights and interests of Aboriginal people either at common law or in some statutory manner. I think we've got now a statutory response to the common law situation, which is a lesser position than the position that the Land Rights Act in the Northern Territory enables. So the common law has, in fact, enabled far more drastic actions by government than prior to native title being determined.

But does land have to be part of the answer for justice?

In most Aboriginal people's contemplation it does. There are obviously a diversity of Aboriginal groups in Australia today for whom land is not necessarily the first point of their consciousness in terms of their Aboriginality. They would see the recognition of their attachment or association by descent as Aboriginal people from some part of this country. They might see the broader rights in the Constitution as something better, a right to self-determination, whatever that might mean, in terms of the political complexity of Australia or some other form of recognition.

But what's the point of recognition of rights to land and recognition of Aboriginal culture in the Constitution without jobs, without decent health, without decent housing?

The rights to land that have with them the right to negotiate is a recognition of Aboriginal people's rights to the country and to have a say of how they're going to be impacted. It also allows them to enter into negotiations about commercial arrangements or other forms of development. Jobs and other things are not necessarily the source point for indigenous people's identity. They're a means to a livelihood; they're a means to an end. The ability to work and to do things is an important thing but it's not what makes people Aboriginal people. Having a job as a truck driver doesn't make you an Aboriginal. Having a job as a clerk in a firm, even an executive director of a large mining company wouldn't make you an Aboriginal person. Being a radio personality doesn't make you an Aboriginal.

The essence of Aboriginal people's identity is tied very much to their spirituality, which has its basis in land. It has its basis in a view of life that is quite different from capitalism, quite different from individualism and has a notion of community that is essential to it. It has a sense of obligation to maintain and support the broader community through the Aboriginal community and to uphold the traditions of your people. If people's lives have been brutalised by being taken away, being subject to assimilation at every point of their existence in the last sixty years, then there have to be opportunities for Aboriginal people to celebrate and find ways of celebrating what it is their Aboriginality is. That's a matter of choice for many Aboriginal people today.

But aren't a lot of Aboriginal people today in our cities making choices, making lifestyle decisions, say, the young people in the cities wearing their caps back the front, listening to American rap music? Is their connection to land and community an ephemera that they can't grasp?

It has the real potential to lead to those people being floaters. People who wander Australia not knowing where their attachment to this country is. Or they'll float off into the non-Aboriginal world and be quite comfortable there. The relevance or significance of their Aboriginality is something they'll read in the history books and won't be part of their essential being. For many other Aboriginal people the significance and importance of their tradition is linked to land and to ceremony and song and to country and to obligations and practices that are akin to the tradition of life that existed prior to the white people coming here. It is still a very important feature that can be shared with other Aboriginal people who find themselves floating in this country, who may be seeking to understand their own traditions better. At the end of the day it's choice that people will make. But the choice, I think, has got to be fair to the rest of society as well as to the Aboriginal people. I think at some point you've got to stop proclaiming the sense of loss if you're no longer prepared to do something about those losses.

So it's up to people themselves to do something about reconnecting with their country?

You can't make people do these things; but in the first instance it's up to people. But the opportunity to do that is an obligation that all Aboriginal people have got to try and make happen. To assist people to do that through our organisations or through the way we influence governments to make government policies more responsive to those needs rather than continue to try to assimilate Aboriginal people. To have a more enlightened approach to negotiation about how the impacts of westernisation affect Aboriginal people. So on the one hand it is about individuals but, on the other hand, it's about influencing the political strategies and thinking of governments of the day to support the maintenance and the strengthening and the expansion of the ways in which Aboriginal people's values and beliefs can be better supported in this country.

Was it the gap between your position on those sorts of issues and the Prime Minister's position on issues such as practical reconciliation part of why you resigned in November 1997?

Oh, in part, I think. In part underpinning his view was very much an assimilationist view, that we simply have to be assimilated into work ethics and moral standards that are more akin to the acceptable position of middle-class Australia and be less offensive to non-Aboriginal Australia by the way we behave. I don't believe people to be deliberately offensive to others, but there are differences in Aboriginal people that are unique. Those differences have to be accepted and understood and accommodated in different ways within our society. It doesn't mean you corrupt the Aboriginal values and pretend that they're the ones that have to be accepted, but there is some real sense of values that we have to uphold.

The disagreements with him were more about seeing programs to deal with health, housing, education, employment as the end-point of reconciliation. Rather than understanding that it is a process and a dialogue and the need to sustain the ongoing nature of the dialogue in order to find better accommodations in the relationship between Aborigines and non-Aborigines. And ultimately to give us cause for celebration when we've resolved complicated and difficult issues that are the source of division and discord between us. One of those is the fundamental recognition of Aboriginal people as the first peoples of this country. If you continue to deny the Aboriginal people as a significant group of people within our Constitution then it's a nonsense.

There's got to be a rectification of that and you just don't do it through health and housing and education. If you do education properly you'll understand that the land was stolen off the Aboriginal people. So you have to address the nature of what education throws up. Education throws up the nature of Aboriginal languages, that there are many languages that have been lost and that there are languages that are still in existence. It throws up knowledge about kinship structures and about communal arrangements. So what's the value of that knowledge in the context of jobs and education and other strategies? The westernisation process is not just what reconciliation's about. It had to be and always has to be about a dialogue and a negotiation at some point about how best to achieve those practical outcomes. Ultimately it is about how best to recognise the right of indigenous people to be indigenous people within the complexity of our western democratic structure and to accommodate that rather than to suppress it.

In terms of moving forward and resolving those issues and giving us something to celebrate, how important is a fulsome national apology?

It's got to be coupled with reparation or with some practical way in which to address the needs that underpin the need for an apology. An apology is the beginning point, I think, and it always has been the beginning point of what needs to be done. We've had the experience of the outcomes and cost of those appalling cases in the Northern Territory. We cannot simply continue to litigate to try and find answers to moral dilemmas here. The letter of the law is never going to support the indigenous experience and pain and hurt that have gone on. We require some compassion and some generosity to close off on this issue in a way that gives us—gives a broader Australian people—people who weren't taken away, because I wasn't taken away, but people who have suffered under these appalling regimes of the past an opportunity to move forward.

Whether they were deliberately put there, whether they were taken away, whether they got there by some other means, we had an appalling system in this country that sought to destabilise and recreate Aboriginal people in the image of white people without any regard for the uniqueness of who the indigenous people were or are. That's an indictment on our policy making of the past. It's an indictment on the philosophy that simply wants to assimilate and not celebrate the uniqueness of the differences that we've got. An apology is an important statement not only to the people who physically suffered under these schemes, but ultimately to the whole of Aboriginal people, as there are very few Aboriginal people whose lives haven't been affected by the way in which these policies operated.

As a kid I remember being dragged by another young girl who came running through our yard, grabbed hold of my hand, dragged me out and said, 'Run.' We ran and we hid in the long grass and watched the welfare and the police chase two other kids through the bushes and around the flat until they caught them. These kids were screaming and yelling and they bundled them into the back of a truck and sent them off to Croker Island. We were terrified that this was what was going to happen to us. Thankfully it didn't, but the trauma of the lives of those people that have gone through these things is not a matter for litigation. It's a matter for courageous leadership and a responsibility to err on the side of generosity for these things.

An apology is just the starting point. Until we have the maturity to look beyond the bottom line and what the dollar's talking about we won't get the reconciliation between us as many, many Australians want, Aborigines and non-Aborigines. So we can close off this section in a mutually respectful way and with a sense of pride. We can actually move forward and pass on to the future generation of Aboriginal and non-Aboriginal kids in this country a sense that we've achieved something of great substance for the good of the nation. We need to be doing that for the good of the nation, for the good of those Aboriginal people.

At the end of the day do you think reconciliation is more about people than politicians and Parliament?

It's fundamentally about people. It's about the people of Australia; it's about the Australian people continuing to hold very much in their eyes the image that they had when they walked across the bridges in Australia.

Do you regret not walking across the Bridge?

No, I don't, I don't regret that because I didn't participate for a different purpose. I just knew that given the character of this government there is no way it was going to respond positively to the recommendations that the Council that I no longer chaired was going to make. It would let the

Australian people down and we wouldn't see substantive change from the concept of practical reconciliation. We wouldn't see the reductions of people in custody or the improvement in health or the improvement in education. We've got 16-year-old kids in Year 10 who can hardly read, you know, and this is under the three years of practical reconciliation. You can say, 'Well, it's going to take another ten generations.' Well, it might, but it's not going to be done under those sorts of philosophies.

It's the people's movement and, thankfully, there are Australians who are continuing this process. They see we are in need of coming to one spirit, one view, one feeling about our position as Australians. They seek to have achieved resolution to some of these hard issues without being lazy and derelict by handing them on to the next generation. They simply find it intolerable that politicians can simply be so lazy and so poll-driven that they're not prepared to stand up with any courage to assist the Australian people to find closure to issues that have been opened up to us that we know have got to be healed. Just by resorting to some social policy about health, housing and education is not going to do it. It's about how we as people are going to feel about ourselves.

Every time we see celebration on a national scale with Aboriginal participation then slowly we're going to start asking questions. What's the significance of the Wandjina Dreamings that were seen in the Olympic Games? What's the significance of the Yipirinya Festival that was held at Alice Springs or the notion of the Bangarra dancers? What's the essence or the uniqueness of this Aboriginal culture that we've just snuffed out? We've refused to do anything that has enabled it to be far more integrated into the Australian lifestyle and left it pretty much to its own forces to survive, while we've done everything to try and extinguish it. So people in Australia is what reconciliation is about.

How much time have we people of Australia got?

If you have good political leadership these things can move quickly. I would hope that in the next three to six years we'll see some significant addressing of the fundamental issues that have been brought to our knowledge through the Royal Commission into Aboriginal Deaths in Custody, through the Council for Aboriginal Reconciliation itself, through the reports from the Human Rights Commission, through the highlighting of the way in which Australians want to be better regarded rather than simply as people who are ignorant. There's a whole other Australia that's in this country that we don't get to know simply by listening to the shock jocks on the radio stations—there's another Australia that requires leadership by politicians and many other people. I believe that the issues will come to the fore in the next three to six years because we're being forced back to the quality of our essence as Australians and as human beings. If we take stock of those qualities we will simply not allow racist and ignorant people to dominate, not only in their relationship to Aboriginal people but to others who are different in this country. Australians won't tolerate that for much longer.

How important is it to you that way back in the late 1960s the Broome Shire Council Roads Board set aside a ceremonial ground for the Yawuru people and now, through native title processes, you've managed to claim that back, or the Yawuru people have managed to claim that back?

It's tremendously important because it was achieved through the efforts of my grandfather and other leaders at the time to get a reserve created for cultural purposes. The non-Aboriginal person who was in charge of the shire, or the Roads Board, responded to it in a positive way. Achieving native title determination to that area, as a law ground, enables us to build the foundations for the future. It is a central place not only for Yawuru but for other tribes, the Karrajarri people, the Nyikina people. So it has significance for the meeting of other groups. We share a common law structure and now have the capacity to maximise an area of our traditional lands for the purposes of the sustaining of that law and trust and practice. Having that recognised in the western legal system has been a tremendous achievement for us. Especially given the chequered history of our being isolated from the community, being kicked out, being sent to Moola Bulla—being outcast in our own society for so long. We are people who have been able to survive and sustain our traditions in line with the wishes of our old people and have done some justice to what they sought to hand on to us.

That's what you want for Australia?

That's what I want for Australia, to be able to celebrate those good things.

Epilogue

Australia's heritage

'What we call our future is the shadow which our past throws in front of us.'
Marcel Proust (1871–1922) *A l'ombre des jeunes filles en fleurs* (1918)

I was travelling; a short afternoon journey on the western train line through the suburbs of Brisbane. The train stopped at each of the stations and my carriage rapidly filled with the noisy exuberance of students released from school. When I was a high school student in Brisbane I had used the same line. It was familiar territory. The loud conversations of the teenage boys in the nearby seats shifted unpredictably from music and sport to the latest 'cracks' for pirated software. Times have changed I thought as I watched and listened.

The boys' exuberance lifted my spirits somewhat, but failed to dispel my mood. I had spent the day on the sombre task of cleaning out my mother's cupboards after she passed away. In sorting through the family albums and documents, I had found a small history textbook I had used at school in the 1960s. The book was familiar and comfortable, its hard covers and convenient size rested easily in my hand. *Australia's Heritage* was a set text for the History and Civics course introduced into Queensland secondary schools in 1964. The cover art on the worn, old textbook was striking. It was a 1960s version of an Australian coat of arms, done in a style imitating an East Arnhemland bark painting. A lion and a kangaroo faced each other in the rampant position, a gum tree between them, a rose and convict chains beneath. The British lion and Australian kangaroo were decorated with simple cross-hatching that loosely quoted the clan and land based iconography of northern Australia. The cover spoke to a vision of Australian heritage as shared heritage.[1]

Flicking through the book, I found illustrations startling in their familiarity: an English village before enclosure, Hargreave's Spinning Jenny, Watt's steam engine, the growth of Australian democracy, Japan's conquests by 1942, the Commonwealth of Nations and the Colombo Plan at Work. I may not have studied the text closely at the time, but I had certainly looked at the pictures.

The first item in the index, Aborigines, referred me to page 46. There, the authors summarised the 'Aborigines' Way of Life' in three paragraphs. They began with Phillip's descriptions of 1788 that 'they were all naked but seemed fond of ornaments.' The authors discussed the work of historians who 'are learning much by digging up sites of aboriginals' camps':

> This much is fairly certain. In the ten thousand years during which the Australian natives occupied our land before the coming of white men, they never advanced beyond the stone age or hunting stage of development … There was no farming; instead of grinding wheat into flour, the aborigines produced a sort of flour from grass seeds or palm nuts. When one tract of territory was eaten out, the tribe moved on to another. There were no fixed homes, only camps and temporary shelters of bark. This is what is meant by a nomadic existence.

There were no other references to Aboriginal Australians in the index. Reading through I found another indirect reference in the chapter on 'What Nationalism is':

> The actors on our vast stage are we Australians: past and present; white and black; English, Scottish, Irish, German and Italian; 'old' Australians and 'new.' Each has a role to play in our pageant. Some have played it and made their exit. Others have still to come onto the stage.

The old textbook echoed the views and values of Dampier when he described the people living near Broome four hundred years ago. In Dampier's view, a people without agriculture or housing were not tillers of the soil or owners of the land. As they were not doing useful work, the land was ownerless or terra nullius. The people living there had no rights of ownership. Dampier's cargo established the foundation for a system of values and ideas maintained over time at the expense of Aboriginal rights and interests.

As the students of today jostled around me, I reflected that the Australian history texts in their bulging bags were not so dismissive and perfunctory in their treatment of the Aboriginal way of life. Ten thousand years of 'occupation' had shifted to some sixty thousand years of 'ownership.' References to the 'stone age' had been over-written by the recognition of a continuous and ongoing interaction between people and land, not found in any other continent. The adaptation of the hunter–gatherer lifestyle to our dry and ecologically fragile landmass was understood as a remarkable human achievement in sustainable land use. The research carried out 'by digging up sites of aboriginals' camps' told an ancient and powerful story. The ochre-covered, carefully positioned skeletons at Lake Mungo were now recognised as one of the world's earliest known examples of religious funerary practices, worthy of protection under the World Heritage Convention. Research in anthropology had looked beyond the simplicity of adaptive technology and started to analyse the complexity, ingenuity and diversity of social and cultural forms. Linguists had realised that Aboriginal languages were as complex in their grammar as Latin and Greek. The Australian languages that had survived were seen as outstanding universal examples of social and intellectual creativity. No text calling itself *Australia's Heritage* could today ignore the last decades of knowledge, understanding and continuing revelation. Our shared texts, our common cultural literacy, had changed.

Our shared understandings of the significance of Aboriginal issues in the life of the nation had also moved on dramatically. Aboriginal rights to protect their cultural heritage had been enshrined in law across Australia since the 1960s. There were laws enabling Aboriginal groups to establish their ownership of their traditional lands and programs to enable the purchase of lands. Large areas of the continent had been returned to Aboriginal ownership, control and management. Massive government interventions attempted to address the persistence of Aboriginal disadvantage. Aboriginal art was recognised as a signature of Australian identity and as a globally significant expression of the relationship between people and land. Aboriginal histories and biographies brought the Aboriginal experience of colonisation and assimilation onto bookshelves across Australia, while television and radio broadcast Aboriginal stories into our living rooms. Media coverage of contemporary issues mushroomed and Aboriginal voices were no longer unheard. The veil over our shared past had been lifted; although some would claim that it had been re-tied as a black armband. The school students around me would agree that the place of Aboriginal politics, society, culture and history in the Australia of today is a significant national issue. As the old textbook put it, 'this much is fairly certain.'

I was less certain of the significance of Aboriginal issues for the young boys and girls sharing my carriage. Their views on racial relations and the cultural interaction of respect and resistance were more likely to be shaped by the rapping of Eminem in the movie Eight Mile than any history text, however enlightened and inclusive. The notion of a shared Australian heritage and identity remained elusive.

I was also uncertain of the impact of the 'Decade of Reconciliation', especially on their young lives. I wondered whether the Australia they would inherit would be in any way different if there had been no attempt to establish a Council for Aboriginal Reconciliation that brought together representatives of Aboriginal and non-Aboriginal Australians to chart a new vision for the nation by the Centenary of Federation in 2001.

I recalled the morning in 1992 at Acton House in Canberra when the Council for Aboriginal Reconciliation first met. I was there, working in a team led by Pat Turner and Dawn Casey in the secretariat of the Council located in the Department of the Prime Minister and Cabinet.

The carefully planned schedule for the day immediately blew away when, as Chair, Patrick invited the twenty-one members of the Council to share their stories. Around the table, everyone was moved by the personal and family histories shared by the Aboriginal and Torres Strait Islander men and women. Rick Farley remembered the stories:

> The chair, Patrick Dodson, opened the meeting and announced that the first business would be for everyone to tell their own personal story. I thought that was a novel approach, particularly given the weight of the agenda papers. Six hours later, I was emotionally drained, reduced to concealed tears a couple of times and absolutely gob-smacked by the stories I had heard. They were way outside my comfort zone and challenged many of my approaches and perceptions. At the same time, I was humbled by the dignity of the Indigenous Council members and their willingness to forgive and move forward.[2]

The contrast between the collective experiences of the Aboriginal and non-Aboriginal members was stark and revealing. Worldly and experienced members such as Robert Champion de Crespigny, Jennie George, Ray Martin and Ian Spicer listened in quiet respect to the stories of people, place and the past flowing from people such as Archie Barton, Essie Coffey, Lowitja O'Donoghue, Wenten Rubuntja, Alma Stackhouse and Galarrwuy Yunupingu. There were common threads in the telling. All shared in different ways a sense of loss: of land, of language, of family, of identity. All shared too, a recollection of the impact on their lives of unfair, unjust and inhumane treatment served up to them and their families based on their Aboriginality. Remarkable in the telling was any lack of bitterness, anger or resentment; there was a restrained and assertive declaration of the need to acknowledge the facts, witness the past and look to the future.

For the first time in my hearing, Patrick told his family story. He started from his Yawuru identity declaring, 'I am a Yawuru man from Broome in the Kimberley.' He told of his grandfather Paddy's proud heritage as a man of knowledge and high degree. He told his fellow Council members of his Granny Liz, who inherited a station from her Irish father but was denied ownership by the state. He told of his mother, in chains on a cattle truck, carted against her will across the Kimberley. He told of his father, imprisoned for the love of his mother. With a catch in his voice, he briefly mentioned losing his parents in Katherine. He mentioned his entry into the Church and his work in the land councils and on the Royal Commission into Aboriginal Deaths in Custody. He then spoke at length about the road ahead for the reconciliation process. He talked of his hope for a process of reconciliation that could put into place agreements and structures at the highest level to ensure that the future Australia was a place where black and white could be proud of their country, working together in mutual respect and sharing their Australian heritage. It needed to be a national movement, he insisted, building on the goodwill of everyday Australians in their communities.

At the end, Ray Martin broke the silence saying, 'The stories we have heard around this table today are the stories of two worlds, two countries. It is incredible that it all happened in the one place, in the one country. Australians just don't know about it.'

After hours of free-flowing and spirited discussion, the vision of the Council for Aboriginal Reconciliation was agreed. I wrote up the final version on the whiteboard:

> A united Australia, which respects this land of ours, values the Aboriginal and Torres Strait Islander heritage and provides justice and equity for all.

A decade on, this vision, while worthy, seemed remote, unachievable and unrealistic. Despite the energy and commitment of Australians across Australia, black and white, the reconciliation goal had receded. The Australian national will, energy and focus had moved on to issues of immigration, terror and security. In the media, reporting on Aboriginal issues focused either on the issues of corruption, scandal and criminality or on the cycles of Aboriginal poverty, abuse and domestic violence. Reconciliation and native title were yesterday's stories.

As I listened to the steel wheels bumping over the points, my mind buzzed with pointless conjecture. What if the Council had been able to sustain its leadership role for the decade? What if it had been resourced sufficiently to fund television campaigns equivalent to those devoted to road safety or smoking? What if the *Mabo* and *Wik* decisions had not come so early and disrupted the steady building of consensus and agreement making? What if the Aboriginal and Torres Strait Islander Commission had been able to develop the capacity and the goodwill to negotiate meaningfully on behalf of Aboriginal Australia for a treaty or constitutional recognition? Would it have been different if political parties of all persuasions had maintained their initial commitment? What would have happened if the issues of Aboriginal health, housing and education had been addressed with the national determination and vigour that attended the rebuilding of Darwin or other disasters? What if there had not been a change of government halfway into the process or if the new government had maintained the momentum? What if Patrick Dodson had not resigned before the job was done? Would we have been further along the road to reconciliation?

Staring out the train window, I watched the backyards of houses in the inner-city Brisbane streets roll by. I caught glimpses into the lives of Australian families: people coming home from school and work, turning on televisions to watch the latest terrorist scare, preparing meals in microwave ovens and on gleaming stove tops, opening cans of dog food, watering the garden plants. At the next station, the young students grabbed their books, bags and sporting gear to get out, jostling each other in robust, confident good humour.

Across the continent, I knew that Patrick Dodson and other Yawuru lawmen were preparing for a federal Court hearing on a native title claim over areas of unalienated land in Broome. Government and some Aboriginal people in the fractured community of Broome were vigorously opposing the claim. A lengthy process of negotiation and mediation between the parties had stumbled and collapsed. The cultural identity and position of Patrick's grandfather, Paddy Djiagween, was hotly contested in a dispute that had divided both the small town and his extended family. While Australia was yet to be reconciled, many Aboriginal families of Australia were in spirited disagreement with each other and their surrounding communities.

Halfway between my train in Brisbane and Patrick's home in Broome, in the centre of Australia, the sun was setting over a small Aboriginal outstation community I knew. Dogs were yapping at a mob of laughing boys throwing stones at tin cans and kicking a semi-inflated football. They had not seen the inside of a school for months and funds for the visiting outstation teaching service had long since evaporated. The camp was settling down for the evening. Women were tending the fires; throwing rough cuts of meat onto the glowing coals. Young girls filled billycans of water from the one constantly dripping tap that served the camp, stepping carefully through the large puddle of muddy water. The children walked hungrily over to the fires. There was not enough meat to go around. What there was would be shared, the cooked pieces scraped with a knife and placed on a sheet of corrugated iron next to the fire. The children grabbed the meat before the dogs got their chance and huddled together under the half water tank humpy to eat, tell stories and prepare for sleep. Their sleep was disturbed by long, sorrowful keening from the women's camp mourning a young kinsman lost after years of sniffing petrol. In the centre of the camp, by the glowing ashes of the fire, the old man listened and watched over the camp. His back throbbed in pain from an untreated kidney problem. Looking out over his country, he watched the evening star rise. Aboriginal reconciliation was a long way from his thoughts.

Two countries in one continent, with one unknowable future. Reconciliation is a long road for all of us.

Endnotes

Abbreviations used in the notes include: SROWA (State Records Office of Western Australia); DNA (Department of Native Affairs); NAA (National Archives of Australia); NLA (National Library of Australia); and NTAS (Northern Territory Archives Service).

Preface

[1] Grattan, 2000 p. 231.

[2] Ray Martin to Kevin Keeffe interview, May 1997.

[3] Robert Champion de Crespigny to Kevin Keeffe, telephone interview, April 1998.

[4] Chief Ted Moses to Kevin Keeffe interview, May 1997.

[5] All quotes from *Proceedings of the Australian Reconciliation Convention*, 1997.

[6] The decision in the High Court, Mabo and Others v. Queensland (No. 2) (1992) 175 CLR 1 was handed down on 6 June 1992.

[7] The decision in the High Court, Wik Peoples v. The State of Queensland & Ors; The Thayorre People v. The State of Queensland & Ors 134 ALR 637 was handed down on 23 December 1996.

[8] *Canberra Times*, 24 December 1996, p. 1.

[9] Australia. Human Rights and Equal Opportunity Commission 1997.

Chapter One: Yawuru country

[1] All chapter introduction quotes from *Collins Quotation Finder*, Harper Collins, Glasgow, 2001.

[2] Pindan is the name given in the region to the red Dampierland soil. I use spellings as contained in sources quoted. Other than direct quotes, for names of languages and people I follow wherever possible the usage of Hudson 1996. For Yawuru terms, I use Hosokawa 1991 or Yawuru Language Team 1998.

[3] *Carissa lanceolata* from Kenneally, Edinger et al. 1996 p. 60.

[4] See genealogical chart at Plate One.

[5] The description of Yawuru territory is based on Paddy Djiagween's description to Wendy Lowenstein in 1969 which matches Hosokawa 1991, and the description and analysis given to me by Patrick Dodson, Stanley and Cissy Djiagween. *See also* Tarran 1997, Davis & Prescott 1992; Sutton 1995; Benterrak, Muecke et al. 1984; Roe 1983; Kenneally, Edinger et al. 1996. Note that the land–people–language relationship of the Yawuru is contested today with some people identifying as Walman Yawuru or Jukun (Jugun) contesting native title rights in the Federal Court. My limited research on traditional custodianship should not be viewed as excluding any of those parties.

[6] Excavation of a rock shelter at Koolan Island, O'Connor, 1999.

[7] My transcription of Paddy Djiagween's name for Broome as recorded by Wendy Lowenstein in 1969. (Wendy Lowenstein Collection ORAL TRC 2915/43, Oral History Collection, National Library of Australia, recorded in 1969 in Broome WA).

[8] Akerman & Stanton 1994 p. 1.

[9] Western Australia Heritage Committee, nd.

[10] Dodson 1988 p.84.

[11] See Hudson 1996, McGregor 1988; Kimberley Language Resource Centre 2000 for maps showing the location of these language groups.

[12] Williams 1989 p. 87.

[13] Clark 1962 p. 39–41; Dampier, Masefield et al. 1906. Dampier made these comments about the people of Buccaneer Archipelago, to the north of Yawuru country, on his earlier voyage to New Holland in 1688 on the *Cygnet*.

[14] Kenny 1995; Lawton 1979.

[15] Kenny 1995; Lawton 1979. Note that Patrick Dodson now lives on land near the well that Dampier used.

[16] Collins 1991. This is a story written by her at Batchelor College, NT.

[17] *Kardiya* (or *kartiya*) is a common Kimberley term for non-Aboriginal person, or whitefella.

[18] Interview, Broome, April 1998. I conducted many interviews with Patrick Dodson from 1998 to 2002. The original notes of the interviews are deposited with the Australian Institute of Aboriginal and Torres Strait Islander Studies. Patrick Dodson has given his approval for use of the interviews and variations where I have edited them for clarity.

[19] Rose 1991.

[20] NAA:A1, 1904/1329 Trepang Fishing. Report by Stretton, Sub Collector, 19/01/1903. Port Darwin was responsible for the Kimberley coastline at the time.

[21] Stokes 1969 p. 81.

[22] Martin & Panter 1864.

[23] *The Inquirer*, 8 June 1864.

[24] Clement 1990.

[25] Edwards 1983.

[26] Bolton 1954 p. 9.

[27] Hasluck 1942 p. 184–6; Green 1981; Edwards, 1983 p. 28–9.

[28] Durack, Mary 1971.

[29] Thomas Clarke's nephew, Lawrence later shared a dormitory with Paddy.

[30] Walter 1928; Flinders 1933.

[31] Dodson 1996

Chapter Two: Pearlers, priests and pastoralists

[1] His precise date of birth is unrecorded. Events in his life confirm the date given to Wendy Lowenstein of 1887. Some family members, at the time of his death in 1991, put the date as early as 1881. A file note records sighting a baptismal certificate which shows date of birth as 1892. In 1905 Mary Wanan and Patrick Diagwan received blankets in Beagle Bay. His age is given at 12 years, suggesting a birth date of 1893. (State Records Office of Western Australia: Department of Native Affairs; Acc 255 24/1906). His 1956 application for exemption

suggests approximately 1888 (State Records Office of Western Australia: Department of Native Affairs; Acc 49/51). After, referred to SROWA: DNA.

[2] All quotes by Paddy unless indicated otherwise are from Tape 45 of the Wendy Lowenstein Collection ORAL TRC 2915/43, Oral History Collection, National Library of Australia, recorded in 1969 in Broome WA (after, referred to as Lowenstein). For Yawuru skin names see Hosokawa 1991.

[3] Note, in 1956 Paddy signed a declaration seeking exemption, citing his parents as Mary Wanan and Joseph Kami (SROWA: DNA: Acc 49/51).

[4] Shaw 2001 p. 29.

[5] Quoted in Durack 1971 p. 33.

[6] Biskup 1973 p. 19.

[7] Figures from Anderson 1978 p. 63. *See also* Hunt 1986. The Asiatics were probably Japanese or 'Manilamen' (Filipinos). By 1888 only 24 Aborigines would be employed, compared to 783 Asiatics.

[8] Flinders 1933 p. 2.

[9] ibid.

[10] Huegal 1969 p. 52.

[11] Edwards 1983 p. 108.

[12] Lowenstein, Tape 45, side A.

[13] Brennan 1995 p. 91 quoting s106 (2) of *Land Act (Qld) 1933*.

[14] Flinders 1933; Kimberley Language Resource Centre 1996; Pedersen 1980; Pedersen & Woorunmurra 1995.

[15] Biskup 1973 p. 18.

[16] Sullivan 1989 p. 5. Thangoo is 30km southeast of Broome as the crow flies; 120km by road. *See also* Hosokawa 1994.

[17] Pedersen 1980.

[18] Shackcloth 1950 p. 219.

[19] Quoted in Durack 1971, p. 81.

[20] Pedersen 1980 p. 33.

[21] White ca.1898.

[22] Biskup 1973 p. 22 quoting SROWA: WA Police Archives Acc: 3548/1897.

[23] Australia. Royal Commission into Aboriginal Deaths in Custody & Dodson 1991.

[24] McCorquodale 1987 p. 92.

[25] ibid. p. 93.

[26] Pedersen & Woorunmurra 1995.

[27] Marshall 1988 p. 98.

[28] Lawton n.d.

[29] Sullivan 1989 p. 6.

[30] Hosokawa 1994 p. 495.

[31] Francis 1992.

[32] Lawton n.d.

[33] Hunt 1986. *See also* Jones 2002.

[34] Edwards 1983 p. 120.

[35] Quoted in Hunt 1986.

[36] Durack 1971 p.114.

[37] Nailon & Huegal 1990 p. 52. Paddy later told Wendy Lowenstein that the date was 1902. Governor Bedfords's visit was in 1904.

[38] Lowenstein Tape 44 Side A, in which Paddy laughed after telling the story. Also Nailon & Huegal 1990 p. 52.

[39] Bourke 1978; Jones 1995.

[40] Huegal 1969.

[41] Now spelled as Nyulnyul; the language spoken in the area of Beagle Bay Mission.

[42] Bates 1938 p.14.

[43] ibid. p. 30ff.

[44] Stanner 1979 p. 99.

[45] Nailon & Huegal 1990 p. 52.

[46] Lowenstein, Tape 44 Side A.

[47] ibid.

[48] ibid.

[49] Marshall 1988 p. 220.

[50] Nailon & Huegal 1990 p. 52.

[51] Lowenstein, Tape 44 Side A.

[52] Nailon & Huegal 1990 p. 54.

[53] Durack 1971 p. 191.

[54] Nailon & Huegal 1990 p.55.

[55] Durack 1971 p.197

[56] ibid. p.162.

[57] Walter 1928 p. 133.

[58] Zucker 1994.

[59] For discussion on this issue see Alroe 1988.

[60] See Myers 1986 p.217 for an analysis of this concept for the Pintupi.

[61] Huegal 1969 p. 9.

[62] Worms 1970 p. 377.

[63] Biskup 1973 p. 60–2. *See also* Royal Commission on the Administration of Aborigines and the Condition of the Natives (aka the Roth Report), 1904, Reports, Evidence, and Declarations, SROWA: WAS 1694, Acc. 1820.

[64] Letter from Fr George Walter to Chief Protector, 12 October 1906. SROWA: DNA, AN1 Acc. 255.

[65] Biskup 1973 p. 65.

[66] Australia. Royal Commission into Aboriginal Deaths in Custody and Dodson 1991 p. 6.

Chapter Three: An Irishman at Wild Dog

[1] This report is adapted (with thanks to the author) from an article prepared for *Irish Times*, 30 December 2000, by Siobahn McHugh.

[2] Fawcett, Jenny Genseek, Government Immigration Scheme To Australia Immigration Scheme—1856, online <http://www.standard.net.au/~jwilliams/d4.htm>, accessed 1 October, 2002.

[3] Nominal List, *David McIver*, 7 April 1857, courtesy of Geelong Local History Society.

[4] *Geelong Advertiser and Intelligencer*, Saturday 12 April 1856, p. 1.

[5] This is according to Paddy's account of his father-in-law as told to Wendy Lowenstein. Lowenstein, Tape 44 Side A. The Fagan (Fagen) family relocated to Echuca.

[6] As recorded in Ronan's biography of his pioneering father Denis 'James' Ronan 1859–1942. (Ronan 1962 p. 38.)

[7] ibid. p. 173 Victoria River Downs (VRD) and Wave Hill were first stocked in 1883 (Schultz & Lewis 1995 p. 229). Darrell Lewis (pers. comm.) notes that Joseph Fagan is recorded as being at VRD on 28 February of 1887, citing VRD records in the Noel Butlin archives, (Australian National University: 2/876/22). Makin (1970 pp. 99–100) claims that Pigeon Hole was established on its present site in 1910 when Sammy Green built its house and yards in 1910. Before this time there was an outstation at Longreach Waterhole, 10 or 15 kilometres to the south which closed when Pigeon Hole opened. According to Makin, the original forerunner to Pigeon Hole/Longreach was the Stockyard Creek homestead which, once the new homestead was built on the Wickham, was renamed Fagin's Camp after its head stockman. Makin implies that Fagan's Camp was renamed Pigeon Hole and that this name was later shifted to the present site, but this seems unlikely. Anzac Munnganyi told Darrell Lewis that Pigeon Hole was named for the fact that Flock pigeons used to water there in their thousands.

[8] Meggitt 1984 p. 19. Wave Hill was stocked in 1883. The Australian Investment Agency (Vesteys) bought Wave Hill and Gordon Downs in 1913–14. *See* Bowden 2001.

[9] Rose 1989. thanks to Peter Matthews for finding the Matilda Wright connection.

[10] esp. Durack 1959.

[11] This was Fitzroy River Station, according to Paddy's account to Wendy Lowenstein., Tape 43 Side B.

[12] Fagan, Jos, miner of Halls Creek is listed in the WA Post Office Directory for 1899, but not other years. He is not listed as a holder of a mining lease in the 1892–1909 directory.

[13] Durack 1959 p. 276.

[14] Ronan 1962 p. 155.

[15] Photo courtesy of South Australian Royal Geographical Society (Maurice 1902). The term 'East Kimberley Gold-fields' applied to the larger district, including the pastoral

properties, not just the diggings. The photo may have been taken at Wild Dog police station, a temporary police outpost near the Ord River, on the station track between Halls Creek and Wyndham, the port established in that year to service the pastoral industry and goldfields. Wild Dog (officially Argyle) police station was established in 1890. Darrell Lewis suggests that the photo was taken in 1902, which may raise questions about the dates for Joe Fagan's first ventures into the Kimberley.

[16] According to the Berndts in Berndt & Berndt 1987 p. 5 and Cole 1988 p.72.

[17] The old Texas Downs station was located closer to Wild Dog and Spring Creek.

[18] Shaw 1983.

[19] Letter 14 November 1892, M. Brophy, Trooper-in-charge to the Commissioner of Police supplied to Patrick Dodson by Chris Owen.

[20] Mick Dodson, interview, Sydney 17 June 1998. Noala is the name that appears on most official records. For the spelling thanks to Patrick McConvell (pers. comm.)

[21] Cole 1988 p. 71.

[22] For example, she is listed as Nullah (F.B.) on her daughter's file. Elizabeth's application for exemption in 1948 gave her name as Nola, but it was Noala in her 1952 application. (SROWA: DNA; 871/50).

[23] If this was the source of the name, their neighbours, the Warlpiri, would call her Napurrula.

[24] Lowenstein, Tape 43 Side B.

[25] Meggitt 1984 p. 6. Patrick McConvell (pers. comm.) notes re Waringarri: 'In other cases linguists and anthropologists have been given terms such as 'waringarr', which seems to mean 'many people' instead of an actual language or group name.' Darrell Lewis suggests that 'waringarri' is used to refer to 'fighting men', which may suggest that his informants were afraid of those living southwest of Gurindji country.

[26] See the discussion in McGrath 1987 pp. 68–94.

[27] Quoted in Reynolds 1987 p. 73.

[28] Durack 1959 p. 355. *See also* Ted Egan's song, *Drover's Boy* (Ted Egan 1993) and McGrath 1987.

[29] Durack 1959 p. 356.

[30] Clement 1987. See also SROWA:WA Police Archives Acc. 430 – file no 3257/1897 Journal of Inspection to Argyle Police Camp at Wild Dog Springs; Acc. 430–2029/1896, Wyndham Argyle Police Camp; Copy of PC Freeman's journal on patrol for natives who had killed cattle; Acc. 2029/1896 Argyle Police Station. Shooting of Native by PC Freeman no 192. Journal of Patrol 23 9–6 10 1898. Wyndham Police Station Occurrence Books— Accession 741/9 1 1 1907–21 11 1908; 741/24– 23 11 1901–24 12 1906; 741/4 —1 7 1897–24 10 1899; 741/8 26 10 1899–26 7 1902. With thanks to Jean Hobson of the Police Academy, Nedlands.

[31] SROWA: Department of Land and Surveys, 8532/1901 and 5331/1902 files.

[32] Durack 1959 p. 307.

[33] Lowenstein, Tape 43 Side B. Much family and archival confusion exists between the Spring Creek property and the Springvale property to the west (which Spring Creek flows through).

[34] SROWA: Department of Land and Surveys, 8532/1901 and 5331/1902. In the files, the station is variously referred to as Spring Creek or Spring Vale. Pastoral lease 1122/102 of 20,000 acres was taken out on 20 September 1901 and lease 1372/102 of 38,000 acres on 16 April 1902. The leases were originally taken out by the Turner Grazing Company (J. Fegan, J. Pilchowski and R.A. Finlay) but shares changed hands several times, before going to Fegan and Bert Ogden in 1917. The leases are now held by EG Green and Sons, through Balmoral Holdings, a W.A. pastoral company.

[35] Shaw 1987 p. 60.

[36] Personal communication cited in ibid. p. 61.

[37] Durack 1983 p. 123.

[38] Shaw 1987 p. 62. *See also* Coate 2000 p. 238.

[39] Hasluck 1994 p. 276. *See also* Coate 2000 pp. 99, 211, 238, 245.

[40] Broughton 1965 pp. 61–3.

[41] Durack 1959 p. 275.

[42] See discussion in Shaw 1983.

[43] For Wardaman, see the map in Berndt & Berndt 1987 p. 130. Wardaman country lies to the southwest of Katherine in the NT, in the area from Scott Creek and Flora River in the north to the Victoria River in the southwest. For Vincent Lingiari, see chapters four and six.

[44] Ross 1989 p. 69 'All along catch em up them *kartiya* (non-Aboriginal)' suggests that Major had a style similar to non-Aboriginal people, and implies he may have been bold and reckless; not mindful of Aboriginal authority.

[45] Vinnicombe 1996 p. 26.

[46] ibid. p. 28.

[47] Report from Turkey Creek, *Broome Chronicle*, 12 September 1908.

[48] *Broome Chronicle*, 22 August 1908.

[49] Reported in *Broome Chronicle*, 15 August 1908.

[50] Personal communication, Chris Owen to Patrick Dodson, 11 November 2001.

[51] Austen 1998 p. 174 quoting *The West Australian* 12–14 August 1908. Bishop Matthew Gibney was Bishop of Perth from 1887 to 1910.

[52] Shaw 1983.

[53] ibid. p. 19.

[54] *Broome Chronicle*, 22 August 1908.

[55] See the account in Vinnicombe 1996 p. 28.

[56] See discussion in Shaw 1983 and Clement 1989.

[57] Ross 1989 p. 33.

[58] Patrick Dodson, interview, Broome April, 1998.

[59] Quoted in Berndt & Berndt 1987 p. 6.

[60] SROWA DNA Acc: 49/51.

[61] Quoted by Christine Choo in Australia. Human Rights and Equal Opportunity Commission 1997 p. 104.

[62] Mechtilde 1961 p. 7.

[63] Bourke 1978 p. 154.

[64] Bailey 2001 p. 64.

[65] Mechtilde 1961 p. 15. *See also* Bailey 2001.

[66] Quoted in Durack 1971 p. 197.

[67] Nailon & Huegal 1990, p.56.

[68] See Lowenstein, Tape 43 for all quotes from Paddy in this section.

[69] Quoted in Bailey 2001 p. 7.7.

[70] ibid.

[71] Lowenstein, Tape 44 Side A.

[72] Lawton 1979 p. 8. This story has been challenged recently by some Walman Yawuru in a disputed native title case in Broome.

[73] SROWA DNA Acc: 49/51.

[74] Based on their ages in 1917, when applying for exemption.

[75] Forrest 1996 p. 295.

[76] Durack 1971 p. 230. Note that the Church later removed the body and placed it in a 'proper grave'. Alroe 1988 p. 31.

[77] Patrick Dodson, 18 September 2001, interview, NLA: Oral TRC 4796.

Chapter Four: Two laws

[1] Nailon & Huegal 1990 p. 56. No record has been found of his death in official archives, as it is not known what name he would have used to enlist, or his place of enlistment. Many Aboriginal soldiers enlisted at the end of a cattle drove, going off with their white bosses to war, and often using their bosses' or their station's name.

[2] Day 1996 pp. 240–2.

[3] NAA: CRS A 367/1; 1917/ 50 Father Bischoff—German Mission Station at Beagle Bay.

[4] Clement 1989.

[5] Shaw 1987 and Durack 1931.

[6] Quoted in Shaw 1987.

[7] Jebb 2002 p. 26.

[8] Ronan 1972.

[9] See for comparative discussion in Central Australia, Rowse 1998.

[10] Durack 1971 p. 254. This scene could have been a model for Tom Ronan's character in *Vision Splendid*. Tom was in the area at the time and later was manager of the Roebuck Bay station, near Broome. (Ronan 1972).

[11] See account in Lawton 1979 p. 8.

[12] ibid. p. 8.

[13] The comments about Paddy's parentage are puzzling. In a later application for exemption (8 June 1917) Paddy lists his mother as Mary or Wannan, and his father as Joseph Carme, Mexican. Perhaps he sought to exempt himself from the Act in this way.

[14] SROWA: DNA Acc: 155/ 20 653, letter dated 12/3/17.

[15] Information, courtesy WA Police History Association. Flinders, John Franklin Regimental number 943.

[16] Personal communication, Chris Owen to Patrick Dodson, 11 November 2001

[17] This account is reconstructed from file copies provided by the Western Australian Aboriginal Affairs Department.

[18] The will was registered as 531/1918. The probate file is SROWA: CONS 3403/175 on microfilm in the J.S. Battye Library of West Australian History. I am grateful to Steve Howell, senior librarian and Aurora Beasley for research on these papers.

[19] Death Certificate 3/1917.

[20] Haebich 1988 p. 156.

[21] Quoted in ibid. p. 156.

[22] ibid. p. 165.

[23] McCorquodale 1987 p. 95.

[24] Neville 1948 p. 51.

[25] SROWA: DNA Acc: 167 519/25. Elizabeth, alias Grace's, exemption application was sent on 30 June 1917 to the Chief Protector from Const Flinders.

[26] Letter from A.O. Neville to Acting Under Secretary, 16 February 1918.

[27] Letter to Aborigines Department Perth, 30 November 1917.

[28] Elizabeth was known as Grace, or Gracie, to her family in this period, and as 'Granny Liz' by her grandchildren.

[29] SROWA: CONS 3403/175.

[30] Bain 1982 p. 257.

[31] Lowenstein, Tape 44 Side A.

[32] Lowenstein, Tape 44 Side A.

[33] Herbert 1961 p. 15. I am grateful to Jack Waterford for reminding me of the Xavier Herbert yarn.

[34] 27 July 1921.

[35] See Clement 1989 p. 4.

[36] Kimberley Language Resource Centre 1996 translated from Kija and Kriol. But note that Clement (1989 p. 4) does not support the oral account.

[37] See Reynolds 1988 pp. 178–88.

[38] Western Australia 1927 p xiii.

[39] ibid. p. 187. For a critical view *see also* McGuiness 2000, Windschuttle 2000; Windschuttle 2001.

[40] These stories have now reached out into the broader community. They are the subject of paintings, such as those by the Warmun artists of Turkey Creek, and ceremonies.
The ceremonies have been elaborated into theatrical forms, such as 'Fire Fire Burning Bright', an adaptation by the Neminuwarlin Performance Group of the East Kimberley of a story passed down over eight decades of violence on Bedford Downs.

[41] Dodson 1996.

[42] Bolton 1972 p. 9.

[43] See Haebich 1988 p.192ff.

[44] Bolton 1972 p. 202.

[45] One million acres were excised from Marndoc reserve for selection by ex-servicemen (Haebich 1988 p. 366).

[46] Quoted in Austen 1998 p. 206.

[47] SROWA: DNA; A167 519/25.

[48] See references in Haebich 1988; Jacobs 1990; Manne 1999.

[49] Australia. Human Rights and Equal Opportunity Commission 1997 p. 108.

[50] Neville 1948 p. 49.

[51] Quoted in Haebich 1988 p. 302.

[52] For Western Australian protests, see ibid.

[53] Quoted in Australia. Human Rights and Equal Opportunity Commission 1997 p. 109.

[54] Quoted in Manne 1998 p. 37.

[55] National Library of Australia: MSS 2004/12/234 Bessie Reischbeith papers 'To the President and Members of the Royal Commission at Broome'.

[56] See discussion in Haebich 1988 pp. 330–42.

[57] C.T. Stannage, K.E.B. Saunders & R Nile 1998 p. 99.

[58] Quoted in Durack 1971 p. 274.

[59] Haebich 1988 p. 343.

[60] Manne 1998 p. 29.

[61] McCorquodale 1987 pp. 97–8. Neville defined 'quadroons' as one-fourth of the 'full blood', or the off-spring of a 'half-blood' and white parents.

[62] Haebich 1988 pp. 50–1.

[63] Arnold 1996.

[64] Australia. Royal Commission into Aboriginal Deaths in Custody and Dodson 1991 s. 21.1.

[65] SROWA: DNA; 49/51 lists them as Stanley, David, Raymond, Francis and Jean Elizabeth Djiagween.

[66] Lowenstein, Tape 44 Side A.

[67] Lowenstein, Tape 44 Side A.

[68] SROWA: DNA Acc: 49/51.

[69] Stanley and Cissy Djiagween, interview, Broome, 3 May, 1998.

70 Durack-Miller 1994 p. 31.

71 Unsourced clipping from June 1961, Broome Historical Society.

72 Dodson 1996. *See also* Lawton 1979 p. 8.

73 Stanley and Cissy Djiagween, Interview, Broome, 3 May 1998.

74 Dodson 1996.

75 Worms 1998 p. 158–9; Keogh 1981.

76 Several discussions with Patrick Dodson. Patrick declined to reveal any details of the 'inside business' of Yawuru law. For published sources on Gadaranya or Juluru, see Glowszewki 1998; Keogh 1981; Glowczewski 1983; Myers 1982; Wallace 1990.

77 Quoted in Rubibi Community v Western Australia FCA 607, Merkel J ('Rubibi'), 29 May 2001.

78 See ibid.

Chapter Five: Crimes of love

1 File notes quoted from SROWA: DNA; A1227 365/38 Half Caste—Patricia Djiagween—Broome-Personal File. SROWA: DNA; 469/43 Half-Caste-Patricia Djiagween now Dobson of Broome. Personal File Warrant Section 12 (Married W/M John Dobson) 8-9-47. SROWA: DNA: Acc: 326/43 H/C Mrs L Djiagween Personal File. SROWA: DNA; 871/50. Half-Caste Elizabeth Djiagween—of Broome—Personal File. Note that I am quoting the records contained in the Personal Files kept by the Department of Native Affairs, and using the language of the time, which may in some parts be offensive to modern readers.

2 National Australian Archives: B833 Second Australian Imperial Forces Personnel Dossiers, 1939–1947 2002/05085970 ABU KASSIM: Service Number—WX36796.

3 Bailey 2001 p. 141.

4 In gaining access to the personal files, names of other people mentioned are necessarily concealed by the archivists (by whiting out the name before copying). Where a name is in brackets inside a quote, I have inserted the known name with permission of the Dodson family.

5 This is no relation. A man named 'Jack Dobson' ran a general store in Hamersley Street. He died in Mandurah (Chapple 1996).

6 Neville's term as Commissioner expired in 1940.

7 The issue of Commonwealth control of Aboriginal Affairs was under discussion at the time. The Commonwealth sought the agreement of the States at the Adelaide Premiers' Conference in 1936. It was rejected.

8 November 1941, the fourth child of Patricia and Abu Kassim, only two of whom survived.

9 Long 1989; Feuer 1996.

10 National Archives of Australia: Australian War Memorial; AWM54, [Raids (Air) — Enemy (including damage):] Australian and Allied Forces and Civilians. Air Raid Casualties Darwin—Broome and Port Hedland, 1942–1945.

11 Compare Tyler 1987.

12 Durack 1971 pp. 304–5.

[13] Australian War Memorial: PR00534; Stanner, W.E.H., CMG (Lieutenant Colonel b: 1905 d: 1981).

[14] Lowenstein, Tape 44 Side A.

[15] For outlines of Aboriginal service in the second war see Ball 1991; Hall 1980.

[16] Letter to *Sydney Morning Herald*, March 1941 quoted in Hall 1980 p. 88.

[17] Durack 1971 p. 297.

[18] National Archives of Australia: CRS A885; B77 Part 1 Beagle Bay Mission Broome Western Australia 1941–1943.

[19] Durack 1971 p. 306.

[20] Notes taken by Patrick Dodson with Fay Wade, Broome, 1 August 1996.

[21] Her autobiography can be found on an excellent website at Sally Bin Denim, online <htttp://library.thinkquest.org/10236/demin.htm>, accessed 13 February, 2000.

[22] Durack 1971 p. 305.

[23] SROWA: DNA; A167 519/25.

[24] SROWA: DNA; A1227 469/43, 9 January 1943.

[25] Personal correspondence, Most Reverend Chris Saunders DD, August 2000.

[26] Notes taken by Patrick Dodson with Fay Wade, Broome, 1 August 1996. I interviewed Fay in April 1998. She declined a tape recorder, so this version is reconstructed from my notes. For Mick's version see interview with Phillip Adams, Late Night Live, 1999. Georgina recorded a version of the story that is part of the history of Broome display in the National Museum of Australia.

[27] Keneally 2001.

[28] Georgina being forgotten in the official document, although she was also removed.

[29] Mick Dodson, Late Night Live interview, 1999. I recorded the interview but failed to note the date. Phillip Adams (pers.comm.) could find no record of the interview.

[30] Fay remembers two nights in the Broome lock-up. The police records indicate four nights.

[31] 'The White Cliffs of Dover', lyrics by Nat Burton, melody by Walter Kent, 1941.

[32] Letter from Patricia (transcribed as written) to her friend (nickname Chicken) from Bohemia Downs on 9 November 1944, SROWA: DNA; 469/43.

[33] Dawson 1945.

[34] SROWA: DNA; 469/43.

[35] Dodson 2000.

[36] Although his parents are named on his marriage certificate as Alf and Ada Dodson from Launceston, I can find no Tasmanian births or death register entries that match the likely dates. Queries to every Dodson or 'Dobson' family in northern Tasmania also failed to elicit a verifiable connection.

[37] Cole 1992.

[38] Northern Territory Archives Service F 303 Tennant Creek—Police journals—1933–1969. I am grateful to David Nash for finding this document.

[39] Northern Territory Archives Service F68 Correspondence files—alphabetical single number series 1928-1945 Box 6 J5 1–15 Oct 1937 16–31/10/1937.

[40] Kimberley Language Resource Centre 1996 various quotes.

[41] From a letter to A.E. Green MHR, 7 March 1929, National Australian Archives (ACT) CRS A1 1937/16437, Chief Protector of Aborigines, Western Australia—Annual Report. 1929–1937.

[42] Notes taken by Patrick Dodson from Fay Wade, Broome, 1 August 1996.

[43] 29 July 1946.

[44] SROWA: DNA; A1227 365/ 38.

[45] McAdam 1995 p .68.

Chapter Six: On the banks of the Katherine

[1] Lea 1987.

[2] Until the meatworks shut down in 1953.

[3] Berndt & Berndt 1987 p.17.

[4] Merlan 1998 p.186.

[5] All file quotes from SROWA: DNA; A 469/43, 43 Half-Caste—Patricia Djiagween now Dobson of Broome. Personal File Warrant Section 12 (Married W/M John Dobson) 8–9–47. SROWA: DNA; 326/43 H/C Mrs L Djiagween Personal File. WA DNA 871/50. Half-Caste Elizabeth Djiagween—of Broome—Personal File, unless indicated otherwise.

[6] Elizabeth's files are full of correspondence on this issue. Patrick was astounded at their detailed chronicling of years of bureaucratic process that led to little action.

[7] Northern Territory Archives Service: Lands Department; AL 542.

[8] The Maher children were Dennis (Mano), Christine, Danny (Wickey), Pamela, William (Billy).

[9] Northern Territory Archives Service: Lands Department; AL 542.

[10] Maude Ellis, interview, Darwin, 3 July 1996.

[11] An outdoor toilet, the contents of which were doused with petrol and ignited, on a weekly basis.

[12] For a pearl meat recipe from Broome see Goolari media 2002, Broome recipes, online <http://www.abc.net.au/message/tv/ms/pearlmeat.htm>, accessed 10 October 2002.

[13] Allen 1997 pp. 111–13.

[14] McAdam 1995 p.131.

[15] See map of socioterritorial groupings, Merlan 1998 p. 15

[16] ibid. p. 6.

[17] See Merlan & Rumsey 1982 p. 32.

[18] Merlan 1998 p. 187.

[19] Arndt 1962.

[20] I am very grateful to Francesca Merlan for providing copies of Arndt's notes and for sharing insights into 'Old Spud'.

[21] All quotes in this section from SROWA: DNA; 326/43.

[22] ibid.

[23] Australia. Human Rights and Equal Opportunity Commission 1997 p.142.

[24] National Archives of Australia: A452/1, 1952/10, Patrol Officer Evans—Reports on patrol of Victoria River Downs and Kimberleys areas, 1951—1952.

[25] Berndt & Berndt 1987 p. 66.

[26] Lea 1987; McGinness 1991; Day 1996 p. 393.

[27] Berndt & Berndt 1987 p.155.

[28] Cummings 1990 p.12.

[29] Manne 1998 p. 29.

[30] Cummings 1990 p. 24. Compare the exploit of the girls in Pilkington 1996.

[31] Quoted in Australia. Human Rights and Equal Opportunity Commission 1997 p. 140. Sir John McEwan, who served 36 years in the Parliament, was later Prime Minister of Australia from 19/12/1967 to 10/1/1968.

[32] Quoted in Sanders 1998 p. 109.

[33] Quoted in Rowse 1998 p.128.

[34] Harry Giese was Director of Social Welfare from 1954 to 1970 and Director of Child Welfare from1959 to 1970.

[35] Quoted in Rowse 1998 p. 122.

[36] Patrick Dodson interview, NLA Oral TRC 4796, 18 September 2001.

[37] There is only slight contact between the families. Patrick met another woman at Halls Creek in 2002 who had borne one of Snowy's other children, a son, Patrick's half-brother.

[38] Max Stuart 1996, interview, 22 May 1996 Jarlmadanga, WA.

[39] National Archives of Australia: ACT A432/77, 1959/2299; Rupert Max Stuart: Murder of young girl in South Australia 1959–1959. *Also see* Dixon 1988; Inglis 2002.

[40] Inglis 2002 p. 374. Tom Dixon was the MSC priest who advocated Max Stuart's retrial. He was a friend of my father (Bernie Keeffe) on Thursday Island after World War Two. He assisted Tom Dixon in his campaign to seek evidence of Max's innocence in Queensland.

[41] Pixie was the wife of Jack Scanlon.

[42] I have not been able to find documentation of this event in NT Archives.

[43] NTAS: Lands Department, F627 AL 523.

[44] *NT News* 25 March 1960.

[45] Berndt & Berndt 1987 p. 58.

[46] NTAS: F292; Police Station Wave Hill. Police Journal.

[47] Patrick Dodson 2001, interview, 18 September,. NLA Oral TRC 4796.

[48] Patrick Dodson 2001, interview, 18 September, NLA Oral TRC 4796.

[49] 60 Ft Fall to Death, *NT News*, 2 August 1960.

⁵⁰ Patrick Dodson, interview, NLA Oral TRC 4796, 18 September 2001.

⁵¹ Jackson 2001.

⁵² Dodson 2000.

⁵³ see *Weekend News*, 13 August 1960.

⁵⁴ Quoted in Rowse 1998 p. 124.

Chapter Seven: In the arms of the Church

¹ See Fairfax Walkabout Australian Travel Guide, online <http://www.walkabout.com.au>, accessed 30 June 1999.

² Fr Jules Chevalier founded the Missionarius Sacratissimi Cordis (MSC), or Missionaries of the Sacred Heart, in 1854 in France. See Conlin 1945.

³ Personal communication, Buddy Gartlan, 17 September, 2002. I am grateful to the Gartlan family for their hospitality and assistance.

⁴ Mr Malcolm Fraser won the seat of Wannon in the 1955 election and was Prime Minister from 1975 until 1983.

⁵ Mr Paul Hasluck became Minister for Territories in May 1951 in the Menzies Government. He served in this role until 1963. He was Governor-General from February 1969 to July 1974.

⁶ Hasluck 1988 p. 121.

⁷ ibid. p. 86.

⁸ ibid. p. 121.

⁹ ibid. p. 646.

¹⁰ National Archives of Australia: CRS A452/1, 1961/7809 Policy re removal of part coloured children from the Northern Territory. 1932–1964. National Archives of Australia: CRS D4082, WB 260 Northern Territory Welfare Branch case files, South Australia and Northern Territory, 1957–1973 Patrick Dodson SC 165 was his personal file. Michael and Patricia were SC 164. The Australian Archives office in Canberra traced the file to Adelaide and copies have been supplied to the family.

¹¹ See for example the oral evidence in Cummings 1990 and Australia. Human Rights and Equal Opportunity Commission 1997.

¹² Hasluck 1988. Note lack of capitalisation in the original.

¹³ See argument in Ross v. Chambers, Supreme Court of Northern Territory, Kriewaldt J. (1956) NT 43.

¹⁴ National Archives of Australia: CRS A452/1, 1961/7809, Administrator, Darwin to Secretary, Department of Territories, 4/2/53.

¹⁵ National Archives of Australia: CRS A452/1, 1961/7809, Memo, Department of Territories 58/ 465.

¹⁶ Australia. Human Rights and Equal Opportunity Commission 1997.

¹⁷ ibid.

¹⁸ Portrait of Mick 1997.

[19] Patrick Dodson, interview, NLA Oral TRC 4796, 18 September 2001.

[20] National Archives of Australia: CRS D4082, WB378, Michael Dodson, SC 164 and CRS D4082, WB378, Patrick Dodson, SC 165.

[21] His Aboriginality would have closed that option, correspondence courses being the privilege of white station families in the Territory until recent years.

[22] McMillan 2001 p. 283. *See also* Bunbury 2002.

[23] Dodson 1996.

[24] Of a total of 5,801,584 ballot papers issued, 5,183,113 voted in favour of amending the Constitution, s51(xxvi), repealing s.127 thereby giving the Commonwealth power to legislate in respect of Aborigines in the States; and for Aborigines to be counted in the census. See McCorquodale 1987.

[25] See his account in McGinness 1991.

[26] Bandler 1997.

[27] Malcolm Fraser was Minister for the Army from 26 January 1966 to 28 February 1968.

[28] *Daily News*, 30 March 1967, p. 3.

[29] Flanagan 2002.

[30] As he told the journalist, Martin Flanagan when writing a 'blurb' for his book on the history of footy, (Flanagan 1998).

[31] McCoy 2002 p. 34.

[32] Patrick Dodson papers.

[33] Patrick Dodson, interview, Sydney, September 2002.

[34] Hoy 1945 p. 10.

[35] Jack Waterford, interview, Canberra, 15 June, 1998.

[36] Hoy 1945 p. 4.

[37] Rumble 1948 p. 8.

[38] Patrick Dodson papers. A rare copy of a significant letter filed by Patrick.

[39] Conlin 1945 p. 60.

[40] Daniel Mannix Memorial Lecture at Newman College Students' Club Melbourne University, 4 September, 1996, Dodson 1996.

[41] Marian Ann Gartlan passed away on 23 June 1968, aged 59 years.

[42] *Catholic Weekly*, 13 March 1969.

[43] The Anglican Church, which allowed marriage, had a much better record, in ordaining and helping Aboriginal priests.

[44] Newspaper article by Barry Wain, unsourced in Dodson papers.

[45] Mick Dodson, interview, Sydney, 17 June, 1998.

[46] Jack Ah Kit, interview, Darwin, 8 April 1998. Mick went to St Mary's convent for Grade 5 and 6, and St John's in Grade 7, while living with the Roe family (Basil and Janet).

[47] Gill 1969.

[48] Patrick Dodson papers.

49 Patrick Dodson papers.

50 Patrick Dodson papers.

51 Nailon & Huegal 1990.

52 *Canberra News* 7 June 1971.

53 Jack Waterford, interview, Canberra 15 June, 1998.

54 Milirrpum v. Nabalco and the Commonwealth of Australia, (Gove Land Rights Case), 1971, 17 Federal Law Reports, 141 (Milirrpum).

55 See McMillan 2001.

56 Milirrpum, 273.

57 Dow 2000.

58 NAA: CRS A5909/1 Cabinet Minute—Aboriginal campers in front of Parliament House.

59 Bennett 1989 p. 12.

60 Quoted in McMillan 2001 p. 288.

61 Carrodus, et al. 2001 p. 38.

62 The Eucharistic Congress ran from 18–25 February 1973. The first Congress was held in Lille, France, in 1881 on the theme of the social kingdom of Christ.

63 Unsourced newspaper article by Graham Williams, 'The old Church is breaking up' probably 23 February 1973. Patrick Dodson papers.

64 Unsourced newspaper article, 'Church's relations with Aboriginals put under scrutiny' probably January 1973. Patrick Dodson papers.

65 Smith 1973 with thanks to Brian McCoy for providing a copy of the newsletter.

66 Patrick Dodson, interview, Broome 30 April, 1998.

67 Maureen Watson, phone interview, 23 July, 1998.

68 For the Goss and Richards law firm, run by a future Premier.

69 Bishop Hilton Deakin, interview, Melbourne, January, 2001.

70 Fr Brian McCoy, interview, Canberra, 4 April 2001.

71 In the racial terminology promulgated by Neville, an 'octoroon' is an Aboriginal person who has one grandparent who is a 'full-blood' Aboriginal, or the offspring of a quadroon and a white person.

72 Walsh 2002.

73 From Patrick Dodson's recollection. In the native title claim for Kunin (Rubibi 6) Patrick used Patrick Dodson Djagun as his formal name.

Chapter Eight: A troubled priest

1 Ordination account based on recollections of those who attended, including Patrick Dodson, Paul Lane, Fr Kevin McKelson and the reports by Les Teese in the *Catholic Leader* and *Woman's Day* (Teese 1975).

2 See Fr Dodson Our First 1975, The First Aboriginal Priest: Tribe's Father 1975; Lewis 1975; Pope's Message 1975, Gill 1975; Teese 1975.

[3] Pope's Message 1975.

[4] The First Aboriginal Priest: Tribe's Father 1975

[5] Mahoney 1975.

[6] Quoted in Teese 1975.

[7] Also known as Luke Bunduk, now deceased.

[8] In 1981, Patrick would also work with the Foundation for Aboriginal and Islander Research Action (FAIRA) in Brisbane on alcohol issues.

[9] They gave evidence to the Standing Committee on Aboriginal Affairs, chaired by Mr Ruddock, in Darwin on 2 July 1976. Thanks to Maggie Brady for this reference.

[10] Dodson 1981 p. 10.

[11] Fr McKelson was Chaplain at the University of Notre Dame, Broome when I interviewed him in 1998.

[12] Nyangumarta, Karajarri, Yulparija, Juwaliny and Mangala.

[13] Kolig 1988 p. 377.

[14] See, for example, the discussion in Tonkinson 1988.

[15] Pascoe 1975.

[16] Rosser 1978 p. 8.

[17] See discussion in Rowley 1970 p. 129.

[18] Study quoted in Rosser 1978 p. 89.

[19] Pascoe 1975.

[20] His brother Bob was the State Minister for Northern Development and Aboriginal and Islander Affairs from November 1983 to December 1987, responsible for Paddy Killoran's downfall on the award wages issue, and in 1993 was elected to the House of Representatives for Kennedy, Queensland.

[21] Fr Dick Pascoe, 1998, phone interview, 6 August.

[22] Kidd 1997.

[23] ibid. p. 267.

[24] Norman Katter & Dick Pascoe, phone interviews, August, 1998.

[25] Sir Gerald Brennan was in 1974, senior counsel for the Northern Land Council in the Woodward Commission into Aboriginal Land Rights in the Northern Territory. He became a Justice of the High Court of Australia in 1981, and was appointed Chief Justice in 1995, retiring in 1998.

[26] Used in Catholic race education materials (Stempf 1984).

[27] Fr Brian McCoy, interview, Canberra, 4 April, 2001.

[28] O'Loughlin 1986.

[29] Fr Brian McCoy, interview, Canberra, 4 April 2001 ; as told to him by Deacon Peter Brogan, himself a Garden Pointer.

[30] Australia. Human Rights and Equal Opportunity Commission 1997 p. 145. As Aboriginal and Torres Strait Islander Social Justice Commissioner, Mick Dodson, with Sir Ronald Wilson, took primary responsibility for conducting the hearings.

[31] O'Loughlin 1986 p. 1.

[32] 16 August, 1977.

[33] Australia. Council for Aboriginal Reconciliation 1997.

[34] Navarre 1987 p. 16 Fr McCoy points out that there were several such guides, but it was the action that was important.

[35] Falkenberg 1962 p. 19.

[36] Pye 1973 p.44.

[37] ibid. p.48

[38] ibid. p6.

[39] Hawley 1981.

[40] ibid. (Carbines 1981).

[41] Hawley 1981.

[42] ibid. I had to explain to Patrick what a front-row footballer was.

[43] Northern Territory Archives Services. Jack Doolan interview NTRS 226; TS499.

[44] Fr Brian McCoy, interview, Canberra, 4 April, 2001.

Chapter Nine: To the Centre

[1] Mick and Alecia's daughter, Inala was born in 1979. Their son, Minirra Michael Dodson was born in January,1981. He passed away in March 2002.

[2] Aborigines Scores a Bar First 1979; First in Victoria 1979; He Did It His Way 1979.

[3] Mick Dodson, interview, Sydney 6 June, 1999.

[4] He Did It His Way 1979. *See also* First in Victoria 1979; Aborigines Scores a Bar First 1979. Ms Pat O'Shane was admitted to the bar earlier in NSW.

[5] Kelly, et al. 2001 p. 37.

[6] Jopson 2001.

[7] Hawke & Gallagher 1989.

[8] See the account in Palmer 1988 p. 137.

[9] Carne, et al. 1980 p. 61.

[10] See photo and article in 'Strong meeting calls for support', 1980

[11] Including Les Malezar, Pat O'Shane, Ribnga Green, Gary Foley and Kerri Rhandriamhefra.

[12] Des Carne, 2000, telephone interview,17 January. See Carne, et al. 1980.

[13] ibid. p. 107.

[14] Connor 1981.

[15] Unsourced press clipping (Fr Pat is a man with a mission) in Dodson papers.

[16] Jeannie Devitt, interview, Darwin, 20 June 1999.

[17] *See also* his comments in a television documentary in 2001 (Jackson 2001).

[18] Yami Lester, telephone interview, 4 April, 2001.

[19] Gordon 2001 pp. 99, 103.

[20] Yami Lester, telephone interview, 4 April, 2001.

[21] *Australia: Multinationals Are Invading* 1982 p. 15.

[22] MSC archives. Roman Catholics today are bound by the 1983 Code of Canon Law promulgated by Pope John Paul II which reformed the Code of Canon Law of 1917.

[23] Barbara Shaw, telephone interview, 30 July, 2001.

[24] Scambary 1985 p. 13.

[25] ibid. p. 14.

[26] Wright 1998 p. 98.

[27] John Ah Kit was Director of the Northern Land Council from 1984 to 1990. He has been the Member for Arnhem since October 1995, and is now a Minister in the Northern Territory Government.

[28] H. Pareroultja, interview, 16 January 1985, for a report to the Central Land Council on the social and economic history of the Mereenie region.

[29] Wright 1998 pp. 95–102.

[30] Shakespeare 1999 p. 419.

[31] Chatwin 1987 p. 49.

[32] Shakespeare 1999 p. 419.

[33] De Groen 1998 p. 261.

[34] ibid. p. 270.

[35] Ralph McInerney, When the Priesthood Isn't forever, online, <http://www.beliefnet.com/author/author_112.html>, accessed 14 October 2002.

[36] Lester 1993 p. 164.

[37] Quoted in *Land Rights Alert*, 1985.

[38] Warren Snowdon is now the Federal member for Lingiari and was previously the member for Northern Territory. He has held these seats from 1987 to 1996 and from 1998 to the present.

[39] Marcia Langton, interview, Darwin 3 April, 1999.

[40] Tape of conversation, P Dodson, D Ross, Peter Yu, Kevin Cook, 13 November 1999 (recorded by P. Torzillo). Cook & Goodall (in press). Story also told by Marcia Langton and Jack Ah Kit.

[41] Australian National Opinion Poll 1985. For a sceptical analysis of the use of these polls, see Rowse 1988.

[42] John Ah Kit, interview, Darwin 8 April, 1996.

[43] At Patrick's request I was appointed national coordinator; probably on the basis of being known to the CLC and based in Canberra with some time to spare as a part-time student.

[44] Patrick Dodson, interview, Sydney 28 September, 2002.

[45] Barbara Shaw, telephone interview, 30 July, 2001.

[46] Tape of conversation, P. Dodson, D. Ross, Peter Yu, Kevin Cook, 13 November 1999 (recorded by P. Torzillo). Cook & Goodall (in press).

[47] Reproduced in Dodson 1985.

[48] Charlie Perkins became Department Secretary in 1984. Later he clashed with Minister for Aboriginal Affairs Gerry Hand and, following charges of maladministration, resigned from the Department in 1988. *See* Read 2001.

[49] The Uluru Kata Tjuta Land Trust received their title on 26 October, 1985.

[50] Radio broadcast on 8HA in Alice Springs, 17 March 1985. Cited in Toyne v. Everingham No. 272/85 Defamation (1993) 91 NTR 1, Supreme Court of the Northern Territory.

[51] Clyde Holding was Minister for Aboriginal Affairs from 1983 to 1987. Gareth Evans was Minister for Resources and Energy from 1984 to 1987.

[52] Gerry Hand was Minister for Aboriginal Affairs from 1987 to 1990.

[53] Tape of conversation, P. Dodson, D. Ross, Peter Yu, Kevin Cook, 13 November 1999 (recorded by P. Torzillo). Cook & Goodall (in press).

[54] Tickner 2001 p. 41.

[55] Arnold 1996.

[56] Note that the *Encyclopedia of Aboriginal Australia* is inaccurate in stating that Patrick worked in Hand's office.

[57] Read 2001 p. 319.

[58] See tape of conversation, P. Dodson, D. Ross, Peter Yu, Kevin Cook, 13 November 1999 (recorded by P. Torzillo). Cook & Goodall (in press).

[59] The break up of the relationship between Patrick and Barbara Shaw was controversial at the time in Alice Springs. I have not discussed the issues with Barbara Flick, but Patrick and Barbara Shaw have asked me to not report the details in this book.

[60] Elliott Johnstone, telephone interview, 4 October 2001. Patrick also met the Commissioners in Canberra.

[61] Yami Lester, telephone interview, 4 April, 2001.

Chapter Ten: Towards reconciliation

[1] Kimberley Land Council and Waringarri Resource Centre 1991.

[2] Tickner 2001 p. 39.

[3] Kennedy 1989.

[4] Australia. Royal Commission into Aboriginal Deaths in Custody and Dodson 1991 p. xvii.

[5] Smith 1989.

[6] Australia. Royal Commission into Aboriginal Deaths in Custody and Dodson 1991 p. 2.

[7] ibid. v1, 1.3.3.

[8] ibid. v5, 38.32.

[9] Tickner 1990.

[10] Smith 1991.

Epilogue Australia's heritage

[1] Logue et al. 1964. Cover art by B. Dean.

[2] Farley 2001.

Bibliography

60 Ft Fall to Death, *NT News*, 3, 2 August, 1960.

Aborigines Scores a Bar First, *The Australian*, 2, 2 March, 1979.

Akerman, K. & J. Stanton, *Riki and Jakuli*, Northern Territory Museum of Arts and Sciences, Darwin, 1994.

Allen, G., *The Gun Ringer: Outback Legends of Jack Vitnell from Queensland to the Kimberley*, Central Queensland University Press, Rockhampton, 1997.

Alroe, M. J., A Pygmalion Complex among Missionaries: The Catholic Case in the Kimberley, *Aboriginal Australians and Christian Missions*. A. Swain & D. Rose (eds), Australian Association for the Study of Religions, Bedford Park, 30–44, 1988.

Anderson, L. P., *The Role of Aboriginal & Asian Labour in the Origin and Development of the Pearling Industry, Broome, Western Australia 1862–1940 [Manuscript]*, Thesis (B.A. Hons) Murdoch University, Perth, 1978.

Arndt, W., 'The Interpretation of the Delamere Lightning Plainting and Rock Engravings', *Oceania*, 32(3), 163–77, 1962.

Arnold, A., 'WA's Black Chapter', *Radio National's Background Briefing*, ABC, Sydney, 1996.

Austen, T., *A Cry in the Wind: Conflict in Western Australia, 1829–1929*, Darlington Publishing Group, Darlington, 1998.

'Australia: Multinationals Are Invading', *Multinational Monitor,* 12, 14–15, 1982.

Australia. Council for Aboriginal Reconciliation, *Proceedings of the Australian Reconciliation Convention*, 'Renewal of the Nation', Melbourne, 1997.

Australia. Human Rights and Equal Opportunity Commission, *Bringing Them Home: Report of National Inquiry into the Separation of Aboriginal and Torres Strait Islander Children from Their Families*, HREOC, Sydney, 1997.

Australia. Royal Commission into Aboriginal Deaths in Custody & P.L. Dodson, *Regional Report of Inquiry into Underlying Issues in Western Australia*, AGPS, Canberra, 1991.

Australian National Opinion Poll, *Land Rights: Winning Middle Australia*, Department of Aboriginal Affairs, Canberra, 1985.

Bailey, J., *The White Divers of Broome: The True Story of a Fatal Experiment*, Macmillan, Sydney, 2001.

Bain, M. A., *Full Fathom Five*, Artlook Press, Perth, 1982.

Ball, D., *Aborigines in the Defence of Australia*, ANU Press, Sydney, 1991.

Bandler, F., 'Speech at 30th Anniversary Ceremony', Proceedings of the Australian Reconciliation Convention, Melbourne, 1997.

Bates, D., *The Passing of the Aborigines: A Lifetime Spent among the Natives of Australia*, John Murray, London, 1938.

Bennett, S. *Aborigines and Political Power*, Allen & Unwin, Sydney, 1989.

Benterrak, K., S. Muecke, et al., *Reading the Country*, Fremantle Arts Centre Press, Fremantle, 1984.

Berndt, R. & C. Berndt, *End of an Era: Aboriginal Labour in the Northern Territory*, AIAS, Canberra, 1987.

Biskup, P., *Not Slaves, Not Citizens: The Aboriginal Problem in Western Australia 1898–1954*, UQP, St Lucia, 1973.

Bolton, G.C., 'The Kimberley Pastoral Industry', *University Studies in History and Economics*, 2(2):9, 1954.

——, *A Fine Country to Starve In*, University of Western Australia Press, Nedlands, 1972.

Bourke, D.F., *The History of the Catholic Church in Western Australia*, Archdiocese of Perth, Perth, 1978.

Bowden, T., *Penelope bungles to Broome*, Allen & Unwin, Crows Nest, 2001.

Brennan, F., *One Land, One Nation: Mabo Towards 2001*, UQP, St Lucia, 1995.

Broughton, G.W., *Turn Again Home*, Jacaranda Press, Brisbane, 1965.

Bunbury, B., *It's Not the Money It's the Land : Aboriginal Stockmen and the Equal Wages Case*, Fremantle Arts Centre Press, Fremantle, 2002.

Carbines, L., Bishop Rebukes Black Priest, *The Age*, 23 June, 1981.

Carne, D., Catholic Commission for Justice and Peace (Australia), et al., *Land Rights: A Christian Perspective: A Social Justice Resource Book*, Alternative Publishing Cooperative, Chippendale, 1980.

Chapple, T. D., *Broome: The Exciting Years: 1920s*, T. Chapple, Perth, 1996.

Chatwin, B., *The Songlines*, Elizabeth Sifton Books, Viking, New York, 1987.

Clark, M., *A History of Australia*, Melbourne University Press, Carlton, 1962.

Clement, C., *Pre Settlement Intrusion into the East Kimberley*, East Kimberley Assessment Project, Canberra, 1987.

——, 'Homes for the Million, Land for Nothing' n.d.

——, *Historical Notes Relevant to Impact Stories of the East Kimberley*, East Kimberley Assessment Project, 1989.

Coate, Y., *More Lonely Graves of Western Australia*, Hesperian Press, Carlisle, 2000.

Cole, T., *Hell, West and Crooked*, Collins/Angus & Robertson, Sydney, 1988.

——, *Riding the Wildman Plains: The Letters and Diaries of Tom Cole 1923–1943*, Sun, Sydney, 1992.

Collins, L., 'They Thought the Boat Was Some Kind of Fish Monster', *Kularlaga: Journal of Aboriginal Adult Education*, 2(2), 6, 1991.

Conlin, J., *The Society of the Missionaries of the Sacred Heart*, Annals Office, Kensington, 1945.

Connor, S., 'Whites Dodge Aboriginal Land Issue?', *The Morning Bulletin*, n.d. 1981.

Cook, K. & H. Goodall, Struggle for change: black and white activists talk with Kevin Cook about the movements for justice 1970–2003, Aboriginal Studies Press, Canberra, (in press).

Cummings, B., *Take This Child…From Kahlin Compund to the Retta Dixon Children's Home*, Aboriginal Studies Press, Canberra, 1990.

Dampier, W., J. Masefield, et al., *Dampier's Voyages: Consisting of a New Voyage Round the World, a Supplement to the Voyage Round the World, Two Voyages to Campeachy, a Discourse of Winds, a Voyage to New Holland, and a Vindication, in Answer to the Chimerical Relation of William Furnell*, E. Grant Richards, London, 1906.

Davis, S. & J.R.V. Prescott, *Aboriginal Frontiers and Boundaries in Australia*, Melbourne University Press, Carlton, 1992.

Dawson, W.J., North-West Mounted Police: A Variety of Tasks, *The West Australian*, 4, 3 March 1945.

Day, D., *Claiming a Continent: A New History of Australia*, Angus & Robertson, Sydney, 1996.

De Groen, F., *Xavier Herbert*, UQP, Brisbane, 1998.

Dixon, T., *The Wizard of Alice: Father Dixon and the Stuart Case*, Alella Books, Morwell, 1988.

Dodson, M., *Assimilation Versus Self-Determination: No Contest*, ANU, North Australia Research Unit, Darwin, 1996.

——, 'Corroboree 2000 Speech', *Encounter*, ABC Radio National, 11 June, 2000.

Dodson, P., 'Alcohol Prevention' *Identity*, 4(2), 10–11, 1981.

——., 'Address to the National Press Club', *Land Rights News*, (34) 2, 1985.

——, 'From Little Things Big Things Grow', Vincent Lingiari Memorial Lecture, 22 August, 1996.

——, 'Daniel Mannix Memorial Lecture', *Eureka Street,* October 1996.

——, 'The Land Our Mother, the Church Our Mother', *Compass Theology Review*, 22(Autumn/Winter), 1–3. 1988

——, *Beyond the Mourning Gate: Dealing with Unfinished Business*, The Wentworth Lecture, AIATSIS, Canberra, 2000.

Dow, C., *Aboriginal Tent Embassy: Icon or Eyesore?*, Dept of the Parliamentary Library, Canberra, 2000.

Durack, M., *Rudolph Philchowski: Tale of a North-West Tragedy. West Australian*, 5, 1931.

———, *Kings in Grass Castles*, Constable and Company Ltd, London, 1959.

———, *The Rock and the Sand*, Corgi, London, 1971.

———, *Sons in the Saddle*, Constable, Hutchinson, London, 1983.

Durack-Miller, M., 'The Legend of Long Mac'. *North of the 26th: A Collection of Writings, Paintings, Drawings and Photographs from the Kimberley, Pilbara and Gascoyne Regions*. H. Weller (ed), Access Press, Northbridge, WA. 2: 29–32, 1994.

Edwards, H., *Port of Pearls*, Rigby, Adelaide, 1983

Falkenberg, J., *Kin and Totem: Group Relations of Australian Aborigines in the Port Keats District*, Oslo University Press, Norway, 1962.

Farley, R., 'A Personal Journey', University of Newcastle's inaugural Human Rights/Social Justice Lecture, Newcastle, 7 October, 2001.

Feuer, A.B., *Commando!: The M/Z Unit's Secret War against Japan*, Praeger, Westport, Connecticut, USA, 1996.

The First Aboriginal Priest: Tribe's Father, *Daily Telegraph*, 17, 18 March, 1975.

First in Victoria, *The West Australian*, 25, 5 March, 1979.

Flanagan, M., *The Call*, Allen & Unwin, St Leonards, 1998.

———, *In Sunshine or in Shadow*, Picador, Sydney, 2002.

Flinders, C., Kimberley days and yesterday: a chronicle of 45 years in the great north-west and Kimberleys of Western Australia, as told to J.F. Christie by C.E. Flinders, 1933 (Manuscript), Alexander Library, Perth.

Forrest, K., *The Challenge and the Chance: The Colonisation and Settlement of North West Australia 1861–1914*, Hesperian Press, Carlisle, 1996.

Fr Dodson Our First, *NT News*, 1, 6 April, 1975.

Francis, I., *Broome: A Pictorial History*, Access Press, Northbridge, 1992.

Gill, A., 'Aboriginal to Become Priest', *Sydney Morning Herald*, 13, 20 April, 1975.

Gill, B., 'A Gentleman and a Scholar', *Melbourne Herald*, 3 March, 1969.

Glowczewski, B., 'Manifestations Symboliques D'une Transition Économique: Le 'Juluru', Culte Intertribal Du 'Cargo'. (Australie Occidentale Et Centrale). *'L'Homme*, 23(2), 7–35, 1983.

Glowszewski, B., 'The Meaning of "One" in Broome, Western Australia: From Yawuru Tribe to Rubibi Corporation', *Aboriginal History*, 22, 203–22, 1998.

Gordon, M., *Reconciliation: A Journey*, University of New South Wales Press, Sydney, 2001.

Grattan, M., *Reconciliation: Essays on Australian Reconciliation*, Bookman Press, Melbourne, 2000.

Green, N., 'Aborigines and White Settlers in the Nineteenth Century', *A New History of Western Australia,* C.T. Stannage (ed.), University of Western Australia, Nedlands, 1981.

Haebich, A. *For Their Own Good: Aborigines and Government in the southwest of Western Australia, 1900–1940*, University of Western Australia Press, Nedlands, 1988.

Hall, R. 'Aborigines, the Army and the Second World War', *Aboriginal History*, 4(1), 73–97, 1980.

Hasluck, P., *Shades of Darkness: Aboriginal Affairs 1925–1965*, Melbourne University Press, Melbourne, 1988.

——, *Black Australians—a Study of Native Policy in Western Australia 1829–1897*, Melbourne University Press, Melbourne, 1942.

——, *Mucking About: An Autobiography*, University of Western Australia Press, Nedlands, 1994.

Hawke, S. & M. Gallagher, *Noonkanbah: Whose Land, Whose Law*, Fremantle Arts Centre Press, Fremantle, 1989.

Hawley, J., 'Priest Ministers to a Culture Apart', *The Age*, 1–3, 22 June, 1981.

He Did It His Way, *The Age*, 1, 2 March, 1979.

Herbert, X., *Seven Emus*, Seven Seas Books, Berlin, 1961.

Hosokawa, K., 'Retribalization and Language Mixing: Aspects of Identity Strategies among the Broome Aborigines, Western Australia', *Bulletin of the National Museum of Ethnology*, 19(3), 491–534, 1994.

——, The Yawuru Language of West Kimberley: A Meaning-Based Description, Thesis (Ph.D.), ANU, Canberra, 1991

Hoy, C., 'The Vocation to Be a Missionary of the Sacred Heart', *Annals Pamphlet*, 15, 1945.

Hudson, J., T. Carr & M. Reid, *Languages of the Kimberley Region*, Catholic Education Office, Broome, 1996.

Huegal, F., 'Beagle Bay Mission—How It All Began', *Northern Times*, 10, 30 January, 1969.

Hunt, S., *Spinifex and Hessian: Women in North-West Australia 1860–1900*, University of Western Australia, Nedlands, 1986.

Inglis, K.S., *The Stuart Case*, Black Inc., Melbourne, 2001.

Jackson, A., 'Aborigines Left out of Celebrations: Long', *The Age*, 4, 4 April, 2001.

Jackson, L., 'For Shame', *Four Corners*, ABC, Sydney, 2001.

Jacobs, P., *Mister Neville*, Fremantle Arts Centre Press, Fremantle. 1990.

Jebb, M.A., *Blood, Sweat and Welfare: A History of White Bosses and Aboriginal Pastoral Workers*, University of Western Australia Press, Nedlands, 2002.

Jones, I., *Ned Kelly: A Short Life*, Thomas C. Lothian Pty Ltd, South Melbourne, 1995.

Jones, N., *Number 2 Home: A Story of Japanese Pioneers in Australia*, Fremantle Arts Centre Press, Fremantle, 2002.

Jopson, D., 'Black, Rich and Proud', *Sydney Morning Herald*, 6, 1 March, 2001.

Keneally, T., *A New Chant for Jimmie Blacksmith. Sydney Morning Herald*, 4, 25 August, 2001

Kenneally, K.F., D.C. Edinger & T. Willing, *Broome and Beyond: Plants and People of the Dampier Peninsula, Kimberley, Western Australia*, Dept of Conservation and Land Management, Como, 1996.

Kennedy, D., 'Dodson: Aboriginal on a Vital Mission', *West Australian*, 9, 23 June, 1989.

Kenny, J., *Before the First Fleet: Europeans in Australia 1606–1777*, Kangaroo Press, Sydney, 1995.

Keogh, R.D. The Two Men: An Aboriginal Song Cycle from the Kimberleys, Thesis (B.Mus. Hons), University of Sydney, Sydney, 1981.

Kidd, R., *The Way We Civilise*, UQP, St Lucia, 1997.

Kimberley Land Council & Waringarri Resource Centre, *The Crocodile Hole Report*, Conference on Resource Development and Kimberley Aboriginal Control, Rugan Community, Crocodile Hole, Kimberley Land Council, 1991.

Kimberley Language Resource Centre, *Moola Bulla: In the Shadow of the Mountain*, Magabala Books, Broome, 1996.

——, *Guide to Writing Languages of the Kimberley*, Kimberley Language Resource Centre, Halls Creek, 2000.

Kelly, P., 100 Years: The Australian Story, Allen & Unwin, Crows Nest, 2001.

Kolig, E., 'Mission Not Accomplished: Christianity in the Kimberleys', *Aboriginal Australians and Christian Missions: Ethnographic and Historical Studies*, T. Swain & D.B. Rose. (eds), Australian Association for the Study of Religions, Bedford Park: 376–91, 1988.

Lawton, K., *From Shinju to Shinju: tales from Broome*, Artlook, Perth, 1979.

Lea, J.P., *Government and the Community in Katherine, 1937–78*, ANU, Northern Australia Research Unit, 1987.

Lester, Y., *Yami: The Autobiography of Yami Lester*, IAD Press, Alice Springs, 1993.

Lewis, J., 'Soon, He'll Be Father to His Tribe', *The Age*, 1, 3 March, 1975.

Logue, W.P., A. McLay et al., *Australia's Heritage*, Jacaranda Press, Brisbane, 1964.

Long, B., *'Z' Special Unit's Secret War: Operation Semut 1*, Transpareon Press, Hornsby, NSW, 1989.

Mahoney, P., 'Historic Church Ceremony for Aboriginal', *Sun Herald*, 23, 27 April, 1975.

Makin, J., *The Big Run: The Story of Victoria River Downs Station*, Rigby, Adelaide, 1970.

Male, A., 'To the Electors of Kimberley'. *Broome Chronicle*, 2, 22 August, 1908.

Manne, R., *The Way We Live Now: The Controversies of the Nineties*, Text Publishing, Melbourne, 1998.

——, 'The Apology You Make When You're Not...', *The Age*, 30 August, 1999.

Marshall, P., ed., *Raparapa: All Right Now We Go Alongside the River*, Magabala Books, Broome, 1988.

Martin, J. & F.K. Panter, *Journals and Reports of Two Voyages to the Glenelg River and the North-West Coast of Australia*, Shenton, Perth, 1864.

McAdam, C. *Boundary Lines*, McPhee Gribble, Ringwood, 1995.

McCorquodale, J., *Aborigines and the Law: A Digest*, Aboriginal Studies Press, Canberra, 1987.

McCoy, B., 'The Hidden Culture of Indigenous Football', *Overland* 166: 30–4, 2002.

McGinness, J., *Son of Alyandabu: My Fight for Aboriginal Rights*, University of Queensland Press, St. Lucia, 1991.

McGrath, A., *Born in the Cattle: Aborigines in Cattle Country*, Allen & Unwin, Sydney, 1987.

McGregor, W. & Kimberley Language Resource Centre, *Handbook of Kimberley Languages*, Dept. of Linguistics, Research School of Pacific Studies, ANU, Canberra, 1988.

McGuiness, P.P., 'Sunday Bloody Sunday...It Was a Massacre among the Chattering Classes', *Sydney Morning Herald*, 9, 13 November, 2000.

McMillan, A., *An Intruder's Guide to East Arnhem Land*, Duffy & Snellgrove, Sydney, 2001.

Mechtilde, S.M., The Missionary Adventures of the Sisters of Saint John of God, manuscript in posession of author, 1961.

Meggitt, M.J., *Desert People: A Study of the Walbiri Aborigines of Central Australia*, Angus & Robertson, London. 1984.

Merlan, F., *Caging the Rainbow: Place, Politics and Aborigines in a North Australian Town*, University of Hawai'i Press, Honolulu, 1998.

Merlan, F. & A. Rumsey, *Jawoyn (Katherine Area) Land Claim*, Northern Land Council, Darwin, 1982.

Myers, F.R., 'What Is the Business of the "Balgo Business"', paper given at AIAS Conference on Contemporary Aboriginal Religious Movements, 1982.

——, *Pintupi Country, Pintupi Self*, Smithsonian Institute Press and AIAS, Washington and Canberra, 1986.

Nailon, B. & Huegal, F. (eds), *This Is Your Place: Beagle Bay Mission 1890–1990: birthplace and cradle of Catholic presence in the Kimberley*, Beagle Bay Community, Broome, 1990.

Navarre, A., *Handbook for Missionaries of the Sacred Heart Working among the Natives of Papua New Guinea*, Chevalier Press, Kensington, 1987.

Neville, A.O., *Australia's Coloured Community: Its Place in the Community*, Currawong Publishing Company, Sydney, 1948.

O'Connor, S., *30,000 Years of Aboriginal Occupation: Kimberley, North West Australia*, ANH Publications ; Centre for Archaeological Research, ANU, Canberra, 1999.

O'Loughlin, J.P., *The History of the Catholic Church in the Northern Territory*, Library Services of the Northern Territory, Darwin, 1986.

Palmer, I., *Buying Back the Land: Organisational Struggle and the Aboriginal Land Fund Commission*, Aboriginal Studies Press, Canberra, 1988.

Pascoe, M., 'Your Blacks Live in Fear', *Courier Mail*, 4, 4 November, 1975.

Pedersen, H., *Pigeon: An Aboriginal Rebel. A Study of Aboriginal-Eurpoean Conflict in the West Kimberley, North Western Australia During the 1890s*, Murdoch University, Perth, 1980.

Pedersen, H. & B. Woorunmurra, *Jandamarra and the Bunuba Resistance*, Magabala Books, Broome, 1995.

Pilkington, D., *Follow the Rabbit-Proof Fence*, University of Queensland Press, St Lucia, 1996.

Pope's Message, *Catholic Leader*, 1, 25 May, 1975.

Portrait of Mick, *Australian Story*, Australian Broadcasting Corporation, Sydney, 29 March, 1997.

Pye, J., *The Port Keats Story*, Bishop of Darwin, Darwin, 1973.

Read, P., *Charles Perkins: A Biography*, Penguin Books, Ringwood, 2001.

'Report from Turkey Creek', *Broome Chronicle*, 12 September, 1908.

Reynolds, H. *This Whispering in Our Hearts*, Allen & Unwin, Sydney, 1988.

Reynolds, H., *Frontier: Aborigines, Settlers and Land*, Allen & Unwin, Sydney, 1987.

Roe, P., *Gularabulu: Stories from the West Kimberley*, Fremantle Arts Centre Press, Fremantle, 1983.

Ronan, T., *Deep of the Sky: An Essay in Ancestor Worship*, Cassell, London, 1962.

——, *Vision Splendid*, Lloyd O'Neil, Hawthorn, Victoria, 1972.

Rose, D., 'Ned Lives!' *Australian Aboriginal Studies*, 2, 51–9, 1989.

——, *Hidden Histories: Black Stories from Victoria River Downs, Humbert River and Wave Hill Stations*, Aboriginal Studies Press, Canberra, 1991.

Ross, H., *Community Social Impact Assessment; a Cumulative Study in the Turkey Creek Area, Western Australia*, East Kimberley Assessment Project, Canberra, 1989.

Rosser, B., *This Is Palm Island*, AIAS, Canberra, 1978.

Rowley, C., *The Remote Aborigines*, Penguin Books, Ringwood, 1970.

Rowse, T., 'Middle Australia and the Noble Savage: A Political Romance', *Past and Present: The Construction of Aboriginality*, J. Beckett (ed), Aboriginal Studies Press for the AIAS, Canberra, 161–179, 1988.

——, *White Flour, White Power: From Rations to Citizenship in Central Australia*, Cambridge University Press, Melbourne, 1998.

——, 'The Modesty of the State: Hasluck and the Anthropological Critics of Assimilation', *Paul Hasluck in Australian History: Civic Personality and Public Life*, K. Saunders, T. Stannage & R. Nile (eds) UQP Australian Studies, St Lucia, 119–32, 1998.

Rumble, D., 'To Be a Priest', *Annals,* Pamphlet/Sacred Heart Monastery, (21), 1948.

Sanders, W., 'An Abiding Interest and a Constant Approach: Paul Hasluck as Historian, Reformer and Critic of Aboriginal Affairs', *Paul Hasluck in Australian History: Civic Personality and Public Life*, K. Saunders, T. Stannage & R. Nile, (eds) UQP Australian Studies, St Lucia, 106–32, 1998.

Scambary, R., 'Dodson Talks', *Catholic Leader*, 1985.

Schultz, C. & D. Lewis, *Beyond the Big Run: Station Life in Australia's Last Frontier*, UQP, St Lucia, 1995.

Shackcloth, I., *The Call of the Kimberleys*, Hallcraft, Melbourne, 1950.

Shakespeare, N., *Bruce Chatwin*, Harvill, London, 1999.

Shaw, B., 'Heroism against White Rule: The Rebel Major', *Rebels and Radicals*, E. Fry, (ed.) Allen & Unwin, Sydney: 8–27, 1983.

——, 'The Tale of Wallambain and Philchowski', *Australian Aboriginal Studies*, 11(1), 58–76, 1987.

Shaw, C., *The History of Broome's Street Names*, Carol Shaw, Broome, 2001.

Smith, S., 'What Happened in Melbourne', *Aboriginal and Islander Catholic Steering Committee Newsletter* 1, 1973.

Smith, S., 'Sad Loss of Kimberley "King"', *The Broome Bulletin*, 2, 1 October, 1991.

Smith, W., Dodson the Million Dollar Man, *The Kimberley Echo*, 2, 6 November, 1989.

Stannage, C.T., K.E.B. Saunders & R. Nile, (eds), *Paul Hasluck in Australian History: Civic Personality and Public Life*, UQP Australian studies, St Lucia, 1998.

Stanner, W.E.H., *White Man Got No Dreaming: Essays 1938–1973*, ANU Press, Canberra, 1979.

Stempf, K., (ed.) *Walk in My Shoes: A Social Justice Resource Book*, Dove Communications, Melbourne, 1984.

Stokes, J.L., *Discoveries in Australia: With an Account of the Coasts and Rivers Explored and Surveyed During the Voyage of H.M.S. Beagle in the Years 1837–38–39–40–41–42–43*, Libraries Board of South Australia, Adelaide, 1969.

'Strong Meeting Calls for Support', *Land Rights News*, 34:4, 11, 1980.

Sullivan, P., *Traditional Affiliation, History and Social Circumstances of Yawuru People*, Aboriginal Development Commission, Canberra, 1989.

Sutton, P., *Country: Aboriginal boundaries and land ownership in Australia*, Aboriginal History, Monograph 3, ANU, Canberra, 1995.

Tarran, M., 'People, Country and Protection of Culture and Cultural Properties', *Tracking Knowledge in North Australian Landscapes*, D. Rose & A. Clarke (eds), North Australia Research Unit, ANU, Darwin: 82–7, 1997.

Teese, L., 'Australia's First Aboriginal Priest', *Woman's Day*, 18 August, 1975.

——, Teese, L., Historic Day for our Aborigines, *The Advocate*, Melbourne: 12–13, 22 May, 1975.

'The First Aboriginal Priest: Tribe's father', *Daily Telegraph*, 17, 18 March 1975.

Tickner, R., *Aboriginal Reconciliation: A Discussion Paper*, Minister for Aboriginal Affairs, Canberra, 1990.

——, *Taking a Stand: Land Rights to Reconciliation*, Allen & Unwin, Crows Nest, 2001.

Tonkinson, R., 'Reflections of a Failed Crusade', *Aboriginal Australians and Christian Missions: Ethnographic and Historical Studies*, T. Swain & D. B. Rose (eds.) Australian Association for the Study of Religions, Bedford Park: 60–73, 1988.

Tyler, W.H., *Flight of Diamonds*, Hesperian Press, Carlisle, 1987.

Vinnicombe, P., *Women's Sites, Paintings and Places: Warrmarn Community, Turkey Creek*, Aboriginal Affairs Department, Perth, 1996.

Wallace, N., The Religion of the Aborigines of the Western Desert, *Ancestor Spirits: Aspects of Australian Aboriginal Life and Spirituality*, M. Charlesworth, R. Kimber & N. Wallace (eds), Deakin University Press, Geelong: 49–92, 1990.

Walsh, M., 'Language Ownership: A Key Issue for Native Title', *Language in Native Title*, J. Henderson & D. Nash (eds), Aboriginal Studies Press, Canberra: 231–44, 2002.

Walter, G., *Australia: Land People Mission*, Pallottine Society, Limburg (Eng trans. Bishop of Broome), 1928.

Western Australia, *Report of Royal Commission of Inquiry into Alleged Killing and Burning of Bodies of Aborigines in East Kimberley and into Police Methods When Effecting Arrests*, Government Printer, 1927.

Western Australia Heritage Committee, *Lurujarri Heritage Trail: Retracing the Song Cycle from Minarriny to Yinara*, Heritage Council of Western Australia, East Perth, n.d.

White, C., ca 1898, The Story of the Blacks: Aborigines of Australia (electronic resource), http://www.culturelanguage.com.

Williams, G., 'The English Approach', *Studies from Terra Australis to Australia*, A. Frost & J.P. Hardy, (eds), Australian Academy of the Humanities, Canberra: 85–93, 1989.

Windschuttle, K. 2000 'The Myths of Frontier Massacres in Australian History', *Quadrant*, XLIV(10), November, 2000, pp17–25.

——, National Press Club Debate, Keith Windschuttle v. Henry Reynolds, 19 April 2001, [http://www.sydneyline.com/fabrication.htm].

Worms, E.A., 'Observations on the Mission Field of the Pallottine Fathers in North West Australia, *Diprotodon to Detribalisation: Studies of Change among Australian Aborigines*, A. Pilling & R. Waterman, (eds) Michigan State University Press, East Lansing: 367–79, 1970.

——, *Australian Aboriginal Religions*, Spectrum Publications, Richmond, 1988.

Wright, A. (ed.), *Take Power Like This Old Man Here: An Anthology of Writings Celebrating Twenty Years of Land Rights in Central Australia*, IAD Press, Alice Springs, 1998.

Yawuru Language Team, *Yawuru Ngan-Ga: A Phrasebook of the Yawuru Language*, Magabala Books, Broome, 1998.

Zucker, M., *From Patrons to Partners: A History of the Catholic Church in the Kimberley 1884–1984*, University of Notre Dame Australia, Fremantle, 1994.

Index

Aboriginal Affairs conference (Canberra, 1937), 106–7
Aboriginal and Torres Strait Islander Commission, 278, 280, 281
Aboriginal children, *see* children
Aboriginal deacons, 218–22, 242
Aboriginal Development Commission (ADC), 280
Aboriginal history, 322–4
    Yawuru, 24–32, 40–8, 55, 305
    see also oral history and storytelling
Aboriginal Land Councils, *see* Land Councils
Aboriginal Land Fund Commission, 257
Aboriginal Land Rights (Northern Territory) Act 1976, 244, 256, 278
    Hawke Government preferred model and, 272, 276–7, 313–14
Aboriginal languages, 47, 233, 275, 317, 324
    at Beagle Bay Mission, 54, 55
    Central Land Council meetings, 267
    at Patrick's ordination, 228, 233
    Yawuru and Jukun, 220–1
Aboriginal law and culture, 25–6, 52, 204–5, 236, 244–6, 306
    alcohol, effect on, 233–4
    assimilation policies, aim of, 172–3
    Australian history texts on, 322–4
    Chatwin's interpretation of, 269–70
    constitutional recognition, 315
    Dampier's view, 26–7, 28–9
    Djiagween, Paddy, 111–14, 161, 210–11, 219, 242, 305
    Galambud (Kulumput), 165–6
    Kunin land claim, evidence to, 115–17
    Patrick's theology and, 239, 242–4, 265
    Royal Commission into Aboriginal Deaths in Custody, 298
    section (skin) names, 39, 71
    see also Aboriginal spirituality; ceremonies; identity
Aboriginal Legal Service, Fitzroy, 255
Aboriginal nuns, 242
Aboriginal Offenders Act 1892 (WA), 46
Aboriginal politics, 258–9, 281
Aboriginal priests, 207
    see also Dodson, Patrick
Aboriginal Provisional Government, 281, 293
Aboriginal spirituality, 25–6, 28–9, 230–1, 236–7, 315
    Djiagween, Paddy, 111–12
Aboriginal tent embassy, 213–14
Aboriginal treaty, 256, 270, 279, 291, 293, 307, 310
Aboriginal Treaty Committee, 256
Aboriginality, 24, 39, 201, 236–7, 315–16
Aborigines Act 1905 (WA), 57–8, 94, 97, 102, 106, 107

see also government intervention and control
Aborigines Act 1971 (Qld), 235
Aborigines Protection Act 1886 (WA), 45–6
'Accommodation for Part-Aboriginal Children in other States for Education and Training Scheme', 184, 194–200
ADC, 280
Adelaide, 198, 260, 294
The Age newspaper, 245–6, 263, 264
Ah Kit, John (Jack), 208, 267–8, 272, 273, 279
alcohol, 40, 73, 166, 176, 275
    research projects, 231–4, 260
Alice Springs, 202, 260, 262–74, 282–3
    Bungalow Home, 172
    gaol, 143
All-Australian Trade Union Congress (1951), 170
All Saints, West End, 236
Allen, Geoff, 163–4
Alphonse, Fr, 56
America, 10, 239, 263–4, 314
Anabia, Mrs, 50
Anangu, 271
Andrews, Constable, 140
Andrews, Neil, 280
apology, 14, 318–19
Arbitration Commission, 200
Argyle, *see* Wild Dog
Army, 130–1, 132, 133, 134–5, 170
    World War One, 91–2
Arndt, Walter, 166
Arrente, 174, 258
arrests and charges, 92–3, 165
    Djiagween, Cecil, 168
    Djiagween, Paddy, 109
    Djiagween, Patricia, 130, 135–40, 176–7
    Dodson, Snowy, 136, 139–42, 143, 145
    Fagan, Elizabeth, 102
    Kassim, Abu, 130
    Stuart, Max, 175
Asians, 30, 42, 49, 79, 80, 98, 103, 105, 167
    see also Japanese; Malays
assimilation, 172–4, 213, 237, 244, 310, 318
    'Accommodation for Part-Aboriginal Children in other States for Education and Training Scheme', 184, 194–200
    churchmen's views, 231, 238–9
    John Howard's views, 317
    Royal Commission into Aboriginal Death's findings, 296
ATSIC, 278, 280, 281
Australian Capital Territory, *see* Canberra

Australian Catholic Relief organisation, 257
Australian Council of Churches, 259
Australian Council of Trade Unions, 10
Australian football, *see* football
Australian history and history texts, 322–4
Australian Investment Agency, 157
    see also Wave Hill
Australian Mining Industry Council (AMIC), 273, 277
Australian Missionary Society of the Sacred Heart, 133, 175, 184, 192, 205, 206
    Patrick's priesthood, 204–66, 270–1
Australian National University, 211, 212, 259
Australian Reconciliation Awards Dinner and Presentations (Melbourne, 1997), 15–16
Australian Reconciliation Convention (Melbourne, 1997), 8–16, 202, 304
Australia's Heritage, 322–3
Auty, Kate, 294

Bagot Reserve, 158, 170
Bailey, John, 80, 124
Balagai, Remi, 56
Bandler, Dr Faith, 202
baptism of Paddy Djiagween, 40, 50
Bardi, 55, 108
Barrjarri section, 39
Barton, Archie, 325
Barunga Sports and Cultural Festival, 279–80
Barunga statement, 279–80, 300, 307
basketball, 199, 208
Batchelor, 162
Bates, Daisy, 51–2, 113, 205
Beagle, 30
Beagle Bay, 40–1
Beagle Bay Mission, 50–6, 57, 91, 100, 109, 129, 209, 233
    internment of Fr Bischoffs, 92
    Patricia and Fay at, 126, 130, 133–5
Beazley, Kim, 13
Bedford, Paddy, 101
Bedford Downs, 100
belief systems and values, 28–9, 38–9, 194
    see also Aboriginal law and culture; Catholic Church
Bellear, Bob and Kay, 216
Benedictines, 207
Bennett, Mary, 104
Bennett, Scott, 213
Berndt, Ron and Catherine, 170, 178
Berrimah Reserve, 170
Berry Springs, 238
bicentennial celebrations, 278–9
bicycle riding, 93, 111
Bidyadanga (La Grange), 41–2, 108, 228, 233, 242

Bililuna Pastoral Company, 95
Billiluna, Banjo, 94–5
Bin Denim, Sally, 133
biological absorption, 103–4, 106–8, 171–2, 196
Bird, Ernie, 46
Birrundudu, 177, 179
births, *see* children
Bischofs, Fr, 54–5, 78, 79, 81, 91, 92
Bjelke-Petersen Government, 214
Blackburn, Mr Justice, 213
'the Block', 22–4, 185, 282, 294
Boraine, Dr Alexander, 10–11
Born Free Club, 217
Borroloola, 266
Brady, Pastor Don, 216–17
Bray, Commissioner, 145
Brennan, Gerald, 236
Bringing Them Home inquiry/report, 14, 103, 107–8, 149–50, 197–8, 238
Brisbane, 216–17, 260
Briscoe, Gordon, 211
British Bovril company, 157
Britten, Jack, 77
Brooking Springs, 139
Broome, 24, 42–3, 48–50, 198, 210–11, 233
    'the Block', 22–4, 185, 282, 294
    Dodson, Patrick: birth, 148; condition put to Prime Minister Hawke about, 293; deaconry, 218–22; ordination, 228–9, 230, 233
    Djiagween, Patricia, 124–30, 135, 137, 147–8, 282
    Djiagween Street, 40
    Fagan, Elizabeth, 78–82, 98, 102, 124, 130, 135, 148, 167–8
    'Half-Castes of Broome' petition, 104–5
    in Herbert's *Seven Emus*, 99
    Kassim, Georgina, 180
    Kunin, 16, 113–14, 115–17, 220, 320–1
    medical conditions, post Mosely Royal Commission, 124
    parliamentary election 1908, 75
    World War Two, 131–2
    see also Djiagween, Paddy
Broome Chronicle, 75, 76, 80, 300–1
Broome gaol/lock-up, 45, 132, 135, 137
Broome hospital, 79, 124, 125, 301
Broome Orphanage, 146, 147
Broome police, 102, 109
    Patricia and, 126, 127, 134–5, 137
Broome Shire, 16, 113
Broome Shire Roads Board, 109–11, 113–14, 220, 320–1
brothels and prostitutes, 42, 43, 49, 57, 130
Bryant, Gordon, 273

Buchanan, Nat, 69
'Buffalo', 267
Bugarigarra, *see* Aboriginal law and customs
Bullarra, 54
bullying, 203
Bunduk, Diidji, 232
Bungalow Home, Alice Springs, 172
Bungle Bungle ranges, 72, 75
Bunuba, 24, 43, 46
Burke Government, 272
Burungu, 39
bushranging, 68
bushwalking, 209
Byers, Wasson, 135, 163–4

cadets, 202, 208
'the cage', 162–3
Camden Harbour Association, 31
Cameron, Donald and Linda, 91
Campbell, Mr, 137
Campbell, Graham, 159, 164
Campbell, Jim, 166
Campbell, Myrtle, 171–2
Canada, 314
Canberra, 211–12, 259, 272–8
    Aboriginal Affairs conference (1937), 106–7
    Aboriginal tent embassy, 213–14
    'Come to Canberra' campaign, 16–17, 274–8
canon law, 264–5
Canossian Sisters, 238
Carlton Reach, 73
Carne, Des, 259
carnival, 174–5, 197
Carnot Bay, 131
Casey, Dawn, 325
Casterton Cemetery, 191
Catholic Church, 50–6, 57, 78–9
    Aboriginal elements incorporated in services, 55, 215, 228, 239–40, 270
    Aboriginal relations with, 230–1, 239, 242–5, 259–60, 265–6
    Australian Catholic Relief organisation, 257
    Djiagween, Paddy, 40, 50–1, 53, 54, 79, 111–12
    Dominican Republic, 239
    Emo, Fr Nicholas, 50–1, 79, 81–2
    Eucharistic Congress, 214–17, 228, 230–1: Philadelphia, 239
    Gibney, Bishop Matthew, 41–2, 51, 76
    Task Force on Land Rights for Aboriginal People, 259–60
    Vatican II, 212
    workshop on Aboriginal participation (Yeppoon), 236–7

see also Aboriginal spirituality; Australian Missionary Society of the Sacred Heart
Catholic Commission for Justice and Peace, 259
Catholic Leader, 265
cattle, *see* pastoral industry
Ceduna, 175
Central Land Council (CLC), 91, 258, 266–9, 280, 282, 284–5
    'Come to Canberra' campaign, 16–17, 275
    memorial services for Aboriginal people, 237
    Stuart, Max, 174–5
ceremonial grounds (Kunin), 16, 113–14, 115–17, 220, 320–1
ceremonies, 25–6, 28, 44, 47–8, 54–5, 56, 316
    initiation, 47, 52–3, 55, 56, 115, 241
    song cycles, 112
Champion de Crespigny, Robert, 10, 123, 325
Chaney, Hon. Fred, 256, 257
Charles, Anarella, 215
Charlesworth, Max, 214
Chatwin, Bruce, 269–70
Child Welfare Ordinance 1958 (NT), 195
children, 46, 93, 170
    Djiagween, Paddy, 95, 98, 100, 108, 115, 131, 301
    Djiagween, Patricia, 124, 129, 130, 145, 148, 158
    Dodson, Mick, 255
    Dodson, Patrick, 246–7, 274
    Fagan, Elizabeth, 95, 98, 100, 261
    Fagan, Joe, 71
children, removal of, 237–8
    Bringing Them Home inquiry/report, 14, 103, 107–8, 149–50, 197–8, 238
children, removal of, Northern Territory, 168, 169–70, 171, 182
    'Accommodation for Part-Aboriginal Children in other States for Education and Training Scheme', 184, 194–200
    Patrick's memories, 173–4
children, removal of, Western Australia, 53–4, 56–8, 78–9, 107–8
    Cecil, 168
    Elizabeth Fagan's fourth child?, 98
    Fay and Georgina, 146
    Myrtle Campbell and sisters, 171–2
Christmas Creek, 136, 138
Church, *see* Catholic Church
Clancy, Jack, 35
Clark, Geoff, 9, 204, 258, 274, 281, 293
Clarke, Thomas, 32
CLC, *see* Central Land Council
Coconut Well, 131
Coe, Paul, 296
Coffey, Essie, 325
Cole, Tom, 70–1, 142
Collier, Premier, 102

Collins, Louisa, 27, 29
'Colonel Rockjaw', 180
'Come to Canberra' campaign, 16–17, 273–8
common law, 11, 213, 314
    see also High Court of Australia
Commonwealth Arbitration Commission, 200
Commonwealth Government Aboriginal Land Fund Commission, 257
Condren, Joseph, 94
confirmation of Paddy Djiagween, 51
Congill, 27, 29–30
Congoo, Bill, 234
constitutional recognition, 307, 315, 317
Cook, Dr Cecil, 106–7, 171
Cook, Captain James, 27, 29
Cook, Kevin, 258, 274
Coombs, Dr HC (Nugget), 256
Cooney, Barney, 272
Corbett, Helen, 296
Cornish, Anthony, 44
Coronation Hill, 300
Corpus Christi College Werribee, 215
Cossack, 32, 40, 41, 42
Council for Aboriginal Reconciliation, 8–10, 291–3, 299–300, 306–12, 317
    farewell dinner for Dodson, 59–60
    first meeting, 324–6
Council for Aboriginal Reconciliation Bill, 299–300, 307
country, 24–6, 315–16
County Monaghan, 67, 69
Courier Mail, 234
Court, Sir Charles, 257
Coutts, Constable, 178–9
Crocodile Hole, 291–3
Crocombe, Mark, 243
Croker Island, 174
Croydon, Victoria, 209
CSIRO, 166
curate, 237–9, 240–7

Dagoman, 164–5
Daguragu, 201
Daly, Mick, 183–4
Daly, Steve, 183–4
Dampier, William, 26–30
Danayari, Hobbles, 69
Daramalan College, 211
Dartinga, Annunciata, 246–7, 248
Dartinga, Grace Elizabeth Dodson, 23, 246–7, 248
Darwin, 158, 179, 200, 203, 246, 294
    Fannie Bay jail, 136, 141, 176, 177

    Fr Patrick in, 231–2, 237–9, 245
    'Fun Land Carnival', 174–5
    Half-Caste Home, 171–2
    Roe family, 147, 158, 182–3, 208, 255
    strike (1951), 170
David McIvor, 67
Day, Police Constable John, 73–4
De Groen, Frances, 270
de Lisle, Viscount, 162
deacon, 218–22
Deakin, Fr Hilton, 215, 217, 231
Deane, Sir William, 15
deaths
    Djiagween, Paddy, 300–1, 306: siblings of, 79, 91
    Djiagween, Patricia, 180–1
    Dodson, Snowy, 146, 177–9
    Emo, Fr Nicholas, 82
    Fagan, Elizabeth, 261
    Fagan, Joseph, 95
    Galambud, 166
    Gartlan, Marian, 207
    Herbert, Xavier, 270
    Jilwa, 43
    Nawurla, 76, 77
    Riley, Rob, 14
    Shaw, Connie, 274
    Wade, Ron, 184
    see also murders
'Decade of Reconciliation', 306–21, 324–6
    see also Council for Aboriginal Reconciliation
Delamere, 74
Derby, 45, 135, 137, 274
Devitt, Jeannie, 260
diamonds, 131–2
dispossession, 294
    see also land
Dixon, Fr Tom, 175
Djagun, 39, 115
Djerrkura, Gatjil, 59–60
Djiagween, Cecil Adrian, 145, 146, 182, 229
    with Granny Liz, 147, 157, 159: committed to Child Welfare Department care, 168
    in Katherine, 160
Djiagween, Charlie, 91
Djiagween, Cissy, 109, 301
Djiagween, Elizabeth, *see* Fagan, Elizabeth Grace
Djiagween, Fay, *see* Wade, Fay Elizabeth
Djiagween, Francis, 115
Djiagween, Joe, 133, 145, 261

Djiagween, Mary, 95
Djiagween, Paddy, 56, 99, 108–14, 282
  adulthood initiation, 51, 52–3
  Catholicism, 40, 50–1, 53, 54, 79, 111–12
  childhood, 39–43, 50–1, 53–5
  death, 300–1, 306: siblings of, 79, 91
  influence on Patrick, 35–6, 38–9, 208, 210–11, 219, 242
  intervention to stop separation of Patricia and Fay, 126
  Lowenstein's recordings of, 39, 41, 71, 221, 305
  marriage to Elizabeth, 81–2, 91–9, 100
  name for Patrick, 148
  note to Patrick (May 1969), 209
  Patrick's memories of, 52, 101, 112–13, 113–14, 222
  at Patrick's ordination, 229
  pearling, 79–81, 108: stories about, 40–1
  recollections of Elizabeth Fagan's people, 71
  recollections of Joe Fagan, 68, 69, 82
  tailor, 79
  World War II, 131–2
  Yawuru and Jugun, view on, 221
Djiagween, Patricia Mary, 123–30, 133–42, 143–8, 163
  Cecil released to care of, 168
  childhood, 100–1, 104
  death, 180–1
  death of Snowy, 179
  relationship with Max Stuart, 174
  relationship with Mark Humphries, 175–6, 177
  stories told by, 161
Djiagween, Ray, 131
Djiagween, Stanley, 109, 301
'Dobson', 126
Docherty, Fr Richard, 240, 242
Dodson, Adrian, 23
Dodson, Alecia, 255
Dodson, Inala, 255
Dodson, John Murray (Jacko), 208, 229
  birth, 158
  childhood, 159–60, 162, 180, 182–3
Dodson, John Murray (Snowy), 136, 138–45, 168–70
  death of, 146, 177–9
  in Katherine, 157–8, 162–3, 176
  marriage to Patricia, 141, 147, 174, 177
Dodson, Michael, 141–2, 195, 229, 255–6, 300
  birth, 158
  'Bringing Them Home' inquiry co-chair, 14, 103, 197–8
  childhood, 159–60, 161–2, 169, 177–9, 180, 182–3
  at Monivae College, 194, 199–200, 208–9
  reaction to Patrick's vocation, 206

Dodson, Patricia, 180, 182–3, 194, 208, 229
    birth, 158
Dodson, Patricia Mary, *see* Djiagween, Patricia Mary
Dodson, Patrick Lionel, 23, 31, 34–6, 149–50, 156–7, 191–321
    Aborigines Act 1905 (WA), description of, 58
    birth, 148
    'the Block', 22–4, 185, 282, 294
    Bugarigarra, description of, 25
    feelings about Joe Fagan, 82–4
    initiation ceremony, 115
    in Ireland, 66–7
    kardiya value systems, 28–9, 194
    Kunin land claim, evidence to, 115–17
    memories of Elizabeth, 130, 173
    memories of Patricia, 123, 179
    memories of Snowy, 143, 162, 174, 176
    recollections of McBeath, Charles Lewis, 141
    see also Central Land Council; Council for Aboriginal Reconciliation; Kimberley Land Council; Royal Commission into Aboriginal Deaths in Custody
Dodson, Patrick Lionel, childhood of, 157, 159–66, 176, 182–4
    death of Patricia, 181
    death of Snowy, 179–80
    'Fun Land Carnival', 174–5, 197
    with Snowy, 169
    welfare, threat of, 173–4
Dodson Dartinga, Grace Elizabeth, 23, 246–7, 248
domestic service, 48–9
    Fagan, Elizabeth, 79, 81, 102, 167
Dominican Republic, 239
Doolan, Jack, 246
Douglas Park, 209
Doyle, Billy, 160
Dreaming, *see* Aboriginal law and culture
drovers and droving, 68–72, 145, 160, 171, 182, 183–4
drownings, 41–2
Drysdale, Sergeant, 126, 127
Duke of Edinburgh, 162
Durack, MP, 69, 71–2, 76
Durack, Mary, 54, 69, 74, 131–2, 133
    Djiagween, Paddy, description of, 110
    Emo, Fr Nicholas, description of, 50
    Fagan, Joe, descriptions of, 72, 73
    Philchowski, Rudolph, descriptions of, 73, 92–3
Durack family, 69, 84, 95
Durack River, 100
Durmigam, 53

Economic Development Commission, 280

Edgar, Lenny, 180
Edwards, Hugh, 43
education, 105, 231, 236, 262–3, 317
    Djiagween, Paddy, 53, 93
    Djiagween, Patricia, 104
    Dodson, Mick, 194, 199–200, 208–9, 255
    Dodson, Patricia, 194
    Dodson, Patrick, 161–2, 182, 183, 184, 191–212, 255–6, 262
    Fagan, Elizabeth, 79
Ellis, Maude, 161, 175–6, 180
Emo, Fr Nicholas, 50–1, 79, 81–2
equal pay, 200–1, 210, 235, 236
equal rights, 170
Eucharistic Congress, 214–17, 228, 230–1
    Philadelphia, 239
eugenics, 103–4, 106–8, 171–2, 196
Evans, Patrol Officer, 169
Evans, Gareth, 278
Everingham, Paul, 277
extinguishment, 12, 312–13, 314

Fagan (Djiagween), Elizabeth Grace (Granny Liz), 78–82, 102, 145, 146, 209–10
    anonymous letter to police about, 130
    birth, 71
    Cecil with, 147, 157, 159, 168
    citizenship applications, 167
    death, 261
    Joe's legacy, 95–9, 102, 159, 167
    marriage to Paddy, 81–2, 91–9, 100
    with Patricia and children, 124–30, 148: at Beagle Bay, 131, 133
    Patricia and children in jail, 135
    Patrick's memories of, 101, 261
    at Patrick's ordination, 229
    relationship with Joe Fagan, 82
    warnings about welfare, 173
Fagan, John, 67–8
Fagan, Joseph, 67–73, 77, 90, 93
    bequest to Elizabeth, 95–9, 102, 159, 167
    Patrick's feelings about, 82–4
    permission for Elizabeth's marriage unnecessary, 81
Fagan, Matilda, 67, 69
Fagan, Nawurla, 70–2, 76–7, 82–3
Fagin's Camp, 68
Falkenberg, Johannes, 241
Fannie Bay jail, 136, 141, 176, 177
Farley, Rick, 325
Federation of Land Councils, 9, 258, 274–8, 279, 281
Ferguson, Nola, 215

Ferguson River, 175
Ferntree Gully, 255
fights, 93, 133, 134, 138, 162
Finlay, R.A., 72
Finnis River Land Claim, 270
first contact, 26–7, 29
first peoples, recognition of, 317
First World War, 91–2, 93
Fischer, Tim, 312–13
Fishermen's Bend, 24
    Kunin, 16, 113–14, 115–17, 220, 320–1
Fitzpatrick, Shane, 243
Fitzroy Crossing, 23, 94, 132, 233
Fitzroy River, 24, 257
Flanagan, Martin, 203
Fletcher, Cecil, 210
Flick, Barbara, 282, 292
Flick, Joe, 282
Flinders, Charles, 42, 43
Flinders, Constable John Franklin (Jack), 94–5, 96, 97–8
Flora Valley, 164
'the flying wedge', 272–4
football, 194, 203, 209, 211, 242
    at Monivae College, 199, 202, 208
Forrest River, 100
Forrester, Vince, 278
Fossil Downs, 136
Foundation for Aboriginal and Islander Research Action (FAIRA), 260
Framlingham, 204, 281
Fraser, Malcolm, 193, 202, 214
Fraser Government, 256
Fremantle prison, 141, 144
'Fun Land Carnival', 174–5, 197
fundamentalist Christianity, 233–4
Fyfe, Fr, 247

Gadaranya song cycle, 112
Galambud, 165–6
Gallacher, Jamie, 272
Galvin, Jerry, 240
gamblers, 68, 94, 111, 147–8
Gantheaume Point, 24, 81
Garden Point, 182, 237–8
Garimba section, 39
Gartlan, Buddy, 194
Gartlan, Jack, 191, 193–4
Gartlan, Marian, 191, 193–4, 198–9, 205–6, 207

Gartlan, Tony, 191, 193
Gates, Thomas, 68
Geelong, 67–8
George, Alf, 137, 144, 145, 146
George, Jenny, 325
Gibney, Bishop Matthew, 41–2, 51, 76
Giese, Harry, 173, 184
Gietzelt, Arthur, 272
Go-Go, 136
gold, 31, 69–70
Goodowel, 52
Gordon, Michael, 263
government intervention and control
    Northern Territory, 164–5, 169–70, 171–4, 181
    Queensland, 214, 234–6
government intervention and control, Western Australia, 42, 45–6, 56–8, 102–8
    Djiagween, Paddy, 94, 95, 98. 109–10
    Djiagween, Patricia, 124–42, 143–7
    Fagan, Elizabeth, 130, 133: citizenship application, 167; Joe Fagan's bequest, 95–9, 102, 159, 167; location to Broome, 78–9; marriage, 81
  see also children; removal of; police
government policies, 42, 56–8
    biological absorption, 103–4, 106–8, 171–2, 196
    see also assimilation; land rights; self-determination
Graceville Parish, 235, 236
'Gracie', 204
Granny Liz, *see* Fagan, Elizabeth Grace
Grant, Harry and Norma, 192
Gregory, Captain, 80
Gribble, Ernest, 100
Grogan, Clarrie, 274, 275
Gumatj Yolngu, 258
Gurindji people, 69, 71, 165, 169
   strike for equal pay, 200–1

Hack, Norm, 192
Haebich, Anna, 96, 107
Half-Caste Home, Darwin, 171–2
Half-Caste Progressive Association, 170
'Half-Castes of Broome' petition, 104–5, 107
Halls Creek, 98, 140, 147, 171–2
  cemetery, 141
  gold-fields, 69–70
  hotel, 139, 145
  mail run, 73
  races, 93–4
Hamilton, Monivae College, 184, 191–209
Hand, Gerry, 272, 278, 279–80, 281, 295

Harris, William, 102
Harrison, Phyllis, 215
Hasluck, Paul, 162, 172–3, 185, 194–6
    with Mosely Royal Commission, 74, 106
Hatfield, Mrs, 102
Hawke, Bob, 272, 279, 293, 300, 307
Hawke Government, 268, 271–81, 295, 300, 307, 313–14
Hawley, Janet, 246
Hawthorn Station overpass, 255
Heath, Ian, 255
Herbert, Xavier, 99, 270
Herron, John, 16
High Court of Australia, 175
    Mabo and *Wik* judgments, 11–14, 236, 308–9, 311–14
history, *see* Aboriginal history
Holding, Clyde, 271–2, 276, 277, 278
Holt, Snowy, 146
Hoosan, Eileen, 274
horse breeding, 70
horse stealing, 68, 72
houses
    'the Block', 22–4, 185, 282, 294
    Broome, 81, 102, 109, 167
    Katherine, 161, 162–3, 176, 177
Howard, John, 16, 59, 150, 312, 317–18
    at Australian Reconciliation Convention (Melbourne, 1997), 12–13
    'Ten-Point Plan', 12–13, 312–13
Howley, Bro. Andy, 243
Huegal, Fr Francis, 43, 51, 54, 134, 136
Human Rights and Equal and Opportunity Commission, *Bringing Them Home* report, 14, 103, 107–8, 149–50, 197–8, 238
Humphries, Mark, 175–6, 177
Hunter, Elizabeth, 168
Hunter, Flora, 133
Hunter, Kathleen, 133
Hunter, Lawrence, 81
Hunter, Theresa, 133

identity, 24, 39, 71, 201, 208, 315–16
Indigenous Peoples and Multinationals conference, 263–4
Indooroopilly, 260
Inglis, Ken, 175
initiation ceremonies, 47, 52–3, 55, 56, 115, 241
inspections at Monivae, 198–200
Institute for Aboriginal Development (IDA), 262–3, 282
Inverway, 169
Ireland and Irish, 54–5, 69, 70, 72, 99, 212
    Patrick's visit, 66–7
Isdell, James, 78, 79

Jandamarra, 46
Japanese, 42, 49, 79, 98, 132
    air raid on Broome, 131
    Paddy's pearling experience with, 80
Jarlmadanga, 292
Jawoyn, 164–5, 267
Jebb, Mary Anne, 93
Jensen, Constable, 139
Jillambin, 92–3
Jilwa, 30, 39, 40, 43
Jirrginngan, 24
Jobst, Bishop John, 228–9, 230
John Mary, Br, 53
John Paul II, Pope, 271
Johnson, Jack, 164
Johnston, Constable, 109
Johnston, Elliott, 281, 282, 298–9
    see also Royal Commission into Aboriginal Deaths in Custody
Jones, Chris, 107–8
Jubilee Downs, 136
Jukun, 220–1
Juluru song cycle, 112

Kalkaringi, *see* Wave Hill
Kanalgundidj clans, 191–209
kardiya values and belief systems, 28–9, 194
    see also Catholic Church
Karrajarri, 26, 115, 228, 321
Kassim, Fay, *see* Wade, Fay Elizabeth
Kassim, Georgina Frances, 176, 182, 229
    birth, 130
    childhood, 133, 135–6, 137–40, 145, 157: removal to Broome Orphanage, 146, 147
Kassim, Gerald Francis, 129
Kassim, Ronald, 181, 228
Kassim bin Marah, Abu, 124–31, 135, 147–8
Katherine, 156–7, 199, 203, 209–10
    Patrick's childhood, 157–66, 173–7, 179, 179–84, 246
Katherine hospital, 165
Katter, Norman, 235, 236
Keasman, Norman, 174
Keating Government, 11–12, 312
Keeffe, Senator Jim, 235
Kelly, Bishop-elect Edward (Ned), 207
Kelly, Jack, 70, 74, 75, 77, 83
Kelly, Ned, 51, 69
Keneally, Thomas, 136
Kennedy, President, 203
Kickett, Daryl, 258, 294

Kidd, Rosalind, 235
Kija country, 72, 100–1
Killoran, PJ (Paddy), 235–6
Kimberley Land Council, 23, 101, 123, 282, 291–3
    Nookanbah campaign, 257–8
Kimberley Land Regulations (1881), 43
King Ranch, 269
King River, 183
King Sound Pastoral Company, 44
Knight, Inspector, 125–7, 128, 133, 134
Knight, George, 73–4
Knott's Crossing, 159
Knowla (Nawurla), 70–2, 76–7, 82–3
Knox, Archbishop, 212, 214
Kolig, Erich, 233
Koolomurt West, 193
Kulminya, Snowy, 275
Kulumput, 165–6
Kunin, 16, 113–14, 115–17, 220, 320–1

La Grange, 41–2, 108, 228, 233, 242
Lake Nash, 269
Lamboo, 139, 146
land, 25–6, 28–9, 41, 315–16
    Patrick on, 35–6, 236–7
Land Councils, 9, 258, 274–8, 279, 281, 309
    see also Kimberley Land Council; Northern Territory Land Councils
land ownership, 31–2, 43–8, 236
    Blackburn judgment, 213
    Dodson, Snowy, 159, 177
    Fagan, Elizabeth Grace, 102, 95–8
    Fagan, Joe, 72–3, 95
    see also native title
land rights, 213–14, 256, 268–9, 271–80, 300, 313–15
    Finnis River, 270
    Hawke Government preferred model, 272, 276–7, 313–14
    Kunin, 16, 113–14, 115–17, 220, 320–1
    Nookanbah, 257–8
    Task Force on Land Rights for Aboriginal People, 259–60
    Wave Hill walk-out, 200–1
    see also native title
Lane, Paul, 22, 23, 66, 90, 294
Langford, Dr 'Spike', 231
Langton, Marcia, 259, 267–8, 272, 278, 294, 304
language, 9
    see also Aboriginal languages
Latin America, 239
Launceston, 142

law students, 229, 255–6, 262
Lawton, Kevin, 47, 48, 81, 94
Leary, Fr John, 231, 232, 240
Lee, Jack, 220
Leichleitner, Dick, 259
Leo XIII, Pope, 32
Leopold Downs, 46
Lester, Yami, 262–3, 271, 283
Liddle, Johnny, 263
Limbunyah, 147, 169, 177
Lingiari, Vincent, 91, 200, 201
Lingiari Foundation, 90
Liveringa, 43, 132
Lombardina, 82, 129, 134
Long, Michael, 182
'Long Mac', 110
Lowenstein, Wendy, 39, 41, 71, 221, 305
Lumbia, 83

Mabel, 108, 115, 131
Mabo judgment, 11–12, 236, 308–9, 311, 312
McAdam, Charlie, 146
McBeath, Charles Lewis, 129, 141, 159
McCoy, Fr Brian, 215, 217, 237, 246–7, 266
    Australian football, remarks on, 203
MacDaniel, Dan, 108, 167
McEwan, 'Black Jack', 172
McGiness family, 270
McGinness, Jack, 170
McGinness, Joe, 201
McHugh, Siobahn, 66
McInerney, Ralph, 270–1
McKelson, Fr Kevin, 233
McKenna, Hugh, 73
MacKenzie, James, 110, 113, 167
McKenzie, Queenie, 75
McKenzie, Sophie, 48
McMahon Fr JJ, 192
McMahon, Fr John F, 207
McMahon Government, 213–14
McMillan, Andrew, 200
McPherson, Shirley, 280
McPhillamy, Fr 'Bomber', 193
Maher, Wiki, 159–60, 181, 183–4
Maher family, 159–60, 161, 175–6, 180, 181
Mahmoot, Rosie, 148
maintenance payments for Patricia and children, 125, 126–8, 130
The Major, 70, 74–7, 83, 91

Malays, 30, 42, 49, 94, 98, 102, 103
    Kassim bin Marah, Abu, 124–31, 135, 147–8
Male, Arthur, 75–6
Male, Mrs Arthur, 81, 218–19
Malngin Land Trust, 91
Malngin people, 72
Manbullo, 166, 170
Mandela, Nelson, 11
Manetta, Sr, 209
Mannion, Sergeant, 165
Mangala, 26, 43, 44, 292, 321
Manne, Robert, 103, 171
Mannix, Archbishop, 132, 206, 209
Mansell, Michael, 274
Manuka Oval, 211
marriage and relationships, 49, 57, 71–2, 93, 103–4, 171
    Daly, Mick and Gladys Namagu, 184
    Djiagween, Paddy, 81–2, 91–9, 100, 108
    Djiagween, Patricia, 136, 138–42, 144–5, 146, 147, 174, 177; Humphries, Mark, 175–6, 177; Kassim, Abu, 124–30, 135; Rose, Cecil, 145, 146
    Dodson, Mick, 255
    Dodson, Patricia, 229
    Dodson, Patrick, 23, 246–7, 265, 266, 274, 282
    Dodson, Snowy, 136, 138–42, 144–5, 146, 147, 174, 177
    Fagan, Elizabeth, 81–2, 91–9, 100, 102, 130
    Fagan, Joe, 70–2, 77
    'Half-Castes of Broome' petition, 104–5, 107
    Wade, Fay, 180, 184, 209–10
Martelli, Dean, 51
Martin, Fred, 171
Martin, Gracie, 135
Martin, Ray, 10, 15, 325, 326
Mataranka, 175
Maurice, R.T., 70
Mechtilde, Sr Mary, 78
Meggitt, Mervyn, 71
Melbourne, 198, 206, 209, 255–6, 260, 294
    Patrick's first impressions, 192
Melbourne Archdiocese, 239
Melbourne Eucharistic Congress, 214–17, 228, 230–1
Melville Island, 231, 237, 238
Menzies Government, 172–3, 194–200
Mereenie oil field, 268
Merkel, Justice, 115–17
Merlan, Francesca, 164–5
Middle Park walkway, 255
Milirrpum v. Nabalco, 213
military, *see* Army

Miller, Mick, 258, 274
Mimili, 263
Minerals Council of Australia, 10
mining industry, 13, 123, 268, 273, 276–7, 300, 312
    Nookanbah, 257–8
    reconciliation and, 10, 309
mining royalties, 258, 267, 268, 272
'Minyirr bul', 148
Minyjirr Yawuru, 24
Mirriwoong, 74
missiology, 238–9, 241
Missionaries of the Sacred Heart, *see* Australian Missionary Society of the Sacred Heart
missions, *see* Catholic Church
Mistake Creek, 91
Mitchell, Major, 191
Monash University, 202, 255, 256, 262
Monivae College, 184, 191–209
Moodewarre, 68
Moola Bulla station, 92, 102, 134, 135–9, 141, 143–6, 147
Morton, Alex, 145
Moseley, F.A., 98
Mosely Royal Commission, 74, 104–6, 124
Moses, Chief Ted, 10
Mt Anderson, 43, 44, 54
Mt House, 132
Mount Nancy Town Camp, 274
Mudbura, 69, 165, 169
Muirhead, Justice, 281, 282
multiculturalism, 260
Multinational Monitor, 263
Murdering Flat, 191
murders, 46–7, 75, 76–7, 100, 191
    kardiya, 44, 73, 75–6, 92–3, 94–5, 100, 101
    Oobagooma Aborigines, 45
    Stuart case, 175
Murphy, Fr Dennis J, 209, 262
Murray, Gelignite Jack, 160
Murray, Matt, 183
Murrinh-Patha people, 240–6
Mutitjulu people, 271

Namagu, Gladys, 184
Nangan, Butcher Joe, 47, 228
Nangiomeri, 52–3
National Aboriginal Conference, 256, 259
National Aboriginal Land Rights Support group, 273
national apology, 14, 318–19
National Farmers' Federation, 12, 312

National Inquiry into the Separation of Aboriginal Children from their Families (*Bringing Them Home* inquiry), 14, 103, 107–8, 149–50, 197–8, 238
National Press Club, 34–6, 276
Native Administration Act 1936 (WA), 106, 107, 126, 140, 141–2
   see also government intervention and control
Native Hospital, Broome, 124, 125
native title, 11–14, 198, 312–15
   Broome, 16, 113–14, 115–17, 220, 320–1
   Mabo and *Wik* judgments, 11–14, 236, 308–9, 311–14
   see also land rights
Native Title Act 1993, 12, 312–13
Naula, 76
Nawurla, 70–2, 76–7, 82–3
negotiate, right to, 312, 315
Neill, Jack, 160
Neville, Auber Octavius, 102, 103–4, 106–7, 144
   Elizabeth and, 96–9, 102
   Patricia and, 126, 127–8, 129
'New Deal', 172
New Norcia, 207
New South Wales, 104, 145, 202, 209, 271
New Zealand, 257
Ngangumarta, 26
Ngikina-Mangala people, 26, 43, 44, 292, 321
Nicholson cartoon, 264
Nickol Bay, 32
night carting, 111
Nightcliff, 237–9
Nixon's Farm, 159
Ngaringman, 275
Noah, 23
Noala (Nawurla), 70–2, 76–7, 82–3
Nookanbah, 257–8
North Australian Workers Union, 170
Northern Land Council, 267–8, 300
Northern Territory, 76, 142–3, 171–4, 207, 237–47
   land rights, 200–1, 213, 268–9, 277
   Patricia's move to, 147–8
   Patrick at Alice Springs, 260, 262–74, 282–3
   Port Keats, 23, 215, 232, 240–7, 264
   reason for Patrick joining MSC, 207
   self-government, 256
   see also Darwin; Katherine; Wave Hill
Northern Territory *Child Welfare Ordinance 1958*, 195
Northern Territory Land Councils, 10, 258, 266–9, 272–8, 300
   Barunga Sports and Cultural Festival, 205–6
   establishment, 256
   see also Central Land Council

Northern Territory Lands Department, 161, 177
Northern Territory Native Affairs Branch, *see* government intervention and control
Northern Territory Supreme Court, 213
Northern Territory Welfare Ordinance 1953, 173, 181, 197
novitiate, 209–11
nuns, Aboriginal, 242
Nyalcas, Bob, 74–5
Nyikina, 26, 43, 44, 292
Nyulnyul, 50, 51–2, 55

O'Brien, Mother Antonio, 54–5, 79
O'Connell, Constable, 109
O'Donoghue, Lowitja, 280, 325
Ogden, Bert, 95, 97–8
Old Spud, 165–6
O'Loughlin, Bishop John, 228–9, 238–9, 240, 244–6, 247, 264
O'Meara, Francesca (Topsy), 211
Onandaga Iroquois people, 263
O'Neill, Inspector, 134, 137, 140, 167
O'Neill, Shorty, 258, 263
Oobagooma Aborigines, 45
Oombulgurri, 123
oral history and storytelling, 92, 115
    Captain Cook tales, 27, 29
    Jack Kelly and the Major, 74–5, 76
    Ned Kelly tales, 69
    Paddy Djiagween's stories of pearling, 40–1
Ord River station, 69, 70
ordination, 228–9, 230, 233
Oscar, June, 23–4
Oscar Range, 139–40
O'Shane, Terry, 274
O'Sullivan, Timmy, 94
outlaws, 68, 70, 74–7
Owen, Chris, 94–5
Ozies, Antonio, 102

Pallottine College, Kew, 215
Pallottines, 51, 55, 56, 132–3
Palm Island, 234–5
Panter, Police Inspector, 31
Papunya School of artists, 112
Pardelup Prison Farm, 144
Parish Priest, 240, 262–6
Pascoe, Curly, 136, 139, 179–80
Pascoe, Fr Dick, 235, 236
Pascoe, Michael, 234, 236
pastoral industry, 12, 13, 309, 312

cattle duffing, 68
Northern Territory, 157, 160, 166, 168–71, 200–1: Joe Fagan in, 68–72
Western Australia, 31–2, 43–8, 74, 93, 95, 101
see also Wave Hill
pastoral leases, 12, 268–8, 312
Patrick, Peggy, 101
Paul, Pope VI, 212, 230, 271
pearlers and pearling, 32, 48, 51, 124
    Djiagween, Paddy, 79–81, 108
    Djiagween's stories about, 40–1
    Mrs Hatfield, 102
    MacDaniel, Dan, 108, 167
    MacKenzie, James, 110, 113, 167
    Male, Arthur, 75–6
    Male, Mrs Arthur, 81, 218–19
    prohibition on Aboriginal employment in, 42
    Yawuru, 25
Pederson, Howard, 294
Pedjert, Deacon Boniface, 242
Perkins, Mr, 110–11
Perkins, Charlie, 202, 276, 280, 281
Perth, 98–9, 104, 260, 294
'Phenyl Kid', 148
Philchowski, Rudolph, 72, 73, 92–3
'Pig Patrols', 217
Pigeon, 46
Pigeon Hole, 68, 69, 166
Pioneer Football Club, Alice Springs, 282–3
Pitjantjatjara, 263
Pius IX, Pope, 207
police, 45–6, 53–4, 78, 109, 141
    Brisbane, 216–17
    Broome, 102, 109, 126, 127, 134–5
    Flinders, Constable John Franklin (Jack), 94–5, 96, 97–8
    Halls Creek, 140, 171
    Katherine, 164, 165, 176–7
    Oscar Range, 139
    Port Keats (Wadeye), 247
    Tennant Creek, 143, 240
    Turkey Creek, 77, 92, 94
    Wave Hill, 178–9
    Wild Dog (Argyle), 72, 73, 76–7, 92
    see also prisoners; Royal Commission into Aboriginal Deaths in Custody
police expeditions, 45, 76–7, 94–5, 100
police trackers, 46, 77
Pope John Paul II, 271
Pope Leo XIII, 32
Pope Paul VI, 212, 230, 271

Pope Pius IX, 207
Port Keats, 23, 215, 232, 240–7, 264
Potato, 165–6
Prentice, Fr, 202
priests, *see* Catholic Church
primary production, *see* pastoral industry
prisoners, 45, 109, 132
    see also arrests and charges
prostitutes and brothels, 42, 43, 49, 57, 130
protection, *see* government policies
Pye, Fr John, 241, 242

Queen of England, 111
Queensland, 164, 216–17, 234–7, 260, 322
    Bjelke-Petersen Government, 214
Queensland *Aborigines Act 1971*, 235
Queensland Aborigines-Torres Strait Islanders Act 1972, 214
Queensland Department of Aboriginal and Islander Advancement, 235–6

Racial Discrimination Act 1975, 235
Raible, Bishop, 132
railways, 254–5
Read, Peter, 280
recognition, 307, 315
    as first peoples, 317
    see also treaty
reconciliation, 8–16, 194, 291–327
    Patrick on, 35–6, 66–7
    at regional level, 23
Redex car rally, 160
referendum (1967), 15, 201–2
Regan, Constable, 100
reparation, 318–19
Reserve 30906 (Kunin), 16, 113–14, 115–17, 220, 320–1
resistance, 44, 66–7, 83, 93
    Jandamarra, 46
    by Yawuru, 26, 30, 31–2
    see also spearings
resource industry, *see* mining industry
Rhatigan, Paddy, 75
right to negotiate, 312, 315
Rights for Whites movement, 210
Riley, Rob, 14, 274, 279, 294
Robeson, Paul, 162
Rockhampton, 260
Rodriguez, Francis, 80–1
Roe, Basil, 182
Roe, Bill, 182

Roe, Janet, 182
Roe, Joseph 'Nipper', 115
Roe, Mary, 147, 158, 182
Roe family, 195, 208, 255
Roebuck, 26
Roebuck Bay, 22, 24, 26–7, 30–2, 39, 42, 47
Roebuck Bay Pastoral and Agricultural Association Limited, 31
Roebuck Plains, 24, 44
Ronan, Jim, 68, 166
Ronan, Tom, 68, 93
Rose, Cecil, 145, 146
Rose, Debbie, 69
Rosewood, 161, 169
Rosie (Nawurla), 70–2, 76–7, 82–3
Ross, David, 263, 267, 268, 274, 279, 282
Roth Royal Commission, 56–8, 81–2
Rottnest Island, 44, 45
Royal Commission into Aboriginal Deaths in Custody, 149, 258, 294–9, 306, 307
    establishment, 281
    Patrick's appointment to, 282, 295
    police as instruments of government policy, Patrick's observations, 46, 108
Royal Commission to Inquire into the alleged killing and burning of bodies of Aborigines in East Kimberley, 100
royal commissions, 56–8, 81–2, 100, 175, 214
    Mosely, 74, 104–6, 124
Rubibi Land, Heritage and Development Council, 16, 294
Rubuntja, Eli, 267
Rubuntja, Wenten, 258, 259, 267, 279, 325

Sandy Point, 40, 56
St Anne's, Warrnambool, 194
St Jack, Constable, 100
St Mary's football team, 203
St Paul's Parish, Nightcliff, 237–9
Sawenko, Toly, 284
Scambary, Rex, 265
Scanlon, Jack, 163
Scanlon, Pixie, 176
school cadets, 202, 208
school captain, 202–4
school holidays, 193–4, 198–9, 200, 203, 207, 255
schooling, *see* education
Scrutton, Stan, 258, 263, 266–7
Second World War, 130–5, 158, 170, 172
section names, 39, 71
self-determination, 213, 232, 236, 242, 280
    Fr Hilton Deakin's view, 231
    Port Keats (Wadeye), 244, 264

seminarian, 211–18
Seven Emus (novel), 99
Shackcloth, Irene, 44
Sharpe, Bert, 135, 136, 137, 139
shaving, 209, 239
Shaw, Adrian, 23, 274, 275, 282
Shaw, Barbara, 264, 265, 266, 274, 282
Shaw, Bruce, 74, 76, 92
Shaw, Connie, 274
Shaw, Geoffrey, 259, 263, 264, 267, 274
sheep, *see* pastoral industry
Shire of Broome, 16, 113
Shire of Broome Roads Board, 109–11, 113–14, 220, 320–1
shootings, 30–1, 46–7, 75, 76, 94
    see also murders
Sisters of St John of God, 54, 78–9, 104, 124
skin names, 39, 71
Smith, Shirley, 215
Smith, Warwick, 295
Snowdon, Warren, 272, 273
Snowy River Stampede, 174, 175
social assimilation, *see* assimilation
Soden, Joe, 133, 145, 261
song cycles, 112
The Songlines book, 269–70
songs, 135, 137–8
    Aboriginal, 112, 210, 219, 316
South Africa, 10–11
South Australia, 175, 198, 260, 271, 294
Southern Cross pearls, 32
spearings, 41
    kardiya, 44, 73, 92, 101
    livestock, 44, 45, 74, 75, 92, 100
Spicer, Ian, 325
spirituality, *see* Aboriginal spirituality
sport, 161–2, 199, 208
    see also football
Spring Creek, 72–8, 90, 91–8, 99, 100
Springvale, 73, 95
Spud, 165–6
Stackhouse, Alma, 325
Stanner, William, 52–3, 132
State Child Number 165, 195–200
state intervention, *see* government intervention and control
station holdings, *see* pastoral industry
Stephen, Sir Ninian, 271
stockmen, 68–72, 145, 160, 171, 182, 183–4
Stokes, John, 30–1

'stolen generations', *see* children, removal of
storytelling, *see* oral history
Streeter and Male, 124, 125, 126
strikes, 170, 200–1
Stuart, Max, 174–5, 197
study materials on land rights, 259–60
Sullivan, Jack, 76
Sullivan, Patrick, 47
Sunday Island, 55
Swan, Charlie, 178, 179

'Tailor Paddy', 79
Tambling, Senator Grant, 295
Tangantyere Council, 269, 285
Task Force on Land Rights for Aboriginal People, 259–60
Tasmania, 142, 274
'Ten-Point Plan', 12–13, 312–13
Tennant Creek, 143, 240, 267
tent embassy, 213–14
Texas Downs, 70, 75
Thangoo, 44, 47, 113
Thargomindah, 68
Tickner, Robert, 17, 273, 291, 293, 299, 300, 307
Timms, Inspector, 126, 127
Timms, Terry, 101
Tipoloura, Bernard, 231
Tiwi, 237–8, 258
Townsville, 260
Toyne, Phillip, 269
Tracer, Inspector, 49
trade, 25, 27, 30, 52
Tranby College, 258
Trappists, 50–1, 53, 55, 92
treaty, 257, 270, 279, 293, 307, 310
Turkey Creek, 74, 76, 77, 92, 94
Turner, Lionel, 259
Turner, Pat, 231, 259, 325
Turner Grazing Company, 72, 90
Tutu, Archbishop Desmond, 10
Twist, Harry, 68
'Two Men' song cycle, 112
Tybingoompa, Gladys, 12

Uluru, 263
Uluru-Tjuta National Park, 271
Union Bar, ANU, 259
United Aborigines Mission, Fitzroy Crossing, 233
United Nations Working Group on Indigenous People, 271–2

United States, 10, 239, 263–4

Valadero, 80
Valadian, Margaret, 215
values and belief systems, 28–9, 38–9, 194
    see also Aboriginal law and culture; Catholic Church
Vatican II, 212, 245
Vesteys, 157
    see also Wave Hill
Victoria, 31, 67–8, 104, 191–200, 209
Victoria River Downs, 68–9, 70, 157, 166, 169
Victorian Aboriginal Legal Service, 255
Victorian Equal Opportunities Commission, 255
Vincent, Victor, 74
violence, 46, 74, 100–1, 105, 162–3
    Port Keats (Wadeye), 247
    between Yawuru and neighbours, 26
    see also fights; murders; resistance
Violet Valley, 92
vocation, 204–7

Wade, Eric, 185
Wade, Fay Elizabeth, 176, 177, 179, 180, 181, 229, 301
    birth, 124
    at 'the Block', 282
    Elizabeth with, 261
    influence on Patrick, 208
    Patrick at Douglas Park, 209
    Patrick at Monivae, 194, 195, 197
    Patrick with, 182–4
    reaction to Patrick's vocation, 205
    relationship with Cecil Fletcher, 209–10
    story of Paddy and Elizabeth's fourth child, 98
    teenager, 162–3
Wade, Fay Elizabeth, childhood of, 124, 125, 127, 148, 157
    Beagle Bay, 126, 130, 133
    Broome Orphanage, 146, 147
    Katherine, 158
    Patricia's arrest and rescue, 135–40, 145, 163
Wade, Ron, 180, 182, 183–4
Wadeye (Port Keats), 23, 215, 232, 240–7, 264
Walcott Inlet, 108
Walker, Dennis, 216–17
Wallace, Ruth, 216
Wallambain, 92
Walsh, Michael, 221
Walsh, Peter, 295
Walter, Fr George, 55, 57

Wanan, 30, 39, 40
Wardaman, 74, 164–5
Waringari, 71
Warlpiri, 165
Warmun, 74, 75
Warrnambool, 194
Waterford, Jack, 205, 212
Watson, Johnny, 53–4, 292
Watson, Len, 216
Watson, Lilla, 216
Watson, Maureen, 216
Wattie Creek, 201
Wave Hill (Kalkaringi), 69, 90, 156, 157, 169, 172
    Cecil Rose's flight to, 146
    Joe at, 70–2
    Snowy at, 170, 177–9
    walk-off (1966), 200–1
welfare, *see* government intervention and control
Welfare Ordinance 1953 (NT), 173, 181, 197
Welford Downs, 68
West Australian, 41–2, 106
Western Australia, 22–147, 200, 207, 233–4, 260
    deaths in custody, 294–5
    Fremantle prison, 141, 144
    land rights, 272, 276, 277: Nookanbah, 257–8
    see also Broome; Kimberley Land Council
Western Australia Aboriginal Legal Service, 257
Western Australian *Aborigines Act 1905*, 57–8, 94, 97, 102, 106, 107
Western Australian *Aborigines Protection Act 1886*, 45–6
Western Australian *Aboriginal Offenders Act 1892*, 46
Western Australian Department of Native Welfare, 113, 220
    see also government intervention and control
Western Australian Museum, 113, 257
Western Australian *Native Administration Act 1936*, 106, 107, 126, 140, 141–2
Wet Season Northern Territory Football League, 203
Whimp, Kathy, 294
White, Charles, 45
Whitlam, Gough, 214
Whitlam Government, 214
Wik judgment, 12–14, 309, 311–14
Wild Dog, 70, 72–4, 76–7, 91
    see also Spring Creek
Willeroo, 74, 183
Wilson, Sir Ronald, 14, 308
Wonaeamirri, Matthew, 258
Woodward Royal Commission, 214
Wooldridge, Dr Michael, 300, 307
Woorabinda, 234

World Council of Churches, 257
World Council of Indigenous Peoples, 259
World War One, 91–2, 93
World War Two, 130–5, 158, 170, 172
Worms, Fr, 56
Worthy, Mr, 199
Wright, Isaiah ('Wild'), 69
Wright, Matilda, 69
Wyndham, 91, 92–3, 95, 101, 146, 174
    mail run, 73

Yankuntjatjara, 262
Yardugarra, 44
Yarrabah, 275
Yarringadi, 71
Yatala Prison, 175
Yawuru history, 24–32, 40–8, 55, 305
Yawuru language, 220–1
'Yellow Rose of Mission', 138
Yeppoon, 236–7
Yolngu, 59, 213
Yorta Yorta case, 314
Yu, Peter, 257, 258, 274, 280, 282, 293, 294
Yungngora community, 257
Yunipingu, Galarrwuy, 213, 258, 267, 279, 325

Zimin's peanut farm, 160